The Development of American Agriculture: A Historical Analysis

The University of Minnesota Press
gratefully acknowledges assistance provided
for the publication of this volume
by the John K. and Elsie Lampert Fesler Fund.

The Development of American Agriculture

A Historical Analysis

Second Edition

Willard W. Cochrane

University of Minnesota Press
Minneapolis   London

Published by the University of Minnesota Press
2037 University Avenue Southeast, Minneapolis, MN 55455-3092
Printed in the United States of America on acid-free paper

Library of Congress Cataloging in Publication Data

Cochrane, Willard Wesley, 1914–
  The development of American agriculture : a historical analysis /
Willard W. Cochrane. –2nd ed.
    p.   cm.
  Includes bibliographical references (p.   ) and index.
  ISBN 0-8166-2282-5 (hc : acid-free). — ISBN 0-8166-2283-3 (pb : acid-free)
  1. Agriculture — United States — History. I. Title.
S441.C62   1993
338.1′0973 — dc20   92-35698
                                    CIP

To

Bushrod W. Allin
John M. Brewster
Winn F. Finner
James G. Maddox
Robert H. Masucci
Patrick E. O'Donnell
H. L. Stewart

*My departed friends and colleagues who
helped me think systematically, yet
realistically, about the development of
American agriculture.*

CONTENTS

PREFACE TO THE SECOND EDITION

Just as the first edition was written in a relatively short time, the work of revising, rewriting, and expanding it to produce this second edition was also accomplished in a short time. But in both cases the final book grew out of years and years of research and study by the author. It also grew out of the research efforts and products of many people. All of this study, information, and research results are pulled together in this historical analysis, *The Development of American Agriculture.*

The first objective in preparing this new edition was to bring the data and the historical analysis up to date. But some new material has been added. Environmental policy, as a force of development, is discussed in a new chapter. A new thesis is presented in connection with the discussion of the watersheds of development. And the conceptual model is used to analyze the volatile economic developments of the 1970s and 1980s. This second edition is thus not a brand-new book, but it does contain some new information and ideas, which it is hoped are effectively integrated into the previous historical analysis.

Numerous people and institutions contributed to the production of the second edition of *The Development of American Agriculture.* Three people in particular encouraged me to undertake the task of revision: W. Burt Sundquist of the Department of Agricultural and Applied Economics at the University of Minnesota; James T. Bonnen of the Department of Agricultural Economics at Michigan State University;

and Lisa Freeman, director of the University of Minnesota Press. As always the Economic Research Service was most helpful in providing many kinds of research support. Four individuals in ERS were particularly helpful: Arthur Mackie, Lloyd Teigen, Eldon Ball, and Victoria Smith. Three old friends came to my assistance at various times when I needed special help or counseling: Vernon Ruttan, John Schnittker, and Abner Womack. Louise Letnes, our departmental librarian, helped me, time after time, locate specific references and sources of data that I did not know existed. Finally, Judy Berdahl, our jewel of a secretary, transcribed my illegible pen scratchings into a neatly typewritten manuscript.

As with the writing of the first edition of this volume the Department of Agricultural and Applied Economics at the University of Minnesota provided the excellent physical surroundings and the stimulating professional atmosphere for undertaking this project. But in the end Cochrane produced this second edition, and he alone is responsible for any errors of fact, logic, or judgment contained in it.

June 1992   Willard W. Cochrane

PREFACE TO THE FIRST EDITION

This book was written in a relatively short time, between 1977 and 1979. But the ideas contained in it developed over a very long time. As a small boy I learned from my grandparents what it was like to grow up and develop a farm in southwestern Iowa during the post-Civil War years. I learned from my parents and from personal experience what ranch life was like in the newly irrigated Imperial Valley of California during the first decades of the twentieth century. As an undergraduate at the University of California at Berkeley, I learned from a course taught by E. C. Voorhies, which was part economic history, part economic geography, and part production economics (and which today would probably be entitled Agricultural Development), what was involved in the agricultural revolution in Great Britain and the Low Countries in the seventeenth and eighteenth centuries, in the development of a modern agriculture in Denmark in the nineteenth century, and in the specialization of agricultural production in the United States. As a beginning graduate student at Montana State College, I learned from R. R. Renne, Peter L. Slagsvold, Carl F. Kraenzel, and Elmer Starch what it was like to try to farm on the Great Plains in the drought and depression years of the 1930s. As an older, but not a traditionally oriented, graduate student at Harvard, I found the historical approaches of such disparate men as Joseph A. Schumpeter, Alvin H. Hansen, Abbott Payson

Usher, and Charles Howard McIlwain to be the exciting and rewarding approaches to economic and social problems. As a young civil
servant in the U.S. Department of Agriculture, I learned through long
hours of discussion with John M. Brewster, Bushrod W. Allin, and
James G. Maddox what it was like to grow up on low-production
farms in the South and what was involved in developing such farms
into viable production units. Concurrently, the nature and significance of the commercial and technological revolutions that were
taking place in food production and marketing in the United States
were impressed upon me by Walter W. Wilcox, Sherman E. Johnson,
H. L. Stewart, Winn F. Finner, Harry C. Trelogan, Patrick E. O'Donnell, Nathan M. Koffsky, and James P. Cavin. In my first effort to put
together the many pieces of the puzzle of agricultural development in
the United States for the first half of the twentieth century, one man,
Robert H. Masucci, was most helpful to me; that effort was published
in the old *Journal of Farm Economics* in the May 1947 issue under the
title "Farm Price Gyrations — An Aggregative Hypothesis."

Many years later, when I returned to the Department of Agricultural and Applied Economics at the University of Minnesota in 1970,
Vernon W. Ruttan suggested that I develop and offer a course that
might be entitled "The Economic Development of American Agriculture." I was agreeable to the idea and began to read extensively in the
broad area of the history of American agriculture. I became fascinated
with the subject and poured a great deal of time and energy into the
development and presentation of such a course. In 1977, W. B.
Sundquist encouraged me to convert my course notes into a book. As
it turned out, that writing effort required much additional work such
as background reading, data and reference searches, and the development of a suitable organization for presenting the subject matter. But it was an enjoyable and satisfying experience, because the
process of agricultural development in the United States unfolds over
time almost as if it were directed by some inner logic — almost as if it
were teleological in nature — and it was my good fortune to concep-
tualize that process and to describe it on paper.

Three people, Wayne D. Rasmussen, Vernon W. Ruttan, and W. B.
Sundquist, read the entire manuscript and made many, many valuable suggestions for improving both the content and the readability of
the text. They also encouraged me to keep writing. Two people, Mary
E. Ryan and James P. Houck, read parts of the manuscript and also
made valuable suggestions for its improvement. My secretary, Mary

J. Strait, edited the manuscript before typing it and improved both its style and readability.

Many persons and things contributed to the actual writing of this book. The staffs and resources of the libraries of the University of Minnesota were invaluable to the project. Michael P. Schenk, illustrator in the College of Veterinary Medicine, drew all the charts in part IV of this volume, as well as several charts in parts II and III; the remaining charts and maps were obtained from the United States Department of Agriculture and private publishers, which are acknowledged on individual charts and maps. My colleagues in the Department of Agricultural and Applied Economics, as well as former colleagues in the U.S. Department of Agriculture, helped by locating diverse pieces of information and data as they were needed by me in the preparation of the manuscript. My wife helped by leaving me alone in my study for long hours at a time, occasionally breaking the silence by serving me a cup of tea. Finally, the long, cold winters of Minnesota are a great inducement to stay indoors and to keep working at one's appointed task.

Thus the book *The Development of American Agriculture: A Historical Analysis* was conceived and written. Errors of fact, logic, or judgment are, of course, the responsibility of the author alone.

February 1979   Willard W. Cochrane

I. Introduction

CHAPTER 1

INTRODUCTION AND OVERVIEW

Economic development is a popular subject these days. The role of agriculture in the development process has been explored in numerous studies. But in the main, these explorations have been limited to less developed countries and regions and to the post-World War II era. It is also true that the long historical development of American agriculture is poorly understood and appreciated by many people with close ties to agriculture — farm people themselves, professional agriculturalists, agribusiness leaders, and political leaders from rural areas. The words and acts of these people often seem to suggest that the present-day agricultural sector of the United States economy jumped fully-developed into the twentieth century from some unknown past romantic age.

But this is not the way it happened. The agricultural sector of the United States developed sometimes slowly, sometimes rapidly, over a very long period — from 1607 to the present day. And it did not develop easily; it developed over much of the period through a trial and error process in which the farmers of one generation learned from the mistakes and failures of the previous generation. The costs of this process in terms of human suffering were very great — so great as to be almost indescribable, except as the process is relived in novels such as *Giants in the Earth*, *Grapes of Wrath*, and *Centennial*.[1] But the physical resources were abundant in the new world. The general climatic and environmental conditions were favorable. The desire to acquire and own land was overwhelming. Thus the process of development in agriculture drove relentlessly on, over nearly four centuries. And it continues to drive on in the 1990s, but the form of that development has changed dramatically over the years.

The Purpose of the Book

The purpose of this book is twofold: first, to describe in some detail the development of American agriculture; second, to explain how the development process took place. The description could prove tedious, but it need not. It need not, because it was an exciting development, liberally sprinkled with high adventure, human tragedy, and conflict. The explanation is formulated and presented at two levels: (1) in terms of the basic forces that motivated, or fueled, the development process and (2) in terms of the operation of a general conceptual model for the post-World War II period.

In a more general sense, the purpose of this book is to introduce the modern student of agricultural development, whether young or old, American or foreign, to the historical development of American agriculture, and to help the student understand and appreciate this long, difficult process. This is our purpose not because of an antiquarian motivation but because an understanding of the forces that generated development in the past is basic to an understanding of the dynamics of agricultural development in the present and future. The process of agricultural development in the United States in the 1980s and 1990s derives out of forces set in motion and decisions taken in the early twentieth century, the nineteenth century, and even the eighteenth century, Modern students of agricultural development must comprehend and appreciate this.

Some Definitions and Concepts

We will be using a number of words and terms that have an everyday dictionary meaning but which have taken on a specific meaning in the literature on economic development. We define those words and terms for use in this book as follows.[2]

Economic development. The term *economic development*, as used here, is a multidimensional concept. The many dimensions include: improvements in the average real income of members of society, the eradication of poverty, changes in the organization and location of production activities resulting in inceased output, changes in technological arrangements leading to increased output, changes in social institutions leading to improvements in production and distribution, and changes in the human agent — physical, mental, and attitudinal — resulting in increased worker productivity. More specifically, by economic development we mean both an increase in the output of goods and services and changes in the technical, organizational, social, and institutional arrangements by which that output is produced and distributed.

Agricultural development. This term means exactly the same as the term *economic development*, except that the unit of inquiry is limited in the main to the agricultural sector. The word *economic* is dropped from the term (as it is in the title of the book) for the sake of brevity, but we could be exact and use the full term: *the economic development of agriculture*.

Economic growth. This is a more restricted term than *economic development*. It is concerned with a change, or increase, in the size of the economy — perhaps the size of the total economy as measured by total output or perhaps a change or increase in some part of the economy as measured by units of input or units of output. The term *economic growth*, however, has two distinct meanings. Those meanings are presented below.

   Extensive growth. By this is meant an increase in the total output of goods and services in which output per capita is constant. In this case output increases as the result of an increase in the use of inputs where all inputs continue to be employed in the same ways under the same institutional arrangements.

   Intensive growth. By this is meant an increase in the total output of goods and services in which output per capita increases. In this case output increases from some combination of an increase in the use of inputs and an increase in the productivity of individual units of inputs as the result of their being employed in new ways under new institutional arrangements. The concept of intensive growth may be viewed as a particular case of economic development.

Institutions. These are agreed-upon arrangements among individuals for governing, or directing, or influencing the way something is done. Some of the arrangements are formalized into law; some take the form of conventions; some take the form of voluntary associations. The laws governing the organization and operation of labor unions illustrate the first case; the tradition that the bride's family will provide a dowry in many Asian societies and will underwrite the cost of the wedding in Western societies illustrates the second; the rules governing the way athletic events are conducted illustrate the third.

Structure. This term refers to the form and characteristics of an industry or a sector of the economy. It is concerned with the size, number, and location of business firms in an industry, with the essential technological and resource characteristics of an industry, and with the basic organizational and institutional characteristics of an industry.

Other more specialized economic terms will be encountered in the course of reading this book. Where the meaning of those terms is not clear, or the terms are used in a special way, they will be defined for the reader.

The General Approach

The subject matter of this book lends itself to various approaches. At one extreme, some type of rigorous quantitative model might be simulated from the agricultural sector of the U.S. economy to describe and "explain" its functioning and transformation over time. For long historical periods of time where the parameters of the system are undergoing continuous and significant change, this approach has severe limitations, but for shorter periods — say, 1950–90 — this approach can be highly rewarding and highly instructive.[3] At the other extreme, one can take a purely literary approach to the subject, as the economic historians Paul W. Gates and Fred A. Shannon have done in describing the historical development of agriculture in the United States in the nineteenth century.[4]

The purpose of this book, as discussed earlier in this chapter, dictates to an important degree the general approach taken. To introduce the modern student of economic development to the historical development of American agriculture, and to explain how this development occurred, it is necessary to include both historical description and economic analysis.

The presentation is divided into three major parts. The historical development of American agriculture from 1607 to 1990 is described in part II. An identification of and analysis of the key forces involved in this development is undertaken in part III. A politico-economic model is conceptualized and employed to explain the development and behavior of American agriculture in the period 1950 through 1990 in part IV. This approach should do three things: first, provide the reader with a descriptive picture of what actually occurred in the long development process with regard to major strands of development and the human drama; second, present a clear perception of the major forces involved in the development of American agriculture and the role that they played in generating development; and third, offer a rigorous model for explaining the development of American agriculture in the recent past, the present, and the future.

An Overview of Agricultural Development in the United States

One hundred and twenty-six years elapsed from the settlement of Jamestown in 1607 to the settlement of Savannah, Georgia, the Thirteenth Colony, in 1733. Economic growth was very slow over this long period; but it was not a time of stagnation, and development began to accelerate in the latter part of the period. In the early years, say, 1607 to 1640, the incidence of death from starvation, disease, and Indian wars was so high among the settlers that the survival of the settlements was in continuous doubt. By 1640 there were probably no more than 25,000 white people in the English colonies, and by 1700 the settlements still hugged the coasts from Charleston, South Carolina, to what is now Portland, Maine.

The principal concern of most of the settlers during the period 1607 to 1640 was survival itself. Thus, when not engaged in protecting themselves from hostile Indians, the settlers were occupied most of the time with the collection and production of food. The typical settler was a combination hunter-farmer. The food production ways of the old country were tried in the new unfamiliar environment and usually found wanting; therefore, new ways had to be discovered and tried. These new ways were often learned from the local Indians and were very often concerned with the growing of two crops: Indian corn (or maize) and tobacco. The first crop provided food for survival, the second a salable product which was used to purchase needed supplies (guns and powder, axes, hoes, cooking pots, sugar, and spirits). The productivity of the hunter-farmer probably rose from near zero in 1607–8 to a subsistence level by 1640, and to a level that produced a surplus over subsistence by 1780. From this surplus a few fortunes were made, and the productive capital of agriculture, including black slaves, increased rapidly in the older, settled areas near the coast.

During the American Revolution and the years immediately thereafter, westward expansion and agricultural development were virtually halted. Nonetheless, a trickle of hardy pioneers was moving across the Appalachian Mountains in the 1780s, and by 1790 the trickle had swollen into a stream. This stream had turned into a great westward movement by 1800 — a westward movement of settlers from Georgia to New England. During the nineteenth century, the entire interior of what is now the continental United States was settled, and the frontier was closed. In general terms, this was a 100-year period of extensive growth. We added one farm or ranch or plantation after another as wave after wave of pioneers moved westward and settled on the new land. Worker productivity in agriculture increased as machines were substituted for human labor. But total output per unit of total input increased very little if at all. This was an age of pioneering, settlement, the adding of resources, and extensive farming. But it was not an easy period; it was cruel to the white settlers who had to learn to live and farm in a new, hostile environment, cruel to the native Indians who were pushed aside, and cruel to the beasts of burden who made the great movement possible. It was also an exciting period with many lessons for the student of agricultural development.

Agricultural development in the United States changed drastically in the twentieth century. The free land was gone, and rapid extensive growth was no longer possible. In the first two decades of the century, the rate of increase in agricultural production was slow, but the rate of increase in demand resulting from surging population growth and World War I was rapid, and agriculture enjoyed unparalleled prosperity. A great dynamic process of technological development began to pay off in the 1920s and continues to do so to the present day. Technological developments in the nineteenth century were primarily mechanical, but the emphasis shifted in the twentieth century to include biological and chemical as well as mechanical developments. As a result, agricultural productivity — output per unit of input — began to increase in the 1930s, and in the 1950s it increased by over 25 percent in one decade. American agriculture was growing once again but this time by the intensive route. The rate of increase in agricultural productivity slowed slightly in the 1960s and appeared to level off in the early 1970s. But fears that the technological revolution in American agriculture was coming to an end soon proved to be unfounded. The rate of increase in agricultural productivity picked up in the second half of the 1970s and raced into the 1980s at an unprecedented pace.

The speed and magnitude of technological developments in farming in the 1980s have caused one observer of the agricultural scene to write in 1990:

Production agriculture in the Western world is now entering the last phase of industrialization — the integration of each step in the food production system. . . . This is true not only in poultry, pork and cattle . . . but also in the production of grains and oilseeds.[5]

This new world of industrialized farming, with its heavy emphasis on technology, capital, and improved management systems, is also a part of another new world, that of a highly competitive international market for farm products. In the 1970s the value of agricultural exports from the United States increased by six times in an unbelievable expansion; in the 1980s the value of those exports has declined by as much as 40 percent depending on the year. And farmers, traders, and the government have struggled to keep agricultural exports from the United States from declining further. How American agriculture will fare in the international market in the 1990s remains to be seen. But one thing is certain: It will be a highly competitive world market.

Suggested Readings

Historical Atlas of the United States, Centennial Edition. Washington, D.C.: National Geographic Society, 1988.

North, Douglass C. *Growth and Welfare in the American Past: A New Economic History,* 2nd ed. Englewood Cliffs, N.J.: Prentice-Hall, 1974. Chaps. 1, 2, and 3.

Rasmussen, Wayne D. "American Agriculture: A Short History." October 1, 1974. (Mimeographed.) Based on *A Documentary History of American Agriculture,* edited by Wayne D. Rasmussen, 4 vols. New York: Random House, 1975.

Smith, Maryanna S., and Roth, Dennis M. *Chronological Landmarks in American Agriculture.* Economic Research Service, U.S. Department of Agriculture, Agricultural Information Bulletin No. 425, Washington, D.C., November 1990.

U.S. Department of Agriculture, Economic Research Service. *A Chronology of American Agriculture, 1776–1976,* January 1977.

II. Agricultural Development:
A Chronological History

CHAPTER 2

THE COLONIAL PERIOD: 1607–1775

The Settlements[1]

Three ships outfitted by a private firm, the Virginia Company, left London bound for the New World in December 1606 carrying 144 colonists, or adventurers. The Virginia Company was instructed by King James I to locate its settlements somewhere between the thirty-eighth and forty-first parallels, or roughly between what is now the entrance to the Potomac River and Long Island. The ships carrying the little band of colonists actually dropped anchor in the James River, somewhat south of the thirty-eighth parallel, in late April 1607. After searching the area, the colonists decided on May 13, 1607, to settle on the Jamestown peninsula. The site selected provided good anchorage for their ships, but it was a swampy, malaria-infested area, ill-suited to settlement.

By January 1608, only thirty-eight settlers were still alive; the rest had died of starvation and disease. A new contingent of colonists arrived in the spring of 1608 with food and other provisions, and the colony was saved. This would be the continuing story of the Virginia Colony for the first twenty years of its existence. It was "saved" almost annually by a new infusion of settlers and supplies. By 1622 some 6,000 settlers had been transported to the colony by the Virginia Company but only 2,000 remained. The rest had died of starvation or disease, been killed by the native Indians, or returned home to England. The company's interest in quick profits led the colonists to expend their energies in searching for gold or becoming involved in other get-rich-quick schemes. As a result, the development of a permanent, productive agriculture was neglected, and the settlers were chronically confronted with the threat of, or actual, starvation.

During this floundering period the settlers did, however, learn two important things from the Indians: how to plant and grow corn, or maize, and how to plant and grow tobacco. The production of corn saved the colony from complete starvation and failure in these very early years, and the production of tobacco provided an important cash crop for export. By 1620 exports of tobacco were sufficiently large — about 100,000 pounds — to cause the stockholders in the Virginia Company to believe that they had at last found the way to turn a profit on their investments. But a large-scale Indian attack on the colony in 1622, in which 350 people were killed in one day, set the colony back once again and retarded its growth. Meanwhile, in England the stockholders and officers of the company continued to disagree and bicker over colonizing policies, where the profits were thin and the prospects dim. Thus in 1624 King James I revoked the company's charter and created a royal colony subject to the direct control of the Crown.

The royal Virginia Colony continued to grow and develop throughout the seventeenth century. The development was based primarily on the production of two crops: tobacco for export, and corn for human and animal consumption. This agriculture was highly exploitive; cleared tracts of land were cropped continuously until the fertility of the soil was exhausted. When the soil of one tract of land was rendered infertile, the large planters with abundant land cleared a new tract and moved their farming operations to it. And they continued to do this until they began to run out of suitable land for cultivation in the latter part of the eighteenth century.

The English government should have learned from the Virginia experience that a business corporation is not well suited to found and administer a colony where quick profits are not likely. The vacillating and inadequate management of the Virginia Colony by a private stock company should have made it clear that some other form of organization was to be preferred when undertaking future colonization ventures. However, the men who governed England closed their eyes to the implications of the Virginia experience and soon created a similar private corporate structure to undertake the settlement of Massachusetts Bay.

But first a religious separatist sect that had moved to Holland in 1608 to escape persecution obtained a grant in 1620 from the Virginia Company of London to settle somewhere in Virginia. This little company of Pilgrim separatists and various and sundry indentured servants and London adventurers, 101 in all, set sail from Plymouth, England, in one ship, the Mayflower, on September 16, 1620. After a relatively short voyage of sixty-five days in which the Mayflower was blown off course either by severe storms or by conscious design, the Pilgrims made landfall at Cape Cod on November 9, 1620. After a month of scouting the area and discussing the propriety of settling in an area to which their grant did not apply, the Pilgrim members of the company entered into a *compact* to govern themselves and to "control" the nonseparatists in the company. Having made the decision to land, they disembarked in Plymouth Harbor on Massachusetts Bay in December 1620. Possessing scant provisions and with no opportunity to produce food and supplies for themselves, the Pilgrims barely survived the first winter. Tradition has it that the local Indians kept them from starving; nonetheless, the mortality rate soared.

Because of the poverty of the Plymouth Colony and the unpopular religious views of its separatist leaders, the colony grew slowly, from 124 persons in 1624, to 300 in 1630, and to 3,000 by 1660. To encourage agricultural production, the settlers abandoned communal farming in 1623, and to survive, the colonists became involved in fishing and trade with the Indians. But returns to the London merchants who financed the enterprise were meager, and the partnership with the London merchants was dissolved in the late 1620s. Thereafter the Pilgrims were on their own. By such enterprises as fishing, and trading in furs with the Indians, they survived — albeit barely. During the latter part of the seventeenth century the Plymouth Colony fell under the influence of the larger, more successful Massachusetts Bay Colony.

In 1630, John Winthrop led the first contingent of about 1,000 Puritan settlers from England to what is now Boston, Massachusetts. Within a decade the population of the Massachusetts Bay Colony had grown to some 20,000 persons. Although this colonizing effort resulted in part from the private profit motive and was organized through a complicated set of private corporate developments, the preeminent motivation for the "great migration" of Puritans to the Massachusetts Bay Colony in the 1630s was religious. Puritans believed that God was closely involved in all human activities and concerns. Many of them thus interpreted the social troubles of England in the 1620s as God's punishment of the nation for its failure to purify the Anglican church. They were further persuaded that because of this failure, God would soon unleash a terrible wrath on the English people. In part, then, New England appeared as a shelter and refuge in which they, the pure and the faithful, could escape the coming devastation. But probably more significant, the Puritan colonists believed that they had a special mission inspired by God to found an ideal community, a Zion, in the New World. And to an important degree they succeeded. They created a theocracy in Massachusetts, with church and state intertwined, that prospered and developed rapidly. Religious zeal provided the drive to migrate to the New World and there to build and to produce; the strong financial position of many of the colonists and the backers of the enterprise in England provided the resources that enabled the colony to develop rapidly.

But the theocracy of Massachusetts Bay would not tolerate dissent. As dissenters appeared in their midst, they were banished. Roger Williams, pastor of the church in Salem, argued for the separation of church and state because in his view meddling with political affairs would cause God's chosen people to be contaminated by the sins of ordinary men. This was certainly not a democratic position, and Roger Williams was no proponent of religious toleration. But he was wise enough to see that if his position of religious elitism was to be protected, the church must be free of state interference.

For his heresy Roger Williams was banished, or permitted to escape, in the winter of 1635–36, with the advice that land free of any government patents was available in the Narragansett Bay area to the south. Other dissenters followed Roger Williams there. After many trials and tribulations, some physical but mostly social strife, Roger Williams obtained a charter for the settlements of Rhode Island from the English government in 1644, which was reconfirmed by Charles II in 1663. Needless to say, the charter authorized complete religious freedom in the settlements of Rhode Island.

With the growth in population of the Massachusetts Bay Colony and its increased productivity and prosperity, it is understandable that the Bay Colony would seek to expand. It is also understandable that the persons involved would seek to expand into a fertile region. This they found in the Connecticut River valley. The people who moved there were not dissenters but orthodox Puritans seeking better land to cultivate and improved economic opportunities. Thus the Connecticut River settlements and New Haven for many years remained closely allied with the Massachusetts Bay Colony. But in 1662 the Connecticut settlements obtained a charter from the Crown giving them independent status as a colony.

Somewhat later, in 1679, the English government recognized the settlements lying to the north of Massachusetts to be independent of Massachusetts and created the royal colony of New Hampshire.

Between 1632 and 1732, eight English colonies not mentioned to this point came into being. Their origin and early settlement are described below.

Maryland. Maryland was founded in 1632 by a grant from Charles I to George Calvert, the first Lord Baltimore. This colony was created out of the Virginia Colony on land lying north of the Potomac River. It was originally founded as a haven for persecuted Roman Catholics, but it granted religious liberty to all Christians, and since it pursued liberal policies in the distribution of land, many Protestants settled there.

The Calverts tried to create a feudal domain in Maryland by granting large manors to wealthy settlers, who were expected to import indentured servants to work the land. But this colonizing policy proved unsuccessful, and the proprietors were forced to offer head-rights, or free grants of land, to individual settlers. The happy combination of religious freedom, a high degree of self-government, free land under the headright system, and the production and export of tobacco caused the colony to grow and prosper.

The Carolinas. Charles II created these colonies out of the region south of Virginia by a proprietary grant to eight powerful English lords in 1663. The grant of land included what are now the states of North Carolina and South Carolina, and that strip of land extended westward to the Pacific Ocean. These proprietors drafted an elaborate quasi-feudal plan for colonizing the region. The Carolinas were to be ruled by hereditary nobility with enormous landed estates. But few Englishmen were interested in becoming peasants on these estates. Thus the grandiose scheme failed. The proprietors did, however, succeed in attracting English planters from the West Indies to produce sugar, rice, and indigo with the labor of black slaves. The settlements around Charles Town developed rapidly. This development was based on a flourishing fur and skin trade with the Indians and the production of rice on large plantations.

The first English inhabitants of the Carolinas had migrated from Virginia into what is now North Carolina. These freeholders resisted all attempts by the Carolina proprietors to attach them to the legal government of the Carolinas, and they eventually broke away from the Carolina Colony (in 1712) to form the separate colony of North Carolina. Isolated by hazardous sandbars and capes along the coast, the colony of North Carolina developed slowly. Its economy was based upon a small-scale subsistence agriculture.

New York and New Jersey. The Dutch colony of New Netherlands, founded in 1624, grew slowly. Its growth was hampered by poor leadership, sporadic wars with the local Indians, and strong competition from the nearby settlers of New England. The Dutch colony capitulated easily to the English forces of the Duke of York, brother to King Charles II, in 1664. The Dutch colony thus became an English colony and was named New York after the Duke of York. The Dutch recaptured the colony briefly during the Anglo-Dutch War of 1672–74 but returned the colony to England as part of the peace settlement.

The local representatives of the Duke of York did not drastically alter the social and governing structure of the colony from what it had been under the Dutch. The Duke was not interested in colonizing ventures but in revenue. Thus his representatives encouraged the Dutch colonists to continue to trade with the Indians for furs, and he gave away what is now New Jersey to Stuart loyalists, Lord Berkeley and Sir George Carteret. In 1665 these two proprietors provided for a government that included a popularly elected assembly. The white population of New Jersey consisted of Swedes and Finns along the Delaware River, Dutch farmers along the Hudson River, and a rapidly growing number of Puritans from New England. In 1702 this proprietorship became the royal colony of New Jersey.

Pennsylvania. William Penn, the son of a famous admiral who had helped restore Charles II to the throne, took a grant of land to be named Pennsylvania in payment for a large debt owed the admiral by the Stuarts. The grant included all the land west of the Delaware River between the fortieth and forty-third parallels. William Penn also inherited land from his father in western New Jersey. Sandwiched in between the Chesapeake Bay colonies to the south and the New York and New Jersey colonies to the north, William Penn and his heirs were involved in boundary disputes for many years.

But William Penn, a converted Quaker who was both very rich and very persuasive, was determined to create a haven in the New World for his persecuted religious brothers, the Quakers. Colonization began in 1681, and William Penn himself came to the colony in 1682 to help lay out the city of Philadelphia. A combination of cheap land and genuine religious freedom quickly attracted many English and German settlers to the colony. The colony grew rapidly, and within some four years its population had reached 10,000. The Friends, or Quakers, provided liberal leadership not only in matters of religion but also in government and economics, and the colony prospered from the beginning. By 1700, the thrifty German farmers around Philadelphia were producing a surplus of corn, wheat, and rye to support the development of the city and also for export to the West Indies.

Georgia. The colony of Georgia was founded in 1732 when George II granted the region between the Savannah and Altamah rivers to a group of wealthy Englishmen. There were at least two motivations for the establishment of the colony: (1) to provide a haven for able-bodied debtors who crowded English jails; and (2) to create a barrier between the English colonies to the north and the Spanish settlements in Florida.

The colony developed slowly owing to poor management and lack of experience on the part of the private trustees. By 1752, the population of the colony of Georgia numbered less than 10,000. In that year Georgia became a royal colony.

Delaware. The three counties of Newcastle, Kent, and Sussex, which now form the state of Delaware, were at various times claimed by the colony of Maryland and the Dutch colony of New Amsterdam. As a result, these counties were populated with English and Dutch, as well as some Swedes, who attempted to colonize this area in the early 1600s. When the Duke of York took over the colony of New Amsterdam by conquest in 1664, all the land claimed by the Dutch colony was in turn claimed by the Duke of York. At a later date, when the colony of Pennsylvania was created, William Penn petitioned the Duke of York to transfer the three counties of Newcastle, Kent, and Sussex to his colony so that Pennsylvania would have a clear and unrestricted outlet to the sea. The Duke of York agreed to this transfer, but it did not resolve the problems of those three counties. First, the colonists in the counties were not happy with governmental arrangements in the principal Pennsylvania colony and sought on various occasions to be freed from the colonial government of Pennsylvania. Second, the British Crown never fully recognized the transfers of the counties to Pennsylvania by the Duke of York and at various times argued that they should be returned to the British Crown. Thus in 1704 the government of England separated the three lower counties — Newcastle, Kent, and Sussex — from the colony of Pennsylvania and granted them a separate and independently elected assembly. Except for the fact that the governor of the three counties continued to be the governor of the colony of Pennsylvania, the separation of the counties from Pennsylvania was complete. It may thus be said that the colony of Delaware came into being in November of 1704, after a long history of uncertainty and confusion.

The Englishmen who colonized North America had to overcome a variety of practical problems and face a host of perils, only some of which they could have anticipated. Inexperience led to misconceptions about geography, agricultural and mineral resources, economic opportunities, and prospective living conditions. There was disease in the ships and in the struggling settlements, and starvation was a constant threat as well as a reality. The climate, soil, and dense forests continued to hamper development. The Indians were a continued worry and sometimes a serious danger. The Spanish, French, Dutch, and Swedes competed with the English for territory, and their rivalry sometimes turned into open warfare. The English colonizing entrepreneurs bickered among themselves, fought with the settlers over the lack of returns, and struggled with the British Crown over rights to govern. Finally, the colonies themselves haggled continuously over boundaries and jurisdictional matters. The problems and perils confronting the settlers and their financial backers at home were endless.

Nonetheless, by 1660 England had launched at least a half dozen settlements that were prospering and growing. Englishmen knew the American coastline from the Carolinas to Maine and were familiar with the island network in the Caribbean. They had avoided the sandy beaches of New Jersey, the uninviting reaches of the eastern shore of Maryland, and the dangerous coastline of North Carolina.

By 1660 there were approximately 75,000 English colonists in North America. About 33,000 resided in New England, about 36,000 in Maryland, Virginia, and what was to become North Carolina. Most of these colonists were, however, crowded together along the coast. In 1660 the great majority of the Massachusetts Bay colonists lived within fifty miles of Boston. In Virginia and Maryland the colonists lined the rivers and estuaries on the shores of the Chesapeake Bay.

Trial and Error in the Early Years of Settlement

The first colonists, in the main, were not farmers. They came from the cities and towns of England and were a diverse group. They were gentlemen adventurers from London seeking their fortunes. They were successful businessmen and professional men — often of the Puritan faith. They were religious dissenters. They were tradesmen seeking new economic opportunities. They were prisoners taken from the crowded English jails and indentured as servants. They were poor children picked off the streets and indentured as servants. They were seamen who jumped ship in the New World. They were soldiers and members of the nobility who had backed a losing political cause. But most colonists had little actual experience in farming and did not expect to become farmers in the New World.

Even when the first settlers were acquainted with agricultural production practices in England, those practices could not be adopted successfully in the New World. This was because physical and environmental conditions in the colonies were very different from those in England. Except for some limited areas in the Connecticut River valley, along the Hudson River in what was to become New York, southeast Pennsylvania, and parts of the Tidewater of Virginia and Maryland, the soil along the Atlantic seaboard was thin, rocky, and infertile. But it was good for growing trees — which it did in profusion. Except for small patches burned over by the Indians for raising corn, the whole area was covered by dense forests that had to be cleared before the land could be planted to small grains. And the hot, muggy climate of Tidewater Virginia and Maryland and the severe winters of New England were new and strange to the English colonists and inhospitable to the plants and animals brought over from England. There were, of course, exceptions. Pigs brought over from England and turned loose in the forests survived, multiplied in great numbers, and grew fat on the produce of nature — principally acorns — in the Virginia-Maryland colonies. But for the most part agricultural production in the North American colonies was a completely new experience. What produced well in the Old World failed in the New World, and methods of crop production and animal husbandry had to be adapted to the new and changed physical and environmental conditions.

But wild game, fish and shellfish, and wild berries and fruits were plentiful. Hence the early colonists became hunters and collectors or they starved. In general, food production activities in the early years of the settlements resembled those of primitive tribes in the hunting and collection stage of economic development.

Slowly, however, the early settlers learned how to farm in the New World. They learned to girdle and kill the trees and let the sun shine through. They learned to plant corn in the hills around tree stumps. They learned to substitute corn for wheat as a human food and survive. The colonists took over directly from the Indians of the Atlantic Seaboard the following crops: corn (or maize), pumpkins, squash, beans, and tobacco. After much trial and error, the first settlers learned to produce corn and other food crops with a hoe and a sharp stick among dead trees and tree stumps. They used little or no animal power; they prepared the land, planted, weeded, and harvested by hand. Thus there was a continuing scarcity of human labor in the colonies to do this hand labor, and a continuous demand for more human hands to work the stump-covered fields.

But production developments in one commodity — tobacco — did not move slowly. The smoking habit was sweeping over England and all of western Europe at this time. It approached a craze. So there was a strong demand for tobacco, which was then supplied largely by Spanish colonies in the New World. Once the colonists in Virginia and later Maryland learned from the Indians how to produce tobacco, there was a ready market for it in England and western Europe. After, say, 1612, most of the energy of the colonists in Virginia was directed into the production of tobacco. This was so much the case that administrator after administrator of the Virginia Colony had to admonish the settlers to produce less tobacco and more corn in order to survive. And before too many years elapsed, the governors of the colony had to issue rules and regulations that directed all colonists to plant some minimum part of their arable land to corn and other food crops. Charles I, who was much opposed to smoking, observed that Virginia was "wholly built upon smoke."

The production of tobacco and food crops by hand methods created an insatiable demand for labor in the colonies. This demand was never fully met during the colonial period, but the colonists strove to meet it in one of three ways. First, they produced their own labor by raising large families. Second, they imported indentured servants from England. Third, they bought black slaves from the slave traders.

Raising large families worked reasonably well in New England, where the settlers came in family units and there was no great shortage of women. But in Virginia the first settlers were exclusively men, and for many years most of the settlers were men. Thus, producing one's own labor by raising large families was not a viable solution in Virginia, and later Maryland. Efforts were made in the 1620s and 1630s to send marriageable young women to Virginia from England — in fact, a private company was organized to provide this service. But in the first decades of settlement there was a great shortage of marriageable women in the southern colonies.

This method of meeting the need for labor in the colonies did, however, have one serious drawback. Because of the ready availability of free or cheap land, sons and daughters, once they were grown, took off to become independent, freeholder farmers. Home-produced labor left the nest as soon as it came of age.

The second solution to the labor problem, namely, the use of indentured servants, was the most successful in the early years of settlement, but it too had its temporary aspects. Private agencies in England would indenture prisoners and other indigents, pay for their transport across the Atlantic, and sell the indentured servants to colonial planters and farmers for a period running from four to seven years. Each of these planters and farmers would have the labor provided by the indentured servant in exchange for the sale price of the servant plus his maintenance for a period of four to seven years. At the end of the period of indenture, the servant became a free man, to work as a laborer or tradesman or to become a farmer on his own as the case might be. There were abuses associated with this practice, as might be surmised, but in a general way it worked well. It provided colonial planters with a needed supply of labor, and it gave the least bad criminals — debtors, for example — and other indigents an opportunity to become productive members of society in the New World. It was the leading solution to the criminal problem in England and the labor shortage problem in the colonies for 150 years or more.

The third solution to the labor shortage problem, the importation of black slaves, was not important in the early years. The first black men were sold in Jamestown, Virginia, by a Dutch slaver in 1619. Some twenty men were sold in this lot. The importation of blacks from Africa continued thereafter, but at a slow rate. There were only about 300 blacks in Virginia by 1650, and their status as slaves was not clear. Their status in this early period was not substantially different from that of white indentured servants. Some did earn their freedom. But after 1650 the institution of black slavery hardened, and black servants and their children became slaves for life. The number of black servants, or slaves, in Virginia also increased rather rapidly after 1650; there were around 2,000 by 1670 and some 6,000 by 1700.

While the early colonial planters and farmers were being saved by
savages by learning to farm along primitive lines, an agricultural revolution was getting under way in England.[2] It centered on the lowly
turnip and other root crops, which were rotated with small grains. By
1800 a new rotation, sometimes called the Norfolk rotation, had
spread throughout much of England. It typically involved a four-year
rotation:
First year: wheat
Second year: root crop
Third year: barley
Fourth year: a cover crop of rye or clover.
The root crops, which were weeded by hand, helped control the
weeds. The new rotation provided an increased amount of fodder for
an expanding livestock industry. The manure produced by the livestock was returned to the land to increase its fertility. Professor Vernon Ruttan calls this *the conservation model* of agricultural development.[3] It played an important role in the development of agriculture
in England during the seventeenth and eighteenth centuries. And it
played a modest role in the older, established agricultural areas in the
United States during the nineteenth century, and in the United States
generally during, say, the period between 1900 and 1930, after the
closing of the frontier and before the widespread use of commercial
fertilizer. But, although this revolution in agricultural production in
England got under way while the English colonies in North America
were being planted, it played no observable role in the development
of agriculture in colonial America. With the possible exception of the
German farmers around Philadelphia, farmers throughout the colonies were highly exploitive and wasteful of their most abundant resource, land.

Abundant Land

Abundant land, often free and if not free then very cheap and sometimes linked to religious motivations, was the great incentive attracting adventurers and settlers to the colonies from 1607 to 1775. Land in
the colonies was distributed in three principal ways with, of course,
an infinite number of variations: first, through great land grants to
friends and supporters of the king; second, by the New England
method of making a grant of land, typically a township, to a church
congregation or corporate group which would settle there; and third,
through the headright system employed in the southern colonies.

In the first method of land distribution, the king would make a grant of land to a single proprietor, or a small group of proprietors, who were expected to colonize that land. The British king made such grants to Lord Baltimore to found the colony of Maryland and to William Penn to found the colony of Pennsylvania; he also made a grant of what is now North and South Carolina to a small group of lords. In Maryland and the Carolinas, the proprietors attempted to create feudal estates in the colonies to be owned by hereditary nobles and to be worked by peasants. But Englishmen did not want to migrate to North America to become serfs, or peasants. Thus the feudalistic schemes of these proprietors broke down, and they were forced to distribute their lands largely as gifts. In other words, to induce people to migrate to these colonies and settle there, the proprietors were forced to give the settlers clear titles to the land either as an outright gift or for a very small payment. Lord Baltimore and his heirs, for example, made huge grants of land to friends and relatives and gentlemen adventurers; they gave 100 acres as a headright to each individual who transported himself to Maryland; and they sold land outright to various kinds of settlers, including Puritans. William Penn proved to be a successful colonizer by offering two things: (1) religious toleration, and (2) land for sale at a low price on easy terms.

In the second method of land distribution — that employed in the Massachusetts Bay Colony — a corporate group, usually a church congregation, would petition the colonial government for a grant of land. If approved, the corporate group would receive a grant of land for the use of the group and for distribution among investing members of the group. The tract on which settlement was to be made was known as the "town grant," and its size varied from four to ten square miles. Near the center of the grant a village would be laid out, with a site for the village green and meeting house, as well as house lots of perhaps a half acre for the settlers. The next step was the division of arable lands and meadows. Large fields of several hundred acres were surveyed and divided into strips, which were numbered. These strips were then distributed among investing settlers by lot. In the distribution of the arable and meadow lands, two criteria were used: (1) the investment of the settler in the original enterprise and (2) his ability to use the land. The allotments of arable and meadow lands were not fenced separately but were surrounded by a common fence; hence they were known as "proprietors' commons." Each settler cultivated his own lot, or lots, within the proprietors' commons subject to restrictions on crops and dates of planting and harvesting. In addition, there were town commons that could be used by all inhabitants of the town. They included all land of the original grant not yet divided among the original proprietors or allotted to latecomers. On such commons any inhabitant might pasture his animals and take wood, stone, or earth, subject to the regulation of the town authorities.

The New England land distribution system, with its community settlements, had important social and political implications. It developed habits of group action and tended to foster a compact, cohesive social life. It provided an effective and equitable method for distributing large areas of land to cultivators in parcels roughly proportional to their ability to use land. In New England during the years when the system of town grants was in operation (that is, up to 1725), land speculation was unknown.

The third principal method for distributing land to settlers was the headright system, a simple but effective method for attracting settlers to the colonies. Under this method any man transporting himself to the colony would be eligible to receive a grant of land once he stepped ashore. He would also receive a grant of land for each person other than himself that he transported to the colony — perhaps members of his family, perhaps indentured servants. Within the colony the individual could select only land that was not yet appropriated, in areas designated for settlement.

This method of land distribution was used in the Virginia Colony for many years. A colonist who transported himself to Virginia received a land grant of fifty acres as his headright. He also received a grant of fifty acres for each additional individual that he transported to the Virginia Colony. Maryland also made use of this method of land distribution for a time, as was noted earlier.

But, as we see from figure 2.1, until 1700 the English settlements in North America were located on the coastline of the Atlantic Ocean, or along accessible rivers flowing into it — the Delaware, Hudson, and Connecticut. After 1700, the settlements moved inland, but they still remained on the Atlantic Seaboard. Until the Revolutionary War, the English colonies were squeezed together on a rocky, generally infertile strip of land lying between the Atlantic Ocean and the Appalachian Mountains.

The population of the English colonies grew steadily but not spectacularly over the long period from 1607 to the Revolutionary War. The growth in population by colony, region, and total may be observed in table 2.1. In rough terms, the population of the English

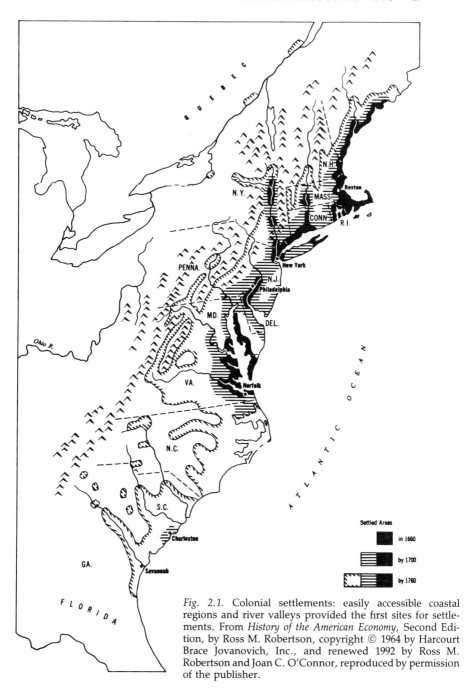

Fig. 2.1. Colonial settlements: easily accessible coastal regions and river valleys provided the first sites for settlements. From *History of the American Economy*, Second Edition, by Ross M. Robertson, copyright © 1964 by Harcourt Brace Jovanovich, Inc., and renewed 1992 by Ross M. Robertson and Joan C. O'Connor, reproduced by permission of the publisher.

colonies more than doubled every thirty years from 1660 to 1780, reaching a grand total of over 2.7 million persons in 1780.

The State of Agricultural Arts, 1700–1775

By 1700 the years of uncertainty with regard to the survival of the colonies were long past, and in the older settled areas a commercial agriculture had developed in which a surplus of agricultural products was available for sale to the growing colonial towns and for export to England and the West Indies. But it would be a mistake to describe

Table 2.1. Population of the English Colonies,[a] 1630–1780

Colony	1630	1660	1690	1720	1750	1780
New England						
New Hampshire	500	1,555	4,164	9,375	27,505	87,802
Massachusetts[b]	1,296	22,062	56,928	91,008	188,000	268,627
Rhode Island	. . .	1,539	4,224	11,680	33,226	52,946
Connecticut	. . .	7,980	21,645	58,830	111,280	206,701
Subtotal	1,796	33,136	86,961	170,893	360,011	616,076
Middle Colonies						
New York	350	4,936	13,909	36,919	76,696	210,541
New Jersey	. . .	. . .	8,000	29,818	71,393	139,627
Pennsylvania	. . .	. . .	11,450	30,962	119,666	327,305
Delaware	. . .	540	1,482	5,385	28,704	45,385
Subtotal	350	5,476	34,841	103,084	296,459	722,858
Southern Colonies						
Maryland	. . .	8,426	24,024	66,133	141,073	245,474
Virginia	2,500	27,020	53,046	87,757	231,033	538,004
North Carolina	. . .	1,000	7,600	21,270	72,984	270,133
South Carolina	. . .	. . .	3,900	17,048	64,000	180,000
Georgia	. . .	. . .	. . .	. . .	5,200	56,071
Subtotal	2,500	36,446	88,570	192,208	514,290	1,289,682
Grand total	4,646	75,058	210,372	466,185	1,170,760	2,780,369[c]

Source: U.S. Department of Commerce, Bureau of the Census, *Historical Statistics of the United States, Colonial Times to 1957* (Washington, D.C., 1960), p. Z-1-20.

[a] Includes both whites and blacks.

[b] The Massachusetts figures include 390 persons from Plymouth Colony and 400 persons from Maine in 1630; 1,980 persons from Plymouth Colony in 1660; and 7,424 persons from Plymouth Colony in 1690.

[c] The 1780 figures do not add up to the grand total because included in the grand total, but not shown in the colonial and subtotal figures, are 96,753 persons who lived in the areas that later became the states of Maine and Vermont, and 55,000 persons who lived in the areas that later became the states of Kentucky and Tennessee.

the agriculture of this period, even in the commercial areas, as a modern, intensive agriculture. It was an extensive type of agriculture, highly dependent on hand labor. The basic tools were the hoe, the ax, and the scythe. A few plows were used, but they were heavy, cumbersome pieces of equipment that often had to be pulled by four oxen and operated by two men. The plowman, where he existed, was not a farmer per se; his was an independent vocation in which he did custom plowing for larger planters or farmers who could afford it. The harvesting and threshing of small grains was done in ways not much different from those of biblical times.

Labor continued to be scarce. Farmers in New England and in the newer settlements on the frontier depended almost entirely on family labor and sought to increase their labor supply by raising large families. Large farmers throughout the colonies imported indentured servants to the extent they could afford it. The large, commercial planters of tobacco in Maryland and Virginia and rice in South Carolina turned increasingly to the importation of black slaves.

Colonial agriculture was a hand-labor agriculture, not because labor was cheap but because the efficient tools and machines that could be substituted for hand labor in agricultural production had yet to be invented and developed. Colonial farmers did, however, substitute cheap land for expensive hand labor to the maximum extent possible. Thus we can characterize colonial agriculture as an extensive, hand-labor agriculture.

In the late 1600s and early 1700s the state of the arts with regard to animal husbandry in the colonies was appallingly bad. Good pastureland was extremely scarce. Fencing almost did not exist. Sheds and fenced enclosures in which to protect animals from the elements and to protect breed standards were virtually nonexistent. Therefore, cattle, pigs, and horses ran loose in the woods and survived as best they could. In the southern colonies where the climate was hospitable, the numbers of these classes of livestock increased to the point where they were sometimes a nuisance. Cattle and pigs were hunted like wild game by whites and Indians alike. Horses and cattle were occasionally rounded up, branded, and then turned loose again. In this process the quality of the livestock deteriorated. Horses became small in size. Cattle produced little meat. Only the pig seemed to do well on a diet of acorns.

But in the eighteenth century the demand for higher quality livestock increased as a result of economic development. Rich planters wanted good horses to ride. Well-to-do townspeople demanded a more reliable supply of better cuts of meat. Freighters and plowmen were in need of improved draft horses and oxen. Thus a cattle-raising and beef-fattening industry began to develop in New England and the middle colonies. Improved breeds of sheep were imported and looked after. The Narragansett Pacer, an excellent riding horse, was developed in Rhode Island and sold from there throughout the colonies and the West Indies. The Conestoga draft horse was developed by the German farmers in Pennsylvania and became known as the finest draft horse in the colonies.

This is not to suggest that the production of high quality livestock was the general rule. The small farmer outside the commercial farming areas had little livestock except pigs. And what he did have he did not take care of. But the beginnings of a livestock industry began to take shape in the 1700s, and the demand for high quality carriage and riding horses was increasing rapidly.

Crops grown in the colonies during this period varied with the geographic area and stage of development. There was one exception, corn (or maize), which was grown everywhere in the colonies. On the frontier it was the staff of life for the settlers, and where a surplus existed, it was probably made into corn whiskey. In the highly commercial tobacco-producing areas of Tidewater Maryland, Virginia, and North Carolina, corn was produced for food for the black slaves and indentured servants, and it was fed to livestock that were to be fattened for slaughter. Corn had a place in the general farming systems of New England, both as a human food and as livestock feed. And in the grain-producing areas of the middle colonies it was one of the principal grains grown.

On the frontier of the colonies the typical farmer was a subsistence farmer. He raised corn on his small clearing for his family use, as was already noted. He probably also raised such things as squash, pumpkins, and assorted varieties of beans. But mainly he was a hunter of wild game and a collector of wild foods, as the first settlers along the coast had been 100 years earlier. In the main he and his family lived off the bounty of the native wilderness, sometimes well, sometimes meagerly, with the assistance of his small patch of corn and other vegetables.

In the older, settled areas of the colonies a clear specialization in the production of crops and animals had emerged. By 1700 the settled areas of New England had become general farming areas involving corn, meadows, hay, some fruit, some wheat, and an improved livestock industry. With respect to food production, it should also be noted that New England had become the leader in and the center of a sea-based fishing and whaling industry. The sea gave New England a ready "crop" to harvest, namely fish, along the banks that extended from Long Island to Newfoundland. And there was a ready market for this "crop" both at home and in the export markets of England and the West Indies.

The middle colonies, New Jersey and Pennsylvania in particular, were the bread basket of the colonial system. All the grains were produced: wheat, corn, rye, oats, and barley. Of these, wheat was the most important grain grown. The wheat that was produced in surplus was used, first, to supply the growing cities of New York, Philadelphia, and Baltimore; second, in the eighteenth century, it was exported as wheat and flour to the West Indies. The middle colonies also produced a surplus of potatoes for sale to the developing cities, and a small livestock-producing and fattening industry developed.

In Maryland, Virginia, and North Carolina, the preeminent commercial crop was tobacco. The production of tobacco, which got under way in Virginia in the first decade of settlement, never stopped growing in the seventeenth and eighteenth centuries. It was the crop that made the large farmers, or planters, of Virginia and Maryland rich and around which a way of life — of gracious living — was built. The field work was done by black slaves; the system of black slavery was firmly institutionalized by 1700. After being cured, the tobacco leaf was shipped off to England and there redistributed throughout western Europe. Exports of tobacco leaf increased from 100,000 pounds in 1620, to 30 million pounds in 1708, to 102 million pounds in 1775. The planters groused about being forced to market their total crop in England, and in some years, owing to overproduction, they did receive very low prices for their tobacco crop. But over the long run the large tobacco planters along the Tidewater built fine homes, sent their sons to universities in England or in the colonies, and became the landed aristocracy of the colonial period.

The second of the great southern staples, rice, was introduced in the late 1600s. By the early 1700s it had become an established crop around Charleston, South Carolina. At first, rice was simply produced in swampy areas subject to intermittent flooding, but before long, an intricate system of flooding was devised that utilized the force of the tide flows. Dikes were built along the lower reaches of the rivers, and as the tide pushed back the fresh water it could be let through gates into irrigation ditches that fed the rice fields. All this required a heavy investment in capital and a great input of human labor. The labor was provided by black slaves imported at a rapid rate in the eighteenth century. The work was backbreaking and had to be done in hot, mosquito-infested swamps. The mortality rate among these black slaves was high. But the profits from rice production were also high. So the importation of black slaves was continued, and a second landed aristocracy was built up in South Carolina during the eighteenth century. The South Carolinians in this period produced some other crops: corn to feed to the slaves, indigo — a dye — for export, and a new crop: short-staple cotton.

It is clear that by the eighteenth century, the older, settled areas of the English colonies had become highly specialized in the production of food and agricultural commodities. Some aspects of this specialization continue down to the present day. But the opening up of the great Mississippi River basin following the Revolutionary War played havoc with some of the specialized agricultural industries along the Atlantic Seaboard.

Trade, Markets, and Policy

Internal trade in the colonies, with some exceptions, was severely restricted. This was the case for several reasons. First, frontier settlers in the back country produced little or nothing to sell; hence they had little or no money with which to buy nonfarm-produced goods and did not constitute a viable market. Second, roads were almost nonexistent. Hence there was no way of transporting heavy, bulky agricultural products that were produced more than a few miles away from the Atlantic coast or from the rivers feeding into the Atlantic Ocean. Third, there was a great shortage of metallic money and no commonly acceptable currency in the colonies. Hence it was not easy to conduct trade in agricultural commodities, or any other commodity for that matter, within the colonies.

But there were exceptions. Trade with the Indians for skins and furs flourished. High-valued furs moved from the interior by pack animal and by canoe along river and lake waterways to such entry ports as New York, Philadelphia, and Charleston. And relatively high-valued items such as beads, muskets, powder and shot, axes, and cooking pots moved back to the Indians by the same means of transport. The second exception was the coastal trade in certain agricultural products, notably wheat and wheat flour and livestock and livestock products. This trade kept the large cities of Boston, New

York, Philadelphia, Baltimore, and Charleston supplied with food items.

The important trade of the colonies was external, or international, and took two principal forms: (1) direct trade with England, which involved the staples produced in the colonies from Maryland to Georgia, and (2) various types of indirect or triangular trade that involved the colonies from Pennsylvania to New Hampshire. Almost all the tobacco, rice, indigo, and naval stores exported from the southern colonies went *directly* to England. England paid for these staple agricultural products by exporting all kinds of manufactured goods directly to the southern colonies. In the eighteenth century, agricultural exports from the southern colonies to England were overwhelming in volume and value as compared with those of the other colonies.

New England engaged in some direct trade with England, exporting fish, lumber, and naval stores and receiving manufactured goods in return. As the external trade of New England and the middle colonies matured, it became increasingly complex. External trade from New England and the middle colonies became triangular, and then even more complex. The best known of the triangles began with the direct exchange of fish, timber, livestock, and wheat and wheat flour shipped from the ports of Boston, Newport, New York, and Philadelphia for rum, molasses, and sugar produced in the West Indies. Before long, this simple system developed into a triangular form of trade in which (1) molasses converted into rum by American distilleries was sent to the African coast to buy slaves, (2) slaves acquired in Africa were brought back to the West Indies and sold there, and (3) molasses was purchased in the West Indies and shipped to New England and the middle colonies to make more rum to repeat the triangle. An infinite number of variations of the above triangle were developed which sometimes involved the importation of black slaves into the southern colonies, the export of food and livestock products to the West Indies, and the exportation of fish, lumber, and wheat products to Spain, Portugal, and the Wine Islands. This international trade, in combination with the fishing and whaling industries, enabled New England to develop an important shipbuilding and shipping industry. In this context New Englanders became known around the world as shrewd and enterprising traders, and many merchant family fortunes were built in New England.

Although exports from the colonies expanded persistently, if not steadily, during the seventeenth and eighteenth centuries, and great merchant fortunes were made in the middle and New England colonies and great landed fortunes were made in the southern colonies, many people in the colonies were not happy with the state of external trade. The southern planters felt they should be free to sell their tobacco on the European continent, and the merchants in Philadelphia, New York, and Boston chafed under the many regulations governing external trade imposed upon them by the mother country. But the British government did not found and support the English colonies in North America to make the colonists rich. The British government founded and supported the colonies as part of a general *mercantilist* policy aimed at making the home country rich and powerful. Thus in the eyes of the men who governed England (known as Great Britain after 1707), the colonies existed to provide (1) a reliable and cheap source of raw materials and (2) a certain and protected market for the manufactured products of England. To this end, the English Parliament passed a series of laws, known as the Navigation Acts, beginning in 1651 to regulate the trade of English colonies overseas so as to benefit the home country. Ross M. Robertson has summarized the principal restrictions to colonial trade of the various Navigation Acts as follows:

1. All trade between England and any of her colonies had to be carried in ships owned by English nationals or by colonials and manned by crews that were at least three-fourths English or colonial.
2. All European imports received by the colonies, with a few minor exceptions, had to come from England. This meant that any imports from continental Europe had to pass first through an English port.
3. Certain commodities, called "enumerated" articles, could be shipped only to England. Putting it formally, we sometimes say that England was made the "staple" for such products. At first the enumerated list was small, but as time went on it was expanded greatly.[4]

The aim of these acts was threefold: (1) to protect and encourage English and colonial shipping, (2) to require that major colonial imports from Europe should come through English ports, and (3) to ensure that all colonial products important to Britain — the enumerated articles — would be shipped to England. In the seventeenth century this set of restrictions probably did not create too much of a problem for the colonists. The list of enumerated articles included only tobacco, sugar, cotton, and certain dyes. And smuggling of these and other commodities was commonplace. But in the eighteenth century the list of enumerated articles was expanded considerably, and the British government made a serious attempt to enforce the Navigation Acts. Thus the regulations governing colonial trade became more restrictive and more effective. How much these restrictions hindered and distorted the external trade of the colonies, and hence slowed the rate of economic development of the colonies, has been debated by economic historians. Some believe that the mercantilistic policies of England as embodied in the various Navigation Acts had a profoundly negative effect on the economic and industrial development of the colonies. Others do not. The Navigation Acts certainly annoyed the colonists, and the merchants of the middle and New England colonies came to believe that they and their domestic clientele were being injured by the operation of the Navigation Acts. Thus the vigorous pursuit of a mercantilistic policy in combination with a series of revenue-raising acts and punitive acts taken by the British government in the 1760s and 1770s pushed the merchant class of the middle and New England colonies a long way down the road toward rebellion.

But why should the wealthy southern planter of tobacco and rice be willing to support a rebellion on the part of the northern merchant class? And why should the frontier settler with little or nothing to sell be supportive of the interests of the merchant class? The answer is to be found in a new and emerging British land policy. Just as English mercantilistic policies in the 1700s tended to restrict and inhibit the growth of colonial trade, so English land policy after 1763 tended to block the way to westward movement and agricultural expansion. For various reasons — the defeat of France in the New World, the fur trade interests, humanitarian concern for the Indians — the British government in 1763 reserved all land from the central Appalachians to the Mississippi for the Indians. This act sent an icy chill down the spine of every land speculator in the colonies, from a rich planter like George Washington to a frontiersman like Daniel Boone. Each saw his road to riches blocked by the new British policy. Thus the rich planter and the destitute frontiersman were united in their opposition to the British Crown. Given these developments, it was relatively easy to take the next step wherein the rich southern planter, the rich northern merchant, and the poor frontier settler joined forces to rebel against the mother country. British colonial policies of the 1760s and 1770s operated to harness the divergent and driving economic forces in American society into a single rebellious effort aimed at the British Crown: the American Revolution.

Suggested Readings

Bailyn, Bernard. *The New England Merchants in the Seventeenth Century*. New York: Harper & Row, Harper Torchbooks, 1964.

Bidwell, Percy W., and Falconer, John I. *History of Agriculture in the Northern United States, 1620–1860*. Washington, D.C.: Carnegie Institution of Washington, 1941. Chap. I–VIII.

Bruce, Philip A. *Economic History of Virginia in the Seventeenth Century*. New York: Macmillan, 1896. Chaps. III–VII.

Edwards, Everett E. "American Agriculture — the First 300 Years." *Farmers in a Changing World. 1940 Yearbook of Agriculture*. U.S. Department of Agriculture. Washington, D.C.: Government Printing Office. Pp. 171–91.

Gunderson, Gerald. *A New Economic History of America*. New York: McGraw-Hill, 1976. Chap. 2.

Holmes, George K. "The First American Farmers." *The Making of America*. Vol. V of *Agriculture*, edited by Robert M. La Follette. Chicago: De Bower, Chapline, 1907.

Robertson, Ross M. *History of the American Economy*, 2nd ed. New York: Harcourt, Brace, and World, 1964. Chap. 2, 3, and 4.

CHAPTER 3

BREAKING OUT OF THE ATLANTIC SEABOARD: 1775–1820

Land Policies of the Revolution and Acquisition of the Public Domain

I n the late colonial period the king of Great Britain and a half dozen English noblemen held title to the vacant land beyond the settlements. The holdings of the king included the ungranted lands of New Hampshire, Vermont, New York, Virginia, Georgia, South Carolina, and the southern half of North Carolina. The royal claims also covered all the present states of Ohio, Indiana, Illinois, Michigan, Wisconsin, Kentucky, Alabama, Mississippi, and parts of West Virginia and Tennessee. This was an empire of some 380 million acres. The heirs of William Penn claimed the unoccupied lands of Pennsylvania; Lord Fairfax claimed a princely state in northern Virginia; Lord Granville had title to much of the northern part of North Carolina, and his claims extended west to include more than two-thirds of present-day Tennessee (some 22 million acres); and the sixth Baron Baltimore claimed all the ungranted lands of Maryland. The form of land tenure in force in these lordly domains was feudalistic; the lords possessed the right to collect annual quitrents, or payments, from settlers who bought, or acquired, any of this land, and this was and could be an important source of revenue to the king and his lords.

The American Revolution brought far-reaching changes in the ownership of these vacant lands. As Professor Curtis Nettels points out, "The men of the Revolution acted on a dual theory. First, they asserted that independence automatically deprived the king of his ungranted land and vested the title to it in the new state governments. Second, the patriots recognized the validity of old royal grants to the extent of claiming for the states the territories which the king had conferred upon the colonies by royal charter."[1] In other words, the patriots evolved and acted upon the principle that independence annulled the king's ownership of ungranted lands but that the authority he had once exercised provided a basis for the territorial claims of the new states. In view of the king's vast landholdings, the acquisition by the states of his ungranted lands was of enormous importance to them. The states added further to their real estate holdings from two sources: (1) they acquired lands that had not already been disposed of by the great landed proprietors, the Penns, Lord Baltimore, Granville, and Fairfax; and (2) they confiscated lands once owned by persons who had remained loyal to the British Crown during the Revolutionary War. As a result of these actions, all the states acquired large real estate holdings, and a few states such as Virginia and North Carolina acquired immense public domains.

Political decisions taken during the Revolutionary period resulted in a situation in which all titles to land within the United States, today, derive their legality from the governments to which the Revolution gave birth. But the question whether a feudalistic type of land law, or a system of freeholds, should prevail in the eastern United States was one of the great social and political questions of the Revolutionary period.

The victory for a freehold land tenure system really occurred through the land policies adopted by the various states during the Revolution. The states pursued five principal policies. First, they swept away the essential elements of a feudalistic tenure system such as quitrents and the right of primogeniture, and they refused to create new feudal or proprietary domains. Second, they stimulated private enterprise by placing land in the hands of private individuals as rapidly as possible instead of holding it in state-owned operations. Third, they sought to build up communities of small farmers by selling small units on easy terms to individuals with limited capital. Fourth, the states that acquired large landholdings sought to use the revenues from the sale of those holdings to pay off debts incurred during the war. Fifth, the states used land grants, or bounties, to individuals as an inducement to them to enlist and serve in the military forces during the Revolutionary War. Different states pursued these policies with different emphasis and different degrees of vigor, depending upon the extent of their landholdings, but all pursued them to a sufficient degree to ensure the establishment of a freehold land tenure system throughout the original thirteen states.

The United States acquired a national public domain in 1784 when the Congress accepted the cession by Virginia to its claim to most of the land lying north of the Ohio River. This cession gave the Union, or Confederation, a clear title to the lands between western Pennsylvania and the Mississippi River, north of the Ohio River and south of the forty-first parallel, for Virginia alone among the states claimed this area. Five other states joined Virginia in ceding to the United States western lands that they claimed under their colonial charters. In 1785, Massachusetts yielded its claim to territory west of New York, and in 1786 Connecticut gave up its claims to land in the Northwest except for the Western Reserve in northeast Ohio. Although the United States did not secure title to present-day West Virginia or Kentucky, it did acquire most of what is now Tennessee, Alabama, and Mississippi for the public domain by ceding actions of North Carolina, South Carolina, and Georgia between 1787 and 1802. The territory of the original thirteen states, four new states created out of Massachusetts and Virginia, and the public domain lying east of the Mississippi River is portrayed in figure 3.1.

The United States thus began as a solid land mass extending from the Atlantic coast to the Mississippi River and from the Great Lakes south to, but not including, Florida and west Florida. Between 1802, when Georgia ceded its rights to western land, and 1898, when the formal annexation of Hawaii occurred, the United States took on its present physical form, with some minor exceptions, through eight principal territorial acquisitions. (The first six of these acquisitions are portrayed in figure 3.1.)

1. The Territory of Louisiana, acquired by purchase from France in 1803.
2. Florida, obtained by treaty and a settlement of claims from Spain in 1819.
3. The Republic of Texas, annexed as a state in 1845. The Republic of Texas had been established nine years earlier when American settlers in Texas won their freedom from Mexico.
4. The Oregon Territory, annexed by treaty with Great Britain in 1846.
5. The Mexican Cession, acquired by military conquest over Mexico in 1848.

40

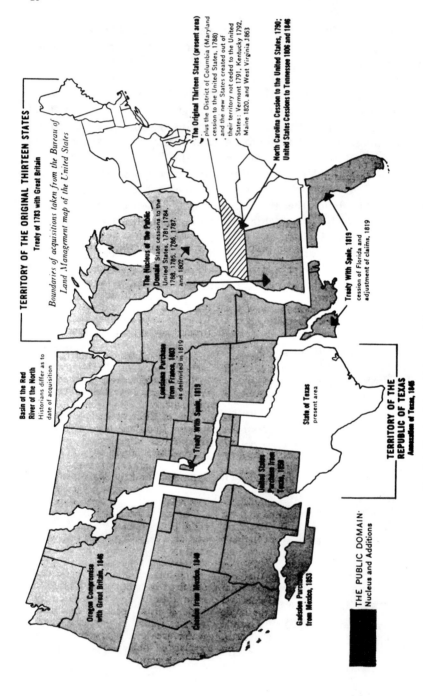

The map contains the following labels:

TERRITORY OF THE ORIGINAL THIRTEEN STATES
Treaty of 1783 with Great Britain

Boundaries of acquisitions taken from the Bureau of Land Management map of the United States

The Original Thirteen States (present area)
plus the District of Columbia (Maryland cession to the United States, 1788) and the new States created out of their territory not ceded to the United States: Vermont 1791, Kentucky 1792, Maine 1820, and West Virginia 1863

North Carolina Cession to the United States, 1790; United States Cessions to Tennessee 1806 and 1846

The Nucleus of the Public Domain State cessions to the United States, 1781, 1784, 1785, 1786, 1787, and 1802

Treaty With Spain, 1819 cession of Florida and adjustment of claims, 1819

Basin of the Red River of the North Historians differ as to date of acquisition

Louisiana Purchase from France, 1803 as delimited in 1819

Treaty With Spain, 1819

State of Texas present area

United States Purchase from Texas, 1850

TERRITORY OF THE REPUBLIC OF TEXAS Annexation of Texas, 1845

Oregon Compromise with Great Britain, 1846

Cession from Mexico, 1848

Gadsden Purchase from Mexico, 1853

THE PUBLIC DOMAIN: Nucleus and Additions

Fig. 3.1. Territorial acquisitions of the continental United States

6. The Gadsden Purchase, obtained from Mexico in 1853.
7. The Alaskan Purchase, acquired from Russia in 1867.
8. The Hawaiian Annexation, ratified in 1898.

By 1853, with the Gadsden Purchase, the continental United States extended from the Atlantic to the Pacific oceans and covered an area of 1.9 billion acres. Of this total, 1.4 billion acres (or 72 percent) were once part of the public domain. By 1853 more than two-thirds of this land was still in the public domain, but many decisions regarding its disposal had already been made. We turn now to a consideration of the decisions made between 1775 and 1820.

Disposal of the Public Domain

With regard to the disposal of the public domain, the Congress of the Confederation had to make three important decisions: (1) Was the New England or the southern system of land distribution to prevail? (2) Should the government seek to maximize its revenues from the sale of land, or should it seek to distribute lands widely through the use of liberal sales terms? (3) What should be the political relationship of the newly settled areas to the thirteen original states?

The third question was settled with relative ease. The principle was affirmed that the new areas should eventually have equal political status with the older areas. To this end, the Ordinance of 1787 passed by the Congress of the Confederation provided for the organization of the Northwest Territory, to be administered by a governor and judges appointed by the Congress. Further, a procedure was established whereby at least three and not more than five states were to be created out of the territory and admitted to the Union on a basis of complete equality with the older states when each had reached a population size of at least 60,000 *free* inhabitants.[2] Contained in the ordinance was a guarantee of civil and religious liberties and a prohibition of slavery in the territory.

Developing solutions to the first two questions, the economic questions, was not easy. With regard to the second question, the terms of sale of the public domain, two fundamentally different points of view emerged. Advocates of the "conservative view" favored selling public lands in large tracts at high prices and for cash, whereas advocates of the "liberal view" favored putting land in the reach of everyone by selling it in small parcels at low prices on easy credit terms. As with most economic policy questions, no clear-cut solution emerged. But in the main the "conservative view" prevailed. In the first land distribution ordinances passed, public lands were sold in relatively large units and for cash. This, of course, led to a set of sales arrangements by which big-time speculators purchased large tracts of land at public auction and in turn tried to sell that land to the pioneer settlers in small parcels, at high prices, and on credit. Such speculative efforts often ended in failure for both the speculator and the pioneer purchaser for one important reason — the typical small pioneer settler had no money. Thus a preeminent political issue in the United States from 1785 to 1862 was that concerned with the terms on which the public domain was to be distributed. Slowly, with much political turning and twisting, the terms of sale, or disposal, were liberalized. But it was an agonizing process.

The New England system of land distribution involved two main features. First, the land opened for settlement was carefully surveyed and laid out in townships, often six miles square, and subdivisions within the townships were laid out in uniform tracts for auction sale, or for distribution by lot, to the settlers. Second, the opening of land for settlement was controlled. It occurred as needed, proceeded with regularity from settled to unsettled land, and no one could own land not previously surveyed. In developing an answer to the first question, that of the land distribution system to be implemented, the Congress of the Confederation in essence accepted the first main feature of the New England system of land distribution and rejected the second. The Congress in the Ordinance of 1785 approved a land survey of the public domain, to serve as a physical basis for distributing the public lands. But it rejected any system of administrative controls that would regularize the distribution of public lands (i.e., offer land on the market only as needed).

Under the provisions of the Ordinance of 1785, government surveyors were to establish on unsettled lands horizontal lines called base lines and vertical lines called meridians. The first of these meridians was laid off in what is now the state of Ohio, and the first surveys covered land north of the Ohio River not included in the "reserves" (i.e., in areas of land reserved for the different states for specific purposes). From the meridians and base lines tiers of townships were laid out. (See figure 3.2.) And within each township thirty-six sections were laid out. Eventually all the land in the United States was included in the survey except the thirteen original states, Vermont, Kentucky, Tennessee, parts of Ohio, and all of Texas. (See figure 3.2.)

The Ordinance of 1785 provided for the sale of federal lands in public auctions to private persons in minimum lots of 640 acres at a price of not less than $1 per acre. The terms were strictly cash. Five sections in each township were to be reserved — four for the United States and one for the public support of public schools in the township. A brief summary of the methods of land disposal established by the several land acts is presented in table 3.1.

The sale of public land and pioneering settlement in the Northwest Territory proceeded slowly following the passage of the Ordinance of 1785 for a number of reasons. First, there were serious Indian troubles north of the Ohio River fomented in part by the British. These troubles were, however, resolved temporarily by the defeat of the Indians

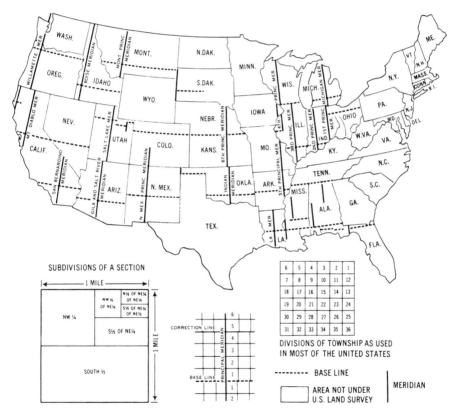

Fig. 3.2. Land survey: principal meridians and base lines made possible precise apportioning of newly opened territories into sections and easily described subdivisions of sections, thus simplifying later property transfers. From *History of the American Economy*, Second Edition, by Ross M. Robertson, copyright © 1964 by Harcourt Brace Jovanovich, Inc., and renewed 1992 by Ross M. Robertson and Joan C. O'Connor, reproduced by permission of the publisher.

Table 3.1. Methods of Disposal by Major Land Acts, 1784–1862

Land Act	Minimum Sale Price	Method of Sale or Disposal	Size of Tract	Terms of Sale
Ordinances of 1784 and 1785	$1 an acre. Discount of one-third to companies and acceptance of government paper	Auction	Half of townships offered entire, other half by 640-acre tracts	Cash until 1787, then one-third cash and rest in 3 months
Act of 1796	$2 an acre. Evidence of public debt accepted at face value	Auction	Half of tracts 5,760 acres, the rest 640 acres	One-twentieth cash, credit of 30 days on balance of first half, and a year on second half
Act of 1800	$2 an acre	Auction	Minimum of 320 acres	8 percent discount for cash. Liberal credit system inaugurated
Act of 1820	$1.25 an acre	Auction	160 acres or 80 acres	Cash
Preemption Act of 1841	$1.25 an acre. Grants to railroads and canals at $2.50	Select and settle, then purchase at minimum price	Not more than 160 acres	Cash
Graduation Act of 1854	Price graduated. For example, if on market from 10–14 years, $1 an acre; 20–24 years, 50¢; over 30 years, 12½¢	Offered for sale at stated minimum price		Cash
Homestead Act of 1862	Free homesteads of 160 acres. Only payment was a fee ranging from $26 to $34	Settle and "prove up"	Not to exceed 160 acres	Only a nominal fee, but other conditions had to be met

Source: Harold D. Guither, *Heritage of Plenty*, 2nd ed. (Danville, Ill.: Interstate Printers and Publishers, 1972), p. 38.

at the Battle of Fallen Timbers in 1794 and by a treaty with the British in which the British agreed to evacuate their military posts in the Northwest. Second, the minimum purchase that a settler could make ($640 for 640 acres) exceeded by far what the typical impoverished settler could afford as an outlay for land. Thus purchases of the public domain were typically made by speculators who hoped to resell that land to settlers at still higher prices. The general state of poverty of the early pioneers reduced the disposal of land under the Act of 1785 to a mere trickle. Third, most of the original thirteen states were engaged in enterprising, and sometimes wild, schemes and programs of land disposal within their borders (e.g., in New York and Pennsylvania) and in territories falling under their jurisdiction (e.g., Maine, Kentucky, Tennessee, and Mississippi). These state schemes and programs of land disposal were in direct competition with the federal program of disposing of the public domain. Fourth, pioneers both within the state jurisdictions and in the federal public domain who could not afford to buy land at any price simply "squatted" on unsurveyed, vacant lands. The squatters then pursued all means open to them to protect their "investment": legal means (i.e., appealing to the government involved to recognize their "rights" by granting title to them) or illegal means (i.e., forming protective associations to drive away by force potential or actual buyers of the land involved). Squatting on vacant public lands was a popular, and in frontier communities an accepted, means of acquiring a farm during this period.

Because the federal government was anxious to increase its revenues from the sale of lands in the public domain and because the Indian troubles in the Northwest Territory appeared to be resolved, the time was ripe for the establishment of a new land policy by the new government of the United States (the Act of 1785 had been passed by the Congress of the Confederation). But the Land Act of 1796 represented another victory for those with a conservative view of land disposal. Under this act, the minimum purchase of land remained 640 acres, and the minimum price per acre was *increased* to $2.00. The minimum outlay that a pioneer had to make to acquire a piece of the public domain was now $1,280 — an amount far in excess of the financial resources of the typical pioneer. The act, however, did introduce a small credit provision; the buyer was given a year in which to pay for the land.

This act further institutionalized the whole process of land disposal. It created a Surveyor General and a Corps of Surveyors to conduct the system of rectangular survey on a systematic and permanent basis. It established land offices at Pittsburgh and Cincinnati near where the land was being sold. And it created a small bureaucracy to deal with land disposal problems.

But as might be expected, sales of land from the public domain continued at a slow pace under the Act of 1796, and there was agitation from the agrarian South and from western representatives in Congress to liberalize the provisions of the land disposal program. Thus Congress passed a new land act in 1800. This act continued the minimum sale price of $2 per acre, but it reduced the minimum purchasable acreage to 320 acres and set down a credit provision by which the purchaser had up to four years to pay for the land.

The above provisions stimulated land sales, but not sufficiently to satisfy westerners. Thus in 1804 the Congress further liberalized the land disposal program. Congress reduced the minimum bidding price to $1.64 per acre and the minimum acreage to 160 acres. Given the four-year credit provision, the down payment on a parcel of land (some $65) was coming close to what many pioneers could afford.

The credit provisions and the lower minimum acreage requirements of the Land Acts of 1800 and 1804 encouraged land sales and land speculation. Only half the land purchased by speculators and farmers by 1819 had actually been paid for. When farmers and speculators found they could not meet their payments, they asked Congress for payment relief. Congress responded by passing twelve such payment relief acts. During this period Congress was in effect underwriting land speculation for anyone who could make a down payment on 160 acres. The federal government sold almost 20 million acres of land from the public domain between 1800 and 1820. In one year, 1818, sales reached a high of approximately 3.5 million acres. The greatest land speculation took place in Alabama and Mississippi in response to the cotton boom. In 1820, one-half of the money owed the federal government for land through the extension of credit was due from planters, farmers, and speculators in Alabama and Mississippi.

In an effort to curb the related evils of credit extension and land speculation, the Land Act of 1820 abolished all credit for the purchase of land. Once again the terms of sale became strictly cash. And the Act of 1820 did some other important things. It cut the minimum bidding price at public auctions to $1.25 per acre, and it reduced the minimum size of purchase to 80 acres. This act went a long way toward creating a land disposal system to serve the small, impoverished pioneer. But it did not go all the way. Land in the public domain was not yet free to the pioneer, and the rights of squatters were not recognized in the act. Squatters were still forced to form protective associations to protect their "land-rights" at public land auctions.

One final point should be made regarding the disposal of land by the states and the federal government. All land distributed during this period was not sold. Large amounts of land were distributed as grants or bounties to men who had served in the Continental Army and to men who had enlisted and served in the army and navy during the War of 1812. To an important degree the men and officers who fought in those wars were induced to do so by the promise of receiving free land with the achievement of victory at the end of the war. Between 1775 and 1855, the federal government disposed of about 73.5 million acres of land through military bounties.

The Westward Movement

Between 1775 and 1800 the westward migration from the Atlantic seaboard was undertaken by similar types of people with common backgrounds and common experiences. As they moved westward, the pioneers from Maine to Georgia had to traverse mountains, grapple with dense forests, and contend with Indians. They used the same modes of travel, employed the same farming practices, and lived more or less the same kinds of lives. The essential unity of pioneering from Maine to Georgia was not broken until slavery spread across the Southwest of that day — across western Georgia, Alabama, Mississippi, and Louisiana after 1800.

At the edge of the frontier dwelt the hunters and woodsmen, who literally lived off the forest. Wild game, berries, nuts, and a patch of corn provided their food. From the sale of furs and skins they earned meager cash incomes. They made small clearings in the forest, built log cabins, and broke the soil to raise a patch of corn. Relying on gun, ax, knife, and hoe, they endured a hard, crude life not greatly different from that lived by the Indians. As neighbors moved in, they sold their improvements (such as they were) and plunged deeper into the forest or across the next mountain ridge.

Behind the hunters were to be found the small pioneer farmers, who had a larger patch of corn than did the hunters, some livestock — each probably owned a cow or two and some pigs — and who did more in the way of undertaking farm improvements. But east of the Appalachian Mountains they were likely to be situated on poor, thin, hilly land, and their cash income from farming was very small. They, too, often supplemented their farm income with hunting and trapping. These men were seeking new economic opportunities to exploit, and when they heard about the rich farmland in the Ohio River valley they were ready and eager to go.

Lying east of the frontier and near the Atlantic coast were the established commercial farming areas. With a few exceptions, the successful farmers in these areas were not interested in joining the westward movement. But some of the younger sons and daughters of these families were. Thus, sometimes with the assistance of the family, and sometimes without, these sons and daughters joined the westward trek.

One important exception to the above generalization was the migration of some tobacco planters from Virginia to the Bluegrass Region of Kentucky. A number of large Virginia tobacco planters on worn-out tidewater lands moved their whole families and slave populations to the rich bluegrass lands of Kentucky.

To summarize: from 1775 to 1800 the hunters and woodsmen showed the way west, and the hardy frontier farmers of the eastern seaboard undertook most of the pioneering settlement west of the Appalachians. This latter group was abetted by the younger sons and daughters of established farmers in the older settled areas, as well as land speculators, adventurers of all kinds, teamsters, and soldiers.

In the period 1775-1800 there were two principal routes to the West. The first followed the valley of Virginia in a southwesterly direction to what is now the southwest corner of Virginia. There this route bifurcated. Some pioneers at this point followed the Boone trail through the Cumberland Gap into the Bluegrass Region of Kentucky, while other pioneers continued to follow the Appalachian valleys in a southwesterly direction toward Knoxville. Here some stopped in the narrow valleys of western North Carolina and eastern Tennessee, while others broke out of the mountains and moved into the level country of middle Tennessee.

The second route involved getting to Pittsburgh in some way — probably by one of the old military roads — and then traveling down the Ohio River by canoe or flatboat. Some of these pioneers migrated into the fertile Bluegrass Region of Kentucky. But most settled along the Ohio River in what are now the states of Ohio, Indiana, and Kentucky.

The influence of these two principal routes on the location of settlements is clearly illustrated in figure 3.3. The line describing the frontier in 1800 forms a wedge that cuts into the west and includes most of present-day Kentucky, parts of southern Ohio, and parts of northern Tennessee. It is estimated that perhaps a quarter of a million people lived in this area in and beyond the Appalachian Mountains in 1790. And the movement that was only a trickle in the first years of the period 1775–1800 had become a torrent by the end of the period. As a result of this great westward migration and settlement, Kentucky was admitted to the Union as a state in 1792, Tennessee as a state in 1796, and Ohio as a state in 1803.

By 1800 the "westward movement" had fanned out in many directions (again refer to figure 3.3). Pioneers were moving northward out of Massachusetts and New Hampshire into Maine and Vermont. New

Fig. 3.3. The moving frontier: census data from 1800 on chronicled the constant westward flow of population. From *History of the American Economy,* Second Edition, by Ross M. Robertson, copyright © 1964 by Harcourt Brace Jovanovich, Inc., and renewed 1992 by Ross M. Robertson and Joan C. O'Connor, reproduced by permission of the publisher.

Englanders crossed the Hudson River near Albany and moved westward along the Mohawk River, taking a trail that touched the present cities of Utica, Auburn, Geneva, and Buffalo. Upon reaching Lake Erie, some traveled by boat to sites along Lake Erie on the Ohio shore; others walked the whole distance. The older routes west described above continued to be important avenues to the West for many years — particularly the route through Pittsburgh and down the Ohio River. Once Pittsburgh was reached, this was the easiest and fastest route west. Lastly and very importantly, after 1800, pioneers from the Carolinas and Georgia swept around the southern end of the Appalachians into the rich lands of Alabama and Mississippi.

This southern migration was in some ways similar to the northern migration discussed above. The hunter and woodsman led the way into western Georgia, Alabama, and Mississippi, closely followed by small, poor, pioneer farmers. But at this point the essential form of the migration changed. The tobacco planters of Virginia and the Carolinas were looking for new lands on which to grow tobacco. The tobacco lands in Virginia and the Carolinas were exhausted from continuous cropping, and the bottom fell out of the world tobacco market in the early 1800s. The cotton planters of the Carolinas and Georgia were also searching for new lands on which to grow cotton. Cotton textile manufacturing was experiencing a great boom in England and western Europe, and the invention of the cotton gin by Eli Whitney[3] made it possible for a slave to clean as much as fifty pounds of cotton a day instead of just a few pounds. Thus the demand for new and more lands on which to grow cotton became a powerful force in support of the westward migration. And with the defeat of the southern Indian tribes during the War of 1812, much of their land in Alabama and Mississippi became available for settlement.

After 1812 the southern planter from the coastal plain of Virginia, the Carolinas, and Georgia, the man of substance, with his great household establishment and his black slaves, migrated into Alabama and Mississippi. The planter with adequate means and credit had all the advantages at the public land auctions and acquired big estates on which to produce cotton with slave labor. A farm population thus developed in the South with large, well-financed planters located on the best lands, and small farmers interspersed among the plantation areas located on the poorer lands. Cotton and slavery went hand in hand in the Deep South to create a unique rural society in the nation.

Referring again to figure 3.3, we see that the line of the frontier by 1820 had been pushed west to a point not far from present-day Detroit, Michigan; from there the line ran southwest to what is now St. Louis, Missouri, and then meandered south through Missouri, Tennessee, Mississippi, and Louisiana. Except for the Deep South, this great expanse of territory was settled by small farmers, some squatting on unsurveyed land, but most living on farm units of 80 to 160 acres purchased on credit from land speculators.

The Pioneer Farmer

Let us consider the pioneer farmer in some detail. The typical pioneer farmer was not destitute; he had, as we shall see, certain resources. But he was almost always terribly poor in terms of ready cash. He and his family might arrive in the area in which they had chosen to settle with between $50 and $150 in cash. If the family had more than $200, they were an exceptional pioneer family. The lucky ones might arrive with a wagon and a team of horses, or oxen, but more typically, the farm family would arrive with one horse, loaded with household belongings, herding a milk cow and some pigs. The household belongings would include a rifle, some cooking pots, blankets, and some spare clothing. The tools with which to begin farming were hand tools — the ax, the hoe, and the scythe. With some cornmeal or wheat flour and salt, these were the worldly goods of the pioneer farmer.

Before 1820 the typical pioneer farmer could not purchase his land at a public land auction because at the minimum price and minimum acreage available to him he could not afford to do so. Depending on the time or place, he might squat on unsurveyed land, or he might buy out the land and improvements of a hunter-woodsman-settler who was moving on farther west, or most likely he would buy his land on credit from a speculator at a price and interest rate that he could ill afford. In any event, the acquisition of his land would take most or all of his ready cash, and he would begin farming destitute of money, probably in debt to some land speculator, and possibly in debt to some merchant for supplies.

Until the prairie land of Illinois was reached (except for the special Bluegrass Region), his land would be densely wooded. Thus his first task was to begin clearing his land of trees: (1) to obtain rails or poles to enclose his clearing so that his pigs and those of his neighbors would be kept out, (2) to obtain logs for building his lean-to, or house, and (3) to let the sun shine through onto his small patch of corn, squash, and potatoes.

Depending on the forest cover, his skill, and the size of his family, the pioneer farmer might clear one to three acres a year. So after ten years of backbreaking drudgery, the farmer might have cleared fifteen acres of land to which he could apply a plow. And that land would probably contain a good number of tree stumps.

Outside the Deep South, the principal crop of the pioneer farmer was corn. Corn had many uses. Corn sustained the family as a staple food. Surplus corn could be made into whiskey for cash sale. Corn was also used to fatten pigs before they were slaughtered in the fall and perhaps to feed the cow during the winter so it would produce some milk.

Whatever may have been the place of origin of the pioneer farmer, his previous way of earning a living was probably easier than pioneering west of the Appalachians in the early 1800s. Life for the pioneer farm family was hard — *unbelievably hard*. For the first settlers there could be little more than a bare subsistence. Housing was crude, involving at first perhaps only a log lean-to, and for the first years a log cabin with no windows and a dirt floor. Clothing was scarce and often limited to the use of skins. There was little or no social life, and Indian attacks, or threats of attacks, were a not uncommon occurrence. Isolation may have protected families against contagious diseases, but once sickness or accident struck, the pioneer settler could do little but let nature takes its course. In sum, from 1775 to 1820 life for the pioneer farmer and his family was both hard and cruel in the area in and west of the Appalachian Mountains.

Economic Problems of the Pioneer Farmer

The pioneer farmer was subject, as we have seen, to all kinds of physical environmental problems (e.g., a dense forest to be cleared) and all sorts of social problems (e.g., isolation, Indian attacks). But these would have been more bearable had he not been plagued with such formidable economic problems. Three economic problems were of overriding concern: (1) the conditions and terms of public land sales, (2) the lack of and/or the high price of credit, and (3) the lack of markets for his produce.

The minimum price of land established by the federal government in the disposal of public lands was not prohibitive. A dollar an acre for good farmland was not exorbitant even in 1785. But the condition that the smallest piece of the public domain that a farmer could buy was 640 acres *was* prohibitive. A pioneer farmer did not need that much land; he probably could not clear it in a lifetime. But most important, the typical pioneer farmer did not have $640; hence he was excluded from the purchase of public lands at auction.

It is difficult to see why the central government established such a high minimum acreage figure in the sale of public lands, since the Confederation and later the United States were anxious to raise revenue from the sale of public lands and to settle the interior. The answer seems to be that some of the wealthy, influential individuals on the East Coast interested in speculating in western land wanted the land disposal law written that way and they got it that way. Rich easterners hoped to become even richer speculating in western land. But in the end, most of these speculations in land failed, and for one simple reason. The pioneers, to whom the speculators expected to sell their land, had no money. For about fifty years, however, the minimum-size-of-tract provision put in the land disposal ordinances at the instigation of the speculators caused pioneer farmers no end of financial troubles and grief.

The second major economic problem confronting the pioneer farmer was that no set of institutions existed in the settlements for extending credit to the farmer except at exorbitant rates of interest. The local merchant might extend credit to a farmer for part of a year to cover the purchase of needed tools and household supplies, but only at extremely high rates of interest. This was the case because (1) the merchant himself was probably borrowing at very high rates of interest, and (2) the risk of default was high. The farmer also probably received credit when purchasing land from a speculator, but again only at a very high rate of interest and on a short-term basis. If the pioneer farmer experienced a bad crop, or met with an accident, and missed a payment, he could well lose his whole investment. Or, if the pioneer farmer could see that he could not meet his payments on his land or to the local merchant, he and his family might well steal away with whatever they could carry and squat on some vacant, unsurveyed land. Such actions, of which there were many, of course contributed to the high price of credit. So for one reason or another the price of credit to the pioneer farmer was extremely high — prohibitively high — thus forcing him and his family to undergo great privation and to develop their pioneer farm more slowly than needed to have been the case.

The third important problem confronting the pioneer farmer (again except in the Deep South where good inland waterways existed) was a lack of markets for his surplus of grain, or livestock, or any fruit or vegetable. Hence there was no great incentive to produce a surplus. There were certain limited exceptions. Some cattle were driven to the East over the Appalachian Mountains to market. Some pigs were sent down the Ohio and Mississippi rivers by flatboat to market in New Orleans. And some surplus corn was made into whiskey and transported by packhorse to distant markets. But in the main, during the period 1775–1820, there were no attractive markets for the surplus produce of pioneer farmers living in the valleys of the Appalachians or farther to the west. The prices of farm products that had to be transported long distances overland were too low to warrant their production in the first place. Hence they were not produced. The pioneer farmer in this period remained primarily a subsistence farmer.

Land Speculation and Farm Practices

As we have already observed, speculation in western land was a national disease during the period 1785–1820. And it continued to be so throughout the nineteenth century. Sometimes we think of the slick easterner, who purchased land at the public land auctions and resold it to the pioneer settlers, as being the principal and perhaps the only land speculator. But this was not the case. Everyone from the father of our country, George Washington, down to the lowliest pioneer was caught up in the land speculation fever.

Let us consider the economic situation of the typical pioneer settler. He acquired a piece of forest-covered land in some way — perhaps at a public land auction, more likely on credit — from a businessman or land speculator, or perhaps he obtained it free of charge by squatting on unsurveyed land. But however he obtained it, it was a large piece of land — perhaps 160 acres — relative to his ability to clear and farm it. Working alone or with some family members, the farmer might clear and prepare for cultivation only ten to twenty acres in ten years. The remainder of his land tract was left in a wild state. In short, the typical pioneer farmer lacked the labor supply to clear and cultivate the relatively large tracts of land that he and fellow pioneers were attempting to buy.

But even if, in some way, he could have cleared 160 acres in ten years and put it into crop production, where would he and his neighbors have marketed the surplus products from such efforts? In 1800, 1810, and 1820, the pioneer farmer outside the Deep South was having difficulty marketing the product surplus from ten to twenty acres of cultivated land. West of the Appalachian Mountains there was almost no market demand for surplus grain, and a very limited, thin market for various types of livestock and livestock products.

Why, then, was the pioneer settler of this period trying to acquire 80, or 160, or 320, or 640 acres of land, *if he lacked the labor supply to work that land and there was no market for the product of his labors if the land could be worked in some way?* He was trying to acquire as much land as he possibly could, perhaps by purchasing on credit, perhaps by squatting on unsurveyed land, *because he, too, was a land speculator.* What the pioneer-farmer-speculator hoped to do was the following: clear a patch of land for crops — perhaps ten acres, perhaps more; build some kind of a suitable house; construct some kind of shelter for the livestock and perhaps for hay or grain storage; enclose some part or all of the land tract with fences; and then sell out the improved homestead to a settler coming along behind him with, it was hoped, greater financial resources. If all went well, the pioneer would take the proceeds from the sale of the first homestead, move farther west and buy a larger piece of land, and become a bigger land speculator. But, of course, in most cases all did not go well. The scenario broke down at some point, perhaps because the husband or wife had an accident or died, or because the pioneer could not make his land payment on time, or because the squatter was pushed off his untitled land. Nevertheless, this was the dream of the pioneer settler for becoming wealthy through land speculation, just as the eastern enterpriser had even more grandiose dreams of future riches.

The combination of abundant, cheap land, scarce labor, and nonexistent markets made the pioneer farmer a poor cultivator. There was little or no economic incentive to become an efficient, productive cultivator. Thus he mined the soil through constant cropping, took what the worn-out soil would give him in the way of yields, and then moved on.

The above set of circumstances also made the pioneer farmer a poor animal husbandryman. He let his animals run loose in the woods. He paid little or no attention to their breeding. Thus his livestock tended to be run-down and scrawny, and they produced poorly.

The above set of circumstances turned the pioneer settler living west of the Appalachian Mountains, at least up to the year 1820, into a poor, unproductive farmer. In his view his best and perhaps only marketable product was his improved homestead and farmland. Thus his energies and his efforts were directed toward the building of a house, a barn, or sheds and fences, and the clearing of the forest to obtain more cultivatable land — not toward increasing his production of crops and livestock. In this economic and physical context, the state of the agricultural arts west of the Appalachians was abysmally low.

Suggested Readings

Bakeless, John E. *Daniel Boone.* New York: Morrow, 1939.

Edwards, Everett E. "American Agriculture — the First 300 Years." *Farmers in a Changing World. 1940 Yearbook of Agriculture.* U.S. Department of Agriculture. Washington, D.C.: Government Printing Office. Pp. 194–205.

Nettels, Curtis P. *The Emergence of a National Economy, 1775–1815.* Vol. II of *The Economic History of the United States.* New York: Holt, Rinehart, and Winston, 1962. Chaps. VII, VIII, and IX.

North, Douglass C. *The Economic Growth of the United States, 1790–1860.* Part 1: 1790–1814. New York: W. W. Norton, 1966.

Robertson, Ross M. *History of the American Economy,* 2nd ed. New York: Harcourt, Brace, and World, 1964. Chap 5.

Schlebacker, John T. *Whereby We Thrive: A History of American Farming, 1607–1972.* Ames Iowa: Iowa State University Press, 1975. Pp. 57–63, 71–80.

CHAPTER 4

FROM PIONEERING TO COMMERCIALIZATION: 1820–1860

Land, Slavery, and Population Policies

The Land Law of 1820, it will be recalled, reduced the minimum acreage that an individual could buy at an auction of public land to eighty acres. But it also abolished all credit provisions in the purchase of public lands. The Land Law of 1820, thus, did not immediately stimulate the sales of public lands. In fact, such sales fell to a low of some 650,000 acres in 1823 as compared with the previous high of 3.5 million acres in 1818. However, the more liberal provisions of the law with regard to the minimum size tract of land that could be purchased eventually did have a positive effect on the sales of public lands. These increased importantly in the 1830s, and in one year alone, 1836, some 20 million acres of public lands were sold at auction. From 1820 to 1841, the period in which the 1820 law was in effect, the federal government sold off some 75 million acres of the public domain, as compared with the sale of only 16 million acres in the period 1800–1819.

The Land Law of 1820 had its shortcomings, as did the administration of it, but it did enable many, many people to become landowners. Such a mass distribution of land to those who tilled the soil was unique in the history of the world up to that time.

This law did not deal in any way with the problem of squatters. From 1785 on, settlers had moved onto public land in advance of its being opened for sale, and perhaps even in advance of its being surveyed. On this land the settler-squatter would erect a cabin, clear some land, cultivate the cleared patch, and fence it. As this became more and more common, claim associations, or squatter associations, came into being to protect the "rights" of squatters, usually by using the threat of force at land auctions to keep buyers from bidding on land already settled upon by squatters. As the West gained more political power in Congress, some thirty-three preemption laws, mostly local in application, were passed between 1799 and 1830, giving the squatters the right to purchase their land at the minimum price without having to bid for it at a public auction. In the late 1820s and 1830s, the right of preemption became a burning political issue. Given this strong demand for the right of preemption and the increased political power of the West, Congress passed five general preemption laws between 1830 and 1840 that foregave squatters already on public lands for the illegal trespass and that gave them the right to purchase their land at the minimum price. But westerners wanted more; they wanted the right of *prospective* preemption, which would sanction, or make legal, squatting on public lands before they were thrown open for sale, and this right they won in the Preemption Act of 1841.

Under the provisions of the Preemption Act of 1841, a farmer could settle legally on the public domain before he purchased his land. Further, he could buy 160 acres of the land on which he had settled for $1.25 an acre when the land in that area was opened for sale. This was not yet a policy of free land disposal, but it was coming close to it.

Despite the efforts of the federal government to sell the public lands, the enterprise and the distribution schemes of the speculators, and the strong desire of the settlers to acquire freeholds, much public land that had been surveyed and offered for sale remained unsold during this period. Paul Gates reports, for example, that of the 167 million acres of public lands surveyed and offered for sale up to 1835, only 44.5 million acres were actually sold, leaving some 122 million acres unsold.[1] This continued to be the case through the early 1850s. Thus there was much agitation to lower the minimum price on lands that had long been on the market and had not sold. It was argued that much of this unsold land was not worth the minimum price and that the only way to move it was to lower its price.

The Graduation Act was passed by Congress in 1854, with the purpose of lowering the price of unsold public lands. Under the provisions of this act, the price of land that had been on the market for ten years would be reduced to $1.00 per acre; if it remained unsold for another five years, its price was to decline to 75 cents per acre; if unsold in another five years, its price would fall to 25 cents per acre; and if it remained unsold after thirty years, its price would be lowered to 12.5 cents per acre. As might be guessed, much of the land sold under the provisions of this act went to speculators. Also, a lot of it ended up in the hands of mining and timber companies, which does suggest that it was not high quality farmland. In any event, this land law was not well received by the public, and it was superseded by the Homestead Act of 1862.

Agitation to liberalize the distribution of public land began, it will be recalled, with the passage of the first land ordinance in 1785. Political action, supported in the main by westerners, was, as we have seen, reasonably successful in achieving this goal. But in the 1840s a new set of land law reformers appeared on the scene. These reformers, often easterners, urged the passage of homestead legislation to distribute lands in the public domain to settlers free of charge, as a means of alleviating the bad economic conditions of urban factory workers. As a result of the continued pressure for free land, the first serious homestead legislation was introduced into the Congress in 1852. This legislation failed, as did other homestead legislation in the 1850s, because it had a formidable array of opposition. Eastern industrialists opposed it for obvious reasons — it could deprive them of their captive supply of labor. Western farmers and land speculators opposed it because they believed that the passage of homestead legislation would act to depreciate land values. Southern planters and slave interests opposed it because they were afraid that it would restrict the area into which a slave-based agriculture might expand. But agitation to pass a free land distribution law continued throughout the 1850s, and in 1860 Congress did pass a homestead act, which was vetoed by President Buchanan.

The questions of slavery, its expansion into the new territories, and the disposal of the public domain were closely related throughout the period 1800–1860. The southerners, striving always to achieve equal voting power with the North in the Senate, fought for and won a series of compromises that enabled them to protect and extend the institution of slavery. In 1819 there were eleven free states and eleven slave states. The Missouri Compromise of 1820 involved two important provisions: (1) Missouri was admitted as a slave state and Maine as a free state, and (2) thereafter, slavery would be prohibited in the territory of the Louisiana Purchase north of 36°30′, or north of a line forming the southern border of the state of Missouri. From 1820 to 1850, states were admitted in pairs, one slave and one free, so that by 1850 there were fifteen slave states and fifteen free states in the Union.

By the early 1850s it appeared that the South was winning its struggle to expand slavery into the new territories of the Far West. Congress in 1848 repealed the provision of the Mexican Cession that required the new territory to remain permanently free; in 1850 it admitted California as a free state but organized the new territories of Utah and New Mexico as territories in which slavery was to be permitted. And in the Kansas-Nebraska Act of 1854 Congress in effect repealed the Missouri Compromise by permitting the question of slavery to be settled by "popular sovereignty" in the still unsettled and unorganized areas of the Louisiana Purchase.

But these legislative victories by the southerners led to new political responses in the North. Farmers in the Northwest came to resist the extension of slavery and the plantation system out of fear of competition from large plantation units based on slave labor with their small family-sized units. Thus farmers in the Northwest broke politically with southern planters in the 1850s. Further, since much of the surplus produce of the Northwest was now moving east by canal and railroad, farmers in the Northwest found their economic interests to be more closely allied with eastern business and industrial interests than with the southern cotton and tobacco planters. The stage was thus set for the realignment of political power, the founding of the Republican party, and the eventual War between the States.

While southerners were winning their struggle to extend slavery into new territories where the plantation system could profitably be developed, northerners and easterners were successful in keeping the doors of immigration wide open. This was of great importance to the growing industries of the North and East, which required for their development an abundant and cheap supply of labor. Antislavery interests in the North were also anxious that the new territories in the West be settled to the maximum extent possible by small freehold farmers, and the settlement of European immigrants on western lands helped them achieve this objective.

In 1820, the first year for which there are good records on immigration, some 8,400 persons immigrated to the United States. Most of these persons, or about 6,000, came from Great Britain and Ireland. By 1830 the tide of immigration had increased to over 20,000 per year, and by 1840 to about 80,000 per year. By 1840 more than a third of these immigrants were from Germany; many came with a respectable amount of capital to invest, and a high proportion settled on lands in the "Old Northwest Territory." These German settlers were not pioneers; they were farmers with assets seeking good land on which to settle and produce commodities for sale. Immigration increased to some 370,000 persons in 1850, and in 1854 it reached a record high for the pre-Civil War period of 428,000 persons. Of this total, almost half were from Germany, and again many sought good farmland on which to settle. Immigration then slackened off in the unhappy years immediately before and during the Civil War.

This great influx of persons into the United States, most of whom settled in the North, and a high proportion of whom were white adult males, had the effect of increasing the work force faster than the rate of growth in population. It is estimated that over half of the adult males in the North in 1860 were foreign-born. Professor Robert E. Gallman, quoting from Michael Shaara (*The Killer Angels*, New York, 1975), writes about this remarkable population development in a description of the Confederate and Union armies on the eve of Gettysburg in the following way:

The Confederate army is "an army of remarkable unity, fighting for disunion. It is Anglo-Saxon and Protestant. Though there are many men who cannot read or write, they all speak English. They share common customs. . . ."

The Union army is "a polyglot mass of vastly dissimilar men, fighting for union. There are strange accents and strange religions and many who do not speak English at all. . . ."[2]

This great and skewed transfer of population from Europe to the United States must have increased the growth of national product as well as the rate of growth in product per head. And overwhelmingly, the fruits of this growth were "harvested" by the North.

Filling Up the Interior

By 1820 the age of pioneering east of the Mississippi River, both north and south, was largely passed. (See the line of the frontier in 1820 in figure 3.3.) The Indian wars, with one or two exceptions, had also ended in this area by 1820; the threat of Indian attacks on isolated settlers had become a thing of the past. Major concerns in the period 1820–60 were (1) populating the area lying east of the line of the frontier in 1820 and (2) pushing the frontier a little farther west and north (i.e., to a line that approximates the western borders of Arkansas, Missouri, and Iowa but includes East Texas). (Again see figure 3.3.) Between 1815 and 1860 fifteen new states were admitted to the Union, and most were located in the Mississippi River valley. Those states were

Indiana	1816	Florida	1845
Mississippi	1817	Texas	1845
Alabama	1818	Iowa	1846
Illinois	1818	Wisconsin	1848
Maine	1820	California	1850
Missouri	1821	Minnesota	1858
Arkansas	1836	Oregon	1859
Michigan	1837		

The population of the United States increased from 9.6 million in 1820 to 31.5 million in 1860. The population of the east north central states (Ohio, Indiana, Illinois, Michigan, and Wisconsin) grew from about 800 thousand in 1820 to almost 7 million in 1860 — more than a sevenfold increase during the forty-year period. The population of the east south central states (Kentucky, Tennessee, Alabama, and Mississippi) increased from 1.2 million in 1820 to 4 million in 1860. This was a rapid rate of increase, too, but considerably slower than that which occurred in the Old Northwest Territory.

Missouri, the first state west of the Mississippi River to be admitted to the Union, increased in population from 66 thousand in 1820 to some 1.2 million in 1860; this was almost a twentyfold increase. Thus the period 1820–60 must be characterized as one of settlement and peopling of that great area falling between the Appalachian Mountains and the Mississippi River.

Indian Removal

The lands beyond the Appalachian Mountains onto which the white settlers poured in floodlike proportions between 1800 and 1860 were not vacant lands. They were the ancient and established lands of many Indian tribes, some of which (the Creeks and Cherokees, for example) were highly civilized. The tribes and individual Indians did not have pieces of fancy paper, registered with a government somewhere, stating that they had title to their lands. But most important, they lacked the military hardware and organization to protect their lands. So when the whites, with their insatiable demand for land, poured over the Appalachians in the early 1800s, the Indians were pushed aside by superior military might and forced to sign treaties ceding the most promising of their lands to the whites. Later, in the 1820s, when the country began to settle up, the cry went up to remove the Indians altogether from their homelands. The whites had to have more land. A policy was thus formalized by the federal government to remove all Indian tribes east of the Mississippi and to resettle them in an Indian territory — a territory which later became the state of Oklahoma.

Gloria Jahoda tells a dramatic story of how the policy of Indian removal came to be formulated:

The winter of 1814 passed with Jackson on an elusive Red Eagle's trail, while Jackson's troops laid waste Creek towns. . . .

One evening, in front of his quarters, Jackson was "accosted by an unarmed, light-colored Indian" who wore buckskin breeches and tattered moccasins.

"General Jackson?"

"Yes?"

"I am Bill Weatherford."[3]

Inside, Red Eagle explained why he had come to surrender to his antagonist. "I can oppose you no longer. I have done you much injury. I should have done you more, but my warriors are killed. I am in your power. Dispose of me as you please."

"You are not in my power," Andrew Jackson answered slowly. "I had ordered you brought to me in chains, but you have come of your own accord. You see my camp. You see my arms. You know my object. If you think you can contend against me in battle go and head your warriors."

"Ah!" Red Eagle's smile was dry. "Well may such language be addressed to me now. There was a time" — he paused — "a time when I could have answered you. I could animate my fighters to battle, but I cannot animate the dead. General Jackson, I have nothing to request for myself, but I beg you to send for the women and children of the war party who have been driven to the woods without an ear of corn. They never did any harm. Kill me instead, if the white people want it done."

Wordlessly Jackson offered Red Eagle a glass of brandy. The warrior drank it. "Save the wives and children of the Creeks, and I will persuade to peace any Red Sticks remaining in my nation," he said. Deliberately, Jackson nodded. Then he extended his hand. Red Eagle took it, looked at his adversary's craggy features for a long moment and then, bowing, departed.

With that handshake, the two principal architects of the ultimate fate of the American Indian had sealed a bargain. Red Eagle's leadership in war had angered America. It had also convinced Andrew Jackson that America's frontiers would always be frontiers while there were Indians to annoy the settlers. The Indians must go. They couldn't be exterminated wholesale because of world opinion. But they could be uprooted and packed off to some remote corner of the country where they wouldn't be in the way. This haven would belong to them, they would be told in the traditional language of America's Indian treaties, "as long as the green grass grows and the water flows," provided they began hiking en masse with a military escort to get there. At the Horseshore Bend of the Tallapoosa River in Alabama, Andrew Jackson silently pledged himself to the policy of Indian Removal which in his presidency was to become law. It would be a simple law: any Indian who remained on his ancestral lands affirming his Indian identity would be a criminal. The Indians would be relocated somewhere on the West's Great Plains. It didn't matter that the Great Plains already had Indian inhabitants who could hardly be expected to welcome red refugees. But the government would tout as a mecca the grasslands and forested river bottoms near the Red and Arkansas and Verdigris rivers, in Red Eagle's time an all but uncharted mystery. Not until five decades had passed did the Choctaw Indian Allen Wright give it a name — perhaps not without irony. The Choctaw word for red was *houma; okla* meant people. Oklahoma was Indian destiny before it graced a single map. Not an Indian alive, except those who already inhabited it, considered it Holy Ground. East of the Mississippi, Ecunchate[4] was lost land, a lost dream, and the road that led out of it forever became the Trail of Tears.[5]

Whether the above story oversimplifies the formulation of the policy of Indian removal is irrelevant. The policy was vigorously pursued in the 1830s, and thousands of Indians east of the Mississippi were rounded up at the point of the bayonet and were driven, or herded by government contractors with the support of the army, over the "Trail of Tears" to their new homes in the Indian Territory. Perhaps one-quarter to one-third of those who started the trek perished. Some died of hunger and cold. More died of white men's diseases. But perhaps most died of heartbreak and despair.

Grant Foreman in his definitive study *Indian Removal* describes the utter desolation that overcame the Indians from the five civilized tribes in the South as they were removed from their homelands:

This tragic phase of American history is best understood if one will remember that for the most part the southern Indians were people of fixed habits and tastes. They were not nomads like some western Indians; they were less inclined to wander to strange places than white people. They loved their streams and valleys, their hills, and forests, their fields and herds, their homes and firesides, families and friends; they were rooted in the soil as the Choctaw chief Pushmataha said, "where we have grown up as the herbs of the woods." More than white people they cherished a passionate attachment for the earth that held the bones of their ancestors and relatives. Few white people either understood or respected this sentiment. The trees that shaded their homes, the cooling spring that ministered to every family, friendly watercourses, familiar trails and prospects, busk grounds, and council houses were their property and their friends; these simple possessions filled their lives; their loss was cataclysmic. It is doubtful if white people with their readier adaptability can understand the sense of grief and desolation that overwhelmed the indians when they were compelled to leave all these behind forever and begin the long sad journey toward the setting sun which they called the Trail of Tears.[6]

The sense of desolation and despair was no less for the northern tribes. Hard and cruel as the age of pioneering and settlement was on the white man and his family, the same period was even harder and crueler for the Indian and his family. He lost his home and his way of life. He lost all.

Opening Markets for the Agricultural Products of the Interior

The first pioneers over the Appalachian Mountains moved along the available waterways — Lake Erie and the Ohio River — by canoe, small sailboat, or flatboat, or they moved along old Indian trails on horseback. And these modes of travel and transport prevailed pretty much until about 1820. Given this severely limited system of transport, there could be no effective market, and there was none, for the surplus product of the pioneer farmers in the valleys of the Appalachians and farther west in the Mississippi River basin. There were, of course, some exceptions. Cattle were driven east along the horseback trails. Corn was converted into whiskey and carried to urban centers by packhorse. And pigs and grain were floated down the Ohio River to New Orleans, or to one of the new river towns such as Cincinnati.

The marketing situation began to change with the introduction of the steamboat. By 1820 steamboats were regularly working the Eastern Seaboard, the Great Lakes, and the western rivers. In the East, steamboats were built for speed and dependability to attract passenger traffic and high-valued cargo. But the steamboats on western rivers were designed from the beginning to be workhorses, and workhorses they were. They sacrificed speed for cargo capacity and operated in very shallow water — as shallow as three feet. With this design they could collect and haul bulky agricultural products such as cotton, grain, and livestock along the Ohio and Mississippi rivers and their many tributaries. And by so doing they widened the market for the agricultural produce of the interior from both the North and the South during the period 1820–60.

Between 1815 and 1840, Americans, primarily through sponsorship by state governments, undertook a major program of canal construction. In 1815 there were less than 100 miles of canals in the United States; by 1840 more than 3,300 miles of canals existed. By and large, this effort was a failure. (We will discuss the relation of transportation to agricultural development in some detail in chapter 11.) But there was one important exception to the overall failure of canal transportation. It was the Erie Canal.

A glance at the map of the United States suggests the great potential of the Erie Canal. When completed, it connected two great waterways: the Great Lakes system on the west and the Hudson River on the east. Further, the Erie Canal could be dug along a relatively level stretch of land following the Mohawk River eastward from the Hudson River and then running across the flat land south of Lake Ontario to the city of Buffalo on Lake Erie. In short, the terrain made it easy and cheap to dig the canal. And its location was perfect for opening up the Northwest Territory. Once the Erie Canal was open, bulky freight, e.g., grain, could be shipped all the way from Chicago to New York City by water.

The Erie Canal was begun in 1817 under the leadership of Governor DeWitt Clinton and under the sponsorship of the New York state government. It was completed in 1825. Since the savings in shipping bulky freight by water rather than by land in those days were enormous, the Erie Canal was an instant success. It opened up to the farmers of Ohio, Indiana, Michigan, and Illinois markets for their production surplus, principally grain, along the East Coast and even in Europe in the period 1820–40.

What the steamboats and the Erie Canal started in the period 1820–40, the railroads completed in the period 1840–60. What the United States, with its great expanse of land, needed by the 1840s was a new form of transportation that could haul passengers and freight speedily and cheaply over great distances. This the railroads provided.

There were less than 100 miles of railroad track in the United States in 1830. By 1840 the miles of track laid had increased to 3,000, and by 1860 there were over 30,000 miles of railroad track. The largest share of this track was located in the Northeast, and in the Old Northwest Territory. These areas were covered by a railroad network. St. Louis was linked to Baltimore by the Baltimore and Ohio line. Chicago had several rail connections with the East Coast. Chicago also had rail connections with New Orleans via the Illinois Central.

By 1860 the railroad had captured most of the passenger traffic east of the Mississippi River and a large part of the freight traffic as well. Freight rates were higher by railroad than by water transport. But the railroads were faster and more dependable. They also connected interior points that could not be reached by water. Thus by 1860 the railroads were hauling an important share of the surplus agricultural products of the Midwest to the large and growing markets along the East Coast.

Early Farm Mechanization

The pioneer farmer, it will be recalled, farmed principally with the aid of the ax, the hoe, and the scythe, and typically was short on labor. So he was not a productive farmer. What he needed to transform himself from a primitive farmer into a commercial farmer was a set of improved tools that would make "his arm longer and stronger" and thus enable him to do the work of several men. This set of improved tools the village blacksmith-mechanic provided him during the early 1800s.

The first piece of improved farm equipment to come along was the plow. The first cast-iron plow, all in one piece, was patented by Charles Newbold in New Jersey in 1797. This plow was improved continuously over the next twenty years, and in 1819 Jethro Wood of New York patented a cast-iron plow with interchangeable parts that was well received by farmers. This plow, and other iron plows with better moldboard designs, worked a revolution in farming in the North. (The iron moldboard plow was not widely adopted in the South.) The iron moldboard plow with interchangeable parts enabled the farmer to do a better job of tilling and preparing the soil and required less human labor and less animal power than did the older wooden plows.

But breaking the prairie in Illinois and Iowa brought new problems. The light, cast-iron plow could not readily cut through the heavy sod; plowshares had to be replaced often; and the rough moldboard would not scour properly. Thus for a time farmers on the prairies had to fall back on cumbersome wooden plows with iron shares. Such plows were heavy and required much animal power, but they did not clog and they would cut the sod. Improvements were not long in coming. John Lane, an Illinois blacksmith, in 1833 put strips of steel over a polished wooden moldboard that made the sticky prairie soil slide off the moldboard and so improved the efficiency of a wooden plow in breaking the prairie. In 1837 John Deere designed a one-piece wrought iron plow with a cutting edge of steel on the share. This plow scoured so well that it became known as the "singing plow." He continued to improve his plow, and by 1846 he and his partner were producing about 1,000 plows a year. By 1857 his plant in Moline, Illinois, was turning out 10,000 plows a year. Hence by the 1850s an efficient, relatively cheap plow made of wrought iron and steel was available to the farmers of America.

During the same period, 1820–60, all kinds of equipment for preparing the seedbed and planting the crop came along for adoption by farmers. In the 1840s a two-horse, hinged harrow with iron or steel spikes appeared; soon, all kinds of land preparation machines followed. In the 1840s a field cultivator attached to several small shovel plows that could be used to break the soil or cover the seeds made its appearance. The use of grain drills for planting the crop was impeded by tree stumps and rocks in the fields. But grain drills began to appear in New York and Pennsylvania in the 1840s, and by the late 1850s grain drills were regularly used in the Middle Atlantic states. The planting of grains, particularly corn, with mechanical planters or drills did not become commonplace in the Midwest until after the Civil War. The walking, single-row cultivator for killing weeds appeared in the East in the 1830s, and the sulky (or riding) two-row cultivator for use in cornfields came along in the 1840s. Although these new cultivators saved many man-hours of labor and took much of the drudgery out of farming, they were just coming into use in the Midwest at the outbreak of the Civil War.

A principal bottleneck in the production of grain was the harvesting and threshing of it. At the time of the Revolutionary War most grain was harvested by hand either with a sickle or with a scythe. Shortly after this war an improved technology for harvesting grain appeared in the form of the cradle. The cradle was a scythe with a frame attached for catching the cut grain. Although a worker who had mastered the art of using the cradle could cut twice as much grain as a worker using a sickle or scythe, harvesting grain remained a hand operation. The cradle, with the various improved versions that came along, remained the principal device for harvesting grain in both the East and the West through 1850.

But work on the development of a mechanical grain reaper was under way during much of the early 1800s. Many people were involved in this work but two names stand out: Obed Hussey and Cyrus McCormick. Hussey patented a reaper in 1833, McCormick in 1834. These first machines did not work too well. However, McCormick combined the best features of both machines in the early 1850s, and by 1855 was turning out a highly successful machine.

During the period when Hussey and McCormick were developing a successful mechanical grain reaper, others were at work on the development of a reaper-thresher: a combine. Such a machine was developed in Michigan in the 1830s and 1840s with the capacity to harvest twenty-five acres of wheat in one day. But for some reason it did not catch on in the Midwest. One such machine was shipped to

California in the 1850s for use in the large grain fields there. The machine performed so well under California conditions that copies of it and modifications of it were used in California for many years.

In 1836 Hiram and John Pitt patented a stationary grain-threshing machine. This efficient and inexpensive machine was quickly and widely adopted by farmers. By the 1840s the use of mechanical threshers was commonplace in the East and much of the Midwest.

It is important to recognize that all these machines — plows, harrows, planters, cultivators, reapers and threshers — came into widespread use at about the same time. They tended to be developed in the 1820s and 1830s, to be adopted commercially on a limited basis in the 1840s, and to come into common usage in the 1850s. This was probably no accident. Advances in one farming operation require advances in others. It is of little advantage to a farmer to be able to undertake and complete one operation speedily and efficiently if other operations in the production process act as a bottleneck. Thus by the 1850s farmers in the North and East had achieved a reasonable degree of efficiency in all aspects of grain production and a fair balance among its principal elements.

Mechanical developments in the South proceeded somewhat differently. The great mechanical technological development in the production of cotton occurred with the invention of the cotton gin by Eli Whitney in 1793. The cotton gin provided an easy, quick, economical way of separating the cotton lint from the green seed in short-staple cotton. This broke the principal bottleneck in the production of cotton. Thereafter, some southern cotton planters adopted some of the machines developed in the early 1800s — cast-iron plows and seed planters. But in the main, southern farmers and planters relied on slave labor with simple hand tools — the hoe and the ax — to prepare the land for cropping and to cultivate the crops. Slave labor in the South reduced the incentive to mechanize the heavy farming operations.

Agricultural Developments in the South

In 1793, the year of the invention of the cotton gin, slavery in the Upper South was in a decline. But the invention of the cotton gin and the expanding market for cotton in Europe reversed that state of affairs. Exports of cotton stood at 21 million pounds in 1801, increased to 128 million pounds in 1820, and then shot up to almost 1.8 billion pounds in 1860. The great expansion in the export of cotton turned the Deep South of Georgia, Alabama, and Mississippi into one great cotton-producing belt. In this area cotton and slavery seemed to be made for each other. The farming operations on a cotton plantation consisted of a series of relatively simple tasks that could be easily learned and readily supervised, that continued through most of the year, and that employed women and children as well as adult males. In the spring the land was prepared by using crude plows that scratched the soil to a depth of two to three inches. The slaves then planted the seed in rows three to five feet apart. During the growing season weeds were kept down and the cotton was thinned by using slave labor and the hoe. In the fall all hands worked from dawn until dark picking the cotton, transporting it to the ginning area, ginning it, and packing and hauling it. On small plantations employing only a few slaves, the owner served as overseer and worked with his slaves in the field and in ginning and packing the cotton. On large plantations slaves would be worked in gangs of twenty or more persons, each gang being supervised by an overseer.

Owing to the mild climate and abundant land, the slaves could be kept in good working condition at a very low cost. Long summers and mild winters reduced the expense for clothing to a trifle. The forest and the labor of slaves provided wood to build cabins and to burn in cooking. Each cotton plantation tried to produce enough corn and hogs to provide the staples, cornbread and salt pork, that sustained the slaves; thus each plantation had its own cornfield to provide food products for its slave labor population. But many cotton plantations were not able to produce their total food requirements and had to depend upon the importation of grain and pork products from the Upper South and from areas lying north of the Ohio River.

The number of acres required to keep an adult field hand fully employed varied from fifteen to forty acres in the Deep South, depending on the quality of the land and the management skills of the overseers, or planters. Poor Alabama pine land might require forty acres, good Mississippi alluvial land only fifteen acres. But at the height of the cotton boom in the Deep South, say in 1850, the rule of thumb was that ten acres of good cotton land and ten acres of corn land would keep an adult field hand fully occupied.

The question whether the slavery system as practiced in the antebellum Cotton South was profitable has often been raised and debated over the past 100 years. It is sometimes argued that because of the cumbersomeness of the system and the low productivity of the slaves, the system would have toppled by itself in due time. This might have happened. Who knows for certain? Certainly, looking at ancient and incomplete farm management records has not resolved the issue, just as modern cost-of-production studies in agriculture have rarely provided definitive answers to the question of the profitability of farming. Imputed land and labor costs tend to fog the issue. But two points do stand out with regard to the spread of slavery in the Deep South between 1800 and 1860. First, cotton and slavery did expand rapidly throughout the Deep South during this period. And slavery continued to expand into sugarcane production in Louisiana. Such an expansion is not suggestive of an unprofitable industry. Second, the price of prime field hands rose from about $700 in 1828 to about $1,800 in 1860. The cotton planters who bid up the price of field hands over this period must have believed, or known, that slavery was profitable in the Deep South.[7]

The prices of prime field hands and young females were, however, bid up so high in the cotton- and cane-producing areas as to make slavery unprofitable in the Upper South in the production of tobacco and grain. Slavery in the Upper South might well have disappeared in the middle 1800s except for one thing — the lucrative business of exporting slaves to the Deep South. Many planters in Kentucky, Virginia, and the Carolinas supplemented their farm income from the sale of slaves into the Deep South. This income from the sale of slaves into the Cotton South helped maintain the political alliance between the Old South and the Deep South in 1860.

Agricultural Developments in the Old Northwest

Pioneer farmers in the Old Northwest until 1820 had essentially the same experiences as settlers along the Atlantic Seaboard during the two centuries of the colonial period. The pioneer farmer first cleared one to three acres of forest land by girdling the trees and grubbing out the stumps. This clearing he planted to corn and vegetables. At this stage the pioneer family depended to an important degree upon wild game and the bounty of the forest for its food supply. As more land was cleared, the pioneer farmer expanded his production of corn and probably planted some wheat. This wheat he hauled to the local gristmill to grind into flour, which was consumed by the farm family and its neighbors. Gradually, and with the aid of the new farm implements and machines that were making their appearance, a farm capable of producing a surplus was created out of the dense forest. Surpluses were shipped to outside markets when the transport became available, and in the Northwest, that transport first appeared in the 1820s. Thus agriculture in the Northwest was ready to take off commercially in the 1820s and 1830s, and it did.

New York and Pennsylvania were the leading wheat-producing states during the first quarter of the nineteenth century. But during this period wheat production was shifting westward in those two states. By the 1830s Ohio had become an important producer of wheat, and wheat and wheat flour began to move eastward through the Erie Canal upon its opening in 1825. Wheat production continued to move westward north of the Ohio River in the 1840s and 1850s. By 1860 the five states of the Old Northwest (Ohio, Indiana, Illinois, Michigan, and Wisconsin) were supplying about one-half of the wheat produced in the United States. Wheat had become the leading cash crop in the Old Northwest. But it would not remain so; wheat production would continue to move westward.

During the age of pioneering, 1800–1820, every settler had a patch of corn which was produced for home consumption. But by as late as 1840 no true corn belt had developed north of the Ohio River. The leading corn-producing states in 1840 were the border states of Virginia, Kentucky, and Tennessee. During the next two decades, however, corn production shifted northward; by 1860 Illinois, Ohio, Missouri, and Indiana had become the leading corn-producing states of the Union.

Corn produced in this new northern Corn Belt was utilized in numerous ways: as food for the family, as feed for the workstock, as grain marketed to New Orleans or into the Deep South, or as feed for marketable livestock, primarily hogs. The hogs, which once were permitted to run wild in the woods and which were later flatboated down the Ohio and Mississippi rivers to market in New Orleans, were now being fattened on corn and driven to, or hauled by railroad to, the meat-packing establishments along the Ohio River. By 1860 a whole new industry had developed in the Old Northwest involving (1) the production of corn, (2) the feeding of that corn to hogs, and (3) the slaughter and packing of hogs in centers such as Cincinnati, which had become known as "Porkopolis."

The range cattle industry had long been associated with the frontier north of the Ohio River. In 1805 a herd of cattle was driven from Ohio to Baltimore and sold for a large profit. Cattle drives to the East continued each year thereafter. By 1840 farmers in southern Ohio were fattening their own cattle. These fat cattle were driven eastward until the growth of the railroads in the 1850s brought an end to the cattle drives. Thus by 1860 an important cattle-feeding industry had also developed in the emergent corn belt of the Midwest.

During the period 1820–60, the region lying north of the Ohio River and stretching from Ohio to Iowa became the leading surplus-producing region for grains in the United States. Surplus wheat produced in this region moved eastward through the Great Lakes and the Erie Canal, and southward along the Ohio and Mississippi rivers to New Orleans. Cheap water transportation now enabled the wheat farmers of the Old Northwest to market their surplus grain in the eastern markets and even to a small degree abroad.

Surplus corn produced in this region was to a limited extent converted into food and whiskey. But to a much greater extent the surplus was utilized to support a livestock-feeding industry. Thus we see that agriculture in the Upper Midwest had by 1860 developed the principal characteristics of its modern form. It had become an efficient and surplus producer of feed grains; this surplus provided the base for a livestock-growing and livestock-fattening industry. Wheat would continue to move westward, but the feed-livestock economy would remain as the principal building block of Midwest agriculture.

Agricultural Developments on the Atlantic Seaboard

Agriculture in New England and the Middle Atlantic states at the beginning of the nineteenth century was, with certain exceptions, extremely primitive. Cultivation was extensive and exploitive; tools were clumsy and inefficient; systematic crop rotation was unknown; and livestock and orchards were badly managed. Competition from the West in grain and livestock production could have destroyed the agriculture of the Atlantic Seaboard. But it did not. It did not because the population of the Eastern Seaboard grew rapidly in the first half of the nineteenth century, creating a market for the food production of local farms. The population of New England and the Middle Atlantic states approximately doubled between 1820 and 1860, and a large part of this population increase was concentrated in the cities and towns.

The growing cities of New England and the Middle Atlantic states, with their flourishing industries and commerce, created a strong demand for dairy products, poultry meat and eggs, vegetables, beef, pork and mutton, dray horses, carriage horses, and the hay and grain to sustain those horses. This development brought a shift from general to specialized farming throughout New England and the Middle

Atlantic states during this period. The form of the specialization in each local area depended upon soil, climate, and the geographical location of the particular area. Market gardening and dairying developed in the immediate vicinity of the urban centers, notably around Boston, New York, and Philadelphia. The cattle-feeding industry was concentrated in the Connecticut River valley and in southeastern Pennsylvania, where there was a surplus of grain, and specialization in the making of butter and cheese occurred in central New York state after the opening of the Erie Canal. A carriage horse — the Morgan horse — was developed in Vermont for sale to urban centers of population. And wool growing became an important industry in the hilly areas of New England and the Middle Atlantic states.

By the 1850s farmers in the Northeast had been largely forced out of the commercial production of wheat and corn. The shipment of cheap grain from the Northwest via the Great Lakes and the Erie Canal brought this about. And through competition from western farmers, eastern farmers were slowly losing their markets for pork, beef, and wool. But their proximity to market saved the eastern farmers in the production of perishable products such as fluid milk, cheese and butter, poultry products, and vegetables. Thus by 1860 agriculture in the New England and Middle Atlantic states had become highly specialized.

In the Upper South, a region which includes Virginia, Kentucky, Tennessee, and the Carolinas, the chief crop in the period 1820–40 was not tobacco, or cotton, or rice. It was corn. Some of this corn was exported to the Deep South in the form of shelled grain, or as pork, since the Deep South with its emphasis on cotton production could not meet its food needs. But most of the corn produced in the Upper South was consumed by the human population and the animal population of that area. Corn was the basic foodstuff of the Upper South.

The most important crop for sale and export — the most important commercial crop in the Upper South — was tobacco. But throughout the period 1800–1860 tobacco was a problem crop. Tobacco is an intensive crop that draws heavily upon the nutritive content of the soil, but at the same time it produces a high yield and brings a high gross return in relation to its bulk and the acreage involved. So it has the potential of producing a high net return to its growers. But the growing of tobacco so depletes the soil that it cannot be produced on the same land for more than three or four years in a row. The practice in colonial times, and still in the 1800s, was to shift tobacco production to a new piece of land as soon as the old piece was worn out. The soil was regarded as an expendable commodity. This practice worked satisfactorily so long as there was an inexhaustible supply of land. But good tobacco land was becoming scarce by 1840. Overproduction, depressed prices, high costs, and declining yields brought economic distress to tobacco planters in Virginia and Maryland periodically throughout the period 1800–1860.

As a result of these continuing problems, serious efforts were made in the 1830s and 1840s to bring about production reforms in tobacco-producing areas. These reforms included the rotation of tobacco with grains and clover to put nitrogen back in the soil, the use of lime and guano fertilizer, deeper plowing, and the introduction of an animal agriculture. These changes in farming practices caused some optimistic observers to say that soil exhaustion was no longer a problem in Virginia in 1860.

Whether this was the case is debatable. But both Virginia and Maryland improved their agricultural positions in the 1840s and 1850s. Tobacco production rose significantly, yields for wheat and corn increased, and there was some increase in the number of cattle.

The preeminent position of Maryland and Virginia in tobacco production was being challenged by Kentucky and Tennessee in the period before the Civil War. Improved water transportation via New Orleans and fresh land gave a strong boost to tobacco production in those states. By 1860, Virginia was still the leading producer of tobacco, but Kentucky was second and Tennessee third. North Carolina's great day in the production of tobacco was still to come.

Rice production began in the coastal areas of South Carolina and Georgia in the colonial period and continued in those areas up to the Civil War. In a limited area extending from five to twenty miles up the rivers from the coast, some 500 planters on not more than 70,000 acres produced the bulk of the American rice crop. Rice was a crop requiring large amounts of human labor, heavy investments in capital, and highly skilled management. In 1860 the greatest concentrations of slaves in the United States were in the rice-producing areas of South Carolina and Georgia, where there were twenty estates with 300 to 500 slaves, thirteen estates with 500 to 1,000 slaves, and one estate with over 1,000 slaves. Nowhere in the United States, except possibly on the sugar plantations of Louisiana, were there such large estates, so amply stocked with slaves, and with such conspicuous displays of luxury as in this rice country.

But rice production was not holding its own in the 1850s. Yields of rice were declining as the result of diminishing soil fertility. Favorable cotton prices were inducing planters to put their land into cotton if the land was suitable for it, and then sell their slaves or transfer them to cotton-producing land. Thus the total production of rice declined from approximately 215 million pounds in 1849 to 187 million pounds in 1859. No other staple crop seemed to offer as little promise as rice in the 1850s.

The Arrival of Commerical Agriculture

By the 1850s there were broad belts of commercial agriculture and highly specialized areas of commercial agriculture established in the United States. Many farmers, perhaps most farmers, in the nation were still subsistence farmers or in a pioneering stage, but east of the Mississippi River there were broad areas in which large numbers of farmers were producing a surplus of products for sale.

There was a rapidly expanding commercial cotton-producing belt that stretched across Georgia, Alabama, and Mississippi and that accounted for more than half of the total U.S. exports before the Civil War. There was a less rapidly expanding, but nonetheless emerging, commercial feedgrain-livestock economy lying north of the Ohio River and stretching from the state of Ohio on the east to the states of Missouri and Iowa on the west. Lying immediately to the north of the feedgrain-livestock area was a commercial wheat belt which was in a state of transition. In the Northeast there were highly specialized areas of dairy products production, vegetable production, and horse production, as well as feed production for urban-based horses. There were enclaves of commercial tobacco production in the Upper South — some of long standing in Virginia and Maryland, and some relatively new in Kentucky and Tennessee. Finally, there were some highly specialized production areas in the Deep South — rice production in the coastal areas of South Carolina and Georgia, sugarcane production in Louisiana.

With certain exceptions (e.g., rice), agriculture in these areas of commercialization did not make intensive use of labor or capital. Cultivation in these areas was not intensive, and yields per acre were low. In expanding output and creating a surplus for sale, farmers and planters typically applied the cheap factor, land, to the scarce and dear factors, labor and capital, to the maximum extent that was technically feasible. A surplus was created and a state of commercialization was achieved, not by increasing yields per acre, but by cultivating as many acres as was technically possible. Commercial agriculture in the United States in the 1850s was an extensive agriculture.

Much has been made of the role of farm mechanization and improved transportation in the development of commercial farming in this chapter. But important to this development was the concurrent development of market centers such as Cincinnati, Chicago, Buffalo, St. Louis, and New Orleans to handle and to distribute the growing agricultural surpluses. Institutions had to be developed to receive, store, finance, and mill the grains, and to distribute the final products. And institutions had to be developed to receive and slaughter the livestock and to pack and distribute the meat products. The story of these "agribusiness" developments before and after the Civil War in the city of Chicago is beautifully told by William Cronon.[8]

Suggested Readings

Danhof, Clarence H. *Change in Agriculture: The Northern United States; 1820–1870.* Cambridge, Mass.: Harvard University Press, 1969.

Gates, Paul W. *The Farmer's Age: Agriculture 1815–1860.* Vol. III of *The Economic History of the United States.* New York: Holt, Rinehart, and Winston, 1960.

Jahoda, Gloria. *The Trail of Tears.* New York: Holt, Rinehart, and Winston, 1975.

North, Douglass C. *The Economic Growth of the United States, 1790–1860.* Part II: 1815–1860. New York: W. W. Norton, 1966.

Robertson, Ross M. *History of the American Economy,* 2nd ed. New York: Harcourt, Brace, and World, 1964. Pp. 115–24.

Schlebecker, John T. *Whereby We Thrive: A History of American Farming, 1607–1972.* Ames Iowa: Iowa State University Press, 1975. Chaps. 7, 8, 9, and 10.

CHAPTER 5

THE LAST FRONTIER: 1860–1897

Physical and Environmental Features of the Great West

With the exception of a few valleys along the Pacific Coast and the Mormon settlements in Utah, all the Great West between the Pacific Ocean and a line drawn roughly from Saint Paul to Fort Worth awaited agricultural exploitation in 1860. This was the farmers' last frontier. It was not, however, an unknown land. It had been thoroughly explored by the fur traders, army units, and adventurers of all kinds. Immigrants from the Midwest and the East in long wagon trains had trudged across it in the 1840s and 1850s seeking fertile lands in Oregon, gold in California, and religious freedom in Utah.

But the Great West, with few exceptions, was not a hospitable land. The Great Plains were known in 1860 as the Great American Desert. Major Stephen Long, who explored the plains region in the early nineteenth century for the army, wrote that the region was "almost wholly unfit for cultivation and, of course, uninhabitable by a people depending upon agriculture for their subsistence."[1] Walter Prescott Webb wrote somewhat more objectively in 1936 as follows:

The distinguishing climatic characteristic of the Great Plains environment from the ninety-eighth meridian to the Pacific slope is a deficiency in the most essential climatic element — water. Within this area there are humid spots due to local causes of elevation, but there is a deficiency in the average amount of rainfall for the entire region. This deficiency accounts for many of the peculiar ways of life in the West. It conditions plant life, animal life, and human life and institutions. In this deficiency is found the key to what may be called the Plains civilization. It is the feature that makes the whole aspect of life west of the ninety-eighth meridian such a contrast to life east of that line. [2]

No one who has tried to live and farm on the Plains has ever said that life was kind or farming easy on those Plains. Hot winds on the southern Plains in July and August can destroy a crop in a few days; everything shrivels and dies before the furnacelike blast of these winds. Blizzards on the northern Plains — a combination of severe cold, high winds, and sleet and snow — cannot be faced by man or beast. Livestock drift great distances before a blizzard, and a person caught out in one will be dead in a few hours unless shelter is found. Farmers must wage a battle with nature each year to produce a crop where the annual precipitation averages less than twenty inches, the distribution of that precipitation through the year is highly variable, and evaporation rates are high. In sum, farming in the Plains environment is a risky business; the hostile physical environment makes it so.

One can gain a mental picture of the Plains environment by following an imaginary line from Kansas City to San Francisco in figure 5.1. A flat plain rises gently and regularly from an elevation near 1,000 feet at Kansas City to over 5,000 feet at Denver. Average annual precipitation declines from between 30 to 40 inches at Kansas City to between 10 to 20 inches at Denver. The Great Plains, or High Plains, which are reached in western Kansas, are practically treeless and in their natural state were covered by short grass — a grass that served as an excellent feed, first for buffalo and later for cattle.

The central part of the Great West is occupied by the several ranges of the Rocky Mountains, all running more or less north and south. A desert plateau extends westward from Salt Lake City some 500 miles until it reaches the Sierra Nevada Mountains of California. This desert plateau, although interspersed with mountain peaks and short mountain ranges, runs between 4,000 and 6,000 feet in elevation on the level areas and has an average annual precipitation of ten inches or less. Webb argues that because of its plainslike physical characteristics and arid climate, this intermountain desert plateau should be considered part of the Great Plains environment. This is debatable, but one thing is certain. Crops cannot be cultivated successfully on this desert plateau except under irrigation. However, under irrigation the desert will bloom, as the Mormons have demonstrated.

Within a brief period of forty years following 1860, much, if not most, of the land that would ultimately be brought under cultivation in the Great West had been plowed up and planted to grains east of the Rocky Mountains and planted to hay and specialty crops in the irrigated areas of the intermountain region and the valleys of the Pacific slope. But much had to happen in that brief forty years. The Plains Indians, who were determined to save their homelands, had to be subdued. The great buffalo herds on which the Plains Indians lived had to be liquidated. The cattle barons and the cowboys had their brief day in the sun. And a generation of farmers and farm families had to be broken financially and physically learning to farm in a semi-arid region. It was hard and it was cruel, but it was done, and done quickly.

Land Policies

The Homestead Law was enacted on May 20, 1862. With the South in

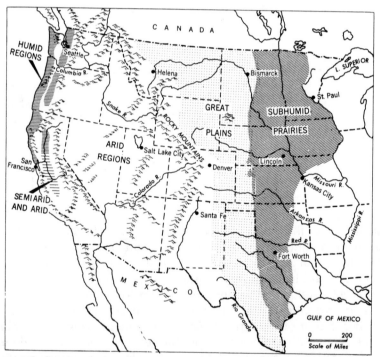

Fig. 5.1. Physical features of the western states and territories. Reprinted from Gilbert C. Fite, *The Farmers' Frontier, 1865–1900* (New York: Holt, Rinehart, and Winston, 1966), p. 5. Reproduced by permission of the University of New Mexico Press.

rebellion, Republicans had enough votes in Congress to enact this piece of legislation into law and thus end a long and bitter struggle for free land. Under the Homestead Act of 1862 any person could file for 160 acres of unappropriated public land if he or she

1. was an American citizen, or had filed his or her papers of intention to become a citizen;
2. was twenty-one years old, or was the head of a family, or had served fourteen days in the army or navy of the United States; and
3. had never fought against the United States.

The last condition was intended to exclude Southerners serving in the Confederate Army. But this condition was dropped in 1866. The man or woman filing on 160 acres of land would then obtain a fee simple title to it when he or she

1. had resided on or farmed the claim for five consecutive years after filing on it;
2. had become a citizen of the United States; and
3. had paid the requisite fees, which in the early years amounted to $10.

The amendments and interpretations of this law were endless, and no attempt will be made to enumerate them. But a few should be mentioned. It was soon decided that both husband and wife could not file on separate homesteads — an excellent excuse for postponing legal marriage, as Professor Fred Shannon points out.[3] The ban against ex-Confederates was dropped in 1866, as was already noted. The original Homestead Act permitted individuals filing on claims who did not wish to live the full five years on that land to buy it for $1.25 per acre; this was the "commutation clause" of the act. This clause was interpreted to mean that if the individual filing on the land lived on it six months and made some small improvements on it, he or she was then eligible to commute it (i.e., purchase it for $1.25 an acre). In the first years of the operation of the act this provision created no serious problems, but in later years the provision was much abused. Cattlemen and timbermen found the commutation provision a quick and easy way of obtaining valuable land at a very low price.

The shortcomings of the Homestead Act were numerous. First, although there was still some excellent land available in western Iowa and Minnesota and eastern Kansas, Nebraska, and the Dakotas in the 1860s, given the hostile physical environment of the Great Plains and the large land grants made to the railroads and to the states by the federal government during this decade, there was very little first-class cropland available for homesteading in the 1870s and 1880s. Second, on the Great Plains a homestead of 160 acres was too small a unit to be economically viable. In the 1900s this provision was changed to allow the individual to file on 320 acres for cropping purposes or on 640 acres for grazing purposes. But these changes came too late to save thousands of families from going broke trying to farm units that were too small. Third, no real attempt was ever made to move impoverished urban workers in the East onto this free land, although efforts in the direction probably would have failed had they been tried. Free land in the West never really became a safety valve for the underemployed and unemployed in the crowded eastern cities. Fourth, the Homestead Act and succeeding acts were *used* by large operators such as cattle ranchers and timber barons to increase the size of their holdings — and hence their operations — at a minimum cost.

The contents of the four major land disposal acts passed largely at the behest of special interest groups in the West to complement the Homestead law are summarized by Professor Ross M. Robertson as follows:

1. *The Timber-Culture Act of 1873.* This law, ostensibly passed to encourage the growth of timber in arid regions, made available 160 acres of free land to anyone who would agree to plant trees on 40 acres of it.
2. *The Desert Land Act of 1877.* By the terms of this law 640 acres at $1.25 an acre could be purchased by anyone who would agree to irrigate the land within three years. (The serious defect of the act was that there were no clearly defined stipulations as to what constituted irrigation.)
3. *The Timber and Stone Act of 1878.* This statute provided for the sale at $2.50 an acre of valuable timber and stone lands in Nevada, California, Oregon, and Washington.
4. *The Timber Cutting Act of 1878.* This law authorized the citizens of certain specified areas to cut trees on government lands without charge. There was a stipulation that the timber should be used for agricultural, mining, and domestic building purposes.[4]

The first of these acts helped small homesteaders on the Plains to enlarge their farm units. But the Congress could not achieve through legislation what nature herself could not do, namely, grow trees on the Plains. Of the 245,000 original claim entries made under the Timber-Culture Act of 1873 for nearly 37 million acres, only about 65,000 clear titles were issued covering about 10 million acres. Professor Shannon states that "nine-tenths of these deeds went to persons that did not comply with 'the letter of the law, to say nothing of the spirit.' "[5] The remaining three land acts summarized above were clearly land-grabbing acts which were little used, and hence of little assistance, to homesteaders and other small farmers.

Public attitudes toward the disposal of public lands began to change in the 1880s. More and more people began to realize that the land resources of the nation were being squandered in a reckless fashion and that there was a need to tighten up the many and varied legal provisions for disposing of the public domain. Thus in 1891 the General Revision Act, which closed several land disposal loopholes, was passed by Congress and signed into law by President Grover Cleveland. This Land Act of 1891 began by repealing the Timber Cutting Act; it next amended the Desert Land Act by specifying that a definite plan for irrigation had to be submitted with each application to take up land under the act; the Preemption Act, which had been in force since 1841, was repealed, and the policy of selling the public domain except under special circumstances was abandoned; and the new law authorized the president to set aside forest lands as public reservations. This act may be viewed as the first concrete step in a conservation movement which was to gain widespread support in the early 1900s.

But the Land Act of 1891 could not undo what had already been done. In this connection, it would be a mistake to think that all or even most of the land in the public domain disposed of between 1862 and 1900 was given away under the Homestead Act. About 500 million acres of the public domain were disposed of between 1860 and 1900. Of that total, only about 80 million acres were distributed under the Homestead Act. During the same period some 108 million acres were sold at auction and by other means; probably most of this land was sold to well-financed land speculators, who in turn sold it to farmers and ranchers. The remaining disposals, some 300 million acres of land, were given as grants to the states and the railroads, which in turn sold these lands to speculators in some cases and to farmers in others.

The national disease of land speculation, which infected everyone from the poor pioneer farmer to the presidents of the United States from 1785 to 1860, continued in virulent form after the Civil War. But land speculation in the post-Civil War period to an important degree passed out of the hands of small farmers and even rich individuals — and into the hands of large corporations and the railroads. It became big business.

Another perspective on the disposal and acquisition of land in the post-Civil War years may be gained from the following numbers. The total land in farms increased from some 407 million acres in 1860 to some 839 million acres in 1900. But of this increase of 432 million acres, only some 80 million acres were added through the issuances of patents, or land titles, to homesteaders. The remainder, some 352 million acres, had to be acquired through land purchases — from the government, from land speculators, from the railroads, or from somebody else. The Homestead Act played a role in the disposal of the public domain in the nineteenth century, but only a small role.[6] Most farmers bought their land from speculators and often became land speculators themselves.

Settling the Great West

Settlement west of an imaginary line running from Saint Paul, Minnesota, to Fort Worth, Texas (figure 5.1), was slow during the 1860s. The preoccupation with the Civil War and Indian troubles on the frontier slowed the tide of migration into the Great West. But settlement picked up in western Minnesota in the late 1860s. And a great land settlement boom took place on the Minnesota-Dakota-Nebraska-Kansas frontier in the early 1870s.

As in earlier periods, many, if not most, of the first settlers came from states immediately to the east of the frontier. These settlers typically traveled by covered wagon pulled by yokes of oxen, with perhaps a horse or two and a cow or two. They had sold a clearing in Wisconsin, or perhaps had been outfitted by their family in Illinois or Indiana, and they were seeking rich prairie land on which to grow grain. A woman in a wagon train of immigrants heading west in southern Minnesota, not far from the present town of Worthington, in June 1873 observed three other wagon trains heading in the same direction.[7] The lure of free rich prairie land between the 95th and 98th meridians from the Canadian border to the Indian Territory was overwhelming in the early 1870s to young native Americans in the older settled regions of the Midwest. They came in droves. Often when they arrived at their destination they found that all the free land was gone. They then had either to buy land from the agent of a railroad, or state government, or private speculator, or to push farther west, perhaps on to the Great Plains west of the 98th meridian, or perhaps on to Oregon, Washington, or California.

But everyone did not arrive by covered wagon from an adjacent state. The railroads were actively recruiting immigrants in northern Europe and the eastern United States. The railroad recruiting agencies would haul the immigrants west into Kansas and Nebraska or to the end of the railroad line in Minnesota and the Dakotas and sell them railroad grant land for between $2 and $10 an acre, depending upon its location.

The new states and the new territories were also not leaving the process of settlement to chance. Each established a land settlement or immigration agency to promote the sale of lands owned by the state and to promote the flow of immigrants into its state or territory. When the established habit of pioneering was coupled with free land policies, the promotion by railroad companies, and the pressure for settlement by states and local communities, the subhumid prairie lands of the upper and central frontier succumbed to settlement in a few short years after the Civil War.

As the subhumid prairies east of the 98th meridian were filled up, settlers pushed on west onto what Professor Webb defines as the Great Plains proper — an arid land with ten to twenty inches of rainfall and a short grass cover that is completely treeless. By 1880 settlers were taking up homesteads and buying land in Kansas as far west as the western border of the state (the 102nd meridian). And by 1890 agricultural settlements covered most of western Nebraska and eastern Colorado as well as western Kansas (figure 5.2).

The first settlers on the Plains usually selected farming sites along streams or in river bottoms where water was readily available and wood could be found for building. But such favorable sites were quickly exhausted, and the settlers who came later, who were most of them, had to establish their homesteads on the open, treeless Plains. These later settlers had to dig deep wells for water, or haul or carry their water great distances. Since trees were nonexistent on the Plains, lumber out of which to build houses and barns was also nonexistent. In this situation, settlers typically built sod houses, and sometimes shelters for their livestock, out of blocks of the grass sod. Such houses did not look elegant and often lacked windows, but because of the thickness of the walls they were relatively warm in the winter and cool in the summer, an important consideration given the fiercely variable climate of the Plains.

Settlers in western Minnesota and the eastern Dakotas usually planted wheat as their cash crop and patches of potatoes and other vegetables for family use. Settlers in Nebraska and Kansas in the 1870s usually planted corn as a cash crop and a garden for family use. But because these settlers almost always came from humid areas, either in the United States or in Europe, and knew little about con-

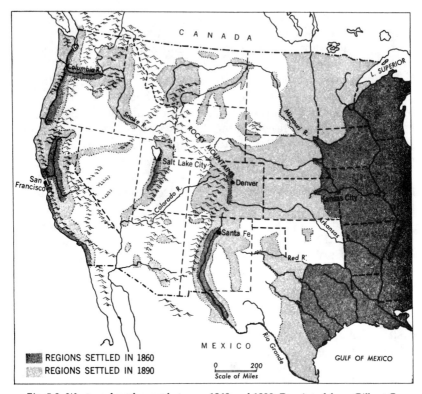

Fig. 5.2. Westward settlement between 1860 and 1890. Reprinted from Gilbert C. Fite, *The Farmers' Frontier, 1865–1900* (New York: Holt, Rinehart, and Winston, 1966), p. 127. Reproduced by permission of the University of New Mexico Press.

serving moisture in the soil, their crops of corn and wheat on the Plains often shriveled and failed. In fact, crop farmers on the Plains seemed to encounter one disaster after another: droughts, hot winds, grasshoppers, prairie fires, low prices, and credit contraction. As a result, a high proportion of the first generation of settlers were starved out and either continued west to the Pacific slope or returned to their families and relatives in the central or eastern United States. And to say that many families were starved out is not an exaggeration; many families literally starved after the grasshoppers ate their crops or the hot dry winds burned them up. The Plains environment was a hard and cruel teacher, and those who did not learn quickly how to adjust to it failed.

But for every family that failed, another soon came along and took its place, so that grain farming on the Great Plains was firmly established by 1890. In the process, however, grain farmers encountered problems other than a hostile physical environment. One was economic hard times, which we will discuss in a later section. Another was the cattlemen, who competed with the farmers for the open plains land. Cattlemen pushed up from Texas in the 1870s with great herds of cattle and covered the Great Plains with cattle and cattle ranches from Texas to Montana. The headquarters of these ranches typically would be established along a river on a few hundred acres, and the cattle would then graze over thousands of acres of unoccupied open range. These ranches were often financed by English capital, and the hired hands, cowboys, were adventurers from all over the United States and even the world. The business of cattle ranching on the Great Plains was exciting and even profitable after the railroads reached the Plains in the 1870s. But the free open range was the problem. Cattlemen wanted it at no cost to themselves, and grain farmers wanted to occupy it and farm it. Thus the "sod-busters" and the cowboys fought many a battle over that land in the courts of law and with guns on the land itself. But the land could not be kept free, open, and unoccupied. Throughout the 1880s and 1890s grain farmers steadily encroached upon the open range land with land deeds and farming operations. And cattlemen not so slowly gobbled up great tracts of that land by direct purchase and under the Desert Land Act of 1877. Hence for the most part the open range had come to an end by the 1890s. Cattle barons fenced their large estates to keep their cattle in, and grain farmers fenced their smaller acreages to keep the cattle out.

The settlement of the Great West in the period 1860–97 was not confined to the central and upper Plains, as we see from figure 5.2. Many farm families pushed on to the Pacific slope by wagon or by railroad in the 1870s and 1880s. Oregon and Washington developed slowly, because they were hard to reach (until the Northern Pacific Railroad reached Portland in 1883) and because they were so far from the eastern markets. But agriculture made good progress in the 1880s, with the number of farms more than doubling in the Pacific Northwest in that decade.

California agriculture developed rapidly in the 1850s as a direct result of the large influx of population in the gold rush period, 1848–50. Vegetable production and fruit growing developed quickly in the valleys around San Francisco and in the bottom lands of the Central Valley around Sacramento. Stockmen pushed up and down the Central Valley in the 1850s. But as soon as these ranchers learned how to grow small grains in the winter season, when the rains came, they turned to the production of wheat, barley, and oats. During the 1860s, cattle and sheep production declined, and thousands of farmers in the Central Valley concentrated their farming efforts on wheat production. California became an important producer and exporter of wheat in this period.

Thus, when settlers began to arrive in California in the late 1860s and early 1870s, they discovered that all the best land — land that would produce grain without irrigation — was already in private hands. Settlers seeking land in the Central Valley suitable for growing small grains had to buy it from large landowners or the railroads for between $2 and $10 an acre. As a consequence, little land was homesteaded in California, and claims filed under the Homestead Law were typically located in the rolling foothills or in very dry areas.

Californians soon came to recognize the limitations of dry-land grain farming. Yields were low relative to yields that could be obtained under irrigation. Higher-valued grape and fruit crops could be raised under irrigation, and more than one crop a year could be produced under irrigation. So California farmers and ranchers spent most of the 1870s and 1880s putting in irrigation works and fighting over water rights. But disputes over water rights were minimized, if not resolved, in 1887 by the passage of state legislation creating irrigation districts with the purpose of developing and distributing irrigation water over broad areas. And the development of irrigation had progressed a long way by 1890. By that year there were nearly 14,000 farms in California with some form of irrigation, involving more than one million acres of land. Most of this land was located in the San Joaquin Valley between Stockton and Bakersfield.

During the 1860s, settlement retreated all along the Texas frontier. Neither the Confederate troops nor the local militia could protect the farmers and ranchers west of Fort Worth from Indian attacks and depredations. And the fierce Comanches stopped migration into northwest Texas until after 1875. But the westward push began in earnest in the late 1860s and early 1870s. During the early 1870s a vast ranching empire was created in west central Texas stretching from Wichita Falls in the north to San Angelo in the south. And in the early 1880s large cattle ranches were established on the High Plains of the Texas Panhandle. But right behind the ranchers came the dirt farmers in covered wagons, with their families and a cow or two, looking for cheap land on which to grow grain and other crops.

Unlike the situation in other parts of the Great West, settlers could not homestead under federal laws in Texas. Under the terms of the admission of Texas into the Union in 1845, Texas retained and disposed of its own public lands. But from the beginning, Texas adopted liberal land disposal policies to attract and hold population. For example, in 1845 its legislature passed a preemption measure that offered 320 acres to a head of family, and 160 acres to a single person who would settle on the public domain, for a price of 50 cents per acre. And in 1854 Texas passed a homestead law granting 160 acres from the public domain to any individual who would live on that land for three years and cultivate it. Thus there were several ways that a settler could acquire land at low cost in West Texas in the 1870s and 1880s.

Corn was the main crop of West Texas farmers at this time. But the production of cotton pushed westward in this period, too, and by the late 1880s cotton was being produced as far west as Abilene. Livestock production played a larger part in farming operations in West Texas than on the Kansas and Nebraska frontiers. A small dirt farmer might have ten to twenty cows, of which three or four were milk cows, and a neighboring small rancher might have 100 to 200 head of cattle. This created problems for small farmers; marauding livestock were forever destroying their crops. The solution came in the form of barbed wire fencing in the 1880s. But often the dirt farmers had to bear the expense of fencing their fields. Steadily, however, in Texas, as in the Central Plains, dirt farmers encroached upon the cattle kingdoms and forced an end to the open range. This was even true in the Texas Panhandle. In 1887 the XIT Ranch began producing grain and vegetables. That marked the passing of the open range and the cowboy.

Technological Developments

The process of farm mechanization, which got under way in the 1830s and which reached widespread proportions in the 1850s, continued and accelerated in the period 1860–97. The shortage of manpower on farms during the Civil War years greatly stimulated the use of laborsaving machines on farms — the use of cultivators, mowing machines, and reapers. And the more than doubling of the land in farms between 1870 and 1900 served to maintain the strong demand for laborsaving farm machinery.

This upward surge in the use of machines on farms occurred primarily in the Midwest, on the eastern fringe of the Great Plains, and in California and the Pacific Northwest. The southern farmer stuck to his hoe, one mule, and shallow plow. Eastern farmers were concentrating on dairying and specialty crops, for which the time of mechanization had not yet arrived. But on the grain-producing prairies of the Midwest and on the Plains, farmers were rushing into mechanization. And this process of mechanization involved principally the substitution of horsepower for human back power.

The new and improved machines that made the greatest impact on cropping operations in this period included the riding, or sulky, plow (of one or two bottoms), the spring tooth harrow, the seed drill, row crop cultivators, forage mowers, the twine binder, and grain-threshing machines. The grain combine also made its appearance in the Far West during this period. The early combines required immense amounts of power; teams of forty or more draft animals were sometimes used with these large machines. As a result, steam tractors began to appear on large farms and ranches in the Far West in the 1890s. But they were inefficient in terms of labor requirements, and there was always the risk that sparks from an engine would set a field of ripe grain on fire. Thus steam tractors had only a brief period of glory in American agricultural history before the gasoline tractor took over.

During this period there were several technological developments of a mechanical nature that had an important influence on the development of American agriculture although they were not concerned with crop production. Two related inventions revolutionized the dairy industry from New England to Minnesota; they were the centrifugal cream separator for separating cream from the milk and the centrifugal cream tester for testing the butterfat content of milk and cream. The first made it possible for every small farmer from New England to Minnesota to milk a few cows, sell his cream to the local butter factory, and have a monthly cash income. The second protected the small farmer who was selling whole milk or cream to a butter factory from being cheated.

Other technological advances included a great expansion in the railroad network, the development of the refrigerator railroad car for shipping fresh meat, fruits, and vegetables, and the birth of a canning industry for preserving perishable commodities. All these developments had the effect of widening the markets for farm producers and, as a result, of increasing their production opportunities and their income-earning possibilities.

Technological developments in the period 1860-97 did three important things for the agricultural industry: (1) they greatly reduced the drudgery of farm work; (2) they greatly increased the productivity of farm workers, and (3) they widened the economic opportunities of farm producers. Thus all should have contributed to an increase in the real incomes of farm workers, and perhaps they did if adequate weight is given to the reduction in drudgery of farm work during the period. It should be recognized, however, that from 1860 to 1897 the toil and drudgery of the farm wife was reduced little, if at all, by the advent of new and improved technologies.

Production Developments

Once the continental United States, with its varied resource and climatic endowments, was settled, and its differently endowed areas were linked by a network of railroads, these areas could and did specialize in agricultural production according to their comparative advantage. The final settlement of the continental land mass and its linkage through a railroad network occurred in the period 1860-97. Thus the specialization of agricultural production by areas, which began in the 1820s and 1830s and which was in transition in the 1840s and 1850s, was largely completed in the period 1860-97. The location of agricultural production in the United States has changed somewhat in the twentieth century but not to any important degree.

The Northeast continued to specialize in fruit, truck crops, and dairy production — particularly dairy production. The Upper South continued to specialize in tobacco production and to produce a surplus of corn, which was fed to hogs and beef cattle, the products of which were consumed in that region or exported to the Deep South, which had a food-deficit. The Deep South continued to specialize in the production of cotton; cotton perhaps ceased to be king, but it remained by far and away the leading crop of the region.

The region lying north of the Ohio River and stretching westward from western Ohio, across Indiana, Illinois, Iowa, and into eastern Nebraska and Kansas, as well as northward into the southern tiers of counties in Michigan, Wisconsin, and Minnesota, became and remains the Corn Belt. Some of the surplus corn of this region was shipped to the Eastern Seaboard and some was exported abroad, but most was converted into pork and beef for shipment through the United States. To the north of the Corn Belt, stretching across the Lake States, an important dairy area developed that specialized in the production of manufactured dairy products. In the western part of this area, in Wisconsin and Minnesota, small grain production remained important in the nineteenth century. But wheat production kept moving westward until it reached the Great Plains, and there it stopped. The Great Plains became one great wheat-producing belt from the Canadian border to northern Texas. Certain limited areas on the Plains (e.g., the Flint Hills of Kansas and the Sand Hills of Nebraska) that did not lend themselves to crop production became enclaves of cattle ranching, but the remainder of the Great Plains with a rainfall of fifteen inches or more became one great wheat field. On the western edge of the Plains where annual precipitation fell below fifteen inches, and in the Rocky Mountain region and the intermountain region outside the irrigated valleys, cattle and sheep ranching became firmly implanted in the 1880s and 1890s and is still to be found there today. The irrigated valleys of the mountain, intermountain, and Pacific regions of the Great West turned to the production of fruit and truck crops in the late nineteenth century, and they continue to produce those high-valued specialty crops in the late twentieth century. Small grain production in the dry land areas of California, Oregon, and Washington became important and specialized in the period 1860–97, and remains so today in Oregon and Washington. A high proportion of the small grain produced on the Pacific slope was and is still exported overseas. Cotton production has made some important locational shifts in the twentieth century, and soybeans have made an inroad into the Corn Belt and parts of the South, but aside from those two crops, the production areas established in the late nineteenth century continue down to the present day virtually unchanged.

The more than doubling of the land in farms, the increased specialization in production, and the widespread substitution of machines for human labor had the expected effect on total farm output. Total farm output increased by some 53 percent between 1870 and 1880, and total farm output increased by 135 percent between 1870 and 1900.

This was a period of extensive growth. Total farm output was increased by the addition of more farms, more acres in crop production, more workers in agriculture, and more machines and equipment. Yields per acre of wheat, corn, barley, cotton, hay, and potatoes were barely increased. And, as might be surmised, estimates of agricultural productivity — output per unit of input — indicate only a modest upward trend. In sum, this was a period of great extensive growth.

During the specific period 1866–1900, the production of wheat increased almost four times, the production of corn some three and a half times, the production of barley some six and a half times, and the production of cotton nearly five times. The number of cattle on farms approximately doubled between 1867 and 1900, and the number of hogs on farms increased by about 50 percent. Output was increasing across the spectrum of commodities, but the greatest growth was in the traditional crops.

Hard Times and the Agrarian Revolt

Prices received by farmers for their products fell irregularly but persistently from the end of the Civil War to the depression year 1896. The price of wheat fell sharply from $2.06 per bushel in 1866 to 95 cents per bushel in 1874 and then declined irregularly to 49 cents per bushel in 1894. Corn followed a similar pattern, declining from 66 cents per bushel in 1866 to 31 cents per bushel in 1878, and then to 21 cents per bushel in 1896. The index of prices received by farmers for all farm products (1910–14 = 100) declined from 119 in 1869 to 66 in 1878 and then to 53 in 1896.

But as Professor Douglass North correctly points out, the terms of trade did not turn against farmers during this period;[8] the prices of nonfarm products were falling at about the pace of farm commodity prices. Why, then, should farmers have been so unhappy between 1870 and 1896? There were numerous reasons — some directly related to the above price relationships, some only indirectly related, and some not related at all. With falling product prices in the 1870s and again in the 1890s, the gross returns of the average, or representative, farmer had to fall. If he was buying his land on time at a fixed price, as many were, this meant that he had to meet fixed land payments out of a declining gross income. The same adverse relationships held for farmers purchasing farm machinery on time.

The fact that nonfarm-produced goods were falling at about the same rate as farm products was of no great consequence for most farmers because most farmers held their purchases of nonfarm-produced consumer goods to a minimum; the day when farmers purchased a high proportion of their operating inputs from the nonfarm sector had not yet arrived. Further, although railroad freight rates were falling during this period, the decline in the official rates did not keep pace with the decline in farm product prices. And where the railroads held spatial monopolies in the great grain-growing regions west of Chicago, the farmer-users were subjected to all kinds of rate and service discrimination and abuse. Thus farmers in the 1870s (to a lesser extent in the 1880s) and in the 1890s knew that their gross returns were down but that their fixed financial commitments were not. They felt they were being pushed around and cheated by the railroads, and they found that because of recurring money panics they often could not obtain credit when they needed it. And for western farmers the price of mortgage credit was about double that for eastern farmers.

The basic farm problem was overproduction. Total farm output, it will be recalled, increased 53 percent between 1870 and 1880, but the population of the United States increased only 26 percent. In other words, approximately one-half of the increased farm output in the 1870s had to find a "market" either abroad or in the form of increased per capita food consumption at home. Farm exports did increase importantly during this period, and domestic per capita food consumption probably increased somewhat. But these two avenues of increased utilization could not cope with the great surge in production during this period over and above the population growth requirement. Thus farm prices and farm incomes lagged and dragged.

Farmers on the western prairies and the Great Plains were confronted with difficult physical hardships in addition to economic problems. As we have seen, prairie fires, hail, drought, and, worst of all, grasshoppers plagued the pioneer settlers in these areas throughout the 1870s. These natural calamities perhaps served to slow the rate of aggregate farm output expansion and thus minimize the downward movement in farm prices. But the farmers beset by one of these calamities would often have their entire crop destroyed. And the areas affected by drought and grasshoppers were often rather wide, involving thousands of farmers. Further, because their financial resources were limited, most of these pioneer farmers could ill afford to lose a crop. The loss of one crop caused many families to go on short rations; the loss of two crops in a row caused many more families to lose their precarious foothold on the frontier.

Destitution was widespread on the central Plains frontier in the 1870s; hunger and outright starvation were not uncommon. Economic conditions improved somewhat in the early 1880s, and the dreaded grasshopper plague seemed to have worn itself out. Farmers were learning to live and farm under semi-arid conditions. But widespread drought in the late 1880s and desperate economic conditions in the early 1890s caused great hardships on the Plains in those years.

By the 1890s farmers had learned that farming on the Plains was a highly risky business, and they began to take steps to conserve that precious resource, water, and to use it wisely. Irrigation was developed where it was feasible, and methods of conserving moisture in the soil were adopted.

The response of farmers to the hard times of the 1870s, 1880s, and 1890s was to organize and act collectively in business and in politics. This was the first widespread agrarian uprising in American history. The membership of the Patrons of Husbandry, better known as the Grange, reached an estimated 1.5 million in 1874. The Farmers Alliance movement, which operated under several different names and which sometimes had separate organizations in the North and in the South, claimed over a million members in 1890. The Populist political party emerged in large measure out of the Farmers Alliances and met with considerable success in 1892 when over a million votes were cast for its presidential candidate, James B. Weaver of Iowa. It reached its high-water mark in 1894 when it received a million and a half votes and elected seven congressmen and six senators to the United States Congress.

The Grange attempted to help the farmer in two general ways: (1) by the enactment of legislation in the states for the regulation of railroads and (2) by the establishment of marketing, processing, manufacturing, and purchasing cooperatives for its members. In a short-run sense the Grange was unsuccessful in both of these economic ventures. Within a few years most of the Granger laws — railroad regulatory laws — were repealed or declared invalid by the courts, and most of the cooperative ventures failed financially. But the right of states to regulate the railroads was affirmed by the Supreme Court in 1876. And in their cooperative business ventures the Grangers learned some valuable lessons which unfortunately went unheeded by other and later farmers' groups.

The Farmers Alliances were active in everything from catching horse and cattle thieves to advocating the free and unlimited coinage of silver. On most issues they met with only limited success, but they were successful in 1891 in conjunction with the Knights of Labor in forming a new political party, the Populist party. The Populist party stood for a national currency issued and managed by the federal government, the free coinage of silver, a graduated income tax, government ownership and control of the railroads and telegraph lines, and the abolition of land monopolies. In 1896 it joined with Democrats under the leadership of William Jennings Bryan in support of the silver issue. A Populist leader, Henry Demarest Lloyd, at the party convention in 1896 called this decision "the most discouraging experience" of his life. The free-silver movement he denounced bitterly as a "fake" and as "the cow-bird of the reform movement." Events bore him out. Bryan went down to defeat in this single issue campaign in 1896, and with him the Populist party.[9]

Government Activities in Agriculture

On May 15, 1862, Abraham Lincoln signed into law an act of Congress establishing the U.S. Department of Agriculture. This agency was a long time in borning. A unit was created within the Patent Office in 1839 with a budget of $1,000 to collect agricultural statistics and "for other agricultural purposes." Agitation for a separate Department of Agriculture gained momentum in the 1840s and 1850s but was turned aside after 1849 by the recurring suggestion that agricultural activities be solidified in a Bureau of Agriculture in the new Department of the Interior. The above suggestion was almost enacted into law in 1862, but in a compromise action a Department of Agriculture was established, to be headed by a commissioner without full cabinet status.

The first commissioner of the U.S.D.A., Issac Newton, outlined in his first report the objectives of the new department. They were (1) collecting, arranging and publishing statistics and other useful agricultural information, (2) introducing new plants and animals, (3) answering inquiries of farmers regarding agriculture, (4) testing agricultural implements, (5) conducting chemical analyses of soils, grains, fruits, plants, vegetables, and manures, (6) establishing a professorship of botany and entomology, and (7) creating an agricultural library and museum. Succeeding commissioners of agriculture enlarged upon this agenda by establishing a Division of Botany, a Division of Veterinary Science, a Bureau of Animal Industry, and other research and regulatory units.

But the basic agenda of the U.S. Department of Agriculture did not change between 1862 and 1896. The department did not in this period become an action-oriented agency to deal with the economic problems of farmers. It moved cautiously but persistently in the direction of physical scientific research. It was laying the foundation for becoming a great science-producing agency of government.

In an effort to give the Department of Agriculture greater status, a law was passed by Congress and signed by President Cleveland on February 9, 1889, making the chief executive of the U.S.D.A. a secretary of agriculture. The law also provided for an assistant secretary of agriculture to be appointed by the president.

The more exciting political action was taking place at the state and local level. We have already noted the effort on the part of the Grange to use the power of state governments to regulate the railroads and the partial success of the Grange in that direction. In Minnesota during the difficult winter of 1871–72, Governor Austin appealed to the public for contributions of cash and food to assist the suffering settlers. A relief fund of nearly $20,000 was created and distributed to destitute families in amounts ranging from $5 to $25 to buy food and seed for the coming year. In February 1872, the Minnesota legislature passed a relief law in the amount of $2,000 for the purpose of helping farmers buy seed wheat and other grains. No individual claim was to exceed $50. The legislature had not done much, but it had recognized the problem and taken some action.

Thereafter the state governments of Minnesota, Iowa, Nebraska, and Kansas, and the territorial government of Dakota regularly wrestled with the problem of relief for their destitute settlers. Sometimes these governments sponsored voluntary relief organizations that raised funds within the state and in the East; sometimes they passed relief legislation earmarking funds for relief — for food, for seed, or for both; sometimes the government authorized the sale of bonds, the proceeds of which were used for relief. The funds raised and distributed by the state governments were not large by modern standards, but these actions helped many, many pioneer families to survive.

Another agency of the government came to the aid of the pioneer farmer and his family on the Plains frontier. It was the army. Army units stationed at posts in Nebraska and Kansas began feeding starving settlers unofficially in the early 1870s. In 1875 Congress formally approved this activity, and it is estimated that the army distributed nearly two million rations to over 100,000 persons in Minnesota, Dakota, Nebraska, Kansas, Iowa, and Colorado in the spring of 1875. The army also issued thousands of clothing items to destitute families on the frontier in 1874–75. Thus the army came to the aid of settlers on the Plains frontier in the 1870s in ways other than through a cavalry charge.

Finally, as we have already recognized, farmers tried to use the power of government, particularly the federal government, to create an economic system that was more responsive to their needs. They tried to use government to curb the power of the great monopolists (e.g., the railroads), to create a more flexible and liberal monetary system, and to reform the tax system. But they failed on all accounts. They failed because they and their leaders did not understand the complexities of the economic system which they sought to reform and because they could not match the power of the entrenched economic interests which they sought to regulate and control. But they would be back in the twentieth century.

Suggested Readings

Cronon, William. *Nature's Metropolis: Chicago and the Great West.* New York: W. W. Norton, 1991.

Degler, Carl N. *The Age of the Economic Revolution, 1876–1900,* 2nd ed. Glenview, Ill.: Scott, Foresman, 1977. Chaps. 3 and 4.

Fite, Gilbert C. *The Farmers' Frontier, 1865–1900. Histories of the American Frontier* series, 18 vols. New York: Holt, Rinehart, and Winston, 1966.

Powers, LeGrand. "Fifty Years of American Agriculture." *The Making of America.* Vol. V of *Agriculture,* edited by Robert M. La Follette. Chicago: De Bower, Chapline, 1907.

Robertson, Ross M. *History of the American Economy,* 2nd ed. New York: Harcourt, Brace, and World, 1964. Chap. 11.

Schlebecker, John T. *Whereby We Thrive: A History of American Farming, 1607–1972.* Ames, Iowa: Iowa State University Press, 1975. Chaps. 11, 12, 13, 14, and 15.

Shannon, Fred A. *The Farmer's Last Frontier: Agriculture, 1860–1897.* Vol V. of *The Economic History of the United States.* New York: Farrar and Rinehart, 1945.

Webb, Walter Prescott. *The Great Plains.* New York: Houghton Mifflin, 1936.

CHAPTER 6

PROSPERITY AND
DEPRESSION: 1897–1933

The Period in Perspective

This period begins in the trough of one of the most severely economically depressed periods of the nineteenth century and ends in the trough of the greatest depression, to date, of the twentieth century. But much happened between those two trough years.

The years 1897 to 1910 were years of sustained economic recovery for American agriculture. Farm prices rose every year during that thirteen-year period; they rose steadily but not dramatically; and they rose relative to nonfarm prices (i.e., farm prices rose more than nonfarm prices). In this favorable economic milieu, with the physical hardships of the pioneering days largely behind them and the drudgery of farm work largely lifted from their backs through the increased use of machines, farm people came to believe that the good life could be achieved on the farm. It is true that the achievement of the good life required hard work, thrift, saving, investment in the farm, and "right thinking" (which in most farming communities meant the tenets of the Grand Old Party), but it could be achieved in the "rational" world of the early 1900s.

Walter Lord describes the sense of confidence, as well as high spirits, that prevailed among Americans as they entered the twentieth century. He writes:

The *New York Times* on December 31, 1899, devoted nearly four editorial columns to a review of the Nineteenth Century. It proudly paraded the list of inventions — steam engines, railroads, telegraph, ocean liners, telephones, electric lights, even the cash register. They would pave the way for even greater advances. "We step upon the threshold of 1900 which leads to the new century," concluded the editorial, "facing a still brighter dawn of civilization."

Sunday sermons struck the same note. The Reverend Newell Dwight Hillis could scarcely contain himself: "Laws are becoming more just, rulers humane; music is becoming sweeter and books wiser; homes are happier, and the individual heart becoming at once more just and more gentle."

No wonder hopes were high. From coast to coast, the country had never seen such good times. The Portland *Oregonian* called 1899 "the most prosperous year Oregon has ever known." The Cheyenne *Sun-Leader* agreed: "Never has a year been ushered in with more promise." The Louisville *Courier-Journal:* "Business in Louisville was never better, if as good." . . .

. . . *Even the usually discontented farmers were happy.* [Italics added.][1]

The good years, 1897–1910, were followed by the Golden Age of American Agriculture, 1910–14. Farm product prices were high and stable. The terms of trade were strongly in the favor of farmers. The country was settled. The world was at peace. Hard work, thrift, and "right thinking" had indeed paid off for farmers; the good life was a reality.

World War I came as a surprise and a shock to most Americans. The world of peace and rationality had collapsed. The great increase in the export demand for, and exports of, foodstuffs, induced by the war, triggered a sharp rise in farm prices in 1916, and by the middle of 1920 the level of farm prices had more than doubled. In this context farmers began bidding against each other for cropland, which by 1915 had become a scarce resource in the United States. The price of farmland rose by 70 percent between 1913 and 1920 for the country as a whole, and by 60 percent between 1916 and 1920. In the best farming areas, such as Iowa, the price of farmland more than doubled betweem 1914 and 1920.

But with the cessation of the war in late 1918 and the tapering off of post-World War I relief efforts in 1920, farm prices in the United States began to fall during the summer of 1920. Within one year the price per bushel of wheat fell from over $2 to under $1, and the overall level of farm prices also fell by almost one-half. Farm prices recovered in the mid-1920s, but only to a limited degree. Thousands of farmers were thus forced to pay for land, purchased on time, with product prices at only half the level that they had anticipated when buying the land. Unable to meet their fixed land payments at their greatly reduced product prices, thousands went bankrupt in the 1920s. Further, although nonfarm prices fell in 1920–21 as well, they did not fall as far or as sharply as farm prices; thus the terms of trade turned against farmers once again in the 1920s. As a result, the 1920s were years of financial failure for many, many farmers and years of economic hardship for all farmers.

The economic depression, which began for farmers in 1920, began for the rest of the nation with the collapse of the stock market in October 1929. This financial debacle was followed by a four-year slide into greatly reduced levels of industrial production and greatly increased levels of unemployment. Between 1929 and 1933 the level of durable goods production declined by 80 percent, and unemployment rose to include over 25 percent of the working force. In this context, farm prices tumbled once again; the index of farm prices fell from 148 in 1929 to 70 in 1933. For reasons that will be discussed later, total farm output held almost constant during the Great Depression years, but gross farm income declined by approximately 40 percent and net farm income by over 50 percent. The present for most farmers in 1933 was intolerable, and the future appeared even bleaker. It would seem that nothing could go wrong for the farming community from 1897 to 1920 and that nothing could go right for it from 1920 to 1933.

The most notable developments in the period 1897–1933 may have been concerned with prosperity and depression and their impact on farmers. But an altogether different kind of development needs also to be recognized and its implications considered. The *beginnings* of a new age in agriculture — a scientific age — may be observed in the period 1897–1933. This age is composed of three essential parts: (1) the discovery of scientific relationships, (2) the development of new technologies based on those scientific relationships, and (3) the adoption of the new technologies on farms. Although (2) and (3) occurred to a limited extent in the period 1897–1933, the first element — the discovery of scientific relationships — was of primary concern. The full flowering of the scientific age of agriculture was to occur after 1933.

Stated somewhat differently, the knowledge base on which a scientific agriculture would later develop was just beginning to take shape in 1897; the personnel and disciplines that would develop and expand this knowledge base were just becoming recognized; and the institutions that would train the personnel, support the disciplines, and thus contribute to expansion of the knowledge base were just becoming well established. A science-based agriculture — an agricultural industry that would grow and develop on the basis of scientific research and development — was still in its infancy in 1897, but all its developmental pieces were in place. Much of the period 1897–1933 would be concerned with growth, expansion, and formalization of these developmental pieces.

A New Direction in Resource Policies: Conservation

Following the passage of the General Revision Act of 1891, the pressure to protect and conserve the land and other physical resources of the nation continued to build. (This is discussed in chapter 5 in the section entitled Land Policies.) In accordance with the provision of this Land Act of 1891, some 50 million acres of valuable timberland were withdrawn from private entry and sale by 1900, despite vigorous opposition from private interests, particularly in the western states. Because Congress failed to adequately fund the Division of Forestry in the U.S.D.A., those reserves were not properly managed nor protected from the depredations of timber thieves. Nonetheless, an important start had been made in protecting and conserving the forest resources of the nation.

When Theodore Roosevelt succeeded to the presidency in 1901, he took the leadership in seeking legislation to establish a broadly conceived national program of resource conservation. In this endeavor he was highly successful.

In 1901 a Bureau of Forestry was created, and in 1905 that bureau became the United States Forest Service. The first chief of the Forest Service was Gifford Pinchot, the leading conservationist of that era, and he initiated a program of scientific forest management on the national forestlands.

By 1907 some 150 million acres had been converted into national forests, 75 million acres of which contained merchantable timber. By 1907 some 75 million acres in the public domain containing valuable minerals were closed to sale and settlement. Much of the land containing valuable minerals had already passed into private ownership, but by this action the government was able to establish some large reserves of coal, phosphates, and oil.

By 1907 the principle had become accepted that it was the proper function of the federal government to carry out programs of public works for the purpose of controlling stream and river flows. In this connection, storage dams and irrigation works were to be constructed on western rivers for the benefit of settlers in that arid region. Further, there was explicit recognition of the future importance of water power sites by the establishment of a policy wherein the ownership of these sites was reserved to the government.

Each of these policy and program actions was bitterly contested by the private interest seeking to exploit the resources involved — particularly in the western states. In fact, the controversy over the conservation of resources became a matter of East versus West in this period. President Roosevelt was keenly aware of the deep-seated differences between the conservationists and the private western interests, and he was fearful that when he left office the achievements that had been made under his administration would be swept away. To help guard against this, he created a National Conservation Commission with Gifford Pinchot as chairman. This commission submitted a report to the nation in 1909, in three large volumes, providing a wealth of information and material in support of the conservation cause.

The conservation movement slowed down in succeeding administrations, but the great achievements of the Roosevelt administration were not undone. And in both the Taft and the Wilson administrations steps were taken to further protect the natural resources of the nation. In the Withdrawal Act of 1910, all known coal, oil, gas, and phosphate lands remaining in the public domain were reserved. And in 1911 the federal government was empowered to purchase forestlands in the Appalachians for the purpose of protecting watersheds. Finally, the Supreme Court in 1917 affirmed the right of the federal government to own and manage power sites in the public interest.

The concept that the public had an interest in the proper management of the resources, land, water, minerals, and timber in the public domain developed very slowly in the United States. The emphasis with respect to resource use was on private exploitation from 1607 to 1891. But the concept of the public interest gained acceptance in the 1880s and 1890s; bold actions were taken to protect and conserve the natural resources of the nation in the first decade of the twentieth century, and that policy of resource conservation was sustained in the second decade.

Belatedly the Homestead Law was made more compatible with the arid Plains environment in the early 1900s. The Enlarged Homestead Acts of 1909 and 1910 made it possible for a homesteader to file on 320 acres of land in most western states. And the Stock-Raising Homestead Act of 1916 allowed the homesteading of 640 acres on land suitable only for grazing.

The Role of the U.S.D.A.

When James Wilson, better known as Tama Jim Wilson,[2] became Secretary of Agriculture on March 6, 1897, a new era began for the U.S.D.A. Tama Jim Wilson had been a professor of agriculture and director of the experiment station at Iowa State College, as well as a member of the Iowa state legislature and a member of the House of Representatives of the U.S. Congress. He believed fervently in the power of scientific research, and he knew how to achieve his research goals through political action. Thus under his leadership the research activities of the department were widened, strengthened, and reorganized. The Department of Agriculture became a great science-producing institution under Wilson's sixteen-year tenure of office, 1897–1913.

The diverse research activities of the department with regard to plants and plant diseases were consolidated into the Bureau of Plant Industries in 1901. With the rediscovery of Mendel's laws of heredity in 1900 and the pioneering work of the Dutch botanist Hugo De Vries and the American geneticist Thomas Hunt Morgan in mutation and gene theory, the new bureau was provided with a basis for scientific plant breeding and the development of the science of genetics. The Division of Entomology was elevated to bureau status in 1904 and its work expanded in many directions. The expanded activities of the Division of Chemistry in both research and regulatory work resulted in its being redesignated the Bureau of Chemistry in 1901. Investigations carried on under the supervision of Harvey W. Wiley of this bureau resulted in the passage of the Food and Drug Act of 1906; regulatory functions of the act were also administered by the bureau. The regulatory functions of the Bureau of Animal Industries and its research activities into animal diseases were expanded in the years 1902–6. As a result, a network of livestock inspection stations was established throughout the country. The Bureau of Soils was created in 1901, the Bureau of Statistics in 1903, and the Bureau of Biological Survey in 1905; and the Bureau of Forestry became the Forest Service in 1905.

In all the above areas Tama Jim promoted scientific research without hesitation, and he pressed hard for the regulatory activities resulting logically from the research findings. But the secretary was more conservative when it came to social change. He viewed motion pictures as the "work of the devil" and opposed their use in the work of the department, and he viewed the automobile with even greater hostility. (However, by 1912 he finally approved the use of one car at the experimental farm at Beltsville, Maryland.) Nonetheless, some important new lines of work were developed during his tenure of office. An Office of Public Roads was formed in 1905 to do research on road building and later to actually build post roads. Farm demonstration work and adult education work were developed and fostered. Economic work in farm management and marketing was initiated.

With succeeding administrations the work of the department was reorganized several times. The office of secretary was strengthened, and the administration of the department was increasingly centralized in that office. The economic work of the department grew both absolutely and relatively, and the Bureau of Agricultural Economics was created in 1922. Extension work was expanded and institutionalized with the passage of the Smith-Lever Act in 1914. And one secretary of agriculture, Henry C. Wallace, tried to interest the White House in an action program, Equality for Agriculture, to deal with the farm depression of the 1920s. (He did not succeed, however.)

But the basic emphasis on research, education, and regulation fixed in the structure of the department by Tama Jim Wilson from 1897 to 1913 did not change in the years 1914–33. The department remained primarily a fact-finding, research, science-producing institution. It would and did undertake various kinds of regulatory activities that resulted logically from research findings on animal diseases, or plant diseases, or pests. But in the main, leadership in the department was not ready to, nor did the research personnel have the capacity to, embark upon action programs to deal with the economic problems besetting farmers.

The Agricultural Colleges

The colleges of agriculture in the Land-Grant University System came of age in the period 1897–1914. The rocky period was passed when they were torn between the preachers and classical scholars on the one side and the practical agriculturalists on the other with respect to what they should teach and what they should research. By the early 1900s, the standard agricultural disciplines had been established, and there was a substantial body of knowledge in each discipline to teach and to use as a base for further research. Those disciplines included:
1. soils,
2. agronomy,

3. plant pathology,
4. horticulture,
5. animal husbandry,
6. veterinary medicine, and
7. even some economics as applied to agriculture.

Research in the above areas made rapid progress in the early 1900s. This was true particularly for plant breeding, causes of plant diseases, causes of animal diseases, and soil chemistry. Farmers were eager for practical information based upon the research findings in these areas. Thus agricultural colleges early in their history developed winter lecture series and all kinds of adult education techniques to transmit to farmers the practical results of the research work going on in the colleges of agriculture and the associated experimental stations created by the Hatch Act of 1887. The Smith-Lever Act of 1914 institutionalized the outreach programs of the state agricultural college by creating the cooperative federal-state extension service. Under the agreement reached between the federal government and the states, all extension work undertaken by the Department of Agriculture in the states should be carried on through the state colleges of agriculture. So although the state and county extension workers were joint employees of the U.S.D.A. and the agricultural colleges, they were in fact off-campus instructors of the colleges of agriculture. And for many years the county extension agent served as the principal conduit through which scientific knowledge and technological advances were transmitted to farmers from the state colleges of agriculture.

The colleges of agriculture never became the training institutions for future farmers that their founders had envisaged. But the colleges of agriculture trained the high school vocational teachers and the extension workers, as well as the research workers who went to work in private and government research agencies. They developed much of the basic science in the agricultural area used by private research and development organizations to produce new and improved technologies for adoption by farmers. And they produced many of the important new and improved technologies adopted by farmers since 1900. The agricultural colleges along with the U.S.D.A. in the period 1897–1933 became the science-producing base upon which the modern highly productive agriculture of the United States was built.

The state colleges of agriculture have performed another role that is less well advertised than their science-producing role. They have served for at least seventy-five years as a wonderfully efficient channel for helping young men and women transfer out of agriculture and into productive nonfarm pursuits. Often the college-trained farm youth has taken a farm-related job; the agribusiness complex has been staffed in large measure by such people. Colleges of agriculture have not been sold to state legislatures on the basis of this role, and certainly it has not been the primary role of these colleges. But the training of farm youth for skilled nonfarm jobs has been a highly successful secondary role of the colleges of agriculture. The ambitious farm-reared youth has for many years found in the college of agriculture an effective mechanism for transferring out of farming, if not out of the enlarged agricultural complex.

In the early years of the twentieth century the U.S.D.A. perhaps took the lead in the science-producing role. It was the first agency to bring together a critical mass of agricultural scientists. But as the agricultural colleges and the associated experiment stations have grown and concentrated on research and education functions, and with the U.S.DA. moving into the economic action arena in the 1930s, the colleges have become the preeminent agricultural science-producing agencies in America. In the period 1897–1933, the production of science and technology became *the* reason for being for the agricultural colleges, and in that role they have prospered mightily.

Technology on the Farm

Technological developments on the farm in the period 1897–1933 were mostly mechanical. Machines became larger and sometimes more efficient. Four-bottom plows pulled by a hitch of eight horses became common in commercial grain-producing areas of the Midwest in the 1890s. Improvements in harrows, seeding equipment, and cultivators occurred almost every year.

Custom grain harvesting became the rule by 1900; custom harvesters started with the harvest in Texas in June and worked their way north with the season to the Dakotas and Montana in September; the rig typically involved a threshing machine, which knocked the grain free of the straw, carried the straw away and dumped it onto a strawstack, and sacked the grain, as well as some type of steam engine to provide the power to operate the thresher. By 1900 a grain combine that could be pulled over hilly ground and not topple over had been perfected. But the steam-powered combines of the 1890s and early 1900s were inefficient and hazardous, even though they had the potential to harvest up to 100 acres a day.

What was needed in 1900 was an efficient source of power to pull and operate the soil preparation and harvesting machines which were becoming larger and larger. By 1900, some 5,000 steam tractors were being produced a year. But they were not the answer. Steam engines consumed huge amounts of fuel and water and hence were inefficient to operate. The steam tractor was heavy, cumbersome, and difficult to move and maneuver. Thus horses and mules continued to provide almost all the power used on farms.

An internal combustion engine mounted on a vehicle — a wagon frame with wheels — was first built in the United States in 1889. But it could not generate enough power to pull a plow. Throughout the 1890s inventors worked to increase the drawbar power, lessen the weight of the engine, and reduce the size of the wagon frame on which the engine was mounted. In 1901, Charles Hart and Charles Parr of Iowa built their first successful gasoline engine tractor. Within a few years they were mass-producing these tractors. The first Hart-Parr tractors weighed about ten tons, but within a few years they were producing a tractor that weighed around five tons and could generate thirty horsepower. In 1906, Hart and Parr gave the name tractor to their machine. It is estimated that by 1909 there were at least thirty companies manufacturing gasoline-engined tractors, and they were producing around 2,000 tractors a year.

Improvements in the design and efficiency of the gasoline-engined tractor were rapid in the period 1910–20. The adoption of gasoline tractors on farms during this period was also rapid. The number of gasoline tractors in operation on farms increased from about 4,000 in 1911 to approximately 246,000 in 1920. And the rapid adoption of gasoline tractors continued through the 1920s; the number of such tractors on farms increased from 246,000 in 1920 to 920,000 in 1930. The mass production of tractors and the standardization of parts in this period contributed to their efficient use and hence to their more general acceptance. Farmers could buy replacement parts without having to have such parts specially machine-made, so that there was no danger of having an inoperable tractor during critical production periods.

Without doubt, the emergence of the gasoline-engined tractor was the most significant technological development of this period. Such tractors provided an efficient and dependable source of power for operating the large soil preparation and harvesting machines that were being developed and sold to farmers. They released millions of acres from the production of grain and forage to support the horse and mule population; this land could now be used to grow food for human consumption. They contributed to more timely farm production operations, hence to increased output per unit of input. And they substituted for an increasingly scarce labor supply in agriculture. An efficient and dependable source of power was required to bring the process of mechanization in crop production to full fruition, and this the gasoline tractor provided in the 1920s, and continues to provide.

But some other technological developments of consequence were occurring too. The use of commercial fertilizers, liming materials, and animal manures increased slowly but steadily during this period. The use of nitrogen fertilizer, for example, doubled between 1910 and 1920 and increased another 50 percent between 1920 and 1930. The application of lime on farmland tripled between 1910 and 1920 and increased, but more slowly, between 1920 and 1930. And wherever livestock were kept in pens, as in dairy farms in the Northeast and on the Pacific slope, animal manures were collected and spread on the cropland to improve the fertility and tilth of the soil. Slowly farmers were learning how to increase the productivity of their land.

Advances in plant breeding and the control of animal diseases were also taking place. The introduction of wheat varieties from abroad and the breeding of new varieties domestically led to wheat varieties that were more resistant to drought and to stem rust than were the traditional varieties. The causes of numerous animal diseases — tick fever, pleuropneumonia, tuberculosis, and hog cholera — became known in the latter part of the nineteenth century. The need for sterile care in treating wounds and the sick was established beyond question, and knowledge of immunization created new opportunities for controlling animal and human diseases. Thus the way was opened for the control of some animal diseases and the eradication of others. A vaccine to protect against hog cholera was developed in 1903, and tick fever in cattle was nearly eradicated by 1914. The struggle to conquer hog cholera would continue till the World War II period and the battle against tuberculosis and brucellosis up to the present time. Knowledge of the causes of plant and animal diseases accumulated rapidly in the period 1897–1933, and techniques and methods for controlling those diseases on the farm followed in most cases not too long after the discovery of the causes of the diseases.

Production and Market Developments

The first decade in the twentieth century was a highly prosperous time for American farmers, but not because the average, or representative, farmer was greatly expanding his production. Total farm output increased only 8 percent between 1900 and 1910. The rate of increase in total farm output slowed down in the period 1900–10 because the rate of adding the extensive resource — land — to the national farm plant had decreased and because the time of the great farm technological payoff had not yet arrived. In fact, the index of farm productivity, output per unit of input, actually declined in the period 1900–1910.

The national agricultural plant was not expanded to any important degree in this decade because it could not be. The land base on which to expand extensively was largely used up; the good arable land was all gone; only land in marginal areas, such as the Great Plains, remained to be brought into cultivation. And the new and explosive technologies, which farmers could substitute for land and thereby increase output, had not yet arrived on the scene.

The period 1910–20 was almost a repetition of the previous decade. Total farm output increased some 9 percent between 1910 and 1920. And the reason total output did not increase more rapidly was that farmers could no longer readily add the extensive resource — land — to the national farm plant, and farm productivity held almost constant over the period.

The rate of growth in total farm output increased in the decade 1920–30 over that achieved in the decade 1910–20. Total farm output rose by some 15 percent between 1920 and 1930. This was achieved by a modest increase in inputs employed in agriculture — mechanical power and machinery — and a modest increase in productivity — output per unit of input.

The entire period 1897–1933 was a time of slow growth in farm output. Land, that seemingly inexhaustible resource, was in fact exhausted in that period. The number of crop acres harvested in the United States increased by some 46 million acres between 1910 and 1932, but these additional acres were low-production, marginal acres. And the total number of crop acres harvested reached an all-time peak in 1932; some 371 million acres of crops were harvested that year. The technological revolution on the farm based on scientific developments was still two decades away. Thus the growth in production that occurred in the period 1897–1933 resulted in part from some increase in the acres devoted to crop production and in part from some increase in farm productivity, which in turn resulted from increased mechanization of the farm.

The demand for, or market for, the total product of American farms varied in the extreme over this period and was the destabilizing factor that moved the farm economy from depression to prosperity and back to depression again. Between 1900 and 1910, the rate of increase in the domestic population was about two and one-half times as fast as that in farm output. This rapid rate of increase in domestic population, both absolutely and relatively, together with the rapid rise in real per capita incomes in this period, explains the steady rise in farm prices. Superimposed on this strong domestic demand for farm products was the sharp increase in foreign demand during the period 1916–19, stemming from the disruptions of World War I. These two strong demands caused domestic farm prices to soar during the period 1916–19. The extraordinary foreign demand for farm products slackened off in 1920, and farm prices in the United States fell disastrously in 1920–21. The foreign demand for American farm products did not recover in the 1920s, and neither did domestic farm prices. The value of agricultural exports fell from a high of $4.1 billion in 1919 to $1.8 billion in 1922. Agricultural exports continued roughly at the 1922 level throughout the 1920s and then declined still further to $662 million in 1932. The sharp decline in farm product exports between 1919 and 1922 was the principal cause of the economic hard times experienced by American farmers in the 1920s. The further decline in farm product exports between 1929 and 1933 added to their economic woes.

The total output of American farms increased at a slow but reasonably steady pace over the period 1897–1933. But the aggregate demand for that output fluctuated wildly. As a result, American farmers were taken for a ride on the farm price roller coaster. They liked the first half of the ride; but they found the second half of the ride to be at best frightening and at worst exceedingly painful.

Credit and Cooperation

Two problems plagued pioneer farmers during much of the nineteenth century: (1) a shortage of credit and (2) inadequate markets. Farmers and their leaders were forever talking about the need for cheaper credit, the need for more relevant credit forms, the need for economic power to compete effectively in markets that were rigged against them, and the need to find ways of combating the power of the great monopolists (e.g., the railroads). Two of the principal thrusts of the agrarian uprising of the 1870s, 1880s, and 1890s were concerned with obtaining easier, or cheaper, credit for farmers and the development of cooperative marketing associations to enable farmers to "control" the marketing of their products. But in both efforts farmers typically were unsuccessful.

Farmers met with greater success in the twentieth century. The Country Life Commission, appointed by President Roosevelt, reported in 1908 that a principal cause of the deficiencies of country life was "a lack of any adequate system of agricultural credit whereby the farmer may readily receive loans on fair terms." In 1912 all the major political parties — Democratic, Republican, and Bull Moose — adopted planks in their platforms advocating action by governments in the field of agricultural credit. In 1913 President Wilson appointed, with congressional approval, an official governmental commission that accompanied a private "American Commission" to Europe to study agricultural credit and cooperation in European countries. Following the release of reports by those commissions, the Moss-Fletcher bill was introduced into Congress in 1914. The bill proposed a system of agricultural credit for the nation, comprising both private profit-making institutions and cooperative associations. It was attacked by agricultural groups that wanted a pure system of cooperative agricultural credit, as was in vogue in Europe, and by some farm organizations that wanted a government agency to make direct loans to farmers. After two years of wrangling, a compromise bill entitled the Farm Loan Act of 1916 was enacted by Congress and signed by President Wilson. It authorized both a cooperative system of twelve federal land banks and a system of joint stock land banks to be organized with private capital for profit. The federal government provided part of the capital required for the cooperative land banks to begin operation and regulated the interest rates that could be charged borrowers in either system.

Thus a system of long-term agricultural credit came into being in 1916. The progress of the land banks was slow in the first few years. Farm incomes in the period 1916–20 were high; hence farmers were less conscious of the need for credit than they had been previously. Further, the plan of organization and capital subscription for the cooperative system was sufficiently novel as to require considerable education on the part of farmer-users.

In the early 1920s, when the need for credit became greater, the private joint stock land banks prospered relative to the cooperative land banks. But the joint stock land banks ran into difficulty in the mid-1920s in making farmland loans, as did many credit institutions. The financial conditions of these joint stock land banks became steadily worse in the late 1920s and early 1930s. Thus in 1933, after a thorough reorganization of the farm credit agencies, the remaining private joint stock land banks were liquidated.

The year 1933 was an important one in the farm credit field. The Emergency Farm Mortgage Act of 1933 made various forms of emergency credit available to farmers through an expansion in the activities of the federal land banks and in the funds provided those banks by the federal government. The Farm Credit Act of 1933 provided for the establishment of production credit associations to make short-term and intermediate-term loans to farmers. The same act also provided for the establishment of twelve district banks and one central bank to extend credit to farmers' cooperative associations.

As the Great Depression widened and deepened, traditional commercial sources of farm credit dried up, whereas the need for farm credit was increased. To meet this need, the federal land banks greatly increased their total loans to farmers. The land banks were authorized to make long-term amortized loans secured by first mortgages on farms. Loans by federal land banks were not to exceed 50 percent of the appraised "normal" value of the land plus 20 percent of the appraised value of the permanent improvements. Loans could be made for the purchase of land, machinery and equipment, and livestock. Most of the funds for loans were obtained from the sale of land bank bonds.

Numerous new marketing agencies came into being in the nineteenth century to handle agricultural products as they moved off the farm. The Board of Trade was established in Chicago in 1848. Cotton exchanges were established in Liverpool and New York in 1870 and 1871. But farmers grew uneasy about these institutions. They suspected that the prices they received for their grain and cotton were determined through various monopolistic arrangements in these markets. Thus economic cooperation became a leading feature of the Granger movement in the 1870s. Whenever a local Grange was formed, one of the first steps was to initiate some form of cooperative buying or selling. These local agencies merged into district and statewide bodies. But as we have already said, these early attempts by farmers to perform the functions of middlemen, manufacturers, and bankers through cooperative enterprise met with short-lived success. Lack of capital, inability to work together, farmers' lack of business experience, and the competition provided by private business, some fair and some unfair, drove most of these cooperative ventures out of business by 1880.

The first successful period in the organization of farm cooperative associations began in the late 1890s and continued to 1920. These cooperative ventures were typically local associations, although some large federated cooperatives came into being on the west and east coasts during this period. The California Fruit Growers Exchange, which handled oranges, was the success story on the west coast, and the Grange-League Federation (later known as Agway), which purchased feed and other production supplies, the success story on the east coast. But most farmers' cooperative associations were concentrated in the states of Iowa, Minnesota, and Wisconsin, and they were concerned with selling grain and livestock and with manufacturing and selling dairy products. Nearly 10,000 farmers' cooperative associations are known to have been organized between 1900 and 1920. Those that succeeded and stayed in business focused on improving the quality of products handled and on becoming more efficient than their private competitors in the handling, storing, and distribution of the products of their patron members. The successful cooperative associations did not return great monopoly gains to their members, but they did return the gains that could be squeezed out of an often inefficient and careless private marketing system.

But farmers wanted more from their cooperative marketing associations. "Orderly marketing" became a popular slogan in the early 1920s, as it did again in the post-World War II years. And many farmers became interested in forming nationwide cooperative marketing associations on a commodity basis that could exercise monopoly control over the sale of that agricultural commodity. Thus there was a need to clarify the legal status of farmers' cooperatives and to make certain they were exempt from the various antitrust laws. This was done in the Capper-Volstead Act, which became law in 1922. Under this act, any producer association, corporate or otherwise, operating for the mutual benefit of its producer members and conforming to one or both of two requirements — (1) that no member be allowed more than one vote regardless of the amount of stock owned by him and (2) that the association not pay dividends on stock or member capital in excess of 8 percent — would be defined as operating legally and not be in violation of the antitrust laws. Jurisdiction with respect to their pricing activities was placed with the secretary of agriculture rather than the Federal Trade Commission.

Armed with the above legal authority, farmers were ready to participate in a movement already under way to gain monopoly control over the marketing and sale of their products — the Sapiro movement. Aaron Sapiro was a young lawyer who served as the attorney for several California cooperatives, and he was convinced that the marketing practices used in connection with localized, specialty crops could be adapted and applied to major national farm commodities such as wheat and livestock. He advocated "cooperation American style," in which farm producers would join in strongly centralized marketing cooperatives that were legally authorized to enter into binding contracts with their members and in which those members were required to deliver all their product to the cooperative involved over a period of years. And *if* the cooperative could get most of the producers of a commodity to sign a binding contract, the cooperative could exercise monopoly control over the marketing and selling of the commodity. In such an economically organized world, farmers, or some farmers at least, could see themselves dictating the price at which their commodity would sell and as a result would reap monopoly gains from the market.

The wheat and corn producers whose prices began to fall in the middle of 1920 first became enamored with Sapiro's ideas. Sapiro worked with the leaders of the wheat and corn growers during the winter of 1920–21. This group, known as the Committee of Seventeen, recommended the establishment of a nationwide grain cooperative marketing association to be known as the U.S. Grain Growers. The plan of organization was ambitious; it called for establishing all the agencies and facilities heretofore provided by the private grain trade. The committee's recommendation and the plan of organization were accepted at a self-appointed ratification conference in Chicago in April 1921. Officers and a board of directors were elected, and the grandiose plan was launched. Internal dissension was rife in the organization from the beginning. The grain exchanges and private trade, of course, fought it. But most important, the membership campaign bogged down. It turned out that more grain farmers were interested in staying out than in joining the organization. Thus the dreams of gaining monopoly control of the marketing and sale of grain, which were held by the leaders of the movement, quickly faded. By the summer of 1922 it was evident that the effort to establish a nationwide grain cooperative had failed.

But this setback did not deter Sapiro. In 1921 he was working with the livestock producers in an effort to establish a National Livestock Producers Association. Soon thereafter he was working with the cotton growers and the tobacco growers to establish centralized commodity-wide cooperative marketing associations for those commodities. In all three of these cases organizations were established and efforts made to sign up producers, and the associations operated after a fashion for a few years. But one after another they collapsed. By 1924 the Sapiro ideas had gone out of style. Farm leaders had learned how difficult it was to put together an effective nationwide business organization. They had further learned how difficult it was to get a majority of producers to sign binding contracts to deliver their products over a long period of time to a centralized marketing association and thereby establish a farmer-operated monopoly in the marketing and sale of their products. Somehow most farmers were unwilling to affix their signatures to binding contracts when the critical time came for them to do so. It was a great idea in theory, but it turned out to be something very different in practice. The monopoly idea, however, was still popular in the late 1970s. And the idea of developing nationwide commodity cooperatives would appear again in the activities undertaken by the Federal Farm Board in 1929 and 1930.

Farmers Turn to Government

As the farm depression deepened in the winter of 1920–21, the various farm organizations in Washington met in April in a ten-day conference to try to decide what their legislative strategy should be. The organizer of the conference, Gray Silver, also held meetings with a bipartisan group of influential congressmen from the farm states. This latter group came to be known as the "Farm Bloc." The Farm Bloc congressmen, with the help of the farm organizations, passed five pieces of farm legislation in 1921. They were:
1. The Packers and Stockyards Act
2. The Futures Trading Act
3. The Emergency Agricultural Credits Act
4. An amendment to the Farm Loan Act raising the interest rate on bonds sold by the Farm Credit system without raising rates to farmer borowers
5. A second amendment to the Farm Loan Act increasing the capital of the federal land banks.

But these acts had limited economic objectives. They lacked the capacity to deal with the general problem of American agriculture in 1921, namely, a reduction in the aggregate demand for farm products stemming in the main from a reduction in foreign demand. The Congress, however, wanted more information about the depressed economic situation in 1921 before attempting to take action to deal with it. Thus in June 1921, by concurrent resolution of both Houses, Congress established a Joint Commission of Agricultural Inquiry. According to Professor Benedict, the commission was directed to determine:

1. The causes of the then current condition of agriculture.
2. The cause of the difference between the prices of agricultural products paid to producers and the prices paid by consumers for the final products.
3. The comparative condition of industries other than agriculture.
4. The relation of nonfarm commodity prices to farm commodity prices.
5. The state of banking and financial resources of the country, as they relate to and affect agricultural credit.
6. The condition of marketing and transportation facilities in the country.[3]

The commission reported in ninety days, as directed, with the following set of recommendations:

1. That the federal government authorize more specifically cooperative combinations of farmers for marketing, grading, sorting, processing and distributing their products.
2. That provision be made, through the existing banking system, for credit to farmers for periods of six months to three years so as to correspond more closely to the periods of turnover in agricultural production and marketing.
3. That improvements be made in the provisions for federally licensed warehouses, and that the states be encouraged to pass uniform legislation regulating the liability and practices of warehousemen operating under state license.
4. That there be an immediate reduction in the freight rates on agricultural products.
5. That the collection of statistics by the Department of Agriculture be expanded.
6. That provision be made for agricultural attachés in the principal foreign countries producing and consuming agricultural products.
7. That trade associations, under state and federal sanction, develop more accurate, uniform and practical grades for agricultural products.
8. That adequate appropriations be made for better record keeping on the costs of production of farm products.
9. That an extended and coordinated program of research through state and national departments of agriculture and the agricultural colleges be undertaken with a view to reducing the hazards of weather conditions, plant and animal diseases and insect pests.
10. That more adequate wholesale terminal facilities be provided, especially for perishables.
11. That the roads from farms to markets be improved, and that joint

facilities for connecting rail, water and motor transport be provided at the terminal markets.
12. That greater effort be directed to the improvement of community life.[4]

But as Professor Benedict further points out, the commission "missed the point of the whole inquiry."[5] It did not focus on the causes of the then current farm depression and what to do about it. It came up with a long list of recommendations — in fact, a grab-bag list of recommendations — that had been discussed in farm circles for years. In an effort to focus on the farm depression, Secretary of Agriculture Henry C. Wallace called a national agricultural conference in January 1922. At the conference George Peek unveiled the plan that he and Hugh S. Johnson, both of the Moline Plow Company of Moline, Illinois, were developing. This plan, to which they gave the name Equality for Agriculture, called upon the Congress and the president of the United States to take the necessary steps to immediately establish "a fair exchange value for all farm products with that of all other commodities." Thus the concept of parity prices for agriculture was born.

The action program proposed by Peek and Johnson for achieving Equality for Agriculture included three essential steps.
1. The total output of each crop would be divided into two parts. The first part would be fed into the domestic market in such amounts, given the domestic demand, as to generate prices that would give farmers a fair exchange value — a parity of prices.
2. The second, or other part, of the total output of the commodity would be sold on the world market for whatever price it would bring.
3. The losses suffered from selling the second part of the crop at lower world prices would be absorbed by, and shared by, the producers of the commodity.

This was the basic concept. The plan, as it was incorporated into legislation, would have numerous variations, particularly with respect to who would absorb the losses. Most farm leaders wanted the federal government to absorb the losses. But the basic concept did not change as it was introduced into Congress every year from 1924 to 1928 by Senator McNary of Oregon and Congressman Haugen of Iowa. It was a bold export-dumping plan; surplus agricultural products were to be dumped on the world market and then restricted from flowing back onto the domestic market by the imposition of a tariff wall. It might have worked for a while if enacted, but it would certainly have induced retaliatory actions by competing nations and importing nations; thus where it would ultimately have led is a matter of conjecture.

But the idea caught on rapidly with farmers. The concept of equality for agriculture, or parity prices, seemed completely fair to farmers in the 1920s, as it did to them in the 1970s. And it provided a simple, direct approach to their difficult price and income problem. Senator McNary and Congressman Haugen introduced a bill into Congress in January 1924 that incorporated the essential features of the Peek-Johnson plan; it had been prepared for them in the Bureau of Agricultural Economics of the U.S.D.A. with the tacit approval of Secretary Wallace. It turned out that the Plan, Equality for Agriculture, was not so simple when translated into a program of action. An export corporation had to be set up. The concept of a fair exchange value, or parity price, had to be defined and made operational. The tariff wall to hold low-priced agricultural commodities in the world market off the domestic market had to be set up. A mechanism had to be established for paying the farmer for his product that would be divided and sold into two different markets at two different prices, and on and on. But a program of action that gave promise of being effective in operation was developed in the U.S.D.A. and introduced into Congress in May 1924. This bill was defeated in the House in June; the opponents charged that the plan was unworkable, unconstitutional, and amounted to price fixing. Similar bills were defeated in Congress in 1925 and 1926.

With some changes in the language of the bill and the provision of a role for farmers' cooperatives in the administration of the plan, the McNary-Haugen bill was passed by Congress in February 1927. But President Coolidge was strongly opposed to farm legislation of the McNary-Haugen type, and he vetoed it. His veto message was a vigorous condemnation of the whole idea. He argued that: (1) the plan was designed to aid farmers in certain areas at the expense of farmers in other areas (i.e., grain farmers at the expense of dairy farmers); (2) the plan constituted price fixing; (3) the plan would be difficult to administer; and (4) the equalization fee in the plan for absorbing export losses represented an unconstitutional delegation of the taxing power of Congress. The veto was sustained, and the plan was dead for 1927.

In 1928 farmers tried again. The new McNary-Haugen bill took account of the president's objections as best it could, and the bill sailed through Congress with overwhelming affirmative votes. President Coolidge once again vetoed the legislation. Farm Bloc congressmen tried desperately to override the veto and came within four votes of doing so in the Senate.

This was the high-water mark for the plan of Equality for Agriculture in the 1920s. It became an issue in the 1928 presidential campaign. But Herbert Hoover, like Calvin Coolidge, was much opposed to the ideas involved in the plan. Thus, with his election to the presidency in the fall of 1928, the plan was dead, although there would be an unsuccessful attempt in 1929 to pass a modified version of the Equality for Agriculture plan, known as the Domestic Allotment Plan.

President Hoover believed that the farm problem could be successfully dealt with through more effective merchandising of agricultural products at home and abroad, reducing the speculation in agricultural commodities, and improving the efficiency of the agricultural marketing system. These ends were to be achieved through the Agricultural Marketing Act of 1929, which established a Farm Board with the authority to make loans to cooperatives for

1. improving the merchandising of agricultural commodities,
2. constructing, or acquiring, handling facilities,
3. forming clearinghouse associations,
4. expanding the membership of cooperative marketing and purchasing associations, and
5. making larger cash advances to grower members of cooperatives than could be provided through regular credit agencies.

In the main farmers and their leaders were not greatly impressed with the program of action developed by President Hoover within the framework of the Agricultural Marketing Act of 1929 — an act passed at his behest. Perhaps if farm prices had not started falling again in 1929, some basic improvements could have been effected in the farm marketing system, improvements which would have been beneficial to both farmers and consumers. But it never got that chance. Prices received by farmers fell almost 50 percent between 1929 and 1932. In this context the Farm Board tried to stem the downward slide in farm prices by making loans to stabilization corporations to acquire surplus products and hold them off the market.

But it was insufficiently capitalized to acquire and hold off the market those amounts of the staple crops — wheat, cotton, and corn — necessary to keep their prices from falling in worldwide markets. And whenever the stabilization corporations released stocks from one crop to make room for commodity from the next year's crop, prices in the market declined still further. The Farm Board with its subsidized stabilization corporations did not have the financial capacity to stem the fall in the world prices of the great staple commodities, and it could not find a way of reducing the stocks it had accumulated without further depressing farm prices. It gave away small amounts of wheat to the Red Cross and bartered some in the international market. But it could find no way out of the economic box in which it found itself, because there was none. Thus in late 1931 and 1932 — in the very pit of the Great Depression — the board became inactive. Its funds were gone, or committed, and if it sold commodity in the open market it contributed to a further decline in product market prices, to say nothing of the losses it would sustain in such selling operations.

Not too much happened on the farm policy front in the latter half of 1931 and 1932. Farmers "hunckered down" hoping for a miracle or just waited for the economic storm to blow over. College professors such as John D. Black of Harvard and M. L. Wilson of Montana were busy developing and promoting the domestic allotment plan. And farm organization leaders were trying to agree on a policy strategy to be pursued with the next, and it was hoped, new administration. It was a period of deep, dark depression, with little hope and even less activity.

Suggested Readings

Benedict, Murray R. *Farm Policies of the United States, 1790–1950: A Study of Their Origins and Development.* New York: Twentieth Century Fund, 1953. Chaps. 7, 8, 9, 10, and 11.

Schlebecker, John T. *Whereby We Thrive: A History of American Farming.* Ames, Iowa: Iowa State University Press, 1975. Chaps. 15, 16, 17, and 18.

Soule, George Henry. *Prosperity Decade: From War to Depression, 1917–1929.* Vol. VIII of *The Economic History of the United States.* New York: Rinehart Press, 1947. Chap. XI.

U.S. Department of Agriculture. *Century of Service: The First 100 Years of the United States Department of Agriculture.* Washington, D.C.: Government Printing Office, February 1963. Chaps. 4, 5, and 6.

U.S. Department of Agriculture. *Farmers in a Changing World. 1940 Yearbook of Agriculture.* Washington, D.C.: Government Printing Office. Pp. 236–326.

CHAPTER 7

THE TECHNOLOGICAL REVOLUTION: 1933–1970

Deep Depression

The farm economy was in a deep depression as this period began. The bottom of the Great Depression was perhaps reached in 1932; prices received by farmers reached a low point in that year, as did the level of industrial production. But economic recovery was slow in the years that followed. This was true for both the farm and the nonfarm sectors. Farm prices and incomes rose slowly in the period 1933–37 and then fell again in 1938–39 (figure 7.1).

Net income per farm *averaged* $454 per year in the period 1930–34 and did not rise above $1,000 per year until the war year, 1941. In this context, thousands of farmers went broke every year in the 1930s, but often the bankrupt farmer simply stayed on the land to which he formerly held title, as a renter, or a new farmer took his place. As a result, the number of operating farms held almost constant during the 1930s at or near 6.5 million. Paralleling this development, the total number of people living on farms in the United States increased somewhat from 1929 to 1933 and then slowly declined from 1933 to 1939. On a trend basis the total farm population held constant at about 31 million over the ten-year period.

The depressed economic conditions of the 1930s, however, had a significant and negative effect on investment in agriculture. Net investment in farm plant and equipment averaged a minus $336 million per year during the period 1930–35, as depreciation in farm machinery, motor vehicles, and buildings exceeded new investments. As a result of this net disinvestment in the national farm plant and the decline in the purchases of current production supplies, the total input of productive resources in farming declined by about 2 percent per year from 1929 to 1934 and then increased slowly between 1934 and 1940.

Fewer total resources were actually employed in farming in 1939 than in 1929. A further reason for this decline in the total inputs employed in farming between 1929 and 1939 was the substantial decline in the man-hours of human labor employed — particularly in the second half of the 1930s. But the labor released — farmers and their families — in the main did not leave the land, or at least did not leave the rural areas. They did not because they could not. Unemployment and lack of economic opportunities in urban areas kept them dammed up as underemployed farm labor in rural areas. What we had then in the 1930s was a large, redundant, or underemployed labor force in the farm sector which did not appear unemployed because the individuals involved shared the forced leisure and the low

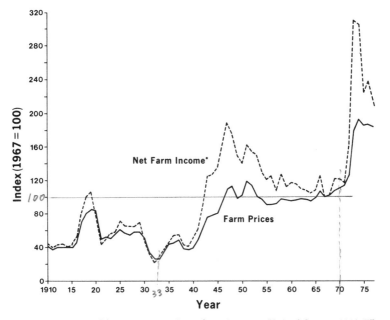

Fig. 7.1. Indexes of farm prices and net farm income, United States, 1910–77.
*Excludes government payments

returns from farming with other members of the immediate families with which they lived. This is the way that farm people survived in the 1930s. A large but underemployed labor force in combination with limited capital, and now limited land, produced to the maximum year after year during the depression years, shared the meager returns in accordance with family modes of living, and waited for an economic miracle to happen.

Wartime and Postwar Boom

The miracle for which farm people were waiting took the form of World War II. The war strengthened the demand for American agricultural commodities in two ways. The increased demand by the combatants for food and fiber products strengthened the export demand. And increased employment and rising wages in war and war-related industries increased the domestic demand for food and fiber products. With both the domestic and foreign demand rising, farm prices began to move up in 1940. Between 1940 and 1946 the prices received by farmers in the United States increased by 138 percent; gross farm income increased by 167 percent; and net incomes of farmers increased by 236 percent. Such an upward thrust in farm prices and incomes would seem to have been great enough to make even the most dour farmer happy.

But there was widespread fear among farmers and farm leaders in 1945 and 1946 that farm prices would break as they did following World War I. This fear and apprehension among farmers was allayed when farm prices did not start falling in 1946. To the contrary, domestic food prices and farm prices took another large upward jump in the period 1946–48. The significant increase in farm prices in the immediate postwar period was attributable to several interacting factors: (1) a two-year price guarantee to farmers following the cessation of hostilities; (2) the avoidance of a postwar economic slump and the maintenance of a strong domestic demand for food; (3) the maintenance of a strong foreign demand realized through a relatively large food assistance program to war-torn Europe and parts of Asia; and (4) the lifting of food rationing and price controls in 1945 and 1946.

Farm prices took a sharp tumble in 1949 but started upward once again in 1950 under the impact of the Korean War. Farm prices reached a peak in the postwar period in 1951 and then began their long downward slide. But it was another exceedingly prosperous period for American farmers while it lasted, and it lasted twelve years. In fact, it lasted long enough to cause many farm people, the younger ones in particular, to forget all about the economic hardships of the 1930s.

Farmers and their families experienced some important developments other than high and rising farm prices and incomes during the period 1939–45. The demands of the military for manpower and the demands of industry for workers broke down the economic wall that was damming up surplus, underemployed workers in the farm sector, and young men and women literally flowed out of the rural areas in torrents. The war created jobs, millions of jobs, and the underemployed in the farm sector were ready and eager to leave farming for higher paying, more productive jobs in the city. In this context, the farm population declined from some 31 million persons in 1939 to approximately 20 million in 1953 — a decline of 35 percent in fourteen years. The war did what the weak recovery of the 1930s and the adjustment programs of the New Deal could not do — it created full employment. And full employment reduced the barriers to labor mobility to inconsequential levels.

The science-producing agencies — the colleges of agriculture and the U.S. Department of Agriculture — continued throughout the 1930s to do what they were supposed to do, namely, discover new scientific relationships and properties. And the same agencies, with private industry, were busy converting this newly discovered scientific knowledge into new technologies for the use of farmers. To an important degree, these new technologies were not adopted by farmers in the 1930s because their adoption required an outlay of funds which those farmers did not have and could not borrow. Thus a backlog of technologies related to farm production built up in the 1930s and remained largely unexploited in 1939.

The war and the postwar boom changed this, too. With rising farm prices and incomes farmers acquired the funds and the credit to purchase the technologies that the Extension Service and the farm newspapers had been telling them they should be adopting to reduce their unit costs. And this they did with a vengeance. They jammed these new technologies into practice, reduced their unit costs, and expanded their farm output. Farmers generally made the rational production decisions as soon as their financial positions would permit, and to the extent that the new technologies could be made available in the war years.

Technological Developments

Technological advances on the farm during the depressed 1930s and the wartime boom were largely mechanical. The tractor was greatly improved in the 1930s. Its weight relative to its horsepower was reduced. Iron or steel wheels were replaced by pneumatic rubber tires, which not only made tractors more comfortable to ride but also reduced fuel consumption significantly. Gear ratios were changed, giving tractors a road speed of up to 20 miles an hour and a field speed of between 3 and 5 miles per hour. As a result of these improvements, the number of tractors on farms increased greatly. In 1940 there were 1.6 million tractors in use on farms; this number increased to 3.4 million tractors in 1950 and to 4.7 million in 1960. The work horse had virtually disappeared on farms by 1950.

With these developments in tractor power came all manner of improvements in farm machinery that took advantage of the greater power and greater speed of tractors. Plows with more bottoms and larger shares came into use. The disk plow became popular — particularly in sticky soils. In the 1940s and 1950s, single-row planters gave way to six- and eight-row drills, and in the 1960s plowing and drilling in gangs and applying one dressing of fertilizer in one operation became commonplace. By 1950 most small grains were harvested by combines. Corn pickers were widely adopted in the 1930s and 1940s, and picker-shellers became popular in the 1950s. Single-row cotton pickers pulled by tractors came into use in the 1940s, and larger, self-propelled cotton pickers came into widespread use in the 1950s and 1960s. This development alone cut the man-hours required in cotton production from 150 hours per acre to about 25 per acre. Dramatic improvements in hay-making equipment were made in the 1940s, and by the 1960s, most hand operations had been eliminated. In the 1950s, improvements in silage equipment brought savings in time and energy and enabled the single operator to handle large volumes of livestock feed. Finally, the milking of cows became almost completely automated in the 1950s, and by 1960 hardly any commercially produced milk was handled in cans; the bulk handling of milk was virtually complete.

The mechanical developments that took place on American farms in the 1930s, 1940s, and 1950s were of the same essential nature as those which had been occurring on farms during the previous 100 years — they substituted for human labor and animal power. But the developments came so fast in the latter decades and reduced human labor requirements so dramatically as to constitute a mechanical revolution in farming. The input of labor in farming declined by some 26 percent between 1940 and 1950, by some 35 percent between 1950 and 1960, and by some 39 percent between 1960 and 1970. The internal combustion engine in combination with sophisticated soil preparation and planting and harvesting machinery had removed practically all the hard physical labor from farming and had reduced the input of labor in farming to a small fraction of total inputs.

But the mechanical revolution was not the only revolution taking place in American agriculture in the period 1933–70. A revolution was taking place in the biological and chemical technologies employed on American farms. Experimental work with fertilization of corn in the first decade of the twentieth century led to an understanding of how hybrid corn could be developed in the next decade, and in the 1920s Henry A. Wallace became the first commercial producer of hybrid seed corn. These early hybrid varieties of corn often doubled or tripled the yield per acre for the adopters and increased the returns to those adopters by 300 percent or more. The Great Depression years slowed the adoption of hybrid corn by farmers, but by the early 1940s hybrid corn had been adopted by most corn growers in major producing areas.[1] Breeding work in wheat and other crops led to somewhat less spectacular results than in the case of corn, but it did lead to more drought resistant and disease resistant varieties of wheat and to yield improvements in almost all corps.

At the same time that new plant varieties were being bred to resist drought and disease and to increase yields, new chemical and biological technologies were being developed to control pests, insects, and weeds. These technologies had the effect not only of decreasing labor requirements but also of increasing yields per acre. But perhaps the greatest source of increasing yields per acre during this period was the increased use of commercial fertilizer. In conjunction with improved plant varieties and an increased number of plants per acre, farmers greatly increased their usage of the plant nutrients — nitrogen, phosphate, and potash — during the period 1940–70. The use of both nitrogen and potash by farmers more than doubled between 1940 and 1950. The use of nitrogen almost tripled between 1950 and 1960, while the use of potash about doubled. In the decade 1960–69, the use of nitrogen by farmers once again more than doubled, and the use of potash almost doubled. More specifically, the use of nitrogen by farmers increased from 419 million tons in 1940 to 7,459 million tons in 1970, and the use of potash increased from 435 million tons in 1940

Table 7.1.   Yields per Acre of Four Important Crops,
Selected Years,[a] 1870–1970

Year	Wheat (bu.)	Corn (bu.)	Potatoes (cwt.)	Cotton (lbs.)
1870	12.7	26.1	52.6	174.2
1900	13.2	24.8	49.9	182.6
1930	14.5	23.6	65.9	177.6
1935	12.3	20.5	66.3	185.4
1940	15.4	30.0	77.4	240.8
1945	17.3	34.4	97.7	263.1
1950	15.7	37.8	145.0	273.4
1955	19.4	42.9	165.6	389.0
1960	24.0	56.5	188.2	448.3
1965	26.2	69.7	203.3	508.0
1970	31.8	80.8	226.3	436.7

Source: *Century of Agriculture in Charts and Tables*, Agricultural Handbook No. 318, U.S. Department of Agriculture, Statistical Reporting Service, 1966; and *Agricultural Statistics, 1972*, USDA, 1972.

[a]Three-year average centered on the year.

to 4,035 million tons in 1970. With these greatly increased rates of fertilization, yields per acre soared during this period.

The magnitude of the yield increases per acre for some of the more important crops that took place during this period may be seen in table 7.1. But there is more to be gleaned from table 7.1. We see that yields per acre for wheat, corn, potatoes, and cotton increased almost not at all, but held constant, over the long period 1870–1935. This condition of constant yields per acre can also be generalized to include almost all crops and almost every year before 1935, back as far as one wishes to go. But in 1935 crop yields per acre took off, and they kept moving up from 1940 to 1970. Yield increases for wheat are less spectacular than for the other commodities because in the United States wheat is grown under low rainfall conditions. But for the other three commodities shown in table 7.1 and for many other crops, yields soared during the thirty-year period 1940–70. This was the product of the biological and chemical technological revolutions in the United States.

There were also some important technological developments in the animal production area during this period. Feed conversion rates in poultry production improved dramatically. The improved control of animal diseases through preventive measures and the use of modern drugs and vaccines was equally dramatic. Knowledge of animal nutrition was greatly expanded, with consequent improvements in animal feeding practices. Finally, improved buildings and facilities for handling livestock contributed to the more efficient production of livestock and livestock products. With the exception of poultry, the productivity gains in livestock production were probably not as great as in crop production, but they were widespread and important.

It can be argued, and certainly it must be observed, that a fourth and different kind of technological revolution also got under way in American agriculture in the latter half of the period 1933–70. It was a managerial revolution. This revolution brought to agriculture much of the managerial technology already in use in other sectors of the economy. As a result of this revolution, some farmers began to adopt managerial practices that involved future contracting and hedging in commodity futures markets, and they began to use computerized information in making decisions with regard to buying inputs, selling products, managing investments, and developing tax strategies. It would be a mistake to envisage this managerial revolution as sweeping over, or engulfing, all farm operators in the 1950s and 1960s; it did not. But it caught up a receptive few — perhaps 10 to 15 percent of all farm operators. And these few operators, who became superior farm managers, in combination with the mechanical, biological, and chemical revolutions, forged ahead in the development process in the 1950s, 1960s, and 1970s to become the large, aggressive, innovative farmers who produce and sell the bulk of the product of commercial agriculture. (This theme will be developed at greater length in chapter 19.)

The Changing Structure of Agriculture

By 1933 most farmers were selling most of their production in commercial markets. But the farm and the farm family continued to provide most of the inputs employed on the farm. This situation changed during the period 1933–70; farmers turned increasingly to the market for their inputs, too. We see the evidence of this in table 7.2. The volume of nonpurchased inputs — inputs provided by the farm enterprise — was cut almost in half between 1933 and 1970, while the volume of purchased inputs — inputs acquired from the nonfarm sector — more than doubled. The farming business, like most businesses in the United States, was highly commercialized by 1970.

The specific nature of this change in the composition of inputs employed in farming may be viewed in table 7.2. We see that the volume of labor employed in farming declined by more than 70 per-

Table 7.2. Indexes of Total Farm Input and Major Input Subgroups, United States, 1930-70
(1967 = 100)

Year	Total Input All[a]	Total Input Non-purchased[b]	Purchased[c]	Farm Labor[d]	Farm Real Estate[e]	Mechanical Power and Machinery[f]	Agricultural Chemicals[g]	Feed, Seed, & Livestock Purchases[h]	Taxes and Interest[i]	Miscellaneous[j]
1930	101	176	50	326	101	39	10	30	75	83
1931	101	178	49	333	99	38	8	26	76	87
1932	97	173	46	321	96	35	5	27	79	84
1933	96	170	46	321	97	32	6	28	75	82
1934	90	156	44	288	96	31	7	27	69	76
1935	91	158	46	299	99	32	8	25	63	76
1936	93	156	50	291	99	34	10	34	68	75
1937	98	165	52	314	100	38	11	32	63	82
1938	96	158	53	293	101	39	11	33	69	76
1939	98	158	57	294	102	40	11	41	72	78
1940	100	159	58	293	103	42	13	42	72	78
1941	100	158	59	288	102	44	14	45	73	79
1942	103	166	60	296	100	51	15	48	73	76
1943	104	166	61	292	98	55	17	52	77	79
1944	105	167	62	289	98	57	20	52	79	82
1945	103	161	62	271	98	58	20	54	80	80
1946	101	155	63	260	102	57	21	53	81	81
1947	101	152	65	246	103	64	23	55	81	83
1948	103	152	67	240	103	72	25	56	79	87
1949	105	152	70	231	104	80	27	61	82	91
1950	104	150	70	217	105	84	29	63	82	87
1951	107	153	73	218	105	90	32	67	82	93
1952	107	150	75	208	105	94	35	69	85	93
1953	106	148	75	200	105	96	36	69	86	92

Year										
1956	103	138	77	174	102	98	41	75	87	90
1957	101	131	77	162	102	97	41	74	86	94
1958	100	127	80	156	100	97	43	79	87	98
1959	102	125	84	151	101	98	49	84	93	103
1960	101	119	86	145	100	97	49	84	94	105
1961	100	116	87	139	100	94	53	88	95	105
1962	100	113	89	133	100	94	58	90	96	108
1963	100	110	91	129	100	93	65	90	98	109
1964	100	108	93	122	100	93	71	92	99	113
1965	98	103	93	110	99	94	75	93	100	109
1966	98	100	96	103	99	96	85	97	100	104
1967	100	100	100	100	100	100	100	100	100	100
1968	100	99	101	97	99	101	105	97	101	106
1969	99	98	101	93	98	101	111	101	100	105
1970	100	97	102	89	101	100	115	104	100	109

Source: *Changes in Farm Production and Efficiency, 1977*, Statistical Bulletin No. 612, U.S. Department of Agriculture, Economics, Statistics, and Cooperatives Service, November 1978, pp. 56–57.

[a] Measured in constant dollars.
[b] Includes operator and unpaid family labor, and operator-owned real estate and other capital inputs.
[c] Includes all inputs other than nonpurchased inputs.
[d] Includes hired, operator, and unpaid family labor.
[e] Includes all land in farms, service buildings, grazing fees, and repairs on service buildings.
[f] Includes interest and depreciation on mechanical power and machinery, repairs, licenses, and fuel.
[g] Includes fertilizer, lime, and pesticides.
[h] Includes nonfarm value of feed, seed, and livestock purchases.
[i] Includes real estate and personal property taxes, and interest on livestock and crop inventory.
[j] Includes such things as insurances, telephone, veterinary, containers, and binding materials.

cent between 1933 and 1970. Most of this decline occurred in the employment of family labor. While the input of human labor in farming declined in a dramatic fashion between 1933 and 1970, the input of farm machinery, agricultural chemicals, and purchased feed, seed, and livestock increased in an equally dramatic fashion. We see from table 7.2 that the input of farm machinery increased by 212 percent over this period, the input of chemicals by some 1800 percent, and the input of purchased feed, seed, and livestock by over 270 percent. Thus once again we observe the tremendous change that took place in farming during the period 1933–70; man-made capital substituted for human labor to an extent that would not have been thought possible at the beginning of the period. During this great transformation in the capitalization of the farming operation, one thing did not change, however. The input of land in farming was almost the same at the end of the period as it was at the beginning.

While the nature of the farming operation was undergoing a major transformation, the size of the average farm and the number of farms were also undergoing a major change. The number of farms in United States agriculture declined from 6.8 million in 1935 to 3.0 million in 1970. (More detailed figures for the period 1939–69 may be seen in table 7.3.) This was a decline of 56 percent in thirty-five years.

As might be expected, as the number of farms declined, the size of the average farm increased. With a little study, this conclusion may be deduced from table 7.3. In this table farms are classified by the value of their gross sales, or gross receipts. Stated differently, farm size in table 7.3 is measured by the value of products sold by each farm. This is a common economic measure of enterprise size. We observe in table 7.3 that the number of farms grossing less than $5,000 per farm declines over the entire period, while the number of farms grossing more than $20,000 per farm increases over the entire period. The number grossing between $5,000 and $19,999 per farm first increases and then decreases. Lastly, the number of farms grossing more than $40,000 per farm increased from 32,000 in 1939 to 219,000 in 1969.

Part of the explanation for the increase in the value of gross receipts per farm between 1939 and 1945 is to be found in the rising farm product price level of that period. Stated differently, gross receipts per farm rose during this period, not because a farm sold more units of product, but in part because it sold the same number of units at a higher price. The latter development obviously does not constitute an increase in the size of the production unit.

The farm price level did not increase over the period 1949–69; it

Table 7.3. Number and Percentage Distribution of Farms Classified by Value of Farm Sales, Selected Years, 1939–69

Year[a]	$100,000 and over	$40,000 to $99,999	$20,000 to $39,999	$10,000 to $19,999	$5,000 to $9,999	$2,500 to $4,999	Less than $2,500	Total All Farms
			number of farms, in thousands					
1939		32[b]	71	245	663	1198	4232	6441
1944		42	102	342	810	1141	3566	6003
1949		51	114	372	807	1030	3348	5722
1954		63	137	398	725	869	2606	4798
1959	20	86	219	503	693	654	1922	4097
1964	32	114	268	482	534	469	1558	3457
1969	51	168	330	400	413	436	1201	2999
			percentage distribution of farms					
1939		0.5	1.1	3.8	10.3	18.6	65.7	100
1944		0.7	1.7	5.7	13.5	19.0	59.4	100
1949		0.9	2.0	6.5	14.1	18.0	58.5	100
1954		1.3	2.9	8.3	15.1	18.1	54.3	100
1959	0.5	2.1	5.3	12.3	16.9	16.0	46.9	100
1964	0.9	3.3	7.8	13.9	15.4	13.6	45.1	100
1969	1.7	5.6	11.0	13.3	13.8	14.6	40.0	100

Source: *Farm Income Statistics,* Statistical Bulletin No. 576, U.S. Department of Agriculture, Economic Research Service, July 1977, pp. 32–52; and *The Expanding and Contracting Sectors of American Agriculture,* Agricultural Economic Report No. 74, USDA, ERS, May 1965, p. 24.

[a]Forty-eight states through 1959; fifty states thereafter.

[b]Figures appearing between the first two categories apply to both categories.

held almost constant. But the number of farms in the low gross receipt classes continued to decline, and the number of farms in the large gross receipt classes continued to increase. Clearly, in this period the average size of farm was increasing. The average farmer was producing more and selling more units of product.

How did this growth in farm size come about? It came about as a result of a combination of actions by the larger, more aggressive farmers. They used their strong financial positions to buy up the productive assets of the smaller, less efficient farmers who were in the process of going out of business. They employed their greater commercial "know-how" to obtain the credit they needed to acquire increased amounts of nonfarm-produced capital (e.g. more chemicals, larger tractors, and related hookups). And they made use of their superior technological "know-how" to adopt new and improved technologies that increased their capacity to produce (e.g. increased yields per acre). In these ways the larger, more aggressive farmers became even larger and more productive in the period 1940–70, as their smaller, less aggressive, less efficient neighbors fell by the wayside.

The increased concentration of agricultural production in the hands of fewer and fewer farmers becomes evident from an analysis of tables 7.3 and 7.4. In 1939 the top 15.7 percent of farmers (or 1,011,000 farmers grossing $5,000 or more per farm) accounted for 62.2 percent of the total agricultural products marketed; in 1969 only 7.3 percent of farmers (or 219,000 farmers grossing $40,000 or more per farm) accounted for 52.7 percent of the total agricultural products marketed and 18.3 percent of farmers (or 549,000 farms grossing $20,000 or more per farm) accounted for 73.1 percent of the total products marketed. At the opposite end of the scale, 68.4 percent of the farmers (or 2,050,000 farmers grossing less than $10,000) accounted for only 13.8 percent of the agricultural products marketed in 1969.

In sum, over the period 1933–70 the structure of farming in the United States changed radically. There was a quantum jump in the number of farms (downward), in the size of farms (upward), in the concentration of production on fewer and larger farms (greater), and in the commercialization and capitalization of farms (greater).

Paralleling this restructuring of farming was (1) the development of

Table 7.4. Percentage Distribution of Total Cash Receipts from Farming,[a] Classified by Value of Farm Sales, Selected Years, 1939–69

Year[b]	$100,000 and over	$40,000 to $99,999	$20,000 to $39,999	$10,000 to $19,999	$5,000 to $9,999	$2,500 to $4,999	Less than $2,500	Total All Farms
1939	14.8[c]		8.7	15.5	23.2	22.0	15.8	100
1944	17.9		9.8	18.3	23.9	17.7	12.4	100
1949	20.6		10.9	18.7	22.4	14.8	12.6	100
1954	23.3		13.6	20.5	20.2	12.4	10.0	100
1959	15.9	14.9	18.1	21.6	15.7	7.6	6.2	100
1964	22.6	17.9	20.0	19.1	10.9	4.9	4.6	100
1969	31.2	21.5	20.4	13.1	6.9	3.6	3.3	100

Source: *Farm Income Statistics*, Statistical Bulletin No. 576, U.S. Department of Agriculture, Economic Research Service, July 1977, p. 53; and *The Expanding and Contracting Sectors of American Agriculture*, Agricultural Economic Report No. 74, USDA, ERS, May 1965, p. 24.

[a] Includes receipts from custom work and recreational uses.

[b] 48 states through 1959; 50 states thereafter.

[c] Figures appearing between the first two categories apply to both categories.

an input service industry to provide farmers with a wide range of producer goods and services for those goods, and (2) the development of a processing and distribution industry to move products from the farm to the consumer. The magnitude of the input service industry by the 1960s may be inferred from the great increase in the use of nonfarm-produced goods in the farm production process. But the development in the processing and distribution sector was even greater. This sector of American agriculture had been developing since the early period of farm specialization and commercialization, 1820–60. But with increased production specialization in the twentieth century and rising per capita incomes in the period 1933–70, the processing and distribution system was called upon to move a tremendously larger volume, to process it more completely and in more diverse forms, to package it more attractively, and to move it to consumers in more convenient outlets. This it did by expanding and improving its facilities and services in assembling, storage and transportation, processing and packaging, wholesaling and retailing, and food dispensing. By the late 1960s the food marketing sector had come to dwarf the food production, or farming, sector.

A perspective on the changed structure of the total agricultural system may be gained from a study of figure 7.2. We see from figure

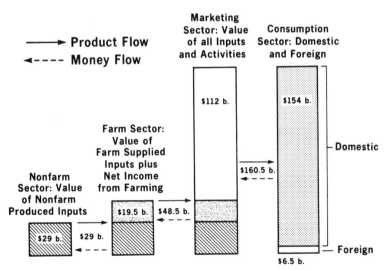

Fig. 7.2. Product and money flows through the food and fiber system, in billions of dollars, 1968

7.2 that the production inputs sold to the farm sector in 1968 from the nonfarm sector amounted to $29 billion. The value added to the total flow of food and fiber products by the farming operation amounted to $19.5 billion: of this total, farm-supplied inputs amounted to $11 billion, and the value added by the farm operation, as measured by net cash farm income, amounted to $8.5 billion. The value added by the marketing sector, as measured by the total marketing bill, amounted to $112 billion, or nearly six times the value added by the farming sector.

The farming operation as of 1968 continued to be critically important in the total food and fiber system. But relatively speaking, it had become a small operation. On the other hand, American consumers were demanding and receiving a vast array of services associated with their food and fiber products; hence the marketing system that provided those services had grown into a giant operation in the national economy.

Some people argue that the marketing system in the late 1960s was pushing many unwanted and unneeded services onto consumers and that the food marketing system had become wasteful and inefficient. The National Commission on Food Marketing in 1966 in part supported that allegation and in part did not. It was the opinion of the majority of commission members that "while some of the selling function — advertising, sales promotion, salesmen — is socially productive, most of the costs incurred to sway consumers toward one seller or product rather than another add little of value to the food consumers buy. The selling function could not be eliminated in most instances, but in principle, it might be substantially reduced without impairing the value of the final product to consumers. . . ."[2] Despite these criticisms and many other suggestions by the commission for improving the marketing system, it concluded "that the contribution of the food industry to a high and rising level of living in the United States was fully comparable with that of other leading sectors of the economy."[3] This latter conclusion is the one that most careful observers of the food and fiber system reach; it is as efficient as any other leading sector of the economy. And the reason it grew so rapidly during the period 1933–70 was that it could and did respond to the demands of consumers for more and more services associated with food products as their real incomes rose (e.g., frozen fruits and vegetables, frozen prepared meals, cake mixes, and the ultimate — eating out in a restaurant).

The Farm Production Response

The technological revolution on farms and the transformation of those farms into highly commercialized and highly capitalized units did not occur by accident. Those things occurred where farmers found it profitable to cause them to occur. The farmers who adopted new technological practices and substituted chemicals and machines for human labor did so because such actions reduced their unit costs of production. On farms where this occurred the supply curve of the farmer-producer shifted to the right; the farmer-producer stood ready to increase his output at any given price. Where many farmers participated in this process the supply curve of the industry shifted to the right, because all these farmers stood ready to increase their output at any given price. Economists will recognize this as the definition of an increase in supply, and this happened almost continuously throughout the period 1933–70. Farmer after farmer increased his capacity to supply the market at any given price by adopting new and improved technologies and by substituting cheaper and more efficient factors of production for dearer and more inefficient factors of production. Those that did not — and there were many — failed and went out of business.

This process moved rather slowly in the 1930s because most farmers lacked the financial resources — the savings or the current income or the available credit — to make the outlays required to adopt the new technologies or to substitute capital for labor. Thus total farm output increased only modestly during the decade of the 1930s; it increased only 11 percent.

But World War II lifted the financial constraint from farmers, and they adopted the new technologies and they substituted capital for human labor with a reckless abandon. As a consequence, total farm output shot up; it increased by 25 percent in the 1940s. Although the level of farm prices declined in the 1950s, farmers' propensity for adopting new technologies and substituting capital items for human labor did not. Total farm output rose by 20 percent in the 1950s.

The technological revolution and the transformation of farms into highly intensive users of capital continued into the 1960s. Thus total farm output continued to expand despite the stable farm price level. Total farm output in the 1960s increased by some 17 percent.

This was a period of intensive growth in American farming. Total output rose dramatically over the thirty-year period 1940–70. But the total input of productive resources increased not at all. Increases in farm output during this period typically occurred through the adoption of new technologies embodied in new producer goods. Thus a technological advance typically occurred on a farm simultaneously with the substitution of a capital item for human labor. The result was an increase in total farm output, no increase in total farm inputs, but a decline in the total labor input and an offsetting rise in the total capital input.

The technological revolution that occurred on American farms during the period 1933–70 did not, however, change the basic location of agricultural production. The regional specialization in the production of agricultural commodities that occurred in the nineteenth century, and which is described in chapters 4 and 5, was not changed to any important degree by the intensive growth of American farming in the period 1933–70. This conclusion is evident from a review of the major types of farming areas in the United States as of 1950. (See figure 7.3.)

Chronic Excess Capacity

Increases in the demand for farm products marched ahead of increases in output in the period 1933–39, not by much, but some, and the farm price level rose irregularly. Increases in the demand for farm

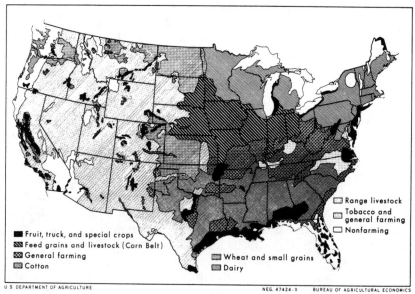

U S DEPARTMENT OF AGRICULTURE   NEG. 47424-X   BUREAU OF AGRICULTURAL ECONOMICS

Fig. 7.3. Major types of farming areas in the United States, circa 1950

products stayed well ahead of increases in output in the period 1939–51, and farm prices soared. But the inevitable occurred in 1952. Foreign demand contracted with the end of the Korean hostilities and the phasing out of post-World War II relief and rehabilitation activities, and farm prices began to fall (figure 7.1). However, farm prices did not fall as sharply or as far in 1952–53 as they had in 1921. They did not because they came to rest on the programs of price support for the major commodities, and they were kept from falling further through the remainder of the 1950s and 1960s by the operation of the price support programs. These programs were in turn rendered effective by the adjunct programs of production control, commodity storage, and surplus disposal.

How much further farm prices would have fallen in the absence of the above battery of farm programs was much debated by agricultural economists during the 1950s and 1960s. But there is evidence to suggest that if all the programs mentioned above had been eliminated in the late 1950s, the level of farm prices would have fallen another 40 percent and the level of retail food prices would have declined about 20 percent. If only the price support and production control programs had been eliminated and the foreign surplus disposal programs maintained, the decline in the level of farm prices might have been closer to 20 percent. But everyone who studied the situation reached the conclusion that the level of farm prices in the 1950s would have declined still further in the absence of the various commodity programs. Or stated differently, the market-clearing, equilibrium farm price level was well below the level that was realized under the programs.[4]

At the level at which farm prices were supported during the 1950s and 1960s the farm sector was producing, or had the capacity to produce, more total product each year than the commercial market, both domestic and foreign, would take at those prices. The farm economy was in a chronic state of surplus.

What happened to those surplus products? The federal government dealt with them in two ways. It paid farmers not to produce them through the operation of production control programs. The commodities that were in fact produced and were in physical surplus, and which would have pushed prices down below the announced level of price support if left on the market, were acquired by the government and removed from commercial channels of trade. Such commodity acquisitions were first stored by the government and later disposed of through various surplus disposal programs, the most important of which was foreign surplus disposal.

What was the extent of the chronic excess capacity of the national farm plant? Numerous studies were undertaken in this period to measure this. One placed the estimate as low as 5 per cent of total production. Other estimates ran as high as 8 or 9 percent. These estimates varied in part because the different studies did not employ the same years in their analyses and in part because they made different assumptions. But it seems reasonable to conclude that between 5 and 9 percent of total farm production, perhaps 7 percent on the average, was surplus — production that could not find a commercial home at the supported farm price level.

Excess productive capacity running at a level of 7 percent of total farm production each year from the mid-1950s to the mid-1960s may not look unduly large. But given the low elasticities of demand for farm products, it gave rise to some very difficult problems. The value of government-owned stocks of storable commodities rose from $1.3 billion in 1952 to $7.7 billion in 1959 and stood at $6.4 billion in 1965. The annual cost of storage programs, production control programs, and surplus disposal programs rose from less than $1 billion in 1952 to $4.5 billion in 1965.[5] And, were the government to dismantle those programs, there was always the possibility, even the probability, that the level of farm prices would fall another 20 to 40 percent. This was something no administration or Congress wanted to happen in the 1950s and 1960s.

Thus the technological revolution on farms and the transformation of farms to intensive users of capital led first to an output response that was considered good and second to an economic problem that was considered bad. This economic problem — chronic excess capacity — did not, or would not, go away by itself. Government was so fearful of the price and income consequences of removing federal farm programs of price and income support that it continued those programs year after year. And with the continuation of those programs, the problem of excess productive capacity became a chronic problem.

The Policy Struggle and Final Compromise

Farmers were in desperate straits when the Roosevelt administration took office in March 1933. This both the president and the Congress recognized, and they moved swiftly to deal with the deepening depression in agriculture. The Agricultural Adjustment Act (AAA) was passed on May 12, 1933. This act did not incorporate the basic features of the long-advocated McNary-Haugen plan or those of the Domestic Allotment Plan, but it did borrow certain features from both of them. The AAA authorized the federal government to enter into agreements with farmers to control production by reducing acreages devoted to basic crops, to store crops on the farm and make payment advances on them, to enter into marketing agreements with producers and handlers in order to stabilize product prices, and to levy processing taxes as a means of financing the crop reduction program. The theory of the farm program that emerged from the Agricultural Adjustment Act is summarized by Nourse, Davis, and Black as follows:

1. Relief was to be brought to the farming population by improvement of incomes through price enhancement and through use of "benefit payments" which would put in their hands at once a substantial amount of money so that they might keep their farm properties intact, make necessary outlays for equipment and farm supplies, and finance expenditures for consumption.
2. The benefit payments were to be drawn in the main from special excise taxes on the commodity, on the theory that in this manner consumers and processors would be brought to pay a "fair exchange value" for such part of the product as was currently consumed instead of an abnormally low price which, it was alleged, had been brought about by the piling up of inordinate stocks because of the farmer's inability to check his operations so as to keep in step with the declining effective demand of the market.
3. Such supplementary income was not to be diverted into the hands of all farmers indiscriminately but was to be a *quid pro quo* to those who agreed to participate in a program of controlled production. This control scheme was designed to produce a supply and demand situation which would bring about a level of prices which would be remunerative to farmers. This goal was defined as "parity," that is, prices which would restore the purchasing power of agricultural commodities to the level which had obtained on the average in a previous period, typically the five years ending July 1914.[6]

Under the AAA program, the government made payments to farmers amounting to over one billion dollars in the two years 1934 and 1935. These payments helped many farmers meet their financial obligations. Further, the program did succeed in reducing the acreages planted to tobacco and cotton. But it is questionable whether the program succeeded in reducing the production of other crops, or production in the aggregate. The drought of 1934, however, was successful in reducing the output of most commodities by more than that called for in the program.

These early efforts to raise farm prices through controlling production were brought to an abrupt halt in January 1936 when the AAA was declared unconstitutional by the Supreme Court. Temporary legislation was passed in 1936 that de-emphasized the objective of raising prices through production control and that focused on production adjustment on individual farms to achieve conservation objectives for which farmers were to be paid. Funds to make these payments to farmers were to be appropriated by the Congress from the Treasury, rather than raised through special processing taxes. (It was the processing tax feature of the original AAA that the Supreme Court objected to.) The government and the farmers limped along with the 1936 legislation for two years. Then in 1938 Congress passed the Agricultural Adjustment Act of 1938, which was intended to be permanent legislation and which remains the organic legislation, amended from time to time, under which many farm programs of price and income support are administered to this day (1991). The general objectives and key features of this important act are summarized below:

The Agricultural Adjustment Act of 1938, approved February 16, provides for a farm program open to participation by all farmers in the United States.

One part of the Act strengthens and continues those provisions of the Soil Conservation and Domestic Allotment Act under which about 4 million farmers took part in the agricultural conservation programs of 1936 and 1937. These provisions will be available, as in the past 2 years, to every farmer. They authorize continued payments to farmers who take part in the agricultural conservation program.

Another part of the new Act supplements the conservation programs with provisions for regulating interstate and foreign commerce in the five commodities listed in the Act — cotton, wheat, corn, tobacco and rice.

Both parts of the Act are designed to safeguard the productiveness of agriculture. All payments are to be conditioned upon participation in measures for soil conservation. Both parts of the Act are designed to stabilize commerce in agricultural products and to give farmers a fair share of the national income.

Broadly summarized, the provisions of the Act are seen to give the basis for a 6-point program designed to assist farmers to produce abundantly year after year. They are designed to protect agriculture against the price collapses that heretofore have penalized heavy production. The Act provides actual methods such as acreage allotments, marketing quotas, and commodity loans, to help give the stability of income that farmers need in order to grow and to maintain ample reserves of farm commodities for the Nation's use. In effect, this means that an Ever-Normal Granary will be started. It is estimated that the Act's provisions affecting reserve supplies will result in about doubling the average annual carry-overs of corn and wheat.

This 6-point program may be outlined as follows:

1. The A.A.A. soil-conservation program is continued and its objectives established as a part of permanent farm policy in the interests of future abundance of food and fiber.

2. National acreage allotments are set at levels to give production ample for domestic consumption, for exports, and for reserve supplies, and payments are made to encourage farmers to produce up to these allotments.

3. Systematic storage of food and feed surpluses from big crop years for use in years of shortage is assisted by loans.

4. Marketing quotas for commercial producers of cotton, wheat, corn, tobacco, and rice, backed by penalties on sales in excess of the quotas can be used, subject to approval of two-thirds of the producers voting, to obtain general participation of farmers in a program designed to hold surplus supplies of the five listed commodities off the market until they are needed.

5. Release of supplies withheld from market under marketing quotas is provided to meet any shortage.

6. Crop insurance for wheat, starting with the 1939 crop, will give wheat producers and bread consumers better protection against crop failure. Gradual accumulations of wheat paid in by farmers as insurance premiums will contribute to the Ever-Normal Granary supplies.[7]

There is more than a little government double-talk in the above six-point statement. Point 2 states that ". . . payments are made to encourage farmers to produce up to these allotments." In reality the payments were made to induce farmers to participate in the program and hold their production *down* to the allotment. Point 3 states that "systematic storage of food and fiber surpluses . . . is assisted by loans." In reality the nonrecourse loan was the primary mechanism by which farmers were induced to remove their products from commercial channels of trade and turn them over to the government. The Agricultural Adjustment Act of 1938 was designed to support the price of farm commodities by controlling production and/or managing supplies; the official government statement presented above seeks to hide that stark economic purpose behind some high-sounding, noncontroversial phrases.

Whether the farm economy could have been pulled out of its depressed state by the operation of the various programs authorized in this act was never determined. The beginning of World War II in Europe in 1939, with its great demands for food and fiber products, caused farm prices to shoot skyward, as we noted earlier in this chapter. And the price- and income-supporting features of this act became inoperative throughout the period 1940–51 with the exception of one year, 1949. One important point with respect to farm price and income support legislation during the war period does, however, need to be noted. As farm prices rose in the marketplace, legal price support was extended to a long list of commodities (fourteen so-called Steagall commodities: manufactured milk, butterfat, chickens, eggs, turkeys, hogs, dry peas, dry beans, soybeans for oil, flaxseed for oil, peanuts for oil, American Egyptian cotton, Irish potatoes and sweet potatoes). The level of price support was raised to 90 percent of parity for these Steagall commodities for two years beyond the end of the war, or through 1948, and, of course, for the six basic commodities: corn, wheat, cotton, tobacco, rice, and peanuts. This was the state of affairs when the farm policy debate began in 1947, preparatory to the passage of new farm legislation in 1948.

Many people and organizations entered into the farm policy debate in 1947, each with his or its particular conceptual view, or slant, and each with his or its particular interest. Hence the debate had many sides and nuances. But in a broad way the participants may be grouped into two camps. The first camp was desirous of lowering the level of price support and reducing the extent of government intervention in the farm economy, or of getting rid of the concept of price support altogether and with it all the paraphernalia of production control, government storage, surplus disposal, and on and on. In this camp were to be found most Republican party leaders, businessmen from the agribusiness complex, and most economists. The second camp was desirous of maintaining a high level of price support as a means of supporting farm incomes, and it would accept whatever programs of government intervention were required to implement the price support objective (although the politicians involved always wanted the weakest set of production controls that could possibly be formulated). In this camp were to be found Democratic party leaders from the South and the Plains, the farm organization leaders who had led the battle for the agricultural adjustment legislation during the period 1933–38, some government economists, and from time to time some union leaders.

This debate, or struggle, continued on year after year, with the actors changing, but the basic issue, the use of the power of government to support farm prices and incomes, did not change (and the debate, or struggle, was at a white heat once again in the 1980s). Farm price and income support legislation was enacted almost every year between 1948 and 1965. It sometimes involved a greater degree of price and income support, and more implementing programs, and sometimes a lesser degree of price and income support, depending upon the economic circumstances at the time and the political power of the contending camps.[8]

Three major attempts were made to break the political stalemate with regard to farm price and income support legislation. Secretary of Agriculture Charles Brannan made the first effort in 1949 with his so-called Brannan Plan. The Brannan Plan contained four new ideas. They were:

1. An income standard to replace the old 1910–14 parity price standard.
2. Production, or income, payments to support gross returns to producers of perishable commodities. (Price support programs would be continued for producers of storable commodities.)
3. A new list of farm commodities (including the important animal products) to replace the old, so-called basic commodity list.
4. No price or income support on production above a certain limit — with that limit to be determined by the size of the typical family farm.

Although the Brannan Plan found strong acceptance among economists, it was not received enthusiastically by lawmakers on Capitol Hill. This was the case for at least three reasons. First, the large commercial farmers, who were well represented in Washington, were strongly opposed to points 2 and 4 listed above. They did not want to see the extent of their income subsidy exposed to public view as it would be under the production payment proposal, and they did not want to see any limit put on the amount of price and income support that any farmer could receive. The latter limitation would obviously be damaging to them. Second, Secretary Brannan proposed an income support standard so high that it drove away his natural allies. Congressmen who were friendly to the basic provisions of the Brannan Plan were appalled by estimates of its costs, which ranged from $3 billion to $8 billion per year. Third, the Republican party was badly frightened by the political appeal of the Brannan Plan — high prices and incomes for farmers and low food prices for the working man. Thus Republicans closed ranks and fought it vigorously and successfully.

Legislation that included some but not all of the important features of the Brannan Plan was defeated in the House and Senate in the summer of 1949. Brannan Plan legislation was revived in 1950, but an upward surge in farm prices in the summer of 1950 drained away farmer support for the legislation. Various elements of the Brannan Plan (income payments, for example) have appeared in farm legislation from time to time since 1950, but the plan as a coherent package was dead by the fall of 1950.

Secretary of Agriculture Ezra Taft Benson, like his predecessor Charles Brannan, had some firm ideas regarding the directions in which farm price and income policy should move. He believed that intervention by the government into the operation of the economy was morally wrong and that the growing surplus condition in agriculture could be cured by letting farm prices fall to their free market level. The morality of a government intervening in the economic affairs of man may be debated, but there is no question that the surplus condition of American agriculture in the 1950s could have been reduced, or eliminated, by lowering the levels of farm price support toward, or to, the free market equilibrium price. The issue was — at what cost to American farmers in terms of lower incomes? The Congress thought that the cost would be too great. Thus Secretary Benson and Congress waged a war for eight years over the level of price support. Secretary Benson won a few battles with Congress and was able to achieve a modest reduction in the level of price support. But Congress won the war; it would never permit the secretary to lower the level of price support sufficiently to correct the surplus problem. Therefore, stocks in the hands of the government built up almost continuously during the period 1952–60.

Secretary Orville Freeman took a very different view of the farm problem. He believed that farm incomes could be raised and the physical surplus problem eliminated through the vigorous intervention of government in the farm economy to control production. President Kennedy, too, was desirous of raising farm incomes, but he was also most anxious that the cost of farm programs to the government be reduced. How was this miracle — raised farm incomes, reduced government costs — to be achieved in the Kennedy-Freeman administration? It was to be achieved through mandatory production controls. Farmers were to obtain higher prices in the marketplace by imposing mandatory production controls on themselves at no cost to the government.

Farmers were strongly in favor of receiving higher prices in the marketplace, but most of them were also strongly opposed to mandatory production controls. This their representatives in the Congress quickly sensed, and they too became strongly opposed to mandatory controls. Thus the production control, or supply management, approach to dealing with the farm price and income problem was defeated piece by piece in the Congress in 1961 and 1962, and defeated in a final sense by the wheat producers voting in referendum in 1963.

The body politic did, however, learn some lessons from the policy struggles and defeats described briefly above. Income payments created fewer resource adjustment problems in supporting farm incomes than did high-level price supports. Price supports at higher than equilibrium levels are not consistent with an agricultural industry that is on an export basis such as the United States's. And voluntary production controls coupled with income payments can be effective in controlling production.

Thus, there existed in 1965 the knowledge and the experience out of which to effect a policy compromise that might last awhile and that could be reasonably effective in achieving its objectives. It may also be the case that the warring factions were worn out and wanted to reach a compromise. In any event, a basic compromise was reached in the Agricultural Act of 1965, which lasted without significant modification for five years and with which most parties to the compromise were reasonably satisfied. It is also true that the Agricultural Acts of 1970 and 1973 added some new features to the commodity programs, but they did not change, or alter, significantly the basic compromise reached in 1965.

What were the elements of that 1965 compromise? They were the following:

1. Levels of price support, commodity by commodity, were lowered to world equilibrium levels. Thus the price support mechanism was transformed from an income-enhancing mechanism to a price-stabilizing mechanism.
2. Farm incomes would be supported, if they were to be supported, through the use of income payments to farmers. But payments would be made to farmers if and only if they participated in the authorized production control program when supplies gave promise of becoming burdensome.
3. Storage and surplus disposal programs would be continued (a) to deal with the surpluses not dealt with under (2) above, and (b) to deal with future short-supply situations at home and abroad.

This was the basic farm policy compromise of 1965. It probably would not have satisfied former Secretary Benson, because it continued to involve the government in the farm economy in a large way. It did not please government budget watchers, because the costs of farm price and income support programs rose significantly in the second half of the 1960s as a result of this compromise. And it failed to satisfy many farmers, because it did not lead to a large increase in their incomes. But the compromise held into the middle 1970s, first, because it was the only policy solution acceptable to all the concerned parties and, second, because farm prices soared in the early 1970s and farmers were happy once again.

The People Left Behind

The story in this chapter has been concerned with agricultural development in the context of a several-sided technological revolution — mechanical, biological, chemical, and managerial. The structural and output consequences of that development were explored, but with one exception, the problem of chronic excess production capacity, the costs to society of rapid agricultural development have been ignored up to this point. Yet one important cost to society cannot and should not be overlooked; it is the state of poverty of "the people left behind" by the process of agricultural development.

In 1965 there were 14 million people living in poverty in rural areas, and a high proportion of them were destitute.[9] Most of these people did not live on farms; only one family in four lived on a farm. The rest lived in shacks and dilapidated houses in the open country, villages, and small towns. Some 11 million of the rural poor were white; the rest were blacks, Mexican-Americans, and American Indians.

These people took varied routes into rural poverty. Declining labor requirements resulting from farm technological advance and capital intensification pushed many laborers, sharecroppers, and tenants off their farms and off the land. Some farmers were unable to cope with the complexities of increased commercialization and advancing technologies and lost their farms in the competitive process. Some became poor during the Great Depression and were unable to respond to the plentiful economic opportunities in the nonfarm sector during the World War II period or to the production opportunities in agriculture resulting from the technological revolution. And some — typically blacks and American Indians — were made poor and kept poor by the continuous and effective discriminatory acts of the white establishment. But whatever the route, some 14 million persons lived in a permanent culture of rural poverty in the mid-1960s.

The rural poor lived then, and many still do, in chronically depressed areas that included much of the rural South, the Indian reservations, and communities in the Upper Great Lakes region, New England, Appalachia, and the Southwest. Typically their housing was and remains atrocious. Rates of unemployment and underemployment are extremely high among the rural poor, and the incidence of disease and infant mortality is shockingly high. The children of the rural poor have gone, and continue to go, to poor schools, and a high proportion of the rural poor are illiterate.

In this culture of rural poverty the members think differently and have different sets of values from other members of society. Among the middle class, for example, education stands for the road to better things for one's children and one's self. But among the rural poor education is viewed as an obstacle to putting one's children to work at as early an age as possible. The poor tend to be fatalistic and pessimistic because for them there is no future; everything is today. When pleasure is available, they take it now. Hence they tend not to save. They were in the 1960s a people without hope and without a future, and the picture has not changed greatly in the 1980s.

In contrast to the urban poor, the rural poor are not organized and have few spokesmen in the nation's capital. Until recent years the nation's major social welfare and labor legislation largely bypassed rural Americans and hence the rural poor. And the farm price and income legislation reviewed in the previous section was not enacted to aid the rural poor; it was enacted to assist commercial farmers. The rural poor have been and continue to be forgotten people in American society. Many, if not most, were pushed into a poverty status by an impersonal, dynamic process of development, with which they were unable to cope, and they have been held in a poverty status by a white middle-class establishment that consistently discriminates against them and by a government that for the most part has ignored their plight.

Suggested Readings

Benedict, Murray R. *Farm Policies of the United States, 1790–1950: A Study of Their Origins and Development*. New York: Twentieth Century Fund, 1953. Chaps. 12, 13, 14, 15, 16, and 18.

Cochrane, Willard W. *The City Man's Guide to the Farm Problem*. Minneapolis: University of Minnesota Press, 1965.

Cochrane, Willard W., and Ryan, Mary E. *American Farm Policy, 1948–1973*. Minneapolis: University of Minnesota Press, 1976. Chaps. 1, 2, and 3.

Griliches, Zvi. "Hybrid Corn: An Exploration in the Economics of Technical Change." *Econometrica*, 25, no. 4 (October 1957), pp. 501–22.

The People Left Behind. A Report by the President's National Advisory Commission on Rural Poverty. Washington, D.C., September 1967.

Schlebecker, John T. *Whereby We Thrive: A History of American Farming*. Ames, Iowa: Iowa State University Press, 1975. Chaps. 22, 24, 27, and 28.

U.S. Department of Agriculture. Economic Research Service. *Changes in Farm Production and Efficiency: Special Issue Featuring Historical Series*. Statistical Bulletin No. 561, September 1976.

CHAPTER 8

U.S. AGRICULTURE IN A WORLD MARKET: 1970–1990

International Trade Trends

The export market has played an important role in the development of American agriculture, as well as in the development of the nation, since colonial times. The export of tobacco, fish, furs, grain, and rum supported the economic development of the colonies up to the time of the American Revolution. From 1820 to 1860 cotton was the preeminent export of the young nation, accounting for 50 percent or more of total exports. After the Civil War, in the period 1870–90, cotton exports declined relative to expanding grain exports, but those two commodities, with assistance from items like leather, meat products, and some fruits and vegetables, constituted approximately three-quarters of total U.S. exports. Agricultural exports were the primary means of earning foreign exchange, which was basic to the economic development of the nation, from earliest colonial times up to 1900.

But with the great increase in the industrial capacity of the United States in the late nineteenth and early twentieth centuries, agricultural exports began to decline relative to industrial exports. By 1950 agricultural exports as a percentage of total exports had declined to 30 percent, and by 1989 they had declined to only 10 percent.

But this does not mean that the export of agricultural products is unimportant to the agricultural industry. The level of agricultural exports is critical to the economic well-being of American farmers. Every period of farm prosperity in the twentieth century has been associated with a high level of agricultural exports, and every period of farm depression has been associated with falling agricultural exports. Stating the importance of the export market for agriculture differently, in the 1970s and 1980s the output of some 30 to 40 percent of the harvested acreage in the United States moved into the international market. Exports of agricultural products have declined relative to nonagricultural exports, but one-fifth or more of farmers' cash receipts in the 1980s were generated by exports.

Agricultural exports reached a post-World War II low in 1953, falling to $2.8 billion in that year. From that low in 1953, agricultural exports slowly grew to $7.0 billion in 1970. At that point in time, U.S. agricultural exports took off. They increased from $7.0 billion in 1970 to almost $44 billion in 1981; in volume, they increased by approximately 160 percent. The U.S. share of the world market for wheat and flour stood at 48 percent in 1981–82, for coarse grains at 60 percent, for soybeans at 86 percent, and for cotton at 32 percent. The United States had become the dominant player in the world market by 1981 for these basic agricultural commodities. And most American observers believed at that time that U.S. exports of these basic commodities would continue to grow in the 1980s, with the United States capturing a larger and larger share of the world market for these commodities.

But this did not happen. Agricultural exports from the United States fell from $43.8 billion in 1981 to $26.3 billion in 1986; in volume, exports fell about 33 percent. The decline ended in 1986, and the dollar value of agricultural exports had climbed back to an estimated $38 billion in 1990. It was a roller-coaster ride for U.S. agricultural exports in the 1970s and 1980s.

Patterns of world trade in the grains for the long period 1934–90 may be observed in table 8.1. It will be noted that total world exports of grain increased importantly from 1934 to 1980, and then leveled off in the decade of the 1980s. U.S. grain exports followed the same general pattern although the movements are more extreme for the United States than for the world as a whole. Exports of grain from the European Community increased dramatically in the 1980s as the EC shifted from a position of a net importer to a net exporter of grains. Exports of grain from Canada and Australia first rose and then fell in the 1980s. The great expansion in the world trade in grains following World War II came to an end in the 1980s, with a general slowing in economic growth worldwide.

Table 8.1. Pattern of World Grain Trade, Annual Averages for Selected Periods, 1934–90 (net exports [+] and net imports [−] in million metric tons)

Region	1934-38[a]	1954-56[a]	1960-62[b]	1970-72[a]	1980-82[a]	1985-87[a]	1989-90[a]
U.S.A.	5	13	31	43	109	74	98
Canada		9	10	17	23	24	19
Western Europe	−24	−21	−26	−25	−7	16	58
Australia and New Zealand	3	3	6	11	16	21	14
Eastern Europe	5	−4	−7	−7	−10	−3	−5
U.S.S.R		2	7	−1	−36	−33	−34
Africa	1	0	−4	−4	−15	−15	−16
People's Republic of China		1	−5	−3	−13	−3	−11
Japan	2	−4	−5	−15	−24	−27	−27
Other Asia		−2	−7	−18	−28	−38	−46
Latin America	9	2	1	1	−7	−5	−11
Total exports of countries and regions listed above	25	30	55	120	222	214	226
Total world exports	33	49	75	123	230	221	230

Source: *FAO Trade Yearbooks*, 1975–90.

[a]Calendar year.

[b]Year beginning July 1 except 1960–62 for Argentina, Brazil, and New Zealand, for which year begins the following December or January.

To this point in this discussion of international trade trends nothing has been said about agricultural imports into the United States. This is because the United States typically enjoys a favorable balance of trade with respect to agricultural products (i.e., the value of agricultural exports exceeds the value of agricultural imports). Further, about one-third of all agricultural imports take the form of noncompetitive products — items such as bananas, coffee, spices, and rubber. The more important competitive agricultural imports include animals and animal products, vegetables and preparations, fruits and preparations, sugar, and beverages (excluding fruit juices). If the United States should, in the future, vigorously pursue a more open trading policy (e.g., a free trade zone that includes Canada and much of Latin America), it could expect to expand its exports of those basic commodities in which it enjoys a comparative advantage, but it should also expect greater competition from foreign producers of sugar, vegetables and preparations, and fruits and preparations, and perhaps animal products as well. A more open world trading system has many advantages for American grain and oilseed producers, but for those producers currently protected by some type of border barrier (e.g., sugar producers and some dairy producers) such a system carries with it the likelihood of serious enterprise adjustments and, possibly, elimination.

Since early colonial times Western Europe has been the principal regional market for American agricultural exports. But that has now changed. In 1979 Asia replaced Western Europe as the leading market for U.S. farm products. The percentage of agricultural exports destined for Asia increased from 32 percent ($12.8 billion) in 1980 to some 41 percent ($15 billion) in 1989. And Japan alone purchased U.S. agricultural products valued at $8.2 billion in 1989 — this in spite of the protectionist agricultural policies pursued by Japan. Meanwhile agricultural exports from the United States to Western Europe have declined from 30 percent ($12.1 billion) in 1980 to 21 percent ($7.8 billion) in 1989. Thus, we see that the international market for U.S. farm products is forever changing.

Understanding World Trade Developments

The question needs to be asked: Why did U.S. exports soar in the 1970s and then fall sharply in the 1980s? Turning first to the export boom of the 1970s, we see that this decline was the direct result of several causes specific to the 1970s. First, the phenomenal growth in

U.S. agricultural exports was spurred by a tremendous increase in world demand for agricultural commodities, resulting in turn from rising incomes and population in the importing countries. Second, many of these importing countries had access to external credit to finance food and other kinds of imports. Third, the United States, as a result of the policy compromise of 1965, was no longer supporting the prices of important agricultural commodities (e.g., the grains, cotton) above world market levels. Fourth, the depreciation of the dollar in the 1970s reduced the prices of U.S. agricultural commodities in terms of the currencies of the importing countries. Fifth, severe drought in many countries stimulated export sales of wheat, corn, and soybeans; this was particularly the case for the Soviet Union. As a consequence of these specific causes, all operating to expand U.S. agricultural exports, those exports reached the unprecedented level of almost $44 billion in 1981.[1]

The sharp decline in U.S. agricultural exports from 1981 to 1986 resulted from another, but very different, set of specific causes. First, a worldwide economic recession in the early 1980s caused the world demand for agricultural commodities to contract and with it the demand for U.S. products. Second, the rapid appreciation of the U.S. dollar in the 1980s, relative to the currencies of competing exporting countries, made U.S. agricultural exports more expensive than those of its competitors. Third, the enormous debt problems of developing countries contributed to a decline in their purchases of agricultural products from the United States. Fourth, the Food Security Act of 1981 broke the policy compromise of 1965 by setting price-support levels for grains and cotton high in relation to world market prices, and made U.S. products less competitive. Fifth, the European Community expanded its export subsidies on agricultural products and as a result increased its market shares in the overseas market. Again, all of these specific causes operating in the same direction, an export-contracting direction, caused U.S. agricultural exports to fall to a level of $26 billion in 1986.

U.S. agricultural exports recovered slowly in the period 1986–90, reaching an estimated level of $38 billion in 1990. This export turnaround resulted from three specific causes. First, the dollar depreciated in value once again, and this effectively lowered the price of U.S. agricultural products in foreign markets, making them more competitive. Second, the Food Security Act of 1986 dropped the level of price support for major agricultural products, thereby making them more competitive in world markets. Third, an aggressive U.S. export policy involving the use of marketing loans for cotton and rice and expanded export subsidies under the Export Enhancement Program all contributed to making U.S. farm export prices competitive with those of foreign suppliers.

The preceding discussion makes it abundantly clear that the world market for agricultural products is extremely competitive. In periods of expanding demand, worldwide, it is easy for an exporting nation to increase its foreign sales, but increasing its share of the world market in such periods requires both aggressive and effective trade policies. In periods of contracting world demand, a nation can easily lose both its volume of exports and its share of the market, as the United States discovered in the early 1980s.

The roller-coaster-like movement in agricultural exports experienced by the United States in the 1970s and 1980s had dramatic consequences, some good, some bad, for the nation. The world market for grains began to tighten in 1970–71. To this tightening world market situation for the grains, add the facts of (1) a poor grain crop in the USSR in 1972 and (2) the decision by the Soviets to enter the world market and acquire supplies of grain to offset their domestic crop losses. Add further a poor grain crop in much of South and Southeast Asia in 1972 and the efforts of those countries to acquire grain supplies in the world markets. In this context, the United States and other exporters increased their exports of grain dramatically and reduced their carryover stocks to near pipeline levels. In this state of reduced stocks, a great fear developed in world grain markets that some unexpected event might further worsen the supply situation. Given this state of fear and uncertainty in early 1973, importing nations and private handlers and processors of grain all tried to improve their stock positions by acquiring additional supplies in the market. The result was a wild scramble for supplies in the summer of 1973, with grain prices shooting skyward. The season average price of wheat in the United States rose to $3.95 per bushel in 1973 and then climbed to the all-time high of $4.04 in 1974. The shortfall in world grain production in 1972 was followed by a good crop in 1973 and then another poor crop in 1974. These fluctuations in world grain production induced further gyrations in world grain prices during those years.[2]

The production of grains and other crops was uniformly good around the world in 1975 and 1976 and reasonably good in 1977. As a result, the world food crisis conditions of 1972–74 came to an end, stocks of grain were built up once again in such diverse areas as India and the United States, and grain prices fell sharply in the United States and the world in the period 1975-77. (The massive movements in farm prices and incomes in the 1970s may be seen in figure 7.1.) Farmers, particularly grain farmers, loved the upward surge in prices in 1972-74, but were back asking the government for price and income assistance in 1977; American consumers, on the other hand, were frightened by the world food crisis and began pressuring the government for an effective reserve stock program.

The downturn in agricultural exports in the period 1981-86 precipitated a farm recession that hit hard those farmers who had borrowed heavily in the late 1970s to expand their operations. Farm prices declined generally in the period 1981-86, and grain prices plummeted. At the same time interest rates rose as the Federal Reserve System tightened the money supply to combat the inflation. In this economic context highly leveraged farmers, both large and small, were caught in a financial squeeze; many failed and went out of business along with the rural banks that had made the loans. A further consequence was a major decline in farm land prices, which turned many good credit risks into poor credit risks and in some cases business failures. With the upturn in agricultural exports in the period 1987-90 farm prices began to rise, farm land prices stopped falling, and the farm recession came to an end. But it was sharp and painful while it lasted. And it was unexpected. The wonderful fifteen-year expansion in agricultural exports unexpectedly came to an end in 1981, and once strong foreign demand slackened, world and domestic prices for the basic crops started to fall and the U.S. farm recession set in. Farmers in the United States learned once again that their economic well-being was linked to the export market — to a strong export market.

Technological Developments[3]

Farm technological developments in the 1970s were a direct continuation of developments in the previous period. Tractors and machines got bigger: the *average* size of tractor on farms increased from 35 horsepower in 1963 to 55 horsepower on January 1, 1978. But monstrous-sized tractors of 200 horsepower or more were developed in the 1970s with the capacity to pull large machine hookups at rapid field speeds; thus the time required to carry out soil preparation and harvesting operations was further and significantly reduced. New chemicals for controlling weeds, insects, and pests were developed and introduced. And plant breeding work across the spectrum of crops continued in an effort to develop varieties that were more disease and drought resistant, and that produced higher yields.

But these technological developments did not produce spectacular results in the first half of the 1970s. All the relevant indicators suggest that increases in agricultural productivity were small to nonexistent in the first half of the 1970s. Yields per acre for wheat, corn, and soybeans held almost constant for the period, and yields per acre for cotton and potatoes increased modestly (see table 8.2). The overall index of crop production per acre holds almost constant over the period 1971–76; even the index of livestock production per breeding units holds constant in this period (see table 8.3).

Why this pause in the march of farm technological advance is not at all clear. It could be one large statistical aberration, but that seems unlikely. It has been suggested that the explanation is to be found in the efforts of environmentalists to ban the use of certain chemicals and to induce farmers to adopt less exploitative practices to protect the environment. But the efforts of environmentalists had not become sufficiently important and pervasive in the 1970s to have had a significant negative effect on crop yield increases. An explanation that would seem to have more plausibility is the following. The technological strategy for increasing crop productivity involving the adoption of plant varieties with a high yield potential, increasing the plant population per acre, and feeding those plants all the commercial nutrients they could use efficiently was in fact still in a crude, early phase. The tactics of getting the right plant variety in the right zone, with the right tillage practices and the right applications of fertilizer, still had to be worked out. And once they were worked out and put into practice agricultural productivity could start marching upward once gain.

And that is what happened. The period 1977–90 is one of steady in-

Table 8.2. Yields Per Acre for Five Important Crops, Selected Years, 1970–90[a]

Crop Year	Wheat (bu.)	Corn (bu.)	Cotton (lbs.)	Soybeans (bu.)	Potatoes (cwt.)
1970	31.8	80.8	436.7	27.2	226.3
1975	29.4	81.7	453.0	26.2	254.0
1980	34.1	103.1	497.6	29.6	271.0
1985	36.9	114.7	594.0	31.8	291.3
1990	35.5	114.4	634.6	33.6	295.3

Source: *Agricultural Statistics*.

[a]Three-year average centered on the year.

Table 8.3. Indexes of Crop and Livestock Production, 1970–89

	CROPS		LIVESTOCK	
Year	Cropland Harvested (Million Acres)	Production per Acre (1977 = 100)	Annual Breeding Units (1977 = 100)	Production per Breeding Unit (1977 = 100)
1970	289	88	100	99
1971	300	96	102	98
1972	289	99	101	100
1973	316	99	102	97
1974	322	88	104	96
1975	330	96	103	92
1976	330	94	101	98
1977	338	100	100	100
1978	330	105	99	102
1979	340	113	100	104
1980	342	100	101	107
1981	351	115	101	108
1982	347	116	99	108
1983	294	100	97	112
1984	337	112	95	113
1985	333	120	92	120
1986	316	116	91	121
1987	293	123	89	127
1988	287	106	89	129
1989	306	119	89	131

Source: *Production and Efficiency Statistics, 1991*, U.S. Department of Agriculture, Economic Research Service, ECIFS9-4, April 1991, pp. 19 and 27.

creases in productivity in both crop and livestock production (see table 8.3). And it will be observed that increases in productivity in livestock production outpaced those in crop production. All manner of technological developments contributed to this increase in productivity in livestock production: increased mechanization of livestock-handling operations, gains in the feed conversion rates of all animal species, better records and controls over the production progress of individual animals, increased knowledge into the causes of animal diseases, and the development and adoption of disease preventive measures.

The increase in overall agricultural productivity of some 28 percent in the 1980s moves this period ahead of the dynamic 1950s in which agricultural productivity increased approximately 22 percent (see table 16.2 in chapter 16). The decade of the 1950s was one of enormous restructuring as over 1.6 million farms went out of business, as well as the rapid adoption of new mechanical, chemical, and biological technologies. The decade of the 1980s, on the other hand, was one more of controlled refinements in production in which increased productivity was achieved through improved control over each farming operation. Soil preparation had become more efficient (e.g., less deep plowing), the choice of plant varieties and seeds was now based on climatic and soil information, the planting operation was more effective, chemicals were used more efficiently, crop harvesting was more timely and less wasteful, and on and on. The better commercial farms by 1990 had become industrialized units in which the production process was as tightly controlled as the state of the arts would permit.

The Changing Structure of Agriculture

The trend toward greater commercialization of farming observed for the period 1933–70 continued into the 1970s (see table 7.2). But some important differences in the pattern of development began to emerge in the 1980s. The employment of nonpurchased inputs — family labor and operator-owned real estate — declined over the entire period 1970–90, with the decline in farm labor leading the way. But in the year 1980, the employment of purchased inputs on American farms began to decline. American farmers reduced their input of mechanical power and machinery nearly 30 percent between 1979 and 1989. Could it be that the long romance of American farmers with machines was coming to an end? Or were they at long last learning to use mechanical power and machinery more efficiently?

The employment of agricultural chemicals reached a high point in 1981 and declined slowly during the rest of the decade. Input of such items as feed, seed, and purchased livestock increased substantially, as did that of such miscellaneous items as insurance, telephone, consulting, and veterinary services. It would appear that farmers in the 1980s were spending more on management services and efficiency-producing inputs and less on traditional inputs such as machinery. The net result of all this was a decline in total farm inputs of about 16 percent between 1979 and 1989.

The number of farms in the United States continued to decline over the period 1970–90 (see table 8.4). But the rate of decline slowed perceptibly. Farm discontinuances occurred at the rate of about 97,000 per year in the 1960s, but at a rate of only 50,000 per year in the 1970s and only 27,000 per year in the 1980s. The average size of farm continued to grow, as measured by cash receipts per farm (table 8.4). The number of farms grossing over $100,000 per farm increased from 53,000 in 1970

Table 8.4. Number of Farms, Percentage Distribution, and Total Cash Receipts from Farming, Classified by Value of Farm Sales, Selected Years, 1970–90

Year	$1,000,000 or more	$500,000 to $999,999	$250,000 to $499,999	$100,000 to $249,999	$40,000 to $99,999	$20,000 to $39,999	Less than $20,000	All Farms
			Farms: Number of, in Thousands					
1970	NA[a]	4	13	36	165	302	2,429	2,949
1975	NA	11	38	96	316	315	1,745	2,521
1980	NA	24	81	166	355	282	1,532	2,440
1985	NA	27	76	223	328	244	1,394	2,293
1990	16	27	64	214	306	259	1,254	2,140
			Farms: Percentage Distribution of					
1970	NA	0.1	0.4	1.2	5.6	10.2	82.4	100
1975	NA	0.4	1.5	3.8	12.5	12.5	69.2	100
1980	NA	1.0	3.3	6.8	14.5	11.6	62.8	100
1985	NA	1.2	3.3	9.7	14.3	10.7	60.8	100
1990	0.7	1.3	3.0	10.0	14.3	12.1	58.6	100
			Total Cash Receipts: Percentage Distribution of					
1970[b]	←———— 33.4 ————→			22.1	19.5	←— 25.0 —→		100
1975[b]	←———— 50.6 ————→			25.2	12.1	←— 12.1 —→		100
1980	NA	28.3	20.0	19.3	18.8	6.7	6.9	100
1985	NA	28.8	18.3	25.1	16.3	5.5	6.0	100
1990	30.9	11.4	13.9	21.2	12.9	4.8	4.9	100

Source: *National Financial Summary, 1990*, U.S. Department of Agriculture, Economic Research Service, ECIFS10–1, November 1991, pp. 53 and 55.

[a] NA = Not Available.

[b] The estimates for these years are taken from *Income and Balance Sheet Statistics, 1979*, U.S. Department of Agriculture, Economic Research Service, Statistical Bulletin No. 650, December 1980, p. 106, and the definitions of categories in the publication differ somewhat from the definitions in the principal source for this table.

to 321,000 in 1990. At the opposite end of the size scale there was a decline in the number of farms; the number of farms grossing less than $20,000 per year fell from 2,429,000 in 1970 to 1,254,000 in 1990. Some of the shift in farm numbers into the higher-valued sales classes can be explained by the rise in farm product prices in the 1970s; certainly no more than half of the 200,000-plus increase in the number of farms falling into the $100,000 and over category between 1970 and 1980 can be attributed to the price rise. Further, prices received by farms did not rise in the 1980s — in fact, they fell over much of the decade — and the number of farms grossing over $100,000 increased by 50,000 between 1980 and 1990. In percentage terms, slightly less than 2 percent of all farms in the United States grossed over $100,000 in 1970, and some 82 percent grossed less than $20,000 per year, while by 1990 some 15 percent of all farms grossed over $100,000 per year and only 59 percent grossed $20,000 or less. A major shift occurred in the size distribution of American farms between 1970 and 1990.

Consistent with the increase in the number of large to very large farms over the twenty-year period 1970–90, the concentration of farm production and sales onto fewer and larger farms gained momentum. In 1970 some 520,000 farms each grossing more than $20,000 produced and sold 75 percent of the national farm product. (These, and the following, estimates of farm numbers and market share are all derived from table 8.4.) Twenty years later some 321,000 farms each grossing over $100,000 produced and sold 77 percent of the total farm product of the nation. Some 200,000 fewer and larger farms were accounting for a slightly larger share of the national farm product in 1990 than in 1970. How did this happen? Three developments were occurring simultaneously: (1) the total number of farms was declining; (2) the number of farms grossing less than $40,000 was declining — primarily by going out of business; and (3) the number of farms grossing more than $40,000 was growing both in size and in number — primarily by acquiring the productive assets of those farms going out of business. Out of this mix the large to very large farms gained command over a greater share of the total productive resources of the nation and the small to very small farms were left with control over a smaller share of the total productive resources. Thus, in 1990 some 1,819,000 small to very small farms produced and sold only 23 percent of the total national farm product, and some 321,000 large to very large farms produced and sold 77 percent of that total. The productive resources of American agriculture had by 1990 become concentrated in the hands of a relatively few large to very large farmers.

Off-farm income had become an important part of family income across the range of farm sizes by 1970. For the average farm grossing over $100,000 in that year net farm income approximated $55,000, and off-farm income amounted to about $8,000. But for the average farm grossing less than $10,000 per year, off-farm income had become all important. The smallest farms, those grossing less than $5,000, had a net farm income of only a few hundred dollars per farm in 1970, including government payments, whereas the average off-farm income amounted to about $7,000. In the next larger sales class, $5,000 to $9,999, the average unit had a net income from farming, including government payments, of a little over $3,000, but an off-farm of almost $5,500. Stated differently, some 2,000,000 farmers had by 1970 become part-time farmers, with their off-farm income far exceeding their farm income.

Throughout the 1970s and the early 1980s the magnitude of off-farm income, and the number of farmers whose off-farm income exceeded their net income from farming, varied with the degree of farm prosperity and employment opportunities in the nonfarm sector. But over time it became an increasingly important source of income for families living on farms — perhaps not in terms of a greatly increased number of families, but certainly with regard to the amounts and stability of that off-farm income. The relationship of off-farm income to net farm income in the second half of the 1980s may be reviewed in table 8.5. For the year 1990, off-farm income greatly exceeds net farm income for the average farmer grossing less than $40,000, and off-farm income and net farm income are almost equal for the average farmer grossing between $40,000 and $99,999.

What we have as of 1990 are some 1.5 million farms operated by part-time farmers whose major source of income is derived off the farm. In fact, for these "farmers" farming is really a sideline. They produce and sell only about 10 percent of the total national farm product, as they earn their living in nonfarm employments. And how should the 300,000 farms falling in the sales class $40,000 to $99,999 be classified? It would seem reasonable to call them medium-sized farms, and as a group they produce and sell some 13 percent of the total national farm product. But the income of the operator families on these farms was, as of 1990, almost equally divided between off-farm sources and farming. It also seems reasonable to hypothesize that this set of 300,000 farms is in transition — transition to one of three possible situations: (1) a larger farm status, (2) a more definite part-time status, or (3) an out-of-business status.

Table 8.5. Net Cash Farm Income and Off-Farm Cash Income, by Value of Sales Class, for Selected Years, 1985–90

	$1,000,000 or more	$500,000 to $999,999	$250,000 to $499,999	$100,000 to $249,999	$40,000 to $99,999	$20,000 to $39,999	Less than $20,000
				Dollars			
1985							
Net cash income	◀—— 549,361 ——▶		130,039	59,939	23,194	8,653	–618
Off-farm income	NA	22,646	14,900	12,994	17,906	21,808	28,204
1990							
Net cash income	1,244,550	272,978	158,267	70,378	25,901	9,192	–370
Off-farm income	28,472	25,916	27,629	18,096	25,335	31,916	35,206

Source: *National Financial Summary, 1990*, U.S. Department of Agriculture, Economic Research Service, ECIFS10–1, November 1991, pp. 44, 49, 52, and 58.

The Farm Production Response

Yields per acre for the major crops leveled off in the first half of the 1970s (table 8.2), and it is also a fact that livestock production per breeding unit held constant on a trend basis (table 8.3). One might guess, then, that total farm output in the United States leveled off in the first half of the 1970s. But that did not happen; total farm output grew by about 13 percent in that period. Total farm output increased in this period as the result of a greater input of cropland and the increased application of fertilizer to that land. The acres of cropland harvested grew by about 14 percent between 1970 and 1975, and the use of agricultural chemicals increased by about 23 percent over the same period.

But this interlude in extensive growth was a brief one. Total farm output continued to grow on a trend basis between 1975 and 1989. But due to variable weather conditions total U.S. farm output fluctuated in an extreme fashion over that fifteen-year period. On a trend basis total farm output increased at a little over 1.3 percent per year between 1975 and 1989. And as we have already noted this increase in output resulted almost entirely from farm technological advance, as the total input of productive resources declined steadily after 1979. Total inputs on American farms declined by over 16 percent between 1979 and 1989.

The increase in farm output over the period 1975–89 was spread evenly over both crops and livestock with both components increasing at about the same rate as overall farm output. As noted earlier the sustained growth in total farm output on a trend basis (there were important year-to-year variations in crop production owing to the weather) was not due to any spectacular technological development comparable to the introduction of hybrid seed corn or agricultural chemicals. It was attributable to controlled refinements in agricultural production methods across the board resulting in turn from better management techniques. Farm output increased in the 1980s with a significant reduction in inputs per unit of output because managers on the highly commercial large to very large farms were refining and improving their methods in all aspects of the farm production process.

The Policy Dilemma[4]

The policy dilemma that confronted American farmers and the federal government representing the general public (taxpayers and consumers) throughout the period 1970–90 (and which continues as of 1992) consisted of three parts. First, farmers petitioned the federal government for, and received, income protection, primarily in the form of direct price and income support, over the long period 1933–90, and they will certainly seek such income protection in the 1990s. Second, the prosperity of American agriculture is absolutely dependent upon exporting one-quarter to one-third of the total national farm production, and any policy, farm or otherwise, that reduces that level of agricultural exports must have the effect of reducing farm incomes and thereby increasing the costs of government programs of farm income protection. Third, the federal government representing the general public (taxpayers and consumers) continuously seeks to hold down the costs of the programs of income protection for farmers, as well as the price of food to consumers.

The Agricultural Act of 1965 did a reasonably good job of reconciling these three, often conflicting, policy objectives through the middle 1970s — holding food prices and government program costs down, operating to expand agricultural exports, and supporting farm incomes at acceptable levels. But this compromise began to unravel in the second half of the 1970s with, first, a decline in farm prices, particularly grain prices and, second, a dramatic increase in prices paid by farmers led by skyrocketing fuel costs. In addition, two new policy objectives assumed importance in the deliberations: (1) protection of the environment and (2) consumer concern with food safety and security.

In the Agricultural Act of 1977 the government tried to deal with the unrest of farmers and the unhappiness of consumers by raising commodity loan levels and target prices and by establishing a "farmer-owned reserve" to protect consumers against food shortages. In response to widespread farm strikes, including tractor parades in the nation's capital, loan rates and target prices were raised again in 1978. As a result of these actions the federal government began to increase its volume of loans to farmers in price-supporting operations, as well as its inventory of commodities taken over in price-supporting operations. These actions, together with an increase in direct payments to farmers, caused the net expenditures of the government in prices and income support activities to rise to $5.6 billion in 1978 — a record up to that time. But these domestic price-supporting programs did not cut into farm exports; farm commodity exports soared between 1978 and 1981, as did the level of farm prices.

Farmers were unhappy in 1981, however, primarily because the prices they paid for inputs were rising more rapidly than their product prices. Countering these farm pressures was a newly elected president, Ronald Reagan, who had pledged to "get government out of agriculture." But the farmers and their congressional allies won the 1981 battle. The Agricultural Act of 1981 contained all the major elements of the farm programs of the late 1970s: target prices, deficiency payments, nonrecourse loans to support prices, acreage reduction programs, the farmer-owned reserve, extension of the P.L.- 480 program, and the food stamp plan.[5] More important, the levels of price and income support (i.e., loan rates and target prices) were actually increased.

It may be asked how the farmers and their congressional allies were able to defeat a popular president. Part of the answer is to be found in the food stamp plan and related food assistance program. Senators and congressional representatives from urban areas were willing to vote for, and did vote for, the farm price and income support programs, in return for rural congressional support for the food stamp plan and other food assistance programs, which by 1980 were running at a level of $14 billion per year and would climb to $24.8 billion by 1990. Another part of the answer is to be found in the fact that this new president had underestimated the political power of the farm lobby; it could perhaps be defeated, but to do so would require the investment of more political capital than the president was willing to expend in his first year in office in the midst of an economic recession.

But just as the government was increasing loan rates for supporting farm prices and target prices for computing deficiency payments to farmers, the export boom came to an end, farm product prices began to sag, real interest rates to farmers began to rise, and the farm depression of the 1980s set in. The consequences of these developments were as follows: government nonrecourse loans to farmers to support farm prices increased dramatically as did government inventories as farmers with nonrecourse loans turned their commodities over to the government when product prices fell below loan rates; and government payments to farmers, primarily as deficiency payments, to support farm incomes increased to $3.4 billion by 1982 and to $9.3 billion by 1983. The net result of all these actions was an outlay by government for farm price and income support of $18.8 billion in 1983.

The farm depression deepened in 1984–86. A major drought hit the Corn Belt in 1983, exports continued to fall, farm product prices fell, real interest rates rose, farm land values began to plummet, and banks, implement dealers, and large commercial farms went out of business in record numbers.

It was in this economic setting that farm, administration, and congressional leaders came together to try to construct a "farm bill" in 1985. First, it should be noted that the resulting Agricultural Act of 1985 contained all the old mechanisms of target prices, deficiency payments, nonrecourse loans, and production controls. But within this set of mechanisms an important compromise was reached that involved (1) a lowering of loan rates between 1985 and 1990 to make commodities such as wheat and corn more competitive in the export market, (2) the holding of target prices near the 1985 level to protect farm incomes, (3) the implementation of large acreage reduction programs to reduce farm surpluses, and (4) the implementation of an export subsidy program, called the Export Enhancement Program, to help expand U.S. exports. In addition to these conventional commodity program features, several new program features were included. "Marketing Loans" were approved for cotton and rice that authorized producers to repay these nonrecourse loans at a lower "market"-level price whenever the world price was less than the loan rate. The Conservation Reserve Program was re-created with the objective of removing 45 million low-production acres from crop production. "Sodbuster and Swampbuster programs" were added in response to environmental pressures to discourage the conversion of highly erodible land and wetlands to intensive agricultural production. Finally, production flexibility provisions were added to the bill to make it more market oriented. One such provision, called the "0–92 Program," allowed wheat and feed grain producers to reallocate all or part of their permitted acreage to conserving uses while continuing to receive deficiency payments up to a maximum of 92 percent of their permitted acreage.

For whatever reason — lower loan rates, a falling dollar, or export-subsidies — or some combination of those and other causes, farm exports increased between 1986 and 1990, and with that favorable development both farm product prices and land values rose over the same period. But because target prices held almost steady over the period 1985–90, whereas loan rates were permitted to decline, the money costs of the farm programs of price and income support actually increased to almost $26 billion in 1986 and to $22.4 billion in 1987. From these astounding program costs — astounding when compared with the historical record — the government costs of programs of price and income support declined to about $10 billion in 1989 and to between $7 and $8 billion in 1990.

The 1990 Farm Bill is in reality an amalgam of the Food, Agriculture,

Conservation and Trade Act of 1990 and the Budget Reconciliation Act
of 1990, the latter of which dictated budget cuts in agricultural programs totaling $13.6 billion over the period 1991–95 as a means of
reducing the federal budget deficit.[6] The 1990 Farm Bill, enacted in a
year of modest farm prosperity, expanding farm exports, and extreme
pressure to reduce the federal budget deficit, thus had these major
goals: (1) reduce the federal deficit, (2) improve agricultural competitiveness in the world market, and (3) enhance the environment. The
question facing congressional legislators was how to achieve these
goals with the least political damage. The compromise solution they
came up with was the "triple-base" plan. Undergirding this plan were
two pricing concepts for the 1991–95 period: (1) target prices would be
frozen, for political reasons, at their 1990 levels; and (2) loan rates, to
realize the competitiveness goal, would be permitted to decline
modestly. The "triple-base" concept continued the idea of splitting a
farmer's historical crop acreage into "permitted" acreage and "idled"
acreage under the Acreage Reduction Program (ARP). Permitted acreage would then be divided into two parts: a base acreage on which
program crops may be grown and are eligible for deficiency payments,
and a "flexible" base, set at 15 percent of the total permitted acreage
for 1991, on which no payments would be made. This "flexible" acreage could be planted to any program or nonprogram crop except fruits
or vegetables. The implicit political bargain was thus: "We will give the
farmer production flexibility, and for this he must surrender a portion
of his deficiency payment." By doing so the farmer would contribute
to a reduction in the governmental costs of the farm price and income
support programs.

Among the many provisions of the 1990 Farm Bill related to the commodity programs several merit mention here. The marketing loan
price support mechanism was extended to soybeans and with a constant loan rate of $5.02 for the 1991–95 period. Producers had the op-
tion to "flex" an additional 10 percent of their permitted crop base. The
limitation of $50,000 for direct payments and deficiency payments was
maintained, and a new $75,000 limit was placed on marketing loan
payments. The farmer-owned reserve was maintained, and reserve requirements of 300 to 450 million bushels of wheat and 600 to 900 million bushels of corn were established.

Environmental concerns were a major driving force behind the 1990
Farm Bill. As a result Congress included a number of conservation and
environmental measures in the bill. The Conservation Reserve Program was maintained with a target of 40 to 45 million acres by 1995.

A voluntary Wetlands Reserve Program was established to enroll up to one million acres of wetland into paid thirty-year or longer easements. A new program was established to help farmers develop plans, or implement practices, that would improve water quality. It expanded the list of benefits denied farmers for not adhering to "Sodbuster and Swampbuster" provisions. It established the Office of Environment Quality within the USDA to evaluate the effects of agricultural programs on the environment and created an environmental council within the USDA at the assistant and deputy secretaries level to guide USDA environmental policies. In sum, the Congress directed the USDA to get serious about protecting the environment; only the future will tell whether the USDA is taking that charge seriously.

The food stamp plan was reauthorized for five years, with additional penalties for fraud and misuse of food coupons. It is interesting that under the terms of reference of the 1990 Farm Bill the 1991 appropriation for domestic food programs, including the food stamp plan, amounted to $27.6 billion, which is more than three times the $8.4 billion appropriated for the agricultural commodity programs.

The 1990 Farm Bill was enacted into law against the backdrop of the radical proposal made to the General Agreement on Tariffs and Trade (GATT) by the Reagan administration in July 1987 for consideration in the Uruguay Round of trade negotiations. The Reagan administration proposed that commodity-specific programs of price and income supports, and, of course, export subsidies for those commodities, be reduced to zero by all nations involved in agricultural trade, and be replaced, if a country so desired, by income payments to farms completely decoupled from specific crops. The Reagan administration, which was unable to reduce the intervening role of government in agriculture in either the 1981 or the 1985 prices of farm legislation, apparently tried to achieve this policy objective through international negotiation. How it thought it could get the Senate to approve a treaty that eliminated all domestic commodity price and income support programs is difficult to understand. Perhaps it reasoned that American farmers would accept the elimination of their commodity price and income support programs if every other nation did the same.

In the Uruguay Round of trade negotiations between September 1986 and December 6, 1990, much progress was made in reducing border barriers and domestic trade-distorting programs for manufactured goods and services. But in the area of agriculture absolutely nothing was agreed to. Important exporting countries of agricultural commodities, such as Australia and New Zealand, strongly supported the U.S. proposals. This was not a new position for them; they had long argued in GATT against U.S. farm programs, which in their view subsidized production and hence exports. Japan and the EC, on the other hand, were strongly opposed to the U.S. proposals. This was not surprising since both areas had effective domestic programs to enhance the incomes of their farm producers and equally effective border protective measures. American farm groups who wanted the agricultural trade negotiations to fail simply let the farm and political leaders of Japan and the European Community fight the battle against the Reagan administration proposal, or some compromised version of it, in the negotiating sessions. The EC balked at a compromise proposal by the Swedish minister of agriculture and chairman of the agriculture group built around reduced export subsidies, increased market access, and reduced domestic measures of support. Korea and Japan immediately joined the EC in opposition to the compromise proposal. These developments occurred on December 6, 1990; that evening the agricultural part of the trade negotiations collapsed. Soon thereafter the multinational meeting as a whole was adjourned and the Uruguay Round of trade negotiations was suspended indefinitely.

Why and how the collapse of the agricultural negotiations brought to a halt, at least for a while, the whole Uruguay Round of trade negotiations is a long and complicated story with more than one version.[7] In the meantime, American agriculture marches into the 1990s under the umbrella of the 1990 Farm Bill.

Suggested Readings

Cochrane, Willard W. *Feast or Famine: The Uncertain World of Food and Agriculture and Its Policy Implications for the United States.* National Planning Association Report No. 136, February 1974. Washington, D.C.: National Planning Association, 1974.

Cochrane, Willard W., and Runge, C. Ford. *Reforming Farm Policy: Toward a National Agenda.* Ames: Iowa State Press, 1992.

Paarlberg, Don. *Farm and Food Policy: Issues of the 1980s.* Lincoln: University of Nebraska Press, 1980.

Rapp, David. *How the U.S. Got into Agriculture: And Why It Can't Get Out.* Washington, D.C.: Congressional Quarterly, Inc., 1988.

U.S. Department of Agriculture, Economic Research Service. *National Financial Summary, 1990.* ECIFS10–1, November 1991.

U.S. Department of Agriculture, Economic Research Service. *Production and Efficiency Statistics, 1989.* ECIFS9–4, April 1991.

U.S. Department of Agriculture, Economic Research Service. *Foreign Agricultural Trade of the United States,* September-October 1991, and earlier issues.

III. The Forces of Development and Structural Change

CHAPTER 9

ABUNDANT LAND

The Magnet

A bundant land — cheap or free, distributed with or without corruption — served as an important stimulus to the overall development of this nation. Land was the magnet that drew the first settlers to English colonies, once the bubble of instant riches had been pricked. It was the magnet that continued to draw them to these shores for almost three centuries. And it was the magnet that drew settlers into the wilderness, over the Appalachians, and across the continent in one century following the Revolutionary War. To the landless and land-hungry people of Western Europe the pull of cheap or free land in North America was overwhelming. They came in droves and they suffered untold misery to make that land their own.[1]

The promise of free land, through land bounties, induced enlistments in the armed forces and supported the military efforts of the United States in three wars: the American Revolution, the War of 1812, and the Mexican War. The sale of public lands provided the funds to support all levels of education in the nineteenth century. And the building of roads, canals, and railroads was financed in part through the granting of public lands to the agencies, both public and private, that were building those transport facilities. Land was the one great resource that the young, struggling government of the United States had in abundance, and it used this resource generously, perhaps recklessly, as a means of inducing and financing economic development.

The federal government disposed of over one billion acres of the public domain in supporting the settlement and development processes of the nation (table 9.1). All authorities are not in agreement with regard to the acreage allocations of the public domain to specific uses, or classes of recipients. And it would be desirable to have disposals of the public domain classified by end use. But the disposal classes and acreage estimates presented in table 9.1 provide a general picture of the methods of disposal and how the land was used. A huge hunk of the public domain was used to support and finance the building of infrastructure (transport, education, and other public improvements); well over 300 million acres were given away for this purpose. The amount of land given away free to settlers under the Homestead Law and later amendments to the law was relatively small; only about 147 million acres were distributed in this manner.[2] Most of the land in the public domain on which the pioneers settled was purchased by them at a low price of one to ten dollars an acre. Some of this land settlers and speculators purchased directly from the federal government at public auction; perhaps 277 million acres fell in this category. The rest they purchased from state agencies, the railroad companies, and private land companies; over 500 million acres fell in this category. In sum, the land, as it was distributed, was cheap, but in most cases it was not free. And therein hangs a tale — long and often unsavory — of sales methods and land speculation.

The Physical Resource

Forests originally covered about one-half of the land in the United States. About four-tenths of the land was covered with grass, ranging from tall and lush grass on the central Illinois prairie to short and sparse grass on the Great Plains. The rest of the land — about one-tenth — was arid and barren.

Most of the humid East, land east of the Mississippi River, was covered with dense forests — hardwoods or conifers depending on the area. Farther west, beyond the Great Plains, there were smaller, scattered forests in mountains interspersed with dry valleys and basins. The West had less than one-fifth of the original forests of commercial quality.

The tall-grass country began in central Illinois and fanned out

Table 9.1. Distribution of the Public Domain[a] by the
Federal Government, as of 1956

Land Category	No. of Acres (Millions)
Land disposals	
Direct grants to railroads [b]	131.0
Grants to states to support education [c]	99.0
Grants to states to support transport and other internal improvements	125.0
Military land bounties [d]	73.5
Homestead and related grants [e]	147.0
Sales and grants primarily to private individuals [f]	455.5
Total disposals	1,031.0
Indian tribal and trust lands	52.8
Reserved for national forests, parks, wildlife, national defense, and other purposes	187.8
Unreserved and unappropriated public domain	170.6
Grand total original public domain	1,442.2

Source: Adapted from tabular material on page 48 of *Land. 1958 Yearbook of Agriculture* (U.S. Department of Agriculture, 1958). This material was developed in turn from the U.S. Department of Interior, *Report of the Director of Land Management*, Statistical Appendix, June 30, 1956; U.S. Congress, Senate, *Inventory Report on Real Property Owned by the United States*, Sen. Doc. 25, 85th Cong., 1st sess., June 30, 1956; U.S. Congress, Senate, *Inventory Report on Federal Real Property of the United States*, Sen. Doc. 100, 84th Cong., 2nd sess., June 30, 1955.

[a]Includes the forty-eight contiguous states of the Continental United States.

[b]This number varies widely depending upon definitions and the authors' interpretations of definitional language in old government documents. For example, some authors place the figure as low as 91 million. Professor Fred A. Shannon in *The Farmer's Last Frontier: Agriculture, 1860–1897* states that over 183 million acres *were given to or reserved for* railroad companies.

[c]Includes grants to support primary, secondary, and higher education.

[d]This is a much disputed figure. Some authors argue that the figure was as low as 61.0 million acres.

[e]This figure varies from 96 million to the number included in the table above depending upon definitions and authors' interpretations of definitional language in old government documents.

[f]This figure is a residual in the above table. It will be larger, for example, if the acreage disposal figure for military land bounties is decreased, and it will be smaller if the acreage disposal figure for grants to railroads is increased.

across Iowa, southern Minnesota, and northern Missouri. It was transformed into short grass on the Plains, stretching from the Canadian border to Texas, and turned into sparse, desert grass on the western side of the Great Plains. As of 1960, more than one-half of the original forestland east of the Mississippi River had been cleared for use as cropland, and the commercial forests of the West had been reduced by about 25 percent.

Most of the original tall-grass land has been converted to cropland, and those original tall-grass prairies of central Illinois, Iowa, and southern Wisconsin and Minnesota now comprise one of the best farming regions in the United States. The better lands of the short-grass regions of the Plains states are used for irrigated and dry-land crops. The rest is used for grazing. The new nation in 1790 was preparing for one of the great achievements in agricultural development in the history of the world — the clearing of 300 million acres of virgin forest and the plowing up of about 300 million acres of virgin grassland in just a little over one century. This achievement was marred, as we know, by waste, human greed, and government corruption. Nonetheless it was a great achievement.

There are approximately 1.9 billion acres of land in the forty-eight contiguous states. Of this total, about 600 million acres have characteristics favorable to crop production. Of this latter total, some 350 to 400 million acres have been cropped during the twentieth century. The remaining land with a cropping potential, some 200 to 250 million acres, could be cropped if product prices rose sufficiently to make it profitable to develop it — to do such things as remove the rocks, install drainage structures, remove second-growth timber, clear brush, and level land.

In the humid areas of the United States a high percentage of the land combines three characteristics favorable to crop production — good moisture conditions, deep, moisture-retentive soils, and gentle slopes. Much of this land lies south of the Great Lakes and stretches from the middle of Ohio to eastern Nebraska (area 1 on the large map in figure 9.1). This is one of the largest areas of highly favored, highly fertile farmland on the earth. Almost all of it is cropped each year; most of it is used to produce feed grains; and it is high-yielding. Furthermore, the central location of this area 1 cropland puts this land at the center of the nation's network of railroads and inland water transport system and gives the area a distinct market advantage.

Other parts of the humid areas are only slightly less favored. The lands designated area 2 in figure 9.1 typically have good, deep soils

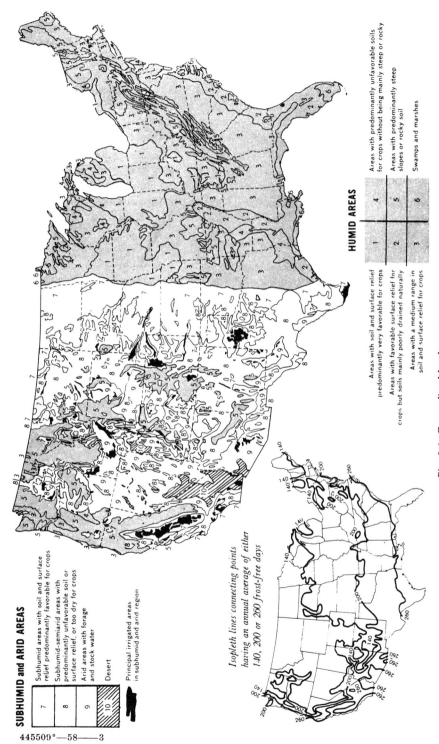

SUBHUMID and ARID AREAS

7	Subhumid areas with soil and surface relief predominantly favorable for crops
8	Subhumid-semiarid areas with predominantly unfavorable soil or surface relief, or too dry for crops
9	Arid areas with forage and stock water
10	Desert

Principal irrigated areas in subhumid and arid region

HUMID AREAS

1	Areas with soil and surface relief predominantly very favorable for crops
2	Areas with favorable surface relief for crops but soils mainly poorly drained naturally
3	Areas with a medium range in soil and surface relief for crops
4	Areas with predominantly unfavorable soils for crops without being mainly steep or rocky
5	Areas with predominantly steep slopes or rocky soil
6	Swamps and marshes

Isopleth lines connecting points having an annual average of either 140, 200 or 260 frost-free days

Fig. 9.1. Generalized land resource areas

445509°—58——3

but suffer from poor drainage. The Mississippi delta is a case in point. Area 2 farmland has the problem of too much water, rather than too little. The portions of area 3 that stretch south from Virginia to Mississippi have soil and surface gradients that are decidedly less favorable than those in area 1, but their moisture supply is good. In many places in area 3 the land has steep slopes, or poor soils, or both; hence a relatively high proportion of this land is covered with forests. But with good moisture conditions and a long frost-free season, area 3 permits the growing of cotton, citrus fruits, peanuts, and vegetables at seasons when northern areas cannot produce them. This advantage of being able to produce products that the rest of the humid area cannot produce has tended to offset the disadvantage of infertile soils.

Areas 4, 5, and 6, scattered throughout the humid region, are for a variety of reasons — e.g., swamps, mountainous terrain — unsuited for crop production. (Refer to the areas and the legends in figure 9.1.)

The transition from a humid to a subhumid climate occurs gradually as one moves westward out of the Mississippi Valley and onto the Plains. A line demarcating the two climatic zones based on an index of precipitation is drawn in figure 9.1; it is approximately at the 96th meridian. Crops can be grown in the moister parts of the subhumid areas without irrigation where the soils and the surface relief favor the conservation of moisture. These subhumid areas (area 7 in figure 9.1) are to be found on the eastern edge of the Great Plains. The choice of crops and the possibility of increasing production by fertilization are more limited in area 7 than in the humid areas because of the lack of moisture.

Within these drier areas, the most productive land resources are those that have water for irrigation. Most of the water for irrigation comes from snow packs in the humid mountain areas (area 5). Acre for acre, irrigated land is among the most productive in the nation, and the 40 million acres of irrigated land (as of 1970) contributed a much greater share of total agricultural production than their percentage of total cropland. But the water available for irrigation in the arid West is severely limited, and the competition for that limited supply of water from urban industrial users increases each year.

Land in area 8 will on occasion produce a crop under dry-land conditions, but it receives so little precipitation on the average that its principal use is in the support of an extensive livestock industry. Area 9 is even drier. Except for occasional irrigated land, land in this area will support only a sparse livestock population. It will provide some forage for livestock, but most of the livestock carried on this land must depend on forage shipped in from other more productive areas.

Although water fixes to an important degree the crop uses to which land may be put, other features of the climate, especially temperature, affect the utility of land resources. We have already noted the advantages the humid South has over the humid North in this respect. The Pacific states have a great temperature advantage. The prevailing winds blow inland off the Pacific Ocean and keep the coastal valleys relatively mild in the winter and cool in the summer. The unique climate of these coastal valleys gives them a distinct advantage in producing many fruit and vegetable crops.

Thus we observe that the physical land resource in combination with the climate in the United States is rich, favorable, and varied. The people who settled and developed the area that became the United States lucked into one of the great and productive pieces of real estate in the world.

Land Disposal Objectives, Policies, and Speculation

The objectives of the federal government in the disposition of public lands were never articulated clearly. They could not be because policy differences arose from the outset over the most desirable way of transferring public land to the persons who were going to occupy it. One view held that the new government sorely needed revenue and hence that land should be sold to the public in tracts and at prices that would maximize revenues to the government. A related view was that the United States should industrialize as rapidly as possible and that land disposal policies should foster that objective. These were the views of Alexander Hamilton and his supporters.

The opposing view was that the public lands should be given to the settlers free of charge. A related view was that the public lands should be distributed in small parcels so as to lead to a nation of small freehold farmers. These were the views of Thomas Jefferson and his followers.

The first important piece of land legislation, the Land Ordinance of 1785, represented a compromise between the industrial and speculative interests on one side and the farming and pioneering interests on the other. The minimum price for which land could sell was established at $1 per acre and the minimum parcel at 640 acres. But that ordinance further established the principle, not always adhered to in fact, that the public domain be distributed in an orderly fashion. It required first that the Indian titles be extinguished; that the lands be surveyed and offered for sale at public auction; that a proper deed granting title in fee simple be issued by the government on land purchased; that sales be completed township by township in order to solidify settlement; and that at least two sections in each township be dedicated to the support of public schools.

The struggle between the Hamiltonians and the Jeffersonians over land disposal policy continued, and each side won a little in the second major land act, the Land Act of 1796. To increase government revenues, the minimum price at which land could sell was raised to $2 per acre. But credit to the purchasers was introduced in this act; the purchaser was granted one year to pay for his land. The year 1796 probably represents the high-water mark of the Hamiltonian position. From 1796 to 1862 the pioneers seeking cheap land won one victory after another. In each succeeding piece of land legislation the conditions of public land disposal were liberalized.[3] And as we all know, free land became a reality under the Homestead Act of 1862.

But as Professor Vernon Carstensen points out, more was involved in disposing of the public domain than passing laws.

The passage of a law was only a prelude. The laws directed, required, or permitted something to be done. And bit by bit, policy and a working bureaucracy were created. The law of 1785 had provided for sale of land by the Board of Treasury, and surveys were to be made under direction of the United States Geographer. In 1796, under the Constitution, the first land offices were created but not yet properly manned; a Surveyor General took the place of the Geographer; and procedures for alienating land from the federal government were outlined. Sale of land remained in the Treasury, but Indian negotiations were to be conducted by the War Department, the issuance of titles to land was managed by the State Department, and the President's signature was required to alienate the land. In 1812 the General Land Office was created and a number of functions were consolidated, but not until 1836 was the Surveyor General made responsible to the Commissioner of Public Lands.

The requirement that Indian title be extinguished before the lands be surveyed, that the lands be surveyed before being offered for sale, and, after 1800, that they be offered for sale at land offices established in the districts — these and other regulations required much tedious administrative work. Men had to be appointed, instructed, and supplied if they were to negotiate with the Indians, who must themselves be rounded up, brought to the designated treaty grounds, and cajoled and persuaded to sign the desired treaties. The treaty had then to be approved by the Senate and the President. Thereafter, the Surveyor General in turn had to seek reliable deputy surveyors who would contract the work of surveying to men who, it was hoped, knew enough about surveying to do the actual work. Much of the early surveying was of a kind that led one student to remark that it was much easier to explain than to admire. No sooner did the surveyors take to the field than they began to complain. From Indiana, Jared Mansfield reported in 1804 that prairie fires each year destroyed the wooden corner stakes, and it was doubtful that settlers would want prairie land anyhow, destitute as it was of wood and water. Two years later he reported that near the rivers life was almost impossible for the men because they were pestered by "such miriads of flies and Moschettoes, that neither man nor beast can live there." From Mississippi, Thomas Freeman wrote in 1811 that flooded land made it impossible to get surveying crews into the field until the middle of August or early September and even then "few men can be found hardy enough to stand the poisonous effect of half-dried mud, putrid fish, and vegetable matter — almost impenetrable cane brakes, and warms of mosketoes — with which these low lands abound after the waters are withdrawn." Lucius Lyon, directed to locate, with the assistance of John Roundtree, the boundary between Wisconsin and Illinois, which was to provide the base line for Wisconsin surveys, wrote his superior early in December, 1831, that the survey was moving slowly. "It was almost impossible to get Mr. Roundtree to come out at all this season — He is an excellent man, but, having been brought up in the south, he is afraid of winter as a Barn Swallow, and about as hard to keep in a cold climate.[4]

The quest for cheap or free land did not, however, bring out the best in American citizenry. It has been said that every corrupt practice ever conceived came into play in the disposal of our public lands. Personal greed, corrupt practices, and speculation pervaded the entire disposal process and involved the whole citizenry from presidents down to the lowliest pioneer. Pioneers, short on cash but long on nerve, pushed ahead of the surveys, squatted on unsurveyed land, and then joined with their squatter neighbors to form "protective associations" to safeguard their squatters' "rights" at public land auctions. The tactic of the "protective associations" at a public auction was to threaten to shoot anyone who would bid on "their" land. On the frontier this tactic was often successful.

Public surveyors and officials in the land office not uncommonly sold information to large land speculators regarding the best land in the surveyed area. Important political and military leaders on the frontier commonly let it be known which pieces of choice land they intended to purchase at public auction at the minimum price, and strongly advised others not to bid against them for that land. Great industrial interests and large land speculators lobbied for and obtained land legislation and land grants favorable to them — the Land Act of 1796, the great land grants to the railroad companies, and the Desert Land Act of 1877, for example.

The land was there for the taking — millions and millions of acres of it — for those strong enough to wrest it from nature, brave enough to wrest it from the Indians, and cunning enough to wrest it from the legal owner, the federal government. In this competitive race for cheap or free land the strong and the brave got some, but the cunning got far and away the most. Again in the words of Professor Carstensen:

The history of the public lands has been full of words such as *speculators, land monopolists, rings, corrupt officials, hush money, fraudulent entry, bogus entrymen, land lawyers, land sharks.* No doubt each new community in the public land states, at one time, had its tales of the "innocent deceits" employed to obtain land. The literal-minded eastern lawyer might regard the land-claim association as a conspiracy to prevent open bidding at a land sale, but westerners were inclined to view such associations as a necessary accommodation to inept federal legislation. Few people in the lead country were disturbed by the story of blindfolding a witness and leading him across land. He could then testify at the land office that he had been on the land and had seen no sign of mineral deposits. A boy might stand on the number 21 and answer truthfully, when asked by the land office official, that he was indeed over 21, and an eight- or ten-year-old girl might serve as a wife of record and so give a man right to claim a double portion of land under the Oregon donation law. A bucket of water poured out in a recently ploughed furrow or a shack measured in inches not feet might be used in testimony as evidence of irrigation or habitation. A group of lumbermen in the Puget Sound area was called into court charged with timber theft. They were fined and also sentenced to one day in jail. Their story, told again and again at the annual meetings of the lumbermen's association, was that they paid their fines and then sent the sheriff out for "segars" and potables. When he returned, lumbermen, sheriff, and judge all retired to the jail, the key was turned in the lock, and all hands remained incarcerated for the day. Thus were the demands of the law satisfied.[5]

What did the squatter, the pioneer-settler, the important political leader, the large land speculator, or the great railroad company do with the land once he/it got it? Specifically, different parties did different things. But in general they all tried to do the same thing. First they made some improvements in the land, and second they tried to sell it at a profit to a settler in the next wave. In general they were all land speculators — whether they owned 80 acres or 8,000,000 acres.

The conventional wisdom among economic historians was, for many years, that speculation in western lands was a losing business. Before the development of an effective transport system by water and rail in the 1840s and 1850s, perhaps most land speculative ventures were losing propositions. This was the case because the typical pioneer-settler to whom the speculator could sell had little or no cash, and no way of earning the money to pay for the land from a farming operation in the absence of a commercial market. But the development of commercial markets, made possible through the development of an effective transport system, made land speculation profitable. The large land speculator, who purchased land from the government at the minimum price of $1.25 per acre, could now break it up and sell it in units of 80 or 160 acres at, say, a price of $3 to $8 per acre; in most instances he would sell it on credit with the reasonable expectation of being paid for that land by the purchasers from earnings on their farm operations. And the railroad company that received a large grant of land from the government free of charge could after 1850 sell relatively small parcels of that grant along its tracks at, say, $3 to $15 per acre on credit, again with the reasonable expectation of being paid for that land by the purchasers from earnings on their farm operations. Depending on the length of time the speculator was forced to hold that land and his selling and supervision costs, returns on his investment in land could vary. Returns of 100 percent were not unheard of, and returns falling in the range of 5 percent to 25 percent were commonplace. Thus, although many, probably most, land speculators died poor in the first half of the nineteenth century, many died rich, some even as millionaires, in the second half of the nineteenth century.

In sum, the land speculator, whether absentee or resident, squatter or banker, local politician or eastern senator, was present on every frontier. He affected every phase of agricultural development on the western frontier. His motives and his deeds one may deplore, but so characteristically American was he, and so dynamic a part did he play in shaping cultural, settlement, and production patterns, that it is difficult to imagine the American frontier without him.

Implications for Farm Operations: Extensive Phase

The pioneers who settled on the new lands in the first half of the nineteenth century typically did not try to become efficient, productive farmers. They too, as we have already noted, were land speculators. Each pioneer family tried to acquire as much land as it could by legal means, or otherwise. Next, the family tried to develop that land as best it could — by building a house, clearing some land, building some fences, and perhaps widening the trail into the farm into a passable road. Then, the pioneer family tried to sell the improved farm to a land-hungry family with some ready cash in the succeeding settlement wave. Depending on the period and access to markets, the second wave of settlers might become commercial farmers.

This process of pioneering and land speculation had the effect of producing an exploitive, unproductive kind of farming. The land in the limited cleared area was mined; crop after crop of corn or wheat would be taken from the land without returning any fertility to it. Tillage practices were superficial. Livestock ran loose in the woods and produced little in the way of meat or milk. The farming operation was designed to support the family, as the family improved the property and readied it to sell to the next family; it was not designed to produce a surplus for sale.

In the second half of the nineteenth century, when a system of transport had been developed and pioneer farmers had access to commercial markets, farming itself became commercialized. That is, farmers became interested in producing a surplus for sale. *But because cheap or free land was available, the commercial farm operation remained an extensive farm operation*. Labor was scarce, capital was expensive, but land was cheap. Thus farmers sought to produce a surplus by combining large amounts of the cheap resource, land, with limited amounts of labor and capital. The land was not worked intensively, and yields per acre did not increase. The commercial farmer produced his surplus by expanding the number of acres that he cultivated, as yields held constant or perhaps even declined.

This behavior was not irrational. American farmers were seeking to make a profit on their farm operations. And one way of making a profit is to keep production costs down. This can be done by employing low-cost resources. In the nineteenth century the low-cost resource was land. Thus each farmer used as much of it as he could combine profitably with his limited labor and capital resources. The result was thus an extensive type of agriculture, with low yields per acre, low livestock productivity, and an operation that was painful for the careful husbandryman of Western Europe to behold.

Secretary of Agriculture James (Tama Jim) Wilson, writing in 1907, demonstrated a full awareness of the extensive nature of American farming in the nineteenth century, and of the forces driving it in that direction. He wrote as follows:

The mighty production of the farm for one-third of a century has come out of an agriculture having many faults. In a large degree there has been one-crop farming; crop rotation, as practiced, has often been too short and unwise; the grasses and leguminous forage crops have been neglected, domestic animals have not sufficiently entered into the farm economy, and many dairy cows have been kept at a loss. The fertilizers made on the farm have been regarded as a nuisance in some regions; they have been wasted and misapplied by many farmers; humus has not been plowed into the ground as generally as it should have been; and in many a place the unprotected soil has been washed into the streams.

This, in few words, is the historic story of agriculture in a new country; yet the course of agriculture in this country, bad as it may seem in its unscientific aspect, has had large economic justification. While pioneers, poor and in debt, are establishing themselves they have no capital, even if they had the knowledge, with which to carry on agriculture to the satisfaction of the critic. . . .

So it has happened, with reason, that the production per acre has been low; but there is no likelihood that low production is fixed and that the farmer must continue his extensive system. When consumption demands and when prices sustain, the farmer will respond. The doors of knowledge and example are opening wider to him.[6]

Implications for Farm Operations: Intensive Phase

That seemingly inexhaustible resource, good farmland, ultimately was exhausted. The closing of the frontier is often said to have oc- curred in the 1890s. Perhaps the frontier, as a wild, lawless area, was closed by 1900. But a great deal of land was homesteaded in Montana and other parts of the Far West in the first two decades of the twen- tieth century. This land was, however, at the extensive margin of cultivation. The good, free farmland in the United States was gone by 1890 or perhaps earlier. As we know, with expanding markets, both foreign and domestic, farm product prices began a long rise after 1896. And land prices started moving up with those product prices.

As the price of land per acre began to rise, farmers had to find ways of holding down, or even reducing, the per unit costs of production. The first, and general, approach to this problem was the substitution of machines for the most expensive factor of production, human labor. Farmers did this first through the substitution of horsepower and machines for labor and later by substituting tractors and machines for labor.

The second approach to this problem of rising land costs was that of increasing the productivity per acre and per unit of livestock. This was achieved through the adoption by farmers of new and improved plant varieties and breeds of livestock. This phenomenon, we will recall, took hold in the 1930s.

The third approach to the per unit cost problem involved the in- creased application of capital items, which acted both to reduce labor requirements and to increase productivity. These capital items included such important items as commercial fertilizer, irrigation water, herbicides, and pesticides. The great increase in the use of these capital items came after World War II.

These approaches, working in combination, had the effect of increasing output per unit of input and thus of reducing per unit costs of production, which is our definition of intensive growth. What we had in the United States from 1933 to 1970 was a period of rapid, unparalleled, intensive growth in American agriculture.

So long as land was cheap, or free, and kept stretching to the west in unlimited quantities, there was no economic pressure to engage in an intensive type agriculture with improved farming practices. So long as land was cheap, or free, it was treated like a free good and squandered like a free good. Resources are conserved only as they become scarce and expensive; this we are now learning with respect to energy, water, and even the air we breathe.

Cropland, land for recreation, water, timber, petroleum, many minerals, and surface air are becoming scarce — scarce relative to current and potential population needs; thus Americans are beginning to worry a great deal about the adequacy of the supplies of these resources. In the meantime the prices of land, water, and energy continue to rise. And the pressure to conserve these resources mounts daily. Where all this will end cannot be foretold in this book. But one thing is certain. The drive to intensify the productive operation on the existing farmland base will increase.

Some General Conclusions

A great deal has been written about the corrupt practices employed in the disposal of the public lands, and perhaps even more has been written about the speculative activities involved. These subjects were discussed briefly again in this chapter. The clear implication of all this writing is that the corruption and speculation were bad for the people involved and bad for the country. Without question, the corrupt practices and the speculation in land led to income transfers among the populace that were inequitable and unjust. In this sense the corruption and speculation were bad. But did they have a significant harmful effect on the nation? Perhaps to some degree. However, it is difficult to measure that degree, either qualitatively or quantitatively.

The land disposal policies pursued, with the corruption and the speculation, certainly did not dampen significantly the settlement of the country or its economic growth. It is difficult to see how the pace of settlement of the country or the rate of economic growth of the country could have been more rapid under any conceivable set of alternative land disposal policies. Professor Douglass C. North draws the following conclusion.

The broad, tentative conclusion to be drawn, therefore, is that . . . land policies in general were consistent with a high rate of economic growth, and it would be hard to develop a hypothetical alternative that would be a very great improvement.[7]

The above position on the rate of economic growth can be conceded, but the following important question can still be raised — What about the quality of that growth in the agricultural sector? The general conclusion with respect to quality must also be favorable. Outside the "Old South" the land disposal policies of the United States resulted in an agricultural sector composed primarily of relatively small production units, or farms, each of which was owned and operated by the family residing there. And the Civil War eliminated the economic and social base of the plantation agriculture in the "Old South," namely, slavery. Thus to an important degree the agricultural sector of the United States at the closing of the frontier comprised small, freehold units in which the families operating those units had a vital stake in the productivity of those units, an important stake in the well-being of the community, and a continuing stake in the welfare of the nation. To a significant degree the Jeffersonian dream had become a reality as of 1900. For the white man in rural America, it was a good society, and the facts make clear that it was a highly productive society.

But one can still argue that the land disposal policies of the nation contributed to, or resulted in, an exploitive type of agriculture: the natural resources of the United States were recklessly exploited in the nineteenth century; the land resources were ill-used; and farming practices by West European standards were bad. But did the land disposal policies of the United States cause, or bring about, those conditions? No, it is argued here. It was the abundance of those resources, the abundance of that land, in combination with the hunger of migrants from the eastern United States and of immigrants from Western Europe to own a piece of that land that led first to the liberal land disposal policies and second to the reckless exploitation of the land. It was the land abundance and the land hunger that led to the reckless exploitation of the land, not the liberal disposal policies. They too were a result, not a cause.

In the judgment of the author the results of the land disposal process in terms of the agricultural economy and the national society were good — not perfect, but good. Compared with the results in Latin America, they were excellent. As of 1900, there were few landed estates in the United States, the labor force was composed primarily of families living on their own farms, and the typical family-owned-and-operated farm was an efficient and productive unit. What more can be said?

Suggested Readings

Carstensen, Vernon, ed. *The Public Lands: Studies in the History of the Public Domain.* Madison: University of Wisconsin Press, 1968.

Schlebecker, John T. *Whereby We Thrive: A History of American Farming, 1607–1972.* Ames, Iowa: Iowa State University Press, 1975. Chaps. 6 and 12.

Shannon, Fred A. *The Farmer's Last Frontier: Agriculture, 1860–1897.* Vol. V of *The Economic History of the United States.* New York: Farrar and Rinehart, 1945. Chap. III.

U.S. Department of Agriculture. *Land. 1958 Yearbook of Agriculture.* Washington, D.C.: Government Printing Office.

U.S. Department of Agriculture. Economic Research Service. *Farm Real Estate Historical Series Data: 1850–1970.* Washington, D.C.: Government Printing Office, June 1973.

CHAPTER 10

FARM MECHANIZATION AND
TECHNOLOGICAL ADVANCE

Scarce Labor

From the day the first English settler stepped ashore in colonial Virginia until the closing of the frontier, the human labor available to develop the abundant land resources was in short supply. Relative to the land resources awaiting development, labor was scarce. In colonial days settlers tried in numerous ways to augment their supply of labor. (See chapter 2.) But in view of the development tasks confronting each pioneer farmer and the young nation, there was a continuous shortage of labor. The money costs of hired labor on the frontier were prohibitively expensive, since every young man, or young family, had the alternative open to him, or it, of acquiring land for development, if not by purchase, then by squatting illegally on it, or later homesteading it. Thus, except in areas where the institution of black slavery existed and until 1840 or 1850, the amount of land that a family could develop and operate was limited by the size of the labor force in each family.

In the early 1800s, the thing that the pioneer farm family needed most to expand the size of its farm, to become more productive, and ultimately to prosper was a cheap, efficient substitute for that prohibitively expensive factor of production — human labor. Since it was virtually impossible to expand the labor supply on individual farms in pioneering settlements by hiring labor, and very expensive to do so in the older agricultural areas, the individual farm family had to find ways of making the arms of its family members longer and stronger. This need was met in the first half of the nineteenth century by the development of machines that enabled the farm worker to do more work more quickly with less input of human energy. Typically, these machines involved the substitution of animal power for human power. And the entire process of developing machines and adopting them on farms — farm mechanization — gained momentum and took off in the period 1820–40 (figure 10.1).

Farm Mechanization in the 1800s

The machines employed by farmers in the United States as late as 1840 were primarily hand tools: the ax, the hoe, the sickle, and the scythe. There were no industrial firms specializing in the manufacture of farm machinery before 1840, and there were no research stations concerned with the design of machines. There were some educated men interested in the art of farming who wrote on the subject: Thomas Jefferson and Edmund Ruffin of Virginia, and Daniel Webster and Ezekiel Holmes of New England. These men had ideas about the various technical aspects of agriculture, including the design of machines, but they could not and did not build the needed laborsaving machines. The machines that revolutionized the preparation of seedbeds and the harvesting of grains between 1820 and 1880 were typically developed and built by local blacksmiths. These were blacksmiths who lived among farm people, understood their needs, repaired their hand tools, and loved to tinker with tools, equipment, and machines.

The first great improvements came in the design and construction of the plow. In 1797 Charles Newbold took out a patent with the U.S. Patent Office for a cast-iron plow in one piece. This plow did not prove satisfactory, but it marked the break with the heavy, cumbersome, wooden plows of that period. R. B. Chenaworth of Baltimore patented a cast-iron plow in 1813 with a share, moldboard, and landside in separate pieces so that the worn parts could be replaced. Jethro Wood, who took out patents in 1813 and 1819 on improvements for cast-iron plows, devoted his whole life to the promotion and use of efficient cast-iron plows. John Deere of Illinois built a one-piece plow of wrought iron with a cutting edge of steel on the share in 1837. The Deere plow scoured so well in the heavy, sticky soils of Illinois that it became known as the "singing plow." By the

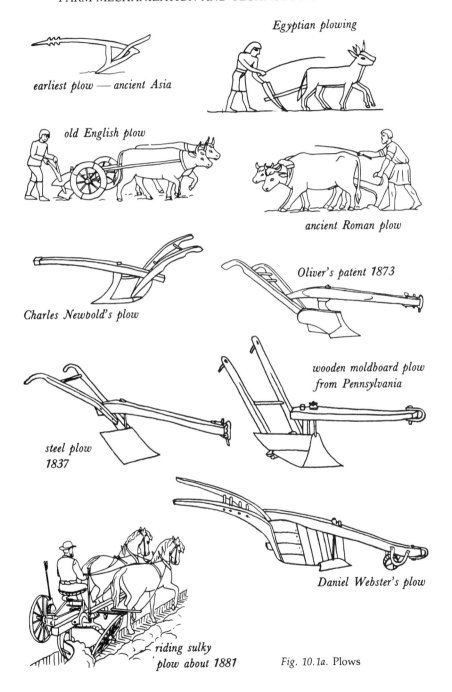

Egyptian plowing

earliest plow — ancient Asia

old English plow

ancient Roman plow

Charles Newbold's plow

Oliver's patent 1873

wooden moldboard plow from Pennsylvania

steel plow 1837

Daniel Webster's plow

riding sulky plow about 1881

Fig. 10.1a. Plows

brush harrow

Roman spike-tooth harrow

Garver spring-tooth harrow 1869

wood-bar harrow

spring-tooth harrow

chisel cultivator

disk harrow

Fig. 10.1b. Soil Preparation

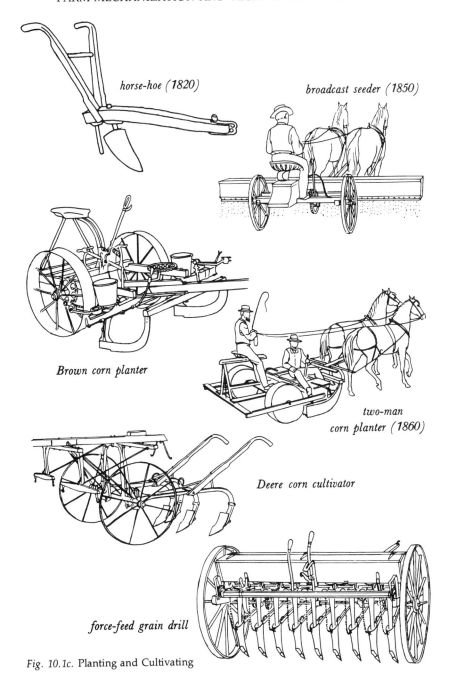

horse-hoe *(1820)*

broadcast seeder *(1850)*

Brown corn planter

*two-man
corn planter (1860)*

Deere corn cultivator

force-feed grain drill

Fig. 10.1c. Planting and Cultivating

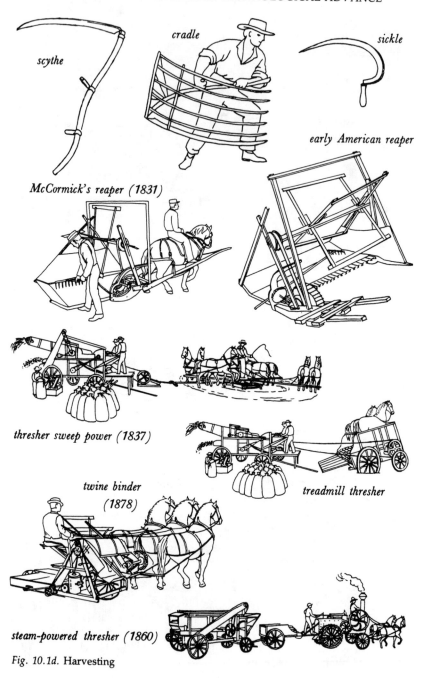

Fig. 10.1d. Harvesting

mid-1840s John Deere was producing a thousand of these plows a year, and by the mid-1850s the John Deere industrial firm was turning out some 10,000 plows a year. The next step was the development of the riding, or sulky, plow with one bottom. This plow was followed by the gang plow of two or more bottoms. By the 1890s large gang plows with four bottoms pulled by eight horses were in common use on large midwestern farms. These large gang plows were often called "horse killers," suggesting that it was time for a new and more efficient source of power to substitute for animal power.

Improvements in machines for harvesting grain during the 1800s were even more dramatic than in the case of plows. The hand sickle for cutting grain was in use as early as 3000 B.C. The only significant advances that occurred in the harvesting of grain over the next 4,800 years were the development of the scythe and the cradle — both hand tools. Then came the mechanical reaper in the 1830s, which opened the way to a complete mechanization of the grain harvest. The mechanical grain reaper of the 1830s was a one-horse machine made mostly of wood. The few metal parts included a ground wheel used to drive gears, which transmitted power to a sickle type of cutting bar. The grain was cut near the ground. A revolving reel pushed the cut grain onto a platform from which it was raked off by hand into small bundles. The bundles in turn had to be tied and placed into shocks by hand. But the mechanical reaper cut in half the work time required to harvest grain.

That these early reapers had serious shortcomings and often broke down should not come as a surprise. But two men, Obed Hussey and Cyrus McCormick, kept working to improve these machines, and in the 1850s McCormick, by incorporating the best features of his reaper and the Hussey reaper, developed a machine that was reasonably efficient and reliable. This machine caught the fancy of farmers, sales of McCormick reapers shot up, and the McCormick Company became the leading manufacturer of reapers.

The development of grain-threshing machines occurred concurrently with the development of the reaper. By the 1830s about 700 different types of threshing machines were being produced and sold in the United States. These first threshers simply threshed. Someone still had to separate the straw with a rake and then remove the chaff from the grain in a winnowing operation.

In the 1840s and 1850s, two firms, the Pitt Company and the J. I. Case Company, began to produce and sell a combination thresher-separator-winnower that would thresh the grain, separate the straw, and remove the chaff. These were large, expensive machines that were usually acquired by farmers who did custom work for other farmers. By 1860 itinerant threshing rigs and crews had taken over most of the business of threshing in the wheat-growing areas.

In the Far West grain combines came into use in the 1870s and 1880s; these cut, threshed, separated, and winnowed the grain. As many as forty horses were used to pull great combines weighing up to fifteen tons that cut swaths of grain up to thirty-five feet wide. In the 1890s steam engines were mounted on these great combines to provide a more constant source of power for the threshing operation than could be provided from the ground wheels, and steam tractors began to replace horses for propelling the entire machine. Grain-harvesting machines in the late 1900s were getting bigger and bigger to facilitate more timely harvests and to reduce crop losses at harvest time; as a consequence, the search for more reliable and efficient sources of power was intensified.

Along with improved plows and harvesting machinery came many other types of machines — harrows, disks, corn planters, grain drills, mowers, and hay-making equipment. Interestingly, all these machines, regardless of the date of invention, came into widespread use at the same time in the 1850s. Advances in one aspect of farm production required advances in other aspects; if one farm operation became easier or quicker, it was of little use to the farmer unless he could speed up other aspects of the production process. In the 1850s, grain farmers in the United States had achieved a fair balance among all elements of the production process.

High farm prices and acute shortages of labor during the Civil War years speeded the adoption of all kinds of laborsaving machines on farms outside the Confederate South. The process of farm mechanization continued throughout the period 1865–1900. This latter period was not, however, like the period 1820–40, in which a variety of new machines were invented and developed. In the period 1865–1900 machines were refined and improved, they became steadily larger, they were adopted more readily on farms, and the search for more efficient and more reliable sources of power continued. It was not a period of innovation, but one of widespread farm adoption. It was thus a period in which the drudgery of farm work was greatly reduced and the productivity of the farm worker was greatly increased.

Farm Mechanization in the 1900s

The gasoline-engined tractor was developed in the 1880s and 1890s. The first gasoline-engined tractor (hereafter referred to as a *tractor*) was essentially an internal combustion engine connected to wheels and mounted on a steel frame. This crude machine was developed into a reasonably efficient and effective machine by 1905, and several firms had adopted assembly line techniques in the production of tractors by 1910. With the urgent need for an efficient and reliable source of farm power and a supply of mass-produced tractors, farmers had begun to adopt tractors on a widespread basis by 1910. We see this, and the rapid growth in the use of tractors on farms, in table 10.1. There were about 1,000 tractors in operation on farms in 1910, 25,000 by 1915, and 246,000 by 1920. Thereafter, the number of tractors on farms increased to about 4.8 million in 1965 and then fluctuated annually between 4.6 and 4.7 million over the period 1965–88. The average farm tractor was, however, much larger in terms of horsepower in the 1980s than it was in the 1960s. The total amount of tractor horsepower at work on farms increased from 176 million in 1965 to 309 million in 1983. But perhaps more important, the average tractor of the 1980s ran faster, did more things, and was less stressful to operate than its counterpart of the 1960s.

Paralleling the rapid growth in the number of tractors on farms was the growth in the use of motor trucks on farms — from 25,000 in 1915 to over 3.4 million in 1988. The gasoline engine incorporated into the tractor, the motor truck, and more recently self-propelled harvesting machines (e.g., the grain combine) now does all the heavy work on American farms: it hauls nonfarm-produced inputs to the farm, prepares the seedbed, plants the crops, harvests the crops, and hauls the crop and livestock products to urban collection centers. To an important degree, farm mechanization in the 1900s is related to and is an outgrowth of the development of the internal combustion engine and its numerous applications.

The internal combustion engine incorporated into tractors, trucks, and self-propelled harvesting equipment (1) has eliminated its chief competitors in the provision of power, namely, horses and mules and steam engines, (2) has eliminated almost all hard human physical labor on farms, (3) has greatly increased the timeliness of farm operations and hence increased productivity, and (4) has induced the development of a wide range of machines to be used with the tractor (e.g., corn pickers, hay balers, field forage harvesters).

198

Table 10.1. Farm Machinery: Number of Specified Kinds on Farms, and Tractor Horsepower, United States, Selected Years, 1910–88[a]

Year	Tractors (Exclusive of Steam and Garden) Total[b] (Thousands)	Horsepower (Millions)	Motor Trucks (Thousands)	Grain Combines[c] (Thousands)	Corn Pickers and Picker Shellers[d] (Thousands)	Pickup Balers[e] (Thousands)	Field Forage Harvesters[f] (Thousands)
1910	1	...	0	1	...	...	...
1915	25	...	25	...	...	...	...
1920	246	10[g]	139	4	10	...	...
1925	549	...	459	...	...	...	...
1930	920	25[g]	900	61	50	...	...
1935	1,048	...	890	...	...	...	...
1940	1,567	42	1,045	190	110	...	...
1945	2,354	61	1,490	375	168	42	20
1950	3,394	93	2,207	714	456	196	81
1955	4,345	126	2,675	980	688	448	202
1960	4,688	153	2,834	1,042	792	680	291
1965	4,787	176	3,030	910	690	751	316
1970	4,619	203	2,984	790	635	708	304
1975[h]	4,469	222	3,038	524	615	667	255
1980[i]	4,780	304	3,377	656	701	756	293
1983	4,669	309	3,435	644	684	800	285
1988[h]	4,609[i]	[j]	3,437	667	[j]	823	[j]

Source: Base data are derived primarily from *Agricultural Census* reports. For years not covered and items not reported in the *Agricultural Census*, the following information sources were used to derive estimates: *Current Industrial Reports* of the Census Bureau (formerly *Facts for Industry*), annual registrations of motor vehicles, results of surveys, changes in farm income, and estimated discard rates.

[a]Data as of January 1.
[b]Includes wheel and crawler types of tractors.
[c]Data for 1975 and after do not include the flail type of forage harvesters.
[d]Includes cornheads for combines.
[e]Does not include large balers, over 200 pounds.
[f]Data for 1976 and after do not include the flail type of forage harvesters.
[g]Average of 1920–24 and 1930–34.
[h]Latest *Census Report*.
[i]Includes wheel tractors only.
[j]Series discontinued in 1984.

The gasoline engine achieved this preeminent position on American farms for a number of reasons. First, given the low price of petroleum that existed in the first seventy-five years of the twentieth century, the internal combustion engine was a highly efficient source of power. Second, the design of the gasoline-engined tractor permitted it to be operated by one man, whereas a steam tractor or rig might require a crew of four men — two men to operate the steam engine and two men to haul water and coal. Third, the gasoline-engined tractor became a highly convenient machine to operate; it started easily, it was and is easy to refuel, and it could do many different jobs. Finally, with the advent of pneumatic tires and power steering the tractor became a comfortable and even easier machine to operate. Given these attractive characteristics, the internal combustion engine incorporated in tractors, trucks, and self-propelled harvesting machines was, and remains in 1990, the centerpiece of mechanization on American farms. All specific pieces of farm machinery are designed and engineered to relate to and hook up with the internal combustion engine.

A careful study of Table 10.1 indicates a new and important development in the 1980s. The number of tractors and trucks on farms is no longer increasing. And the rate of increase in the number of important pieces of farm machinery slows perceptibly. Something very important is taking place on American farms in the 1980s with regard to the input of mechanical power and machinery — a development that will require our attention in the pages to come.

Power on the farm has been provided by electricity as well as by the internal combustion engine. Milking machines, feed mixing units, and many, many smaller machines on farms are powered by electricity as well as many home appliances.

The Consequences of Farm Mechanization

The process of farm mechanization in the United States has been concerned primarily with the substitution of machines for men, first powered by animals and later powered by the internal combustion engine. Hence we should not be surprised to discover that labor requirements in agricultural production have declined persistently and dramatically since the early 1800s. And that is what we do find.

Between 250 and 300 man-hours were required to produce 100 bushels of wheat on five acres with a walking plow, brush harrow, hand broadcast of seed, sickle, and flail in 1830. By 1890, some 40 to

50 man-hours of labor were required to produce 100 bushels of wheat on five acres with a gang plow, seeder, binder, thresher, horses, and wagons. By 1930, some 15 to 20 man-hours of labor were required to produce 100 bushels of wheat on five acres with a three-bottom plow, tractor, tandem disk, combine, and trucks. By 1975, only 3 to 4 man-hours of labor were required to produce 100 bushels of wheat on three acres with a tractor, thirty-foot sweep disk, twenty-seven-foot seed drill, twenty-two-foot self-propelled combine, and trucks. Comparable declines in the man-hours of labor required to produce corn, cotton, and other field crops were achieved through mechanization over the same general period.

There were two direct results of these great decreases in labor requirements in agricultural production. First, the size of farm that an average size farm family could operate efficiently grew steadily during the 1800s and has grown dramatically in the 1900s. Second, total farm output increased importantly from 1920 to 1990, while farm employment declined from 13.4 million to 2.9 million. In other words, farm mechanization, as it has occurred in the United States, has had the direct effect of first causing the average farm to increase significantly in size over the years and of then enabling the total farm output to be produced with a smaller total labor force than would have been required with a slower rate of mechanization. As a result of farm mechanization, labor was released from agriculture at a rapid rate for reemployment in nonfarm pursuits, even as total farm output expanded and kept pace with increasing demand.

Whether the way it happened and the rate at which it happened were good or bad may be debated. The rate at which labor was displaced in agricultural production by machines in the 1900s certainly worked a great hardship on many of the people involved and created acute problems for the urban areas that received the rural migrants. But the general direction in which the process worked was and is consistent with economic progress, since it contributed to an increase in gross national product in which the real income of the average person in the United States increased.

Farm Technological Advance

The process of farm mechanization — the development of new and improved machines and their adoption on farms — was a form of technological advance. Between 1820 and 1920, it was the principal, almost the exclusive, form of farm technological advance. Farm people in this period thought of technology as machines and mechanics, and of improvements in technology as involving improvements in machines.

What do we mean by an advance in technology? By a technological advance we have in mind a situation wherein resources are combined in a new form, or a new configuration, such that the same volume of resources measured in value terms yields an increased output,[1] or a lesser volume of resources measured in value terms yields the same output. Resources are combined in a new form, or a new configuration, so that output per unit of input increases; this is the essence of a technological advance. For the economist this means that the production function of the farm involved shifts upward and the cost structure of the farm shifts downward. This means in turn that the farm that has experienced a technological advance stands ready to produce and sell a larger quantity of its product at a given price, or the same amount of product at a lesser price.

It will be recalled from the historical analysis of part II that scientists in the Department of Agriculture and the colleges of agriculture in the Land Grant universities from the 1870s on were at work trying to understand the causes of various animal diseases, searching for cures for those diseases, seeking to unravel the mysteries of plant and animal genetics, studying the causes of plant diseases, studying the properties of the soil, breeding new plant varieties for resistance to drought and disease, trying to determine the nutrient requirements of plants and animals, and on and on. But learning the cause of, say, hog cholera and finding a way to control it, or learning that crossing two inbred plant lines would create a hybrid vigor in the cross such that its yield would increase, and finding an efficient method for producing the hybrid seed, were very different propositions from improving the plow. The latter could be achieved by a tinkerer with some knowledge of metallurgy and a vision of what was needed by farmers. The former could be achieved only as a body of knowledge was built that could explain the functioning of plants and animals. This took time, and it required intellectual discipline. But once the U.S. Department of Agriculture and the state colleges of agriculture turned their attention in a disciplined way to the understanding of the functioning of plants and animals, the necessary body of knowledge was built, field after field. From these bodies of knowledge in agronomy, plant pathology, veterinary science, animal nutrition, soil science, and agricultural engineering, new *techniques* began to surface in the form of new and higher-yielding plant varieties, ways of controlling plant and animal diseases, efficient animal feeding rations, recommendations for soil fertilization, and so on.

These new techniques, most of which represented farm technological advances when adopted on farms, came along very slowly before 1920, gathered momentum between 1920 and 1940, and poured forth after 1940. In the period 1940–70 there were really three technological revolutions going on concurrently in American agriculture. There was a mechanical revolution that led to the mechanization of almost every production process in farming. There was a biological revolution that led to drought-resistant and disease-resistant varieties, and greatly increased crop yields. There was a chemical revolution that did many wondrous things: controlled plant and animal diseases, as well as pests and weeds, and provided soil fertilization.

Technological developments in the period 1970–90 were less revolutionary than in the previous thirty years. They were more concerned with refinements, through management controls, in the application of mechanical, biological, and chemical technologies to the production process. Thus after a brief pause in the early 1970s, the rate of increase in farm productivity speeded up to a record-breaking pace in the 1980s. Over the long period, 1940–90, then, thousands upon thousands of farmers had the unique experience in history of adopting one new technique after another which had the effect of continuously increasing the productivity of the resources employed by each of those farmers. Thus these farmers had the unique experience of standing ready to produce, and of producing, more product in each new year, or each new production period, than they did in the previous period at any given price. This each was willing to do, and did, because each was adopting new production techniques that represented technological advances in the production process of his farm.

Capital and Financial Implications

The total value of physical assets in farming grew importantly over the long period 1870 to 1950, except for the period 1920–40. The value of those assets in current dollars rose from nearly $12 billion in 1870 to approximately $22 billion in 1900, to $84 billion in 1920, declined to $40 billion in 1935, and then rose again to $107 billion in 1950.

Total physical capital in farming measured in constant 1910–14 prices grew rapidly between 1870 and 1920, leveled off between 1920 and 1940 in the farm depression years, and then increased again between 1940 and 1950. The principal reason for the high rate of capital formation in the period 1870–1920, despite frequent weaknesses in the prices of farm products, was the availability of land for settlement. Farmers, as we know, obtained this land at little or no money cost from the federal and state governments, the railroads, and private land speculators and converted it into operating farms through their own and their families' hard physical labor. Thus in this period farmers to a remarkable degree financed the increase in farm capital through their own physical toil and savings.

But with the closing of the frontier, the increased mechanization of farms, and widespread technological advance on farms, the composition of farm capital changed; this may be seen in a general way in figure 10.2. The value of land in constant dollars leveled off after 1900, while the value of implements and machinery increased dramatically. The value of land and buildings as a percentage of total physical assets stood at 80 percent in 1870; by 1950 it had declined modestly to 78 percent. But the value of implements and machinery as a percentage of total physical assets increased from 1.3 percent in 1870 to 8.2 percent in 1950. We see also in figure 10.2 the absolute and relative decline in the value of horses and mules. The changing composition of physical capital on American farms over the long period 1870–1950 clearly reflects the technological developments of that period.[2]

Since 1950 the total value of physical assets on farms in current prices has increased tremendously. The total value of physical assets increased from about $111 billion in 1950 to approximately $796 billion in 1990. Much of this great increase was due to price inflation, but some of it was due to an increase in real physical assets.

The composition of total farm assets (physical and financial) over the period 1950–90 reversed the trends described above for the long period, 1870–1950. Farm real estate as a percentage of total assets actually increased from 62 percent in 1950 to about 72 percent in 1990. The value of farm machinery as a percentage of total assets, on the other hand, holds constant at about 11 percent over the entire period. Real estate (land and buildings), which has long been the dominant physical asset in farming, assumed an even more dominant role in the decade of the 1980s.

But more is involved in farm production than physical assets. Labor once played a dominant role, and operating capital is playing an increasingly important role. As we see from table 10.2, human labor provided 65 percent of the total inputs employed in farming in 1870. The proportion of total inputs provided by labor declined steadily over the long period 1870–1990, reaching a low of 19 percent in 1990. The input of land and buildings held reasonably constant over the same period, fluctuating between 18 and 24 percent of total inputs employed. (The modest fluctuations that are observable in table 10.2 are, in the judgment of the experts, more the results of changes in the statistical weights than of changes in real conditions.)

Capital employed on farms in the United States provided only a small proportion of the total inputs employed — some 17 percent — in 1870. But reflecting the increased mechanization of farms over the long period 1870–1990, and the widespread technological advances in farming from 1930 to 1990, the proportion of total inputs provided by

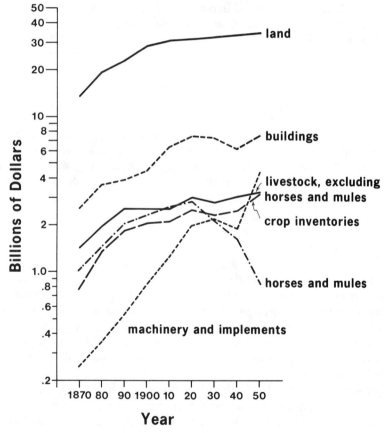

Fig. 10.2. Types of capital used in farming, United States, 1870–1950, values in 1910–14 prices

Table 10.2. Changes in the Percentage Composition of
Agricultural Inputs, United States, Selected Years, 1870–1990

Year	Labor	Real Estate	Capital[a]	Total
1870	65%	18%	17%	100%
1900	57	19	24	100
1920	50	18	32	100
1940	41	18	41	100
1960[b]	27	19	54	100
1970	19	23	58	100
1980	20	22	58	100
1990	19	24	57	100

Source: 1870–1940, *Productivity of Agriculture, United States, 1870–1958*, U.S. Department of Agriculture Bulletin No. 1238, April 1961, p. 11; 1960–76, unpublished estimates provided by Donald Durost of the Economic Research Service of the U.S.D.A.

[a]Includes all kinds of capital items: operating capital and physical capital other than land and buildings.

[b]The series for 1960 forward employs different, and more modern, weights than for the period 1870–1940.

capital increased steadily. By 1990 capital of all kinds provided 57 percent of the total resources employed in farming. Thus between the years 1870 and 1990 there was almost a complete reversal in the positions of human labor and capital in the structure of farming.

Farm mechanization and technological advance resulted in the substitution of all kinds of capital for labor on farms from the 1850s to the present. This has meant that farmers have had to purchase a larger and larger proportion of their productive resources from off-farm sources. This has meant in turn that farmers have become increasingly dependent upon credit and off-farm financing of the production enterprise. In sum, the modern farm unit has become a highly capital-intensive unit that must have ready access to production credit of all kinds and that must make use of large amounts of that credit, if it is to operate successfully. There is nothing basically wrong with this development, but it means the farm operator, if he is to be successful, must be an expert not only in the complex modern technology of farming but also in credit and finance.

The Engine: Farm Technological Advance[3]

Let us consider how the engine — farm technological advance — operates to develop the agricultural sector. We will describe and analyze that process with the aid of a hypothetical example. The example runs as follows: A scientist working on a basic problem in a state university theorizes that a plant treated in a particular way by electrical energy during its growth will develop certain desirable mutations and produce twice as much fruit in succeeding generations. For the moment, this is a hypothesis put forth by a scientist in a research paper.

Now a geneticist in the United States Department of Agriculture picks up the idea and begins to experiment with it. He discovers that the mutations do occur, but unpredictably. He then enlists the aid of a plant breeder and they continue to develop plant sports, breeding those sports that have the desired characteristic — that produce twice as much fruit. They continue until they get a plant that will breed true: that is, the seed from the mutated plant will consistently yield the characteristics of the parent plant. These men in turn write a paper, and their results become common knowledge among plant breeders.

The research and experimental phases are past, but much developmental work remains to be done. The new variety may yield twice as much as the original variety, but it may not be resistant to certain plant diseases, and the plant stalk may be too weak for the weight of the head, hence not stand up well for mechanical harvesting.

At this point, a private seed-producing firm may enter the picture and start cross-breeding the new variety with other varieties to develop a disease-resistant variety with a strong short stalk. After three or four years, the firm may come up with a variety ready to be put on the market — one that yields, say, only a third more than the original variety, but which is disease-resistant and has a strong stalk.

Between the writing of the original paper and the offering of the new variety on the market by the private seed firm, ten or twenty years may have elapsed. At each stage, researchers will have been lured up blind alleys and some research teams will have failed and given up. But with many researchers involved, free access to research experiences and results, and a generous expenditure of money, breakthroughs occur. It is impossible to say when or where breakthroughs will take place, but they do happen, and after a course of events somewhat like that described above.

Will farmers adopt this new variety when the seed company's salesman comes around? In the first year probably most farmers will not adopt it, but a few will. The innovator — the man constantly on the lookout for new production practices that will lower his costs and who has the technological background to read and understand the literature about the new variety — will adopt it if he believes its potential is good. Assuming that the variety proves out under farm production conditions, the output per unit of productive resources will have increased on the innovator's farm. His costs of producing a bushel will have gone down and, assuming prices are unchanged, his net return will have increased. The innovator is thus rewarded for his superior business and technological judgment and skill.

The next year more farmers will adopt the new variety; the news about the higher yields will have gotten around. The neighbors of the innovator will have seen the increased yields, the county agent will have held meetings to discuss the new variety, and the seed salesman will have told everyone who would listen. In a few years the variety will be widely adopted, and *total* production on each farm and in the producing area will have increased significantly.

The process of farm adoption in this case is fairly simple. The cost of adoption would be low; the price of seed of this improved variety would be very little more than that of previous improved varieties that had gone through a comparable development process. Production practices in the field would be little different. The only question at issue was whether the new variety increased output by one-third. Once this was established under practical growing conditions, the new variety's widespread adoption would be ensured.

But the case is not always so simple. The new technology may require a major capital investment, or a major reorganization of the farm operations. And the question is often asked — If farming is unprofitable, why does any farmer adopt new practices? Or, if everyone adopts the new practice and total output expands and the product price falls, why does any farmer adopt the practice in the first place?

To fully understand the process of farm technological advance and thus answer such questions, we must first look at the economic structure of farming. Farming is an atomistic industry: each producer is so small compared with the total output of the industry that each has no perceptible influence on output or upon the price of his product.

In other words, *the farmer is a price taker*. But, although he cannot influence the price at which he sells, he can on his own farm do something about his production practices and oraganization and thereby influence his own costs of production. With a price given to him — a price made in the world market, in Washington, or in heaven — which he individually cannot influence, he can, if he can get his unit costs down, improve his economic position. He can reduce his losses or improve his profits as the case may be. And he can get his unit costs of production down by the adoption of a new technology that increases his output per unit of resources employed.

This he does if the new technique is available and if he is an astute business manager. This he does whether he is losing money at the time or making money, for in either case the adoption of the new technology improves his own economic situation. This is why new and improved technologies are adopted, whether economic conditions are good, bad, or indifferent. Each farmer sees the new technology as a solution to his business problem; it is a way of getting his costs down. Thus there is always an incentive for the farmer to adopt a new and improved technology.

If the flow of new and improved technologies to farmers is wide and deep, farm technological advance will be a powerful engine of agricultural development. And this was the case between 1940 and 1970. But the engine appeared to be sputtering in the 1970s. Then, in the late 1970s and the 1980s, it gained strength and powered a great surge in development.

Suggested Readings

Miller, Merritt F. "The Evolution of Reaping Machines." *The Making of America.* Vol. V. of *Agriculture,* edited by Robert M. La Follette. Chicago: De Bower, Chapline, 1907.

Schlebecker, John T. *Whereby We Thrive: A History of American Farming, 1607–1972.* Ames, Iowa: Iowa State University Press, 1975. Chaps. 9, 10, 15, 16, 17, and 24.

Tostlebe, Alvin S. *Capital in Agriculture: Its Formation and Financing Since 1870.* Princeton, N.J.: Princeton University Press, 1957. Chaps. 1, 4, and 8.

U.S. Department of Agriculture. *Productivity of Agriculture, United Stated, 1870–1958.* Technical Bulletin No. 1238, April 1961. Pp. 11–28.

U.S. Department of Agriculture. *Power to Produce. 1960 Yearbook of Agriculture.* Washington, D.C.: Government Printing Office. Pp. 1–74, 132–35, 218–67.

U.S. Department of Agriculture. Economic Research Service. *National Financial Summary, 1990,* ECIFS, 10–1, November 1991.

CHAPTER 11

BUILDING PHYSICAL INFRASTRUCTURE
Transport and Other Elements

What Is Infrastructure?

Infrastructure is defined by the dictionary as "the basic, underlying framework, or features, of a system, as the military installations, communications, and transport facilities of a country." In economic parlance the term "infrastructure" is used to refer to inputs and services that are controlled by society and that are external to the firms or persons making use of them. The term is sometimes used interchangeably with "social overhead capital." The inquiry in this chapter is concerned with the role of *physical* infrastructure in agricultural development.[1] Physical infrastructure as it relates to the agricultural sector is defined as "the physical capital, both public and private, which provides services to, and which has a significant effect on, the economic functioning of the individual farm firm, but which is external to the individual farm firm." Roads and railroads are classic examples of physical infrastructure.

Families living in a traditional or tribal society and practicing a subsistence agriculture require little in the way of infrastructure. But even people living in a tribal society, if they are to be protected from invasion, wars, and capture as slaves, will require some form of police or military infrastructure to provide them with personal security. When a traditional, subsistence type of agriculture begins to develop, it will require infrastructural elements of various kinds to move information and supplies into the area undergoing development and to store surplus products,[2] handle them, and move them out of the area. An agriculture comprising many, many small production units cannot develop unless the society involved provides those units with the necessary infrastructure. Development of the agricultural sector without the services that flow from the required infrastructural elements is impossible.

Emphasis on Transport in the Nineteenth Century

Why was so much emphasis placed on the building of transport systems in nineteenth-century America? Why in the making of internal improvements, as the building of infrastructure was called in the early nineteenth century, did the people and their government focus their attention so completely on transport? The answer is obvious if one looks at a map of the continental United States and recalls some history. With victory at the close of the Revolutionary War all the land stretching west from the Appalachian Mountains to the Mississippi River became part of the new nation and was empty of white settlements. It was covered by dense forests and claimed by various Indian tribes, but to the new nation it was empty and calling for settlement. If that great hinterland was to be settled and a nation created, ways had to be found to open it up. Ways had to be found to facilitate the inflow of settlers, the inflow of supplies to the new settlers, and the outflow of the surplus agricultural products of the newly settled region. Given the great land mass to be settled and exploited, the new nation had an overwhelming need for an efficient transport system within that broad expanse of territory.

Thus much of the efforts of the new nation, at both the federal and state levels, for more than one hundred years would be directed toward the building of an efficient transport system: first roads and bridges, then canals and waterways, and finally railroads. The effort was prodigious, and many mistakes would be made in building a transport system that was both fast and efficient and that would link the entire nation. But it was accomplished by 1900,· just as a new transport technology, the internal combustion engine, was being developed, which would call for a completely new system.

Roads and Bridges

Roads outside the larger cities were unbelievably bad at the close of the Revolution. In most places they were simply broad paths through the forest. They were ungraded, often with large stones and stumps in the pathway. When wet they turned into mud quagmires, and when dry they were covered with a deep layer of powdery dust. A person could ride over these roads on horseback with relative ease; carriages and stages moved over these roads with considerable difficulty; and hauling heavy freight over them in large wagons was virtually impossible.

In the period from 1790 to 1812 considerable progress was made in the New England and Middle Atlantic states toward linking the principal urban centers by means of turnpikes. Turnpikes were improved roads upon which tolls were charged. Typically, these roads were built by private companies, chartered by state governments, and were erected over the most important travel routes. The best ones, like the Lancaster Turnpike, were built on a foundation of solid stone with a top dressing of gravel. The Lancaster Turnpike, which was built between Philadelphia and Lancaster, Pennsylvania, was completed in 1794. The financial success of this turnpike really initiated the turnpike era.

Strong efforts were made in the Congress during the first two decades of the nineteenth century to get federal financing support for the building of "post roads." But efforts to build a national system of roads were unsuccessful — for a number of reasons. Many political leaders, including several presidents, believed that federal support of internal improvements was unconstitutional. But of greater importance was the bitter sectional jealousies that were racking the young nation. New England, which had built a reasonably good road system through state and private efforts, was opposed to federally financed internal improvements (e.g., a federally supported road system). Further, New Englanders looked with alarm at the migration of people from their hills to the Ohio River valley. And, although the South had the poorest roads in the nation, it was well supplied with navigable rivers and had little or no interest in a national system of roads. Only the westerners in the Ohio River valley consistently supported the concept of a national system of roads, partly or wholly financed by the federal government. But they could not carry the day in Congress.

Thus the country turned to privately constructed turnpikes for its internal transport system. The turnpike era ran from approximately 1800 to 1830. During this period thousands of miles of turnpikes were built by private companies throughout the New England and Mid-Atlantic states. The greatest turnpike project during this period was the National Road. This turnpike, built with on-again, off-again aid from the federal government, started at Cumberland, Maryland, ran through Wheeling, Virginia, Columbus, Ohio, and finally reached Vandalia, Illinois, about 1850.

The turnpikes were a great boon to travelers moving by carriage and stagecoach. They literally smoothed the way for immigrants journeying westward. But for heavy, bulky freight moving long distances, the turnpikes were of limited value. So long as freight had to move in large clumsy wagons pulled by large horse or oxen hitches, the cost of transport for most items (e.g., grains) was prohibitively high; it was also terribly slow. Thus heavy freight, for the most part, simply did not move over these private turnpikes. But without this kind of traffic the turnpikes could not show a profit on their investments. As a result, private turnpikes began to go out of business in the 1820s, and the added competition from canals and railroads in the 1830s sealed their doom.

Another kind of road was developed in the 1830s; it was the plank road, sometimes called the "farmers' railroad." Plank roads were built by laying heavy, wide planks across rails, or stringers, the latter of which ran parallel to the direction of the road and were set solidly in the roadbed. The first plank road was built near Syracuse, New York, in 1837. Within the next twenty years several thousands of miles of this kind of road were built in the United States.

There were several reasons for the immediate popularity of plank roads. First, given the abundance of wood and lumber, they were relatively cheap to build. Second, a team of horses could pull much heavier loads on the plank roads than on ungraded dirt roads. Thus they were ideal for short-haul, farm-to-market traffic. Finally, there was a strong aversion to railroads in their early years, and many investors preferred to put their money into something that they considered safer than steam engines.

But the plank-road movement was short-lived. The plank roads were no more successful than the earlier turnpikes in being supported by receipts from tolls. The freight traffic that they required did not materialize. Further, the expense of repairs and upkeep was prohibitively high. The planks, which were expected to last seven to ten years, gave way in much shorter times from hard wear and rot. In the words of George Rogers Taylor, "The failure of the plank-road movement left most short-haul land transportation literally stuck in the mud, there to remain until the later age of the rigid-surfaced road and the internal-combustion engine."[3]

The turnpike and plank-road eras did, however, do one important thing — they gave a great impetus to bridge building. Like turnpikes, the bridges of this period were typically built by private companies chartered for that purpose and were supported by tolls. But unlike turnpikes, the bridges were essential to everyone, and the tolls were easily and effectively collected. Thus many privately owned toll bridges continued in operation long after the turnpikes and plank-road ventures had gone out of business. The toll bridge was one form of transport infrastructure that could be provided by private enterprise at a profit.

The Canal Era

Although there were about 100 miles of canals in operation in various states along the Atlantic Seaboard in 1816, the canal era in the United States really opened with the digging of the Erie Canal. The construction of the Erie Canal was authorized by the New York state legislature in April 1817, and work began in July of that year. Eight years later, at a cost of $7 million and with the enthusiastic support of Governor De Witt Clinton, the canal opened. From tolls collected over parts of the canal before its final completion, it became evident that the canal would be a financial success.

A look at the map suggests why the Erie Canal was an instant success. The topography lent itself to the digging of the canal; at its highest point near Buffalo, the canal was only 650 feet above the Hudson River at Albany. Thus the cost of constructing the canal was far less than for most later ventures. But more important, the Erie Canal linked up with important natural waterways at each end: with the Hudson River on the east and Lake Erie on the west. With the completion of the Erie Canal it became possible to ship heavy, bulky freight (e.g., grains) all the way from Cleveland, or Toledo, or Chicago to the East Coast by water transport. Linking the Ohio River valley, with its surplus of agricultural products, to the growing urban markets of the East ensured the success of the Erie Canal.

This success set off a nationwide craze of canal building. With the need for improved transportation so great in the developing nation and the financial and economic benefits from artificial waterways apparently demonstrated by the Erie Canal, private groups and governmental units in every part of the country rushed into canal building. In general terms, three types of canals were constructed between 1825 and 1840: (1) those designed to improve transport between the upcountry and tidewater in states bordering the Atlantic, (2) those like the Erie Canal designed to connect the Atlantic Seaboard with the

Ohio River valley, and (3) those in the West designed to connect the Great Lakes with the Ohio-Mississippi river systems. Very large sums of money were required to build these canals, since the construction costs per mile rarely fell below $30,000 and ran as high as $80,000. This was more than private parties could typically aggregate; thus canal promoters quickly turned to the government for financial support. The federal government granted some four millions acres of the public domain to canal projects in the western states, and it subscribed over $3 million to the stock of private canal companies. But it was the individual state governments that made the major capital contributions to canal building. And to an important degree the state governments built and operated the canals within their states.

By 1840 the people of the United States, acting primarily through their state governments, had constructed some 3,326 miles of canals. Between 1816 and 1840, some $125 million was spent on building canals, and three states had so strained their credit that they were on the verge of bankruptcy. No major canals were begun between 1840 and 1860. In the 1840s less than 400 miles of canals were added to the system, and in the 1850s abandonments exceeded new construction. The great era of canal building in the United States was over. The canal network that existed in 1860 may be seen in figure 11.1.

The construction of canals came to an end in the 1840s because construction costs on most of the later canals greatly exceeded the estimates of their promoters, and revenues from tolls fell far short of expectations. In short, the canal sites with the best economic and financial potentials had been exploited, and most of the later canals were financial failures. But the canal development as a whole was no failure. The development of water transport via canals greatly reduced the cost of moving heavy freight, an important consideration in the development of agriculture west of the Appalachians and in the development of heavy industries. Further, the traffic on and the earnings of several of the more important canals did not reach their peak until after the Civil War. Traffic on the Erie Canal, for example, increased steadily until the 1880s.

As a means of moving heavy freight, canal transport was vastly superior to land transport over turnpikes or roads, and it offered stiff competition to the railroads for many years. Observe the freight rate advantage of canals over railroads throughout the 1800s in figure 11.2. But water transport via canals was far from a perfect answer to the need for improved transportation. The movement of freight through the canals was extremely slow. But more important, it was

215

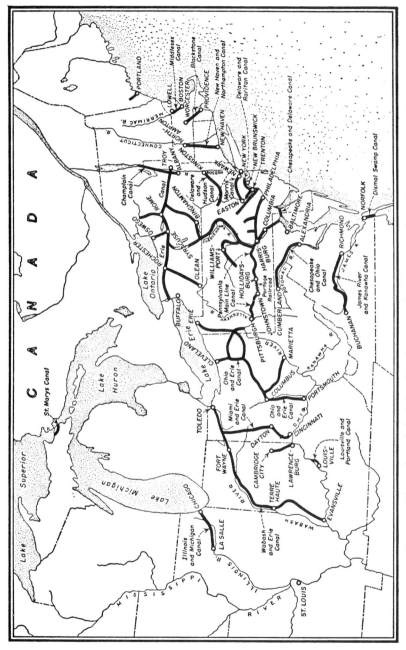

Fig. 11.1. Principal canals built by 1860. Reprinted, by permission from George Rogers Taylor, *The Transportation Revolution, 1815–1860* (New York: Holt, Rinehart, and Winston, 1951), p. 35.

not dependable. Canals were forever being washed out by heavy rains. Further, canals commonly ran short of water in the summer and fall. For extended periods traffic would be interrupted or halted owing to too much water or not enough. Finally, water transport via canals was severely limited by the location of the canals; only a few geographic sites lent themselves to successful canal construction and operation. Thus the canals slowly lost out to the railroads.

Before we turn to the role of railroads in the economic development of the United States, we need to look briefly at one other form of water transport, namely, the steamboat on inland waters. The river steamboat was developed in the United States in the first decade of the 1800s. The first successful river steamboat, the Claremont, was

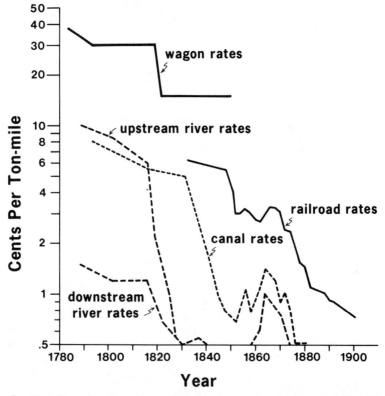

Fig. 11.2. General pattern of inland freight rates by type of transport, 1784–1900. Based on table 4 in Douglass C. North, "The Role of Transportation in the Economic Development of North America," *Les grands voies maritimes dans le monde XV–XIX Siècles* (Paris: SEVPEN, 1965), pp. 244–46.

built by Robert Fulton and launched in 1807 to carry passengers up and down the Hudson River. Following this pattern, the steamboat in the East developed into a specialized vessel for carrying passengers and express cargo. And by the end of the second decade in the 1800s, fast, sleek steamboats moved up and down the Atlantic coast and up and down the eastern rivers in considerable numbers competing vigorously for the passenger trade.

On the western rivers the steamboat developed very differently. What was needed on the western rivers was a workhorse that could carry bulky freight upstream as well as down and that could operate in very shallow water. Thus a steamboat was developed for work on the western rivers that was wide relative to its length and that sacrificed speed to gain cargo space. By 1817 there were seventeen such vessels operating on the Ohio-Mississippi river system with a combined tonnage of 3,290 tons; by 1820 the number of these steamboats had increased to sixty-nine; and by 1855 there were 727 such vessels with a total tonnage of 170,000 tons. It is further estimated that at least twenty steamboats operating on the Ohio River in 1838 could function in thirty inches of water.

The western river steamboat carried bulky agricultural products such as grain and cotton downriver and transported all kinds of supplies (hand tools, cloth, traps and guns, and railroad equipment) required by the developing economy upriver. The relatively low freight rates charged by the river steamboats may be seen in figure 11.2. These low rates, in combination with the ability of these steamboats to ply up and down all the principal western rivers and many of the smaller ones, enabled the western river steamboat to play a key role in the development of the Ohio and Mississippi river valleys.

The Railroads

The key elements of a railroad — rails and locomotives — were developed over a long period of time in England. Metal rails with cars that ran on those rails were first developed for the coal mines. By 1820 a rather advanced system of rails and cars was employed in horse-drawn tramways. Attempts to combine a steam engine with a wheeled carriage began in the late 1700s. Attempts were made to develop a locomotive to pull coal cars in the mines in the early 1800s, but none could generate enough power to be serviceable.

The first successful railroad was placed in operation in England in 1825; the designer of the locomotive and its engineer was George

Stephenson. Four years later he built an engine, the Rocket, for the Liverpool and Manchester Railway. It weighed approximately five tons, could pull a load three times its own weight, and could travel up to speeds of twenty-four miles an hour. Interest in railroad construction in the United States was aroused immediately. The Baltimore and Ohio Railroad, designed to extend westward from Baltimore to the Ohio River, was chartered in 1828, and thirteen miles of track were in operation by 1830. The Charleston and Hamburg Railroad, designed to connect the rich cotton region of the Piedmont with the port of Charleston, was open for passenger traffic in 1831 and had 136 miles of track in operation by 1833 — the longest railroad in the world at that time. Over the strong opposition of investors in turnpikes and canals, and of many people who felt that the steam locomotive was the work of the devil, railroad construction continued during the 1830s up and down the Atlantic Coast. By 1840 railroad mileage in the United States totaled 3,328 miles. This mileage just about equaled the mileage of canals at that date, and all but a fraction of it was located east of the Appalachians. The construction of railroads moved ahead rapidly in the 1840s. By the end of that decade there were some 8,879 miles of railroad in operation in the United States, and the railroads had crossed the Appalachian Mountains and were inching into the Ohio and Mississippi river valleys. A flurry of railroad construction occurred in the 1850s, and by 1860 the United States east of the Mississippi was linked by a railroad network (figure 11.3). Between 1850 and 1860 more than 20,000 miles of railroad track were added to the transportation system, bringing the total mileage up to about 30,000 miles.

The development of a railroad network in the United States between 1830 and 1860 did not occur automatically. Numerous technological advances had to take place before the railroads could become an effective means of transport. The first rails, which were wood, or wood with metal straps affixed to the top, were not serviceable; they wore out quickly and could not carry heavy loads. Through trial and error the "T" type of steel rail evolved, and over the years those rails became heavier and heavier, thus permitting the carrying of heavier and heavier loads. The roadbed had to be improved to meet the needs of heavy steam engines and loaded freight cars. Almost everything was tried. But gradually, wooden sleepers, or ties, firmly imbedded in gravel were found to provide the best support for rails; such an arrangement had some give to it as the train passed over it but still held firm. More powerful steam engines had to be de-

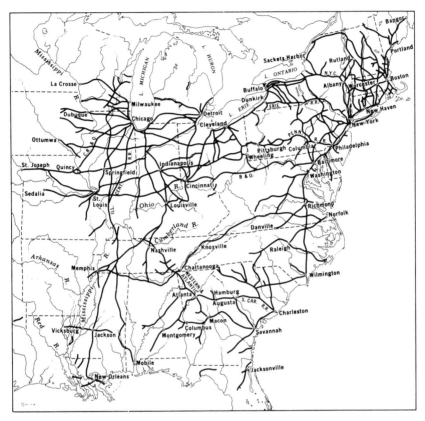

Fig. 11.3. Major railroads built by 1860. Adapted from Henry F. Graff and John A. Krout, *The Adventure of the American People,* 2nd ed. (Chicago; Rand McNally, 1970) p. 212. Reprinted by permission of Houghton Mifflin Company.

veloped to pull larger cars and more cars and thus become efficient in the transport of heavy freight. The first passenger cars, which were designed like stagecoaches, had to be redesigned to handle more passengers in more comfortable surroundings. This was achieved through the development of the swivel truck, which allowed passenger cars to become longer and as a result more comfortable.

All these things did occur, and a comprehensive railroad network was in place and operating by 1860. But it would be a mistake to think that the railroads quickly took the freight business away from the canals and the river steamboats. The first railroads engaged principally in passenger traffic. They were fast and dependable, and passengers were willing to pay a premium for that service. The railroads could not compete effectively with water transport for heavy freight traffic in the 1830s and 1840s for two reasons. First, their roadbeds, rails, and equipment would not permit the hauling of heavy freight; mechanically the railroads had not progressed to the point where they could haul heavy freight. Second, and reflecting the above condition, railroad freight rates were high and greatly in excess of water transport rates during the period 1830–60 (figure 11.2).

But it was also the case that railroad freight rates declined by approximately 50 percent between 1830 and 1860, and technologically railroads had developed by 1860 to the point where they could carry heavy, bulky freight without fear of physical breakdown. Thus it is not surprising that the volume of freight traffic handled by railroads in 1860 equaled that handled by canals. From 1860 on, the volume of railroad freight traffic increased steadily throughout the latter half of the nineteenth century and did not go into a decline until the Great Depression years of the 1930s. The mileage of canals and the volume of freight traffic on canals, on the other hand, began to decline in the 1850s, and declined steadily throughout the second half of the nineteenth century. Even the Erie Canal system, the most successful of all canal systems, reached a high point in the volume of freight carried in 1880 and slowly declined thereafter.

Railroad construction did not slow down in the post-Civil War period, at least not in absolute terms. This was the period in which the great transcontinental railroads were built and in which a comprehensive network of railroads for the entire nation was constructed. Between 1867 and 1913 more than 2,000 miles of track were laid every year except for four years, 1875, 1894, 1895, and 1896 — all depression years. In one year alone, 1872, more than 7,000 miles of track were laid. During this period, too, track rails became heavier, boxcars and passenger cars longer and bigger, and locomotives much more powerful. In Civil War days a single freight car could carry a maximum load of ten to twelve tons; by 1914 the typical freight car could handle up to seventy tons. A typical locomotive in 1860 might pull twenty-five cars or so; the typical locomotive in 1914 could pull fifty to 100 cars. By 1914 the railroads had triumphed over all other forms of transport.

How is the triumph of the railroads in the second half of the nineteenth century to be explained? It is not to be explained by freight rates alone. Although rail freight rates declined steadily throughout the second half of the nineteenth century, they never reached the low levels of water transport. (See figure 11.2.) The triumph of the rail-roads must be explained in other terms. Four reasons are commonly advanced for the great success of the railroads. First, railroads could, within reason, be built into areas and link up markets in which rivers did not run and canals could not be built. This was particularly true of east-west traffic in the United States. Second, the railroads were highly dependable and operated the year round, in comparison with canals, which were not dependable and often could not operate in the winter when they were frozen over. Third, the railroads were fast and convenient compared with canal traffic. And speed and convenience have always been prized highly by Americans. Fourth, and perhaps for some of the above reasons, railroads were highly profitable in the nineteenth century, and many people at home and abroad were happy to invest in their development.

It is true that the railroads were heavily subsidized in the nineteenth century by federal and state governments. The federal government made grants of lands that totaled at least 130 million acres to different railroad companies to help them finance the con-struction of their routes. And if land grants by the states to railroads are taken into account, the gift of land to the railroads by all levels of government runs perhaps as high as 183 million acres. It is, further, estimated that in the period 1845–60 the various state governments borrowed $90,000,000 mainly to finance the construction of railroads. But the canals were heavily subsidized by the state governments too. The ultimate triumph of railway transport over water transport in the United States would seem to rest on the following set of conditions: (1) American businessmen, including farmers, valued highly speed and convenience in the movement of their products; (2) the railroads could, within reason, go wherever the freight originated and take it wherever it needed to go; and (3) when rail freight rates became somewhat competitive with water transport in the second half of the nineteenth century, the railroads won over all other forms of trans-portation.

The influence of railroads on the growth of the American economy is a much debated subject. Before 1960 it was fashionable for economic historians, on the basis of qualitative analysis, to argue that the railroads had an overriding influence on the growth of the Ameri-can economy and on the location of industry and agriculture. In 1964 Robert W. Fogel advanced the argument that the railroads had a rather small influence on the growth of the economy.[4] Employing quantitative methods, Fogel estimates, for example, that the social savings of railroads as of 1890 were equal to approximately 1 percent of gross national product in the handling of agricultural products and approximately 5 percent in the handling of all commodities. Or stated differently, if the United States in 1890 had been forced to depend on alternative forms of transport, primarily water transport, the gross national product would have been only some 5 percent less. Since 1964, other researchers using quantitative methods but different assumptions with regard to cargo losses and inventory costs, and taking account of passenger traffic, have found that the contribution of the railroads to growth in the gross national product may have been twice that estimated by Fogel, but still small compared with the contribution attributed to the railroads by the earlier qualitative historians.

The quantitative type of analysis employed by Fogel and members of the new school of economic history is perfectly legitimate but very "iffy." Many questions can be raised about the assumptions made in an analysis that asks the question, "What would have been the rate of growth of the American economy *if* there had been no railroads?" In conclusion, we will ask two such questions. First, "In the essentially static analysis employed by Fogel, was the dynamic effect of investment in railroad construction on the growth of the economy properly taken into account?" A review of the Fogel analysis suggests that it was not. Thus the failure to take into account the multiplying effect of investment in railroads on the growth of the gross national product would appear to have caused Fogel to understate the effect of railroads on the development of the economy of the United States.

But of more direct relevance to this analysis is the second question, "How would the agriculture of the United States have developed differently *if* there had been no railroads, or any comparable technological development?" Or stated differently, "If the agriculture of the United States had been forced to depend almost entirely on water and wagon transport, how would it have developed?" Certainly, it would have developed much differently. Agriculture would have had to develop more intensively in the Ohio and Mississippi river valleys where there were navigable rivers and where canal linkages could be developed relatively economically, whereas the agricultural resources lying west of the western borders of Minnesota, Iowa, Missouri, Arkansas, and Louisiana, where navigable rivers are almost nonexistent, could not have been developed as intensively as they were with the existence of the railroads. Wheat and small grain production could have moved west onto the Plains only with the greatest of difficulty; in all likelihood the Plains would have remained an extensive grazing operation. Whether this would have meant that the real product of agriculture would have been increased or diminished in the long, long run would depend upon the course of technological developments in agriculture. But for the second half of the nineteenth century, it almost certainly would have meant that the total real product of agriculture would have grown more slowly than it in fact did as farmers were forced to increase output through the costly process of intensifying their use of those scarce and expensive inputs — labor and capital — in areas adjacent to water transport (i.e., the Ohio and Mississippi river valleys). The option of producing the increased output of agriculture through the use of more of the cheap resource, land, would have been foreclosed to them in the absence of the railroads.

Infrastructural Elements in the Twentieth Century

Roads and Highways

Areas of emphasis in the building of physical infrastructure changed in the twentieth century, but not immediately and not completely. Technological improvements in the internal combustion engine and the development of the motor car and trucks created a need for an improved road and highway system. But the building of a better road and highway system lagged far behind the development of motor cars and trucks in the first two decades of the twentieth century. There was no agreement with respect to who or what unit of government should plan for and pay for a national road and highway system. Local units of governments, which traditionally built and maintained roads, were not interested in a national road system, and the federal government was hesitant about becoming involved.

It was pressure from the farmers to get them out of the mud that finally induced the federal government to act. Legislators from rural constituencies piloted the first road and highway legislation through the Congress in 1916. With the passage of the Federal Aid Road Act of 1916, the federal government began in a timorous way to develop a national highway system. The federal government committed itself to spending $75 million a year to build rural post roads; state and local governments were to match the federal funds so that the federal contribution was not to exceed 50 percent of construction costs. This was a beginning, but it was a small beginning, and the effort remained small throughout the 1920s. Travelers in the 1920s often found that the smooth strip of concrete on which they were traveling came to an end at a county line or a state line, and they were confronted with at best a gravel road or at worst a sea of mud. Road and highway improvement in the nation was spotty; California and some eastern states built some excellent roads, but many midwestern states did very little. Thus nothing approaching a national highway system existed in 1930.

The Great Depression created serious economic problems for almost everyone, but it did provide one blessing — it provided the impetus to improve the national road system. Public expenditures undertaken to reduce unemployment and to stimulate the economy were devoted in large measure to road and highway construction. The federal contribution to the building of roads and highways rose from approximately 10 percent in 1930 to 40 percent in 1933. This increased federal support for road and highway improvement continued throughout the 1930s and was institutionalized in various ways.

In 1944 the Congress passed the Federal-Aid Highway Act in anticipation of a road-rebuilding program after the war. This law made available for expenditure $1.5 billion in the three fiscal years following the end of the war, and it provided for the designation of an interstate highway system of some 40,000 miles. In 1956 Congress authorized the building of the interstate and defense highway system. This system was to provide 41,000 miles of limited-access, multi-lane highways connecting the principal population centers of the United States, and it was to be completed over a thirteen-year period. That system, as of 1978, is virtually complete, but through heavy use and wear it is also deteriorating rapidly. Maintenance of the heavily used interstate highway system in a state of good repair will require massive infusions of federal funds over the long-run future.

The United States, as of 1980, had a well-designed system of interstate highways, and some of the heaviest users of that system were trucks carrying agricultural produce. Much of that produce is perishable and high-valued and must move with speed (e.g., fresh fruits, vegetables, and meats). But large quantities of heavy, bulky grains were also moving in trucks on the highways. Once again American farmers, middlemen, and consumers seem to have opted for convenience and speed at high cost over the slower, more economic forms of transport — in this case the railroads.

But the fifty-year trend away from rail freight and to trucks appears to have come to an end in the 1980s. Between 1980 and 1988 the ton-miles of freight handled by the three principal types of carriers held almost constant: railroads at 37 percent of the total, trucks at 25 percent, and pipelines at 23 percent. Costs per mile may have ended the shift to truck transport; in 1987 rail costs per ton-mile were 2.9 cents while truck costs were 32 cents per ton-mile.

Water Resource Development

The Army Corps of Engineers was involved throughout the nineteenth century in improving the navigability of the nation's rivers. But the first great effort of the federal government to develop the water resources of the nation took place in the early part of the twentieth century. With the passage of the Reclamation Act of 1902, the federal government made use of its proprietary powers over great areas of the public lands in the West to build reservoirs and delivery systems to supply irrigation water to farm settlements. It also used these powers to set standards, in the public interest, for state and private development of water power. The concept of multiple-use projects involving navigation, flood control, irrigation, and water power also originated in this period.

During the Great Depression public works programs instigated by the federal government to stimulate business and to provide jobs were utilized to develop water resources. Plans developed by the Bureau of Reclamation and the Corps of Engineers were made the basis of huge reservoir projects; these projects typically involved the multiple-purpose use of water resources. The newly created Tennessee Valley Authority was given the authority to develop the water resources of the entire Tennessee River basin for the multiple purposes of flood control, navigation, power generation, and regional economic development. And a nationwide program of flood control improvements was initiated.

During the 1930s the federal government created a succession of national planning organizations, the last of which was called the National Resources Planning Board, to coordinate federal construction projects at the river basin level and to prepare advance plans for public works construction. The federal government also provided technical assistance and financial support to state and local governmental units so that they could do their own advance planning for water resource development during this period. During World War II much of the machinery for this centralized planning was abandoned.

But construction was not abandoned. During the post-World War II period there was a great expansion in the two largest construction programs: flood control and navigation improvements by the Corps of Engineers and irrigation development by the Bureau of Reclamation. The programs of both these agencies emphasized multiple-purpose reservoirs and water power development. At the same time the Soil Conservation Service of the U.S. Department of Agriculture added the construction of small, upstream flood control structures to its ongoing work of watershed protection. During the 1950s this latter program provided planning and financial assistance to local units of government in the construction of small improvements for flood control, agricultural uses of water, and other useful purposes.

As a direct result of the above programs, the number of acres of farmland receiving irrigation increased from 3.7 million in 1890, to 14.7 million in 1930, to 25.9 million in 1950, and up to 50 million in 1990.[5] Farmers have benefited from the efforts of the federal government to develop water resources in two other ways. First, upstream flood control projects have reduced the amount of water erosion in many areas. Second, power generation projects have in some areas reduced the cost of electric power to farmers.

But it seems unlikely that farmers will benefit in the future as much as they have in the past from the development of water resources. In the allocation of new supplies and even existing supplies of water, the increased demands of urban and industrial users, as well as the greater demands for water in environmental protection, will offer strong competition to farmers in their use of irrigation water. Unfortunately, since the abolition of the National Resources Planning Board in 1943, the executive branch of the federal government has no agency with the authority or the capability to prepare overall water resource plans and to evaluate the merits of the construction projects of such agencies as the Corps of Engineers and the Bureau of Reclamation. The formulation of plans for the development of water resources and the carrying out of the projects is, and has been for a long time, a strictly *ad hoc* business. Congressmen typically favor projects that benefit their constituents, and Congress as a whole tends to operate on the basis that the ultimate decision regarding a water resources development project should be made by the congressional delegation of the district concerned. This type of *ad hoc* decision making works reasonably well when resources are abundant, but it does not work well when resources become exceedingly scarce, as the resource water has now become. The allocation of water among competing uses has already given rise to serious problems in many parts of the nation, and as water becomes more scarce relative to needs those allocative problems will become frighteningly acute. In such future periods it seems unlikely that the national society will permit decisions to be made on the development and allocation of water resources in an almost accidental fashion — accidental in the sense of a political boundary drawn in the distant past, or who happens to chair an important committee of Congress at the time that a key decision is made with respect to the development of a natural resource. But how the society of the United States will move to a more rational decision process with respect to the development and allocation of its water resources, as of 1990, is far from clear.

Rural Electrification

The electrification of farms in the United States was slow prior to the creation of the Rural Electrification Administration (REA) in 1936. Less than 2 percent of all farms were electrified in 1919, and only 11 percent had electricity in 1935. But with the creation of the REA, the provision of electrical service to American farms increased rapidly. Some 30 percent of farms had service in 1940, some 77 percent in 1950, and 97 percent in 1960.

Two things occurred to speed the electrification of American farms after 1935. First, a series of technological developments occurring between 1910 and 1935 greatly lowered the cost of building electrical transmission lines; other advances permitted the use of higher voltages and involved the use of simplified and improved transformers at the farm site. These technological advances made it feasible to transmit electricity long distances to farmers living in the country. Second, rural electrification was stimulated by the creation of the REA. The REA was (and still is) empowered to make loans to cover the full cost of constructing power lines and other facilities to serve persons in rural places who were without central electrical service. In making loans, the REA was to give preference to nonprofit and cooperative associations and to public bodies.

Lines constructed by REA borrowers are designed to serve entire rural areas, including less densely settled sections as well as the more populous areas. "Area coverage" became the guiding principle of the REA as the task of electrifying rural America progressed. Under this principle, the test to determine whether electrical service should be extended to users in a particular section was not whether that extension of service would be self-supporting but whether the entire local system would be self-supporting.

The rural electric systems financed by REA are relatively small. There were more than one thousand such systems in operation in 1989. They operated 2.2 million miles of line, and they served some 11.6 million consumers.[6] The REA also makes loans to improve and extend telephone service in rural areas. Loans have been made to more than 635 commercial companies and to 241 cooperatives to finance modern dial telephone service for nearly three million rural subscribers. Farmers may also obtain loans from their REA cooperatives to install grain drying and farm storage facilities to enable them to hold their grain and engage in more orderly marketing.

Farm families in the United States, as of 1990, use electricity in numberless ways. They light their homes and barns with it. They use electricity to operate all kinds of laborsaving machines in the home: clothes washers and dryers, food freezers, sewing machines, and on and on. They use electricity to pump water for the home, to pump irrigation water, to water livestock automatically, and to heat water tanks in the frigid north. They use electricity to operate milking machines, mechanical feeders for cattle and poultry, brooders for chicks and pigs, and cooling systems for milk, eggs, and fruits and vegetables. Electricity provides the power to do literally hundreds of different jobs on American farms.

Complementary Developments in the Input and Marketing Industries

This development began, of course, in the nineteenth century with the work of the blacksmiths, tinkerers, and small machinery manufacturers on the input side and the operations of small flour mills and meat-packing establishments on the marketing side. The role of these industries expanded importantly throughout the nineteenth century. The machinery manufacturers developed retail outlets and spare parts inventories, and machinery repair shops gradually substituted for the blacksmiths. The marketing firms expanded in two ways: (1) by taking on more functions (e.g., assembling products, processing, storage, wholesaling, retail distribution) and (2) by taking on more products. By 1900 almost all products produced on farms moved through an involved marketing system before reaching the consumer.

But the great development of the input and marketing industries has occurred in the twentieth century. It will be recalled from table 10.2 that capital items used on the farm but purchased off the farm accounted for only 24 percent of all farm inputs in 1990, but by 1990 those capital items accounted for 57 percent of all farm inputs. For this transformation to occur on farms, a development had to take place in the complementary input industries. The petroleum industry, the tractor and farm machinery industry, the fertilizer industry, the pesticide industry, and the livestock feed industry had to develop the production plants and the distributive organization — the infrastructure — to permit and facilitate the capital transformation on farms. We will look at this infrastructure in some detail for one of these input industries — fertilizer.

Few industries have undergone as much change in the volume and quality of product as the fertilizer industry did in the 1950s and 1960s. During the ten-year period 1956–66, dollar sales of fertilizer to farmers increased by 64 percent, gross fertilizer tonnage consumed increasd 56 percent, *but the amount of primary plant nutrients consumed increased 106 percent.*

Each of the three primary plant nutrients — nitrogen, phosphorus and potassium — has specific production characteristics. The principal source of nitrogen is air and is, therefore, practically unlimited. Nitrogen combined with hydrogen under controlled conditions produces synthetic ammonia. Natural gas is the major feedstock for producing hydrogen. At least 88 percent of American ammonia production comes from the use of natural gas. Commercial production in the United States was begun in 1921 by one company. By 1940 there were seven firms in the United States producing ammonia with a capacity of 475 thousand tons. This industry-wide expansion continued up to 1982 when 136 establishments were producing ammonia in the United States with a capacity of 16 million tons.

Phosphorus is found in all rocks, but the concentration of phosphorus in most rocks is too low for economic recovery. Domestic deposits that yield a relatively high proportion of phosphorus are being worked in Florida, North California, Tennessee, Idaho, Montana, Utah, and Wyoming, with about 80 percent of the mine production of phosphate rock being mined in Florida by about twelve firms. After mining, phosphate rock is washed and ground and then routed through a chemical process. Its end products include ammonium phosphate, triple superphosphate, normal superphosphate, and other products. In response to both an expanding domestic demand and an expanding overseas market phosphate production capacity in the United States increased to 11 million tons in the early 1980s. This production capacity was distributed among some 128 firms in the late 1970s. With the onset of the farm depression in the early 1980s the number of producing firms declined to 109.

About 90 percent of the domestic production of potash comes from mines in New Mexico. There were seven firms producing potash in New Mexico in the late 1960s. The remainder of domestic production comes from California and Utah. The United States is a net importer of potash, with most imports coming from Canada. In 1990 imports accounted for about 60 percent of total domestic utilization.

Early distribution patterns for fertilizers followed classical lines: raw material producers sold only to fertilizer mixers, mixers sold only to retail dealers, and dealers sold to consumers. But this traditional distribution pattern has largely disappeared. Faced with a highly seasonal demand, many producers of primary nutrients have warehouses scattered across the country. Warehousing in the market areas reduces the risks of delivery interruptions at the height of the consumption season. Delivery from the warehouse to the mixer is usually by truck. In this way the storage function has shifted away from the mixing plant to the raw material producer, and the raw material producer has shifted the warehousing from the production plant to the market area.[7]

Plant nutrient use in the United States peaked in 1981 at 23.7 million tons. Since that date total plant nutrient use has slowly declined (see table 11.1). This decline resulted from a combination of causes: the income squeeze on producers induced by the farm depression of the 1980s and the pressure on producers to refine their production processes and thereby increase their production efficiency.[8]

Table 11.1. Fertilizer Utilization in the United States, 1980–89 (includes Puerto Rico)

Year	Primary Nutrient Use			
	N (Nitrogen)	P_2O_5 (Phosphates)	K_2O (Potash)	Total
	Million tons			
1980	11.4	5.4	6.2	23.1
1981	11.9	5.4	6.3	23.7
1982	11.0	4.8	5.6	21.4
1983	9.1	4.1	4.8	18.1
1984	11.1	4.9	5.8	21.8
1985	11.5	4.7	5.6	21.7
1986	10.4	4.2	5.1	19.7
1987	10.2	4.0	4.8	19.1
1988	10.5	4.1	5.0	19.6
1989	10.6	4.1	4.8	19.6

Source: *Agricultural Resources*, U.S. Department of Agriculture, Economic Research Service, AR-17, February 1990.

After farmers have converted inputs into product outputs, those products flow into the third component of the food and fiber system — the product marketing sector — for processing and distribution. The food marketing system of the United States entered the 1990s considerably changed in size, competitiveness, and performance from that of the 1970s and early 1980s. There were fewer firms in 1990 — some 380,000 as compared with 600,000 in the 1970s. This resulted from a record number of mergers, leveraged buyouts, and business failures. The surviving firms were more concentrated and deeper in debt. This huge food distribution system composed of processing, wholesaling, retailing, and food service firms — the largest marketing system in the nation — was also a slow-growing system. In 1980 these firms employed 11.5 percent of the total workers of the nation compared with 10 percent in 1990. A contributing factor to this relative decline in the food marketing system is that the share of disposable personal income Americans spent for food declined from 13.8 percent to 11.8 percent over the period 1980–90.

Another way of looking at the vast array of activities that comprise the product marketing sector — the marketing infrastructure that complements the farming sector — is through the marketing bill. The marketing bill describes the marketing sector in terms of its major cost components such as labor, packaging, transportation, and so on. The cost components of the marketing bill for farm food products may be seen in table 11.2. It will be noted that labor costs in the marketing sector account for almost one-half of total costs in recent years. To a significant degree, the product marketing sector is involved in supplying labor — labor employed in those tasks of food preparation and handling that no longer take place on the farm or in the home. It is concerned with the handling of food products — processing, packaging, movement and storage, and final preparation — that make intensive use of human labor. Thus the product marketing sector is a high cost sector. It undertakes many of those expensive labor-intensive operations that neither farmers nor housewives are willing to undertake in recent decades.[9]

Implications for Agricultural Development

In the first section of this chapter it was argued that "development of the agricultural sector without the services that flow from the required infrastructural elements is impossible." Does this mean that the pioneers would not have pushed across the continental United States

Table 11.2. Components of the Marketing Bill for Domestically Produced Farm Foods, Selected Years, 1960–90

Year	Labor[a]	Packaging Materials	Intercity Rail and Truck Transportation	Fuels and Electricity	Corporate Profits Before Taxes	Other[b]	Total Marketing Bill[c]
				Billion Dollars			
1960	19.7	5.4	4.1	N/A	2.1	13.3	44.6
1970	32.2	8.2	5.2	2.2	3.6	23.7	75.1
1975	48.3	13.3	8.4	4.6	7.1	29.7	111.4
1980	81.5	21.0	13.0	9.0	9.9	48.3	182.7
1985	115.6	26.9	16.5	13.1	10.4	76.5	259.0
1990	153.8	36.2	19.6	16.3	14.1	94.2	334.2

Source: *Food Cost Review, 1990*, U.S. Department of Agriculture, Economic Research Service, Agricultural Economic Report No. 651. N/A = Not available.

[a]Includes employee wages or salaries and their health and welfare benefits. Also includes estimated earnings of proprietors, partners, and family workers not receiving stated remuneration.

[b]Includes depreciation, rent, advertising and promotion, interest, taxes, licenses, insurance, professional services, local for-hire transportation, food service in schools, colleges, hospitals, and other institutions, and miscellaneous items. Data for 1960 also include fuels and electricity.

[c]The marketing bill is the difference between the farm value and consumer expenditures for these foods both at foodstores and away-from-home eating places. Thus, it covers processing, wholesaling, transportation, and retailing costs and profits.

and settled that great land mass if the requisite infrastructural elements for development had not been forthcoming? Not at all. The pioneers were crossing the Appalachian Mountains and settling the Ohio River valley during the period 1775 to 1820, it will be recalled. They were doing this in the almost complete absence of all infrastructural elements. Thus there is little reason to argue that those hardy pioneers would not have completed their westward movement to the Pacific in the absence of all those infrastructural elements discussed in this chapter.

But once the settlements were planted, the development scenario would have been very different in the absence of all the requisite infrastructural elements. The pioneer settlers would have remained pioneer settlers. Except for enclaves where natural waterways made it profitable to produce and sell surplus agricultural products — tobacco in the tidewater of Virginia, rice around Charleston, South Carolina, sugarcane along the Mississippi in Louisiana, and cotton along the Mississippi River and its principal tributaries — the pioneer settlers would have remained primarily subsistence farmers. This subsistence condition would have been forced upon them because markets for their surplus products could not have developed without an effective system of transport. In the absence of the requisite infrastructural elements, the agricultural sector of what is now the United States, as of say 1950, would have looked much like the agricultural sector of much of Latin America, as of 1950. Enclaves of commercial agriculture, possibly a plantation type of agriculture, would have existed where natural waterways made the production of a surplus economically feasible; the remainder of the agricultural plant would have taken the form of a low production, subsistence type of agriculture with low per capita incomes and grinding poverty.

What precisely then is the role of infrastructure in agricultural development? It is *to provide farm operators with favorable economic options.* The effective water and rail transport system built in the United States in the nineteenth century provided ambitious, aggressive farm operators with the option of shifting out of subsistence crop and livestock production and into the production of commodities for which their area had a comparative advantage. They could now produce a surplus of those commodities for which they had a comparative advantage, sell that surplus in the commercial market, and then purchase supplies that they needed from the proceeds of the sale of their surplus. The development of the complementary input and marketing industries further widened the options of farmers —

provided them with new and improved production options and new and more profitable commodity options. The development of water resources and electric power widened still further the options of farmers.

The building of infrastructure does not guarantee agricultural development; it provides the opportunity for development. If the farmers involved are literate and understand the economic implications of the options confronting them, if they are not excessively constrained from reaping economic rewards, if they are industrious, and if they know or believe that they, their families, and their immediate community will gain from the exploitation of a favorable option, then the provision of infrastructure by society will serve as a powerful motivating force to agricultural development. These conditions were met to an important degree in the United States in the nineteenth and twentieth centuries. Farmers were economically literate. Farmers reaped close to the full gains, as well as the losses, of their enterprise. Farmers and their families were hard workers. And as owner-operators of viable-sized units they had a vital stake in the development of their farm units and their community. Thus to a great extent farmers and their families took advantage of the favorable options made available to them by society through the building of physical infrastructure. In this context the agricultural sector developed rapidly, the real incomes of farm people increased significantly, and rural communities prospered in the long run.

Suggested Reading

Frederick, Kenneth D., and James C. Hanson. *Water for Western Agriculture.* Washington, D.C.: Resources for the Future, 1982.

Johnson, James C., and Donald F. Wood, *Contemporary Logistics,* 4th ed. New York: Macmillan, 1990. Part II, Chaps. 4 and 5.

North, Douglass C. *Growth and Welfare in the American Past: A New Economic History,* 2nd ed. Englewood Cliffs, N.J.: Prentice-Hall, 1974. Chap. 9.

Robertson, Ross M. *History of the American Economy,* 2nd ed. New York: Harcourt, Brace, and World, 1964. Chaps. 6, 12, and 19.

Taylor, George Rogers. *The Transportation Revolution, 1815–1860.* Vol. IV of *The Economic History of the United States.* New York: Harper and Row, 1951. Chaps. 2, 3, 4, and 5.

U.S. Department of Agriculture. *Power to Produce: 1960 Yearbook of Agriculture.* Washington, D.C.: Government Printing Office. Pp. 69–88.

U.S. Department of Agriculture. Economic Research Service. *The Food and Fiber System — How It Works.* Agricultural Information Bulletin No. 383, March 1975.

U.S. Department of Agriculture. Economic Research Service. *A History of Water Resources Programs, 1800–1960.* Miscellaneous Publication No. 1233, June 1972.

CHAPTER 12

BUILDING SOCIAL INFRASTRUCTURE
Education and Research

Faith in Education

The Puritan settlers of the Massachusetts Bay Colony had an abiding faith in education. But the purposes of education in the early years of the colony were not those ascribed to education in the present day. The purposes of education were not to undergird the democratic process or to foster new ideas or to promote creativeness; they were to teach children discipline and to reinforce the religious orthodoxy of the puritans. The acts of 1642 and 1647, which required all parents and masters to teach children and apprentices to read and write and to establish schools in every town of fifty or more households, had as their objective to teach children and apprentices "to understand the principles of religion and the capital laws of the country." And the principles of religion were not those of any religion; they were the principles of the strict Calvinist faith of the Massachusettes Bay Colony.[1]

Although religious motives loomed large in the establishment of universal education in Massachusetts in the 1600s, there were secular motives involved from the beginning, and those secular motives became increasingly important in the 1700s as the Puritan orthodoxy began to break down. From the beginning New Englanders viewed education as a way of "getting ahead." Parents viewed education as a vehicle for their children to learn a legal means of support: for learning a trade, for becoming an astute trader or businessman or perhaps a professional man. Thus education in the Bay Colony always had a practical side and a developmental side which became increasingly strong as the colony grew older.

It is also true that education, even dogmatic religious education, has a way of stimulating people to think for themselves. Education in the Massachusetts Bay Colony was no exception to the rule; heretical thinking with respect to religious theology soon manifested itself in the colony. Challenging official church doctrine was not only a personal sin; it operated to undermine and destroy the tight theocratic state that had been established in the colony. Thus such heretics as Roger Williams and Anne Hutchinson were driven out of the colony and into the wilderness. The result was the establishment of new colonies in New England with different and/or more tolerant views on religion.

So strong was the faith of the Puritan colonists in education that within a few short years after they sailed into the Boston harbor in 1630, they had established a complete school system: elementary schools to educate all young people sufficiently so that they could read and understand the Bible and the religious and civil laws of the colony; secondary schools to train future leaders of the church and state for college; and a college that would ensure an educated ministry as well as an adequately prepared professional class. New Englanders carried this faith in education west with them. In 1803, when the Congress admitted Ohio into the Union under the Ordinance of 1787, Section 16 in every township was reserved for the support of public schools within each township. The pattern of support for public education established in Ohio became the accepted pattern of educational support throughout the Old Northwest and later the Far West. Time after time Congress reaffirmed in legislation that Section 16 in each township (or if Section 16 were already occupied, that comparable land be provided) should be reserved for the support of public education in the new states being admitted to the Union. It is estimated that some 77 million acres of land were reserved in new states admitted to the Union for the support of common schools.

But it would be a mistake to visualize this strong faith in education as being universal throughout the colonies and in the early years of the nation. Where the Puritans adopted universal education as a means of instituting discipline and perpetuating religious orthodoxy, Governor Berkeley of Virginia elected to pursue the opposite policy, namely, keeping the masses in ignorance, for achieving the same ends. And this was the general educational policy pursued in the southern colonies and the southern states in the early years of the nation. It was unlawful to teach black slaves to read or write; little or no provision was made for educating the main body of white citizens; education was viewed as a luxury to be afforded by the rich through the vehicle of private tutors and private schools.[2] The landed aristocracy of the South produced some well-trained men — lawyers, physicians, and writers — who had an important impact on the young, developing nation. But the masses, blacks and whites, for the most part remained in a state of ignorance through the end of the nineteenth century. Universal education was not perceived as a necessary and integral part of a developing society in the Old South before the Civil War. And it took a long, long time to replace that negative view of education for the masses following the Civil War. In fact, it is not fully replaced as of 1978.

Rural Primary Education

As the country was settled in the nineteenth century, the one-room schoolhouse located every few miles, with grades one through eight, presided over by a young teacher, either male or female, became the rule in rural areas. This pattern became well established in the post-Civil War years and continued until the 1920s when improved roads and the automobile led to consolidated rural schools. A common size for one-room country schoolhouses was sixteen by twenty feet with windows on each side. One end might be partitioned off for coal storage and a coatroom. In later years the schoolroom was probably equipped with a blackboard. In the winter the room would be heated with some kind of iron or potbellied stove. Maintenance of the schoolhouses varied with the community; some schoolhouses were kept in a state of good repair, but others were not. The school yard was usually large enough to permit the playing of various kinds of informal games; it would contain two outhouses, one for girls and one for boys; and there might be a small barn for the stabling of horses. The physical facilities were typically spartan.

The number of students might vary from ten to thirty, with none, or one, or a few students in each of the eight grades. Depending upon the time period, the teacher might or might not have a certificate to teach issued by the state, and his or her training probably would consist of education through the eighth grade plus one to several years of advanced training of some kind, although many teachers would begin teaching in a country school with only an eighth-grade education. Each teacher was expected to maintain discipline at all times and to teach all subjects in each grade. Textbooks in the nineteenth century were scarce and teaching materials even scarcer. Students often learned to write and did their "sums" on small individual slates. Individual teachers varied greatly in their ability to teach and to stimulate their students. Some writers extol the abilities of the country schoolteachers to inspire their students to learn and to take advantage of their limited educational experience; others describe the country schoolteacher as little more than a drillmaster, or disciplinarian, who made liberal use of the rod. Perhaps the typical teacher was to be found somewhere between these two extremes.

It should be of interest to read how one country school, District 26, got started in Martin County, Minnesota, in the late 1860s.

In 1865 and 1866 several families came out in covered wagons from Pennsylvania, New York, and Wisconsin, and made a small settlement on a little stream, known on Joseph Jean Nicollet's first map of this territory as Chanyaska or Shinneiska river.

The M. A. Seymour family home became the nucleus of the settlement. These people were all homesteaders. Mrs. Seymour had brought along a number of school books from their old home in New York state. As soon as they were settled in their sod and log cabin, she began to teach her children from these books. Other neighboring homesteaders sent their children to her home to be taught. Within that first year the homesteaders within a radius of five or six miles came together and organized a school district, receiving the number 26 from the county commissioners. Since the Seymour home was too small to accommodate all the pupils, it was necessary to build a schoolhouse. They dug a hole in the high bank of the creek, with a floor space about 16 by 16 feet. They cut down elm and oak trees which grew nearby, cut out planks by hand for roof supports, for the front of the schoolhouse, and for benches for the teacher and children to sit on. Since there were only summer sessions of school at first there was only an opening in front for an entrance. But they did afford two panes of glass for windows.

From the first day school started, a record was kept. Fortunately one of the first teachers, Mrs. M. L. Pope, kept that old record book and from it this information is given. The Teacher's Daily Register was started for the summer term of two months, May and June, 1870; Miss Emma Griswold, teacher. There were 21 pupils registered in ages ranging from 6 years to 23 years. A year later school was again opened with one of the former pupils, Ella Weber, 17, as the teacher. The number on the register was increased by three. Wages were from $12 to $20 a month and the teacher boarded 'round from one family to another during the term. There was also a visitor's register showing that parents frequently visited school and that, at such times, "the older pupils assisted with declamations and anecdotes which enabled us to pass the time pleasantly indeed." . . .

A larger frame building was put up a few years later more centrally located in the district, situated on a knoll on the prairie alone with the nearest farm place a mile distant. This building was equipped with a stove so terms could be held in the winter. There were windows on two sides. On June 15, 1892, a cyclone struck the buildings and all records were destroyed. One of the pupils, Matt Posivio, tells the story: "Miss Maggie O'Hara was the teacher. She called us inside when she saw the funnel cloud coming. . . .

"The last thing I remember was the teacher standing up in front repeating over and over the Lord's Prayer and the kids trying to follow. Then came a lifting feeling, I gripped my desk to brace myself. The next thing we knew we were lying up at Woods (the nearest farm place) on straw strewn on the floor with our mouths filled with dirt. Old Doc Harnden was looking us over." Several were badly injured but no one was killed.

A new frame building was put up a half mile away on a higher knoll with a view of the countryside for miles in every direction.[3]

But regardless of the abilities of the typical country schoolteacher, his or her teaching responsibilities were so broad, the teaching materials so scant, and the physical facilities so limited that the educational experience of the student had to be extremely limited. But limited as it was, it could be thorough and it was utilitarian. The subjects studied were spelling, grammar, reading, writing, and arithmetic. Students were required to go over the limited teaching materials time and time again, until the better ones at least became good spellers, took pride in their penmanship, could compose a gramatically correct sentence, and could solve simple arithmetic problems. To repeat, it was a limited educational experience, but it did produce a rural society of literate farm men and women.

The graduates of rural primary schools could read advertisements and catalogs with some judgment, understand the content and conditions of contracts they entered into, make rough calculations of enterprise costs and returns, compute simple interest, and in general behave like rational businessmen in the operation of their farms. They could also read their state and local newspapers with pleasure and interest, follow national and community affairs, and participate in an informed way in the political and social affairs of their nation and their community.

It is easy to become nostalgic about the one-room country schoolhouse and attribute educational results to it that were rarely, if ever, achieved. But it would be a greater mistake to underestimate the contribution that rural primary education, as provided in one-room country schoolhouses across the land, made to the development of rural society. *That educational experience lifted farm people in the United States out of the class of peasants.* It enabled some of them to become farm businessmen who could appraise accurately the options open to them. It enabled others to transfer to nonfarm employment with relative ease. And it enabled most of them to become effective participants in the social and political processes of which they were a part. Farm people who could read and write and make simple arithmetic calculations no longer had to live by tradition; they could and did become rational decision makers in economic and social processes. This is not to say that they always made the best or the correct decisions. But it is to say that basic literacy emancipated American farmers from the dead hand of tradition.

The Push for Higher Education for Agriculture

During the period 1820–60, local and country agricultural societies were organized across the nation. Some 300 such organizations were sufficiently active in 1852 to report their existence to an emerging national organization. These local associations federated into state societies in most states. These state societies formed the United States Agricultural Society in 1852.

Agitation for the creation of scientific schools, industrial schools, and technical agricultural schools became one of the principal activities of these state and local agricultural societies. Their efforts met with success in many states; various kinds of small technical schools were established during this period with the support and backing of the state governments and local agricultural societies. The Agricultural College of the State of Michigan, located on a large farm near Lansing, was established in 1855. During the years 1845–47, a Department of Philosophy and the Arts came into being at Yale with three professorships for the study of agriculture and the arts. This unit was later known as the Yale Scientific School. In 1854 the Pennsylvania legislature passed an act creating a "Farmers High School" with the purpose of educating the youth of Pennsylvania "in various branches of science, learning, and practical agriculture as they connected with each other." This institution later became the Pennsylvania State College and now is the Pennsylvania State University. Provision was made for the establishment of a state university in the Congressional Enabling Act of 1846, which created the state of Wisconsin. The new state of Wisconsin incorporated the University of Wisconsin in 1848. A professorship of chemistry and natural science was created in 1854 to offer lectures in agricultural chemistry and "the application of science to the useful arts." After a heated struggle the

University of Wisconsin was reorganized in 1866 to include an agriculture unit, and the federal land grant under the Morrill Act was given to the university.

Efforts to establish a system of state agricultural colleges across the nation with federal support were stepped up during the 1850s. The new United States Agricultural Society pressed for the establishment of agricultural schools, colleges, and model farms with federal support. The state of Illinois, acting on the Turner plan for a system of industrial universities, memorialized the Congress of the United States in 1853 to pass legislation "donating to each state in the Union an amount of public lands not less in value than five hundred thousand dollars, for the liberal endowment of a system of industrial universities, one in each State in the Union. . . ." But these efforts, including the first land grant college bill introduced into Congress in 1857 by Congressman Justin Morrill of Vermont, were unsuccessful. In the main, they were unsuccessful because the southern congressional leaders, who held most of the key committee chairmanships in the Congress, were opposed to the public support of education in general and were strongly opposed to federal support of higher education in particular. Bills proposing federal support for industrial universities or agricultural colleges were simply bottled up in committees by unfriendly committee chairmen. A modestly revised land grant college bill introduced by Congressman Morrill in 1859, which was enacted by Congress, was vetoed by President Buchanan. In his veto message President Buchanan argued that the legislation was extravagantly expensive and that it was unconstitutional. The veto could not be overridden; thus hopes for the early establishment of a system of federally supported agricultural and mechanical arts colleges were dead.

The secession of the southern states from the Union in 1861 greatly changed the political complexion of the Congress. Further, presidential candidate Abraham Lincoln committed himself to supporting the establishment of a system of state universities that emphasized the study of agriculture and the industrial arts. Thus the second land grant college bill, introduced by Congressman Morrill in December of 1861, was passed by Congress in June 1862 and signed into law by President Lincoln on July 2, 1862. As has been repeated many times, the purpose of this legislation was the endowment, support, and maintenance of at least one college in each state (accepting the terms of law) ". . . where the leading object shall be, *without excluding other scientific and classical studies,* and including military tactics, to teach such branches of learning as are related to agriculture and the mechanic arts. . . ." [Italics added.]

Under the provisions of the Morrill Act, each state accepting the terms of the act was to receive 30,000 acres of public land for each member of its congressional delegation. This meant that New York state received some 990,000 acres and Kansas obtained only 90,000. Further, states like New York, which had no public lands within its borders, received land script which could be located in any western state or territory in which there were public lands open for settlement. This procedure for making land grants was hardly fair to new, poor, western states (for example, Kansas), which received small land grants and which were required to locate those grants within their own borders. But the older, eastern states would not have supported the land grant college legislation without some such land allotment formula. Thus the land allotment compromise was accepted, and the land grant colleges and universities came into being.

Only seventeen of the states and territories turned their land grant over to the established state university. All the rest of the states established separate agricultural and mechanical arts colleges — A & M colleges. And many of the states, especially in the South, established two A & M colleges — one for whites and one for blacks.[4] So many states saddled themselves with a financial overhead and duplication of facilities that came close to crippling them in the dark days of their early existence.

For many years after the opening of the new colleges, whether as part of existing state universities or as separate A & M colleges, very little was done toward training rural youth to become expert agriculturalists. Professors of agriculture had to be found where none had previously existed. Students had to be found where those with the necessary secondary background were more interested in becoming medical doctors and lawyers than in becoming expert agriculturalists, and those interested in studying technical agriculture typically did not have the necessary prerequisites. And the agricultural sciences had to be developed where none had existed before.

These new colleges had other and equally serious problems. There was the question of the proper mission of these colleges. The men who fought the battle for industrial education shared a common goal: the elevation of agriculture and mechanical arts to the prestige of the learned professions. These were the "narrow gaugers," who wanted to exclude from the curriculum of these new colleges or universities all subjects that did not contribute to the "practical" education of farmers and mechanics. At the opposite extreme were the classical scholars and preachers, who up to this point in time had provided the intellectual leadership for institutions of higher learning and who had no concept of, and no interest in, the educational goals of proponents of industrial education. Somewhere in between were the "broad gaugers," who wanted to combine the new education with the old by adding agricultural, scientific, and engineering courses to the established curriculum rather than by subtracting from it. These factions were at war with one another in the land grant colleges and universities throughout the latter half of the nineteenth century. In some cases these wars of mission, which involved the administrators, the faculties, the trustees, and outside pressure groups, practically wrecked the fledgling institutions. In other cases, where the practical agricultural forces won out, the colleges of agriculture forged ahead in terms of buildings and enrollment, if not in the development of the sciences. And in still other cases, where the classical scholars and preachers were victorious, the concept of agricultural education atrophied.

In general, the growth in agricultural education at the college level was slow and uneven during the 1870s and 1880s. It took a long time to dispel the idea that agriculture was a subject that could be taught by one instructor in one course, and there were many disappointments. But a number of the better agricultural colleges had by 1900 developed departments of animal husbandry, dairy husbandry, agricultural chemistry, agronomy or soil science, horticulture, and entomology. Such colleges also had an experiment station, an extension department, and one to several demonstration farms. By 1900 some of the better agricultural colleges had become effective instruments of agricultural education; they had a specialized faculty, a respectable number of students, and some course content in the agricultural disciplines to teach those students. For these colleges the rough, rocky period was past.

Adding the Research Component

As the colleges of agriculture in the land grant institutions struggled in the 1870s to become viable organizations, it became clear to some of the leaders in those institutions that there was a need for experimentation and research in the agricultural area to build knowledge and to create a set of agricultural sciences. In 1875 the state of Connecticut established an independent agricultural experiment station. In 1886 the Committee on Agriculture of the House of Representatives noted that twelve states had established agricultural experiment stations, attached to the agricultural colleges in all cases except Connecticut, and that several more were undertaking experiment station work without a formal experiment station organization. This activity led, as might be expected, to one request after another for federal support for the experiment station work. As a result of the agitation, Congress in 1887 passed the Hatch Act, which provided each state $15,000 a year *from the sale of public lands* to support the work of the agricultural experiment stations. This money was to be given to the land grant colleges except in the few cases where independent experiment stations had already been established. The Hatch Act spelled out in some detail the *practical* nature of the work that should be pursued in these new agricultural stations.

The center of struggle between the practical-minded agriculturalists, or "narrow gaugers," on the one hand, and the more theoretically inclined, whether classical scholars or chemists, on the other hand, simply shifted from the college to the experiment station. Except for one area, agricultural chemistry, there was no tradition, no set of guiding principles, to direct the research and experimental work of these new stations. The work of Justus Liebig in Germany and his book, *Organic Chemistry and Its Application to Agriculture and Phynology*, published in 1840, had a major impact in America. Liebig's work, particularly in soil chemistry, gave the many agricultural societies in the United States something solid to discuss and a base from which to make recommendations regarding soil fertilization. Challenged by the Liebig ideas, several Americans went to Germany to study with Liebig: Eben Norton Horsford, John A. Porter, and Samuel W. Johnson. On their return to the United States, these men met with varying degrees of success in presenting the Liebig ideas to the American farm public. But they, with John Pitkin Norton, who studied at Edinburgh, did succeed in implanting the science of agricultural chemistry in American universities. These men established the principles for guiding and directing the work of their students and their students' students in the science of agricultural chemistry.[5]

But outside the area of agricultural chemistry, should these fledgling experiment stations be concerned with plowing a straight furrow or studying plant genetics? No one really knew, but the opinions were varied, extreme, and strident. What these experiment stations required, and what a few were fortunate enough to find, were leaders who had a commitment to and an understanding of the world of scientific disciplines and who at the same time were able to forge political alliances with farm leaders and businessmen to the mutual advantage of all concerned. Professor Charles Rosenberg calls such leaders "research-entrepreneurs," and he describes the experience of three highly successful "research-entrepreneurs": William H. Henry of Wisconsin, Eugene Davenport of Illinois, and Eugene W. Hilgard of California. Each built a highly productive experiment station for his state out of practically nothing. Each was able to do this by first recognizing the technical needs of his lay constituents and tailoring a research policy to meet their needs, and second by placing a high priority on professional values and scientific realities and in this context seeking out and hiring men of ability and talent and providing them with a reasonably satisfactory research environment in which to work.[6] Walking this sociopolitical tightrope was no easy task; few land grant colleges found leaders who could do it, and only comparatively few agricultural experiment stations prospered. But some did. Perhaps a dozen agricultural experiment stations were doing highly professional work in the agricultural sciences by 1900. Once the scientific properties and relations of plants, animals, and the soil were understood, the technologies for combating plant and animal disease and for increasing yields could begin to flow forth. And they did so after 1900. But the great technological payoff from investments in agricultural research and experimentation did not occur until the 1930s.

The state agricultural experiment stations in the second half of the twentieth century have become great research centers involved in both basic scientific work and adaptive research work. The research work of the stations is funded from three sources: the federal government, the state governments, and private business. Most research workers in the stations hold positions in the agricultural college and divide their time between teaching and research.[7] The typical agricultural experiment station is thus an integral part of the land grant college of agriculture, and the two components are indistinguishable to the outside observer. The only difference is that the work of the agricultural college and that of the agricultural experiment station fall under separate categories in the university budget.

It would be a mistake, however, to think that all research in agriculture takes place in the state agricultural experiment stations. Work in the state experiment stations has been complemented since the 1870s by work in the U.S. Department of Agriculture. It is probably the case that in the nineteenth century scientific work progressed more rapidly in the U.S. Department of Agriculture than in the state experiment stations. The mission of the U.S. Department of Agriculture with respect to research was more clear-cut, and it was easier for this department to get funding. Thus by 1900 many of the best-known professional workers in the agricultural sciences were members of the research units of the U.S. Department of Agriculture, and those individuals were playing a leading role in the development of the agricultural sciences. But in the twentieth century the U.S. Department of Agriculture has lost its preeminent role in agricultural research, primarily as a result of the continuous strengthening of the professional staffs of the land grant colleges of agriculture and pressures on the U.S. Department of Agriculture to assign higher priorities to its action programs dealing with the economic ills of farmers.

The expanding research budgets of the state agricultural experiment stations and the USDA may be seen in table 12.1. Much of the budgetary expansion shown in table 12.1 is due to price inflation. But if the combined research budgets of the state experiment stations and the USDA are deflated for the price inflation, it is still true that the resources devoted to agricultural research increased many, many times between 1920 and 1990.

Research in agriculture is not limited to public institutions. Private firms have become increasingly important in this regard. Although hard figures for the total expenditures of private firms on agricultural research and development are difficult to come by, it is estimated that the R&D budgets of private firms totaled $2,359 million in 1984.[8] In rough terms this means that private firms accounted for approximately 57 percent of the total R&D budget for agriculture in 1984, and public agencies for 43 percent. Thus, it is clear that the national budget for R&D in agriculture, as of the 1980s, is very large — in excess of $4 billion.

Further, a rough division of labor in the R&D area of agriculture has developed in the twentieth century. The public institutions have come to concentrate on the training of scientific personnel and the more basic aspects of research. The private firms tend to concentrate on the development of technologies that can be sold to farmers in a specific geographic area. Private firms are likely to focus on the development of such things as a hybrid variety of corn for a particular area, or a feed mixture for baby pigs, or a new harvester for a specific tree fruit. In this rough division of labor the public institutions produce the knowledge that enters the public domain, whereas the private firms produce tech-

Table 12.1 Public Expenditures in Millions of Dollars for Research and Extension in Agriculture, Selected Years, 1920–90

Year	State Agricultural Experiment Stations	U.S. Department of Agriculture	Federal-State Extension
1920	5.0	7.7	14.7
1930	13.1	15.5	24.3
1940	16.8	22.1	33.1
1950	48.2	46.8	74.6
1960	120.3	105.2	141.7
1970	296.1	238.7	290.7
1980	853[a]	367[b]	683[c]
1985	1,259[a]	496[b]	997[c]
1990	1,807[a]	593[b]	1,662[d]

Sources: SAES: 1915–60, "Report on the Agricultural Experiment Stations," published by Office of Experiment Stations through 1953 and by Agricultural Research Service from 1954 through 1960; 1961–73, "Funds for Research at State Agricultural Experiment Stations," Cooperative State Experiment Station Service, U.S. Department of Agriculture.

USDA: 1915–53, "Report of the Director of Finance," U.S. Department of Agriculture; 1954–73, "Appropriations for Research and Education," prepared by Office of Budget and Finance, U.S. Department of Agriculture.

Extension: 1915–55, "Annual Report of Cooperative Extension Work in Agriculture and Home Economics," Federal Extension Service, U.S. Department of Agriculture; 1956–73, unpublished data from the extension service.

[a]Obtained from Cooperative State Research Service, U.S. Department of Agriculture, Washington, D.C. Includes funds to forestry and veterinary schools and Tuskegee University.

[b]*USDA Budget Summary*, U.S. Department of Agriculture, for the relevant years.

[c]Wayne D. Rasmussen, *Taking the University to the People: Seventy-five Years of Cooperative Extension* (Ames: Iowa State Press, 1989), appendix C.

[d]Obtained by telephone call to Federal Extension Service, U.S. Department of Agriculture, Washington, D.C.

niques for which there is a ready market.

Finally, it should be recognized that a state of science and technology can be reached with respect to agriculture where the R&D establishment must keep turning out new and improved technologies and practices at a rapid pace in order for the consumers of food and fiber products to hold their consumption levels even. This is the case for many reasons: the increased scarcity of certain inputs (for example, petroleum); the rapidly growing world population; the incidence of new plant and animal diseases; the mounting problem of pollution. Just to offset and hence negate the above set of forces so that the level of consumption of the average American consumer holds constant, a continuous flow of new and improved technologies based upon research and development is required. And to lift the level of consumption of the average consumer requires an increased flow of new and improved technologies, which requires in turn an increased flow of resources into the R&D establishment. This appears to be the position that the United States now finds itself in; it must invest at least four billion dollars a year on research and development in the food and agricultural sector so that the average consumer does not experience a decline in food consumption. And should the force of the adverse factors noted above become more powerful, the volume of resources devoted to research and development would need to be stepped up to hold constant the level of food consumption of the average American consumer. In this sense, research and development in food and agriculture have become an unending process.

Adult Education

The educational efforts of the land grant colleges of agriculture quickly took an outreaching form. One of the things that the new agricultural colleges discovered in the 1870s was that they had a hard time attracting full-time students. Most farm boys did not, or could not, attend secondary schools and hence were not eligible to enter college. Also, it was often the case that well-to-do farmers who did plan to send their sons to college did not want them to study agriculture; they wanted their sons to study for one of the prestigious professions — to become a lawyer or medical doctor. So to survive, the new agricultural colleges went looking for students. This meant developing educational materials and educational institutional arrangements for those people who had struggled long and hard to bring the land grant agricultural colleges into being, namely, adult farmers with an incentive to improve their production practices.

Various kinds of institutional arrangements were pioneered during the period 1870–1900 to reach farmers. Lecture series on special topics were developed; winter short courses were developed for young men and women lacking the necessary prerequisites for regular college entrance; and all kinds of training institutes were developed. By 1900 almost all the agricultural colleges were engaged in this kind of educational work, and it was highly popular with farm people.

Cornell University was the leader in this adult education work. By 1897 it had an adult education program that covered the entire state, supported by an annual state appropriation of $25,000. The Cornell University program was composed of five elements: (1) local experiments as a means of teaching, (2) popular, readable farmers' bulletins, (3) itinerant horticultural schools, (4) instruction in nature study in rural schools, and (5) instruction by means of correspondence and reading courses. In 1902, some 30,000 persons were enrolled in the farmers' reading course, some 9,500 in a reading course for farm wives, 20,000 in a junior naturalist course, and 26,000 in a course for beginning gardeners. This extension work attracted national attention, and many other states adopted variations of it in the early 1900s.

Interest in adult education, or extension work, developed rapidly in the early 1900s. The Association of Agricultural Colleges established a standing committee on extension work in 1905. That committee defined extension work as follows:

Extension teaching in agriculture embraces those forms of instruction, in subjects having to do with improved methods of agricultural production and with the general welfare of the rural population, that are offered to people not enrolled as resident pupils in educational institutions.

By 1913 colleges in thirty-eight states had extension departments, and appropriations for this kind of work from state and local sources aggregated more than one million dollars. Without question, the extension type of education was popular among farm people, and the demand for it was increasing so rapidly that state and local governments and the agricultural colleges felt they could not meet this need. Thus the agricultural colleges and their farmer clients turned once again to the federal government for funding support.

The Smith-Lever Cooperative Extension Act, which was passed by Congress in the spring of 1914 and signed into law by President Wilson on May 8, 1914, greatly increased the extension work within each state and fundamentally changed the relations of the agricultural colleges to the federal government on the one hand and their relations with rural communities on the other. This act provided each state that accepted the provisions of the act with an appropriation of $10,000 annually, plus an additional amount based on a formula involving the size of the rural population of the state. But the state would receive this additional amount only to the extent that it was matched with funds from within the state. The act was passed with the understanding that the county extension work sponsored by the federal government, which in 1914 was under way in 900 counties, would be incorporated into the state extension work now to be supported by the Smith-Lever Act. Further, the act permitted contributions by counties, local authorities, or private individuals and organizations, as well as the states and colleges, to be used to match federal funding in the support of county extension work. This latter provision was to create difficult problems in the years to come, since one of the program features of the emerging American Farm Bureau Federation during this period was providing funding support and program guidance for the work of the county agent.

The land grant colleges of agriculture at first had considerable difficulty adjusting to the concepts of *continuing* adult education at the county level through the vehicle of the county agent and the close supervision of the use of federal funds in state and local education. But the U.S. Department of Agriculture and the agricultural colleges worked out a joint memorandum of understanding that was satisfactory to the leaders in the land grant colleges and universities. The memorandum provided: (1) that each state shall organize and maintain a definite and distinct administrative division within the college of agriculture for extension work, (2) that the head of this division, called the extension director, shall administer *all* the extension work within the state as the joint representative of the college and the U.S.D.A., (3) that all funds for extension work in agriculture and home economics work shall be expended through such extension divisions, and (4) that the U.S.D.A. shall cooperate with the extension divisions of the colleges in all educational work done by the U.S.D.A. within the states.[9]

The development of the cooperative extension system developed rapidly under the Smith-Lever Act once the memorandum of understanding between the agricultural colleges and the U.S. Department of Agriculture was approved. By 1917 all the principal features of the system were in place. Total funding from federal, state, and local sources for this work increased from $3.6 million in 1915 to $6.1 million in 1917. The number of counties with agricultural agents increased from 928 in 1914 to 1,434 in 1917; the number of home demonstration agents increased from 279 to 537 over the same period. The total number of persons engaged in extension work in the United States in 1917 was 4,100 — 2,983 men and 1,117 women.

Extension work in rural communities was firmly institutionalized by 1917. The county agent traveling about in his Model T Ford became the symbol of technological advance on American farms for the next decade or so. He was the principal vehicle through which new production practices and new technologies developed in the agricultural colleges and in the U.S. Department of Agriculture were transmitted or extended to farmers. But all was not success and harmony. Some difficult problems had to be resolved. The relationship of a private farm organization, the American Farm Bureau, for example, to a public educational program had to be resolved. It was resolved by requiring the Farm Bureau to withdraw from the public extension program, but in some states that was not easy. The status of extension workers in the land grant colleges and universities was resolved in different ways in different states. The strange role of a federal employee, the extension worker, working in a state institution, the land grant college, required considerable adjustment by all parties over the years. But this hybrid organization, the Cooperative Federal-State Extension Service, prospered and became a highly succesful organizational system for carrying the fruits of scientific research to farmers.

As technology has become more complex and the technological needs of farmers have become more exacting, the organizational form of the extension service has changed. This is particularly true in the post-World War II period. The county agent is no longer the principal technological conduit to farmers. The extension service in each state has developed many and varied specialists whose function it is to carry specific technical information to farmers. In this context the county extension agent serves as something of a program chairman for his farmer clients. He arranges meetings and conferences on different technical subjects to which he brings extension specialists and other technical specialists to provide farmers with the latest technical information in subject areas in which they are interested or are having problems. In this organizational arrangement the extension service is providing farmers with essentially the same service in 1990 as it did in 1917, but the new organizational arrangement recognizes the increased specialization in science and technology.

The extension service is not, as of 1990, the only supplier of technical information to farmers. There are numerous other suppliers of technical information that should be mentioned. The various breed associations, crop improvement associations, and farm management associations regularly supply their members with up-to-date technical information. The farm newspapers and journals continue to be an important source of technical information, as has been the case for many decades. Important new sources are the feed, seed, fertilizer, and machinery salesmen, or representatives, of private firms and farmer-owned cooperatives. The information provided by salesmen may in some cases be biased, but it is likely to be more specific and possibly more relevant to production conditions of a particular geographical area than, for example, the information provided by a state extension specialist. Thus farmers are increasingly obtaining their technical information regarding inputs from the area sales representatives of private firms and farmers' cooperative associations. Finally, some of the larger, more aggressive farmers are hiring technical consultants and consulting services to provide them with technical information as it relates to their specific production situations. As the size of farms continues to grow, this source of technical information will almost certainly become increasingly important.

In sum, as new and improved technology, based upon research and scientific development, has played a larger and larger role in farm operations, farmers have sought and have obtained more effective means for informing themselves of those technological developments. This is the clear historical record in the United States for the past 100 years. Adult education did not have to be forced upon farmers. The better ones came looking for it. Given this strong demand, the state and federal governments, working primarily through the land grant colleges of agriculture, and private associations and firms as well, have developed effective institutional arrangements for providing farmers with the technical information, knowledge, and skills they were seeking.

The Modern Agricultural College Complex

The modern agricultural college of a land grant university is a large and complex establishment. The annual budget for all functions of one of the larger colleges of agriculture, as of 1990, will run in excess of $40 million. The number of permanent professional staff members will approach 400. It will operate numerous experimental stations and farms across its state. And it will undertake many and varied activities, only some of which relate directly to farming.

The agricultural college, as it has evolved over time, has three principal functions: resident instruction, research, and extension. The work and budgets of the college are thus divided functionally into those three categories. But for purposes of administration, colleges of agriculture are typically divided into subject matter departments (e.g., horticulture, agronomy, agricultural engineering, agricultural economics). There are likely to be some twenty departments in the larger colleges of agriculture. The number of professional staff members in these departments may range from ten to fifty.

Within the departments it is not unusual for a staff member to spend half of his or her time teaching and half time on research, or half of his or her time teaching and half time on extension. And the work of some staff members may be split three ways: part-time resident instruction, part-time research, and part-time extension. Two points regarding the work of the modern agricultural college should thus be recognized: (1) three very distinct lines of work or activities are undertaken, and (2) there is much administrative flexibility in the way that work is carried out.

It should further be recognized that these three distinct work functions tend to complement one another. The teaching and extension activities are enriched and enlivened by the research activity. And questions and problems that surface in the teaching and extension activities act to challenge the research worker and give focus to his or her work. Without question, the interaction that takes place between teaching, research, and extension in the typical college department, either in the same persons or among different persons, operates to strengthen and give a sense of purpose to each functional activity.

Since their inception the primary mission of the agricultural colleges has been the development of the agricultural sciences as the means of making available to farmers new and improved technologies and production practices. This work continues at a rapid pace, as does work in the physical sciences in all institutions of higher learning. And it seems clear that the production-oriented activities of the colleges of agriculture in the future will be firmly grounded in the basic sciences and scientific methods; this will be necessary for the discovery and development of new and advanced production systems. Such production systems are also likely to go beyond the strictly farming sector of agriculture to include the handling and processing of the products of farms.

In the twentieth century the mission of the agricultural college has come to encompass more than the development of new production technologies. Stated more positively, the typical agricultural college now has several missions. We will identify five of these missions in this chapter.

The first mission is the original mission of the agricultural colleges discussed directly above, namely, the development of the physical agricultural sciences and the creation of new production technologies. In this connection the colleges of agriculture will need to continuously broaden their research and adapt their techniques to deal with the new systems of production and need to protect the environment.

The new technologies that have helped solve production problems in agriculture have also helped create new human and social problems. The new mechanical technologies have substituted for human labor and pushed farmers and their families off the land. They have contributed to the production of surpluses and low prices and incomes. For these and other reasons (e.g., changing patterns of trade, impacts of war), the colleges of agriculture have become increasingly concerned with problems of human adjustment, social adjustment, and rural institutions. The second mission of the colleges of agriculture, and one which has grown in relative importance in the twentieth century, thus seeks to cope with the "social, economic and institutional problems of rural people."

A third mission is concerned with the improvement of the environments for plants, animals, and humans, including the protection of the air, water, and soil from contaminants. Colleges of agriculture have much to contribute in this area, and since the end of World War II they have been called upon increasingly to expand their activities in this area.

A fourth mission is to deal with rural-urban resource use problems. Urban and suburban people need guidance, as much as farmers, with respect to land use and the use of renewable resources. And conflicts of interest regarding desirable land use at the rural-urban fringe have increased greatly in the post-World War II years.

Finally, and fifth, there is the mission concerned with international agriculture. Technical assistance to the less-developed world in the area of food and agriculture has increased importantly in the post-World War II period. The question is thus posed — What is the proper role of the American colleges of agriculture in this kind of work?

With the changing emphasis on the missions that they undertake, the colleges of agriculture have in the past several decades, and will in the decades to come, become more complex and more varied institutions. The knowledge centered in them will be devoted to more varied uses than was the case in the past. As instruments of progress and public service they will have an ever widening clientele and they will be increasingly concerned not only with technology per se but with how that technology affects people and institutions. The broadening of the missions of the colleges of agriculture, as outlined above, places them in the mainstream of American society and its development, and should serve to revitalize their purpose as academic institutions.

But it means more. It means that the agricultural college must continue to change in organization and function. More resources must be devoted to problem solving in the areas of food and nutrition, rural-urban conflicts, and human resource adjustments. Some agricultural colleges have already made program and organizational adjustments in these directions. Reflecting these developments several have changed their names: the college of agriculture in Michigan is now the College of Agriculture and Natural Resources; the college of agriculture at the University of California at Davis is now the College of Agricultural and Environmental Sciences; the college of agriculture in Florida is now the Institute of Food and Agricultural Sciences. Others, on the other hand, have tried to stand pat with traditional programs and organization. Finding a proper balance among the different missions will not be easy. Some of the forces will pull in the direction of tradition. Others will push for change. But if the demands by different segments of society for the teaching, research, and extension products under each of these five missions are as strong as has been suggested in the foregoing discussion, the programs and the organization of the agricultural colleges must change. They must change and develop in the future as they have done in the past.

Returns to Society

The returns to society from agricultural education and research have been many and varied. The achievement of a literate farm population enabled the pioneer farmers and later the commercial farmers (1) to analyze the options confronting them and to select options that were advantageous to them, (2) to behave rationally in the combining of their scarce resources and to make enlightened investment decisions, and thereby (3) to become, on the average, relatively efficient and productive farm producers. Research in the agricultural sciences has guaranteed a wide and continuous flow of new and improved technologies and practices to farmers. If technological advance was the principal engine of agricultural development in the twentieth century, research served as the fuel to power that engine. The agricultural colleges provided an attractive and remunerative escape route from the drudgery of farm work for ambitious farm-reared youth for over 100 years. And in recent years the agricultural colleges have begun to fulfill the goals of the early promoters of the agricultural and mechanical arts colleges, namely, the production of and the returning to the farm of highly skilled farm managers. In these and other ways agricultural education and research have contributed to the increased productivity of American farms, of the men and women who work them, and of society as a whole.

Economists prefer, however, to state the returns from an investment wherever possible in more precise terms than is done above. In this connection, considerable work has been done in recent years in measuring the rate of return to investments in agricultural research. Professor Willis Peterson obtains estimates of the marginal rates of return to investments in agricultural research by deriving measures of the *additional* inputs saved over specified time periods stemming from the *growth* in productivity during those periods. Marginal internal rates of return are computed by matching the research and extension expenditures with the corresponding additional inputs saved for each of four periods. The internal rate of return is the rate of interest that makes the accumulated research and extension expenditures at the end of each investment period equal to the discounted present value of the additional inputs saved.[10] The internal rate of return may be viewed in the same way as one would view the interest return on a savings account. It is the number of cents returned each year for each dollar invested.

Estimates of the internal rate of return to expenditures in agricultural research and extension in American agriculture for four periods are given in the accompanying tabulation.[11] We observe that rates of return to expenditures on agricultural research and extension are relatively high for the period 1937–62, but the rate of return declines importantly in the period 1967–72. The question may, therefore, be asked — Is there a reasonable possibility that the marginal rate of return in agricultural research and extension will fall below a minimum acceptable level, say 15 percent, in the foreseeable future? Preliminary work suggests that there does not appear to be any danger of this happening in the short-run future. But in the longer run the rate of return to investment in agricultural research and extension could drift downward unless some significant technological breakthroughs occur.

Period	Internal Rate of Return
1937–42	50%
1947–52	51
1957–62	49
1967–72	34

More recent studies done for later periods by different investigators indicate that internal rates of return for expenditures on agricultural research and extension, ranging between 25 and 50 percent, have been the norm for the United States. The downward drift in rates of return noted in the above tabulation is not confirmed by these more recent studies.[12]

Neither recent measures of the internal rates of return to expenditures for research and development in agriculture nor measures of increased productivity in the 1980s (chapter 8) suggest any falling off in farm technological advance in the United States. This should not come as a surprise, because the body of scientific knowledge on which technological developments take place continues to grow. But if in the name of economy, or budget stringencies, public and private agencies in the United States should start cutting back on funds for research and development in agriculture, then we must expect that farm technological advance will slow down.

Suggested Readings

Kellogg, Charles E., and Knapp, David C. *The College of Agriculture: Science in the Public Service.* New York: McGraw-Hill, 1966.

Kerr, Norwood Allen. *The Legacy: A Centennial History of the State Agricultural Experiment Stations, 1887–1987.* Columbia: University of Missouri, Missouri Agricultural Experiment Station, 1987.

Larson, Elsye Davey. *Country Schoolhouse.* New York: Comet Press, 1958.

Moores, Richard Gordon. *Fields of Rich Toil: The Development of the University of Illinois.* Urbana, Ill.: University of Illinois Press, 1970.

Rasmussen, Wayne D. *Taking the University to the People: Seventy-five Years of Cooperative Extension.* Ames: Iowa State Press, 1989.

Rossiter, Margaret W. *The Emergence of Agricultural Science: Justus Liebig and the Americans, 1840–1880.* New Haven: Yale University Press, 1975.

Shannon, Fred A. *The Farmer's Last Frontier: Agriculture 1860–1897.* Vol. V of *The Economic History of the United States.* New York: Farrar and Rinehart, 1945. Chap. XII.

Thayer, V.T. *The Role of the School in American Society.* New York: Dodd, Mead, 1960. Chaps. 1, 2, 10, and 11.

True, Alfred Charles. *A History of Agricultural Education in the United States, 1785–1925.* U.S. Department of Agriculture. Miscellaneous Publication No. 36, July 1929.

CHAPTER 13

INTERNATIONAL INPUTS

To settlers of colonial America, international trade and commerce were the natural result of their geographic location and state of economic development. The early colonists were highly dependent upon the mother country for basic supplies and manufactured goods of all kinds; thus they had to find, and did find or produce, raw products — furs, timber, fish, and tobacco — for shipment to England as payment for their supplies. The colonists did not confine their interests to that narrow coastline stretching from Maine to Georgia, as those of us engaged in a study of colonial America are prone to do. The American colonists were seafarers as well as landsmen. They ranged over the North Atlantic and the lands bordering it — trading, slaving, fishing, and smuggling — as if it were one part, the easily accessible part, of the new world that lay open to their exploitation. One cannot read the history of Portsmouth, Salem, Boston, Newport, New Haven, New York, Philadelphia, Charleston, or the Tidewater regions of Maryland and Virginia without realizing the dominant role that international trade and commerce played in the development of those communities and regions. International trade and commerce were the lifeblood of colonial America.

By the mid-1700s American colonists were beginning to push into the interior, and their economic interests were turning westward. But this westward migration in the second half of the 1700s was held up by Indian wars, the proclamation of the British government of 1763 prohibiting settlement beyond the Appalachian Mountains, and the

Revolutionary War. With victory over the British at Yorktown in 1781 and the negotiation of a favorable peace treaty in 1783, a new nation came into being with a great new territory that extended west to the Mississippi River. In this context, the development of the United States turned westward and inward. International trade and commerce increased in volume throughout the nineteenth century and contributed to the development of the national economy, but it did not play a dominant, or even a leading, role. The energies of the nation were devoted overwhelmingly to pushing back the frontier, settling the western lands, and building an industrial empire in the continental United States. Americans were concerned first and foremost with creating farms out of the wilderness, building roads and railroads, and establishing major industries. And with certain exceptions, the most notable of which was cotton, the product of this great productive effort could be and was consumed in the domestic market. Economic development in the United States in the nineteenth century was to an overwhelming degree a domestically oriented process.

As a result of many things — two world wars, the preeminent position of the United States in world politics, the growing surplus provided by American agriculture, and the increasing dependence of the United States on foreign raw materials, especially petroleum — the economy of the United States has become increasingly integrated into the world economy in the twentieth century. In the post-World War II period the United States has become the largest trader of goods and services in the international market. For no sector is this more true than for agriculture. The United States has become far and away the leading supplier of grains to the world market. It is also the largest, or one of the largest, exporters, depending on the year, of oilseeds and oilseed products, livestock and livestock products, cotton, and tobacco. The prosperity of American agriculture in the 1970s and 1980s depends to an important degree, just as it did in colonial Maryland and Virginia, upon the state of foreign demand. Whether the rains come, and come on time, in India or the Soviet Union may in the 1970s and 1980s be of far greater importance to grain farmers in the United States than weather conditions at home.

European Heritage and English Legacy

The first settlers, or colonists, along the Eastern Seaboard all came from Western Europe. As we know, most were English in the 1600s, but there were a few Swedes and Dutch scattered through the middle colonies. In the 1700s, the Germans and the Scotch-Irish came in large numbers, and the Scotch-Irish immediately began pushing westward into the Piedmont areas and into the limestone valleys of the Appalachians. The blacks came involuntarily as slaves.

The different West European nationality groups brought with them distinct customs and folkways, some of which have lasted into the twentieth century. But they also brought with them a common heritage — a heritage that emphasized individual initiative, hard work, and a desire to improve themselves economically. Thus, although the different nationality groups often did not like each other and commonly did not mingle socially or settle together, they did work alongside one another toward the common goals of establishing farms, building towns, and engaging in trade. They tolerated each other's different religious beliefs and social customs as they worked and struggled "to better themselves." The great and common goal to create a better life for themselves and their families in the American wilderness held the frictions among the different nationality groups to a minimum and held the individual settlers to a course of industry and enterprise building.

Neither the Dutch, nor the Swedes, nor the Germans, nor the Scotch-Irish could have succeeded in establishing their political, legal, and economic institutions in the thirteen colonies even if they had tried to do so. The political, legal, and economic institutions by which the settlers in the thirteen colonies lived came directly from England. The entire common law of England moved inviolate to the colonies. Enacted laws and established rules governing all elements of economic society — land, labor, trade controls, and business practices — were transplanted directly from England to the colonies. The accepted formula was that the law of any colony, in addition to laws passed by the colonial government, was the entire common law of England, plus English statute laws passed up to the time of colonization, plus later statutes specifically extended by Parliament to the colonies. At the time of the Revolution the common law of England was claimed by the Continental Congress and the new state governments. "As Chief Justice Morrison Waite put it in Munn *vs.* Illinois (1877): 'When the people of the United Colonies separated from Great Britain they changed the form, but not the substance, of their government.' "[1] In other words, the laws of England were the laws of the colonies, and subsequent American law would have to grow from that intellectual root.

Laws governing the tenure rights of ownership in property in the United States today derive from ancient English law and laws and usages in colonial times. Laws governing the rights and duties of masters and servants (laborers) came directly from England. The legacy of the labor contract in the United States was stormier than that of land ownership law, but it has been just as enduring. Laws governing the exchange of property in chattel goods in the United States also came down to us from English law and practices. In sum, the economic institutions of this country from its very beginnings are an English legacy.

This is not to say that Americans have not created any legal institutions of their own. They have. The Northwest Ordinances of 1785 and 1787 for establishing the transfer of land titles, modes of settlement, and procedures for bringing new states into the Union represent innovations in social and legal thought as important as any of the received English law. Further, the development of the American corporation and the laws pertaining to it owe little to English law and practice. But the fundamental English framework of economic institutions, developed for centuries in English experience and law and transported here in the period of colonization, produced an enveloping frame which Americans have changed but not abandoned. Americans in the fundamentals of their economic institutions remain, as of 1990, identifiably English, and some might argue, eighteenth-century English at that.

Immigration

Immigration, America's historic reason for being, has been one of the most persistent and most influential forces in its overall development. The whole history of the United States has been molded by successive waves of immigrants who responded to the lure of the New World and whose labors, with those of their descendants, have transformed an almost empty continent into a great and productive nation. Of the 70 million or so people who migrated from Europe since 1600, about two-thirds came to what is now the United States. In the colonial period, as we know, the immigrants were predominantly English, but even in that period Americans were a conglomerate breed; by the time of the Revolution the colonies contained substantial groups of Germans, Scotch-Irish, Dutch, Swedes, French, and African Negroes. In the great migrations of the nineteenth and twentieth centuries the United States received great blocs of Germans, Britons, Irishmen, Slavs, Italians, Russians, Scandinavians, Canadians, and

Mexicans. In the same period came smaller but still significant numbers of Greeks, Syrians, Armenians, Portuguese, Chinese, Japanese, Filipinos, and Puerto Ricans. American culture is thus a blend of the cultures of millions of immigrants with different languages, religions, and mores, and the American economy is the product of millions of diverse, but eager, immigrant hands.

Immigration into the United States in the period 1783–1815 was slow. It is estimated that no more than 250,000 persons immigrated into the United States during this thirty-two-year period. The reason for this slow rate of immigration was not a reluctance on the part of Europeans to cast their lot with the young republic. The reasons were (1) the Napoleonic wars, which greatly added to the hazards of the Atlantic crossing, and (2) restrictions imposed by European governments, particularly that of Great Britain, upon the emigration of skilled workers and artisans.

But despite the small number of immigrants, the period was a significant time for the United States. An unusually large proportion of those who came were men of outstanding gifts and skills, who were to make important contributions to American government and to business and industrial development. Skilled and talented men and women slipped out of the British Isles and the European continent, sometimes with the connivance of Americans and sometimes on their own, to try their luck in America. As a result, American society was enriched and the developing American economy was given a boost at a critical time.

Immigrants then and at later periods made immense contributions to the development of the American economy by bringing with them new and productive ideas which translated into new and improved productive processes and new and more efficient forms of business organization. The exploitation of the resources of an entire continent required eager and willing workers' hands, but it also required new and effective ideas about the best ways of exploiting those resources. Thus men and women with productive ideas found a receptive home in the United States in the nineteenth century.

The great Atlantic migration from Europe to the United States got under way in the 1820s and reached a peak in the pre-Civil War year of 1854 when 428,000 persons entered the United States from foreign shores. Immigration figures for the pre-Civil War period are given in the accompanying tabulation. Five million people immigrated to the United States from 1815 to 1860, a number greater than the entire population of the new nation in 1790, and the three million who arrived between 1845 and 1855 landed in a country of only about 20 million. This represented in proportional terms the largest influx into the United States that the nation has ever known. Although every European country was represented to some degree in this great exodus, the overwhelming majority of immigrants came from north-west Europe. Over two million came from Ireland alone. About three-quarters of a million came from Great Britain, and about one and a half million came from Germany.

Period	No. of U.S. Immigrants
1820–29	151,000
1830–39	599,000
1840–49	1,713,000
1850–59	2,314,000

There was both a push and a pull to this mass movement. The push forces included the enclosure movement in British, Scotch, and Irish agriculture, the potato famine in Ireland, the development of the factory system in England and Continental Europe and the displacement of skilled artisans, and the political upheavals and revolutions of the 1830s and 1840s. The pull was the lure of improving one's self economically in the New World. This might be achieved through the acquisition of cheap or free land, or the finding of a more productive, hence more remunerative job, or the starting up of a business or enterprise. The fact that the better economic life was not always achieved, and that many immigrants suffered great hardships and great indignities from the then native Americans, did not destroy the lure, or dampen the pull, throughout the nineteenth century. The "pull" of a better life kept inducing Europeans to emigrate to the United States in ever increasing numbers throughout the nineteenth century, except in those panic or depression years when economic opportunities in the United States were in a depressed state.

The impression should not be gained that most of the immigrants in the period 1820–60 entered agriculture and moved onto the frontier. Very few moved to the frontier; it was alien to their background and experience. Probably most did not enter agriculture. Almost none of the Irish immigrants entered agriculture; they bunched together in the large East Coast cities or followed the large construction projects — canal and railroad construction projects. Displaced European artisans and political refugees were not looking for economic opportunities in agriculture.

European immigrants in the pre-Civil War period did, however, play an important role in the development of American agriculture in this period. It was a twofold role. First, they supplied the labor demanded by the rapidly expanding industrial sector in this period and thus facilitated its expansion without drawing labor out of agriculture and slowing down the development of that sector. Second, some immigrants filled in behind the pioneer farmers as the latter kept pushing the frontier to the west. The immigrants of this period who entered agriculture would often purchase the partially developed farm of a pioneer farm family and within a few years turn it into a productive commercial farm. This is a role that German immigrants, with some ready cash and a strong work ethic, often played in the Middle West. They helped build the commercial agriculture of the Upper Midwest in the 1840s and 1850s after the frontier had moved on farther west.

Immigration into the United States slackened off in the years immediately preceding and during the Civil War. But it began to increase again even before the war was over. Immigration rose from a low point of some 92,000 persons in 1862 to approximately 460,000 in 1873, slackened off during the depressed 1870s, shot up to some 780,000 in 1882, fluctuated with economic conditions throughout the 1890s and early part of the twentieth century, reaching a peak of some 1,285,000 in 1907 and a second peak of 1,218,000 in 1914. Immigration into the United States was reduced to a relatively small stream during the World War I years and then shot up once again to 805,000 persons in 1921. But in that year free immigration into the United States was brought to an end by congressional action. In 1924 permanent legislation was passed limiting immigration into the United States to specified quotas of various nationality groups already in the country. As a result of this and later legislation restricting immigration into the United States, the number of immigrants fell off sharply, reaching a low of some 23,000 in 1933. From that low point, immigration increased to a level of some 300,000 persons per year in the late 1950s and continued upward, particularly in the 1980s, reaching a high of slightly over one million in 1989.[2]

The second great wave of immigration into the United States during the nineteenth century, which ran from 1860 to 1890, brought some 10 million persons to these shores. The immigrants of this wave, like those of the earlier pre-Civil War wave, came predominantly from northern Europe — from the British Isles, Germany, Scandinavia, Switzerland, and Holland. But there was a significant shift in the geographic origins of American immigration toward the end of the nineteenth century. The last and greatest of the three immigration waves brought a total of 15 million persons into the United States between 1890 and 1914. The immigrants of this wave came predominantly from Austria-Hungary, Italy, Russia, Greece, Rumania, and Turkey. The extent of the change in the geographic origins of the immigrants can be seen by comparing the immigration of 1882 with that of 1907, the years in which the two post-Civil War waves crested. In 1882, some 87 percent of the immigrants came from northwestern Europe and 13 percent from countries of southern and eastern Europe. In 1907, some 19 percent came from northwestern Europe and 81 percent from southern and eastern Europe. This change in the geographic and nationality composition of the immigrants to the United States around the turn of the century led to a restrictionist immigration policy in the 1920s that had the avowed purpose of maintaining the racial preponderance of northern Europeans in the ethnic composition of the population.

In the two post-Civil War immigration waves, as in the earlier pre-Civil War wave, the greater proportion of the immigrants settled in the large cities. To an important degree these immigrants provided the supply of labor, both skilled and unskilled, that enabled the United States to become second only to England in the production of manufactured goods by 1870 and to become the leading producer of manufactured goods by 1885. But in the period 1870–90 a relatively high proportion of the immigrants from Britain, Germany, and the Scandinavian countries tried their luck at farming on the last frontier — the subhumid Plains and the Great Plains. This happened for several reasons. First, this was the period of free land under the Homestead Act. Second, this was the period when the land grant railroads and immigration offices of the western states were operating advertising and recruiting campaigns in northern and western Europe. And third, many of these recruits were not destitute, as were the Irish in the pre-Civil War wave. Many of these immigrants possessed the capital necessary to get started in farming in America at that time.

But farming on the subhumid Plains and the Great Plains was a totally new experience for these North European immigrants, just as it was for native American migrants from the humid Midwest and East. Both sets of migrants had to learn to farm in an area with a subhumid to arid climate — and that area, the Plains, was a hard teacher. Both sets of migrants made the same kinds of farming mistakes and suffered untold human hardships. In the process many, perhaps most, of the first wave of settlers were broken both physically and financially. But slowly, very slowly, not really until after the droughts of the 1930s, did the farmers of the Plains learn to manage these lands is such ways as to maintain a successful, permanent farming operation.

Immigration into the United States continues to perform a critically important role for certain peoples in certain periods — for example, Vietnamese and Laotian refugees in the 1970s and 1980s, as well as legal and illegal Mexican entrants. But immigration no longer plays the dominant role in the economic development of the United States that it played between 1820 and 1914. In that period immigration (1) provided the needed supply of labor, both skilled and unskilled, for the rapidly developing industrial sector of the United States economy, and (2) supplied the people needed to settle the great hinterland of America, usually but not always behind the frontier, and to create a highly productive commercial agriculture. The great migration of peoples from Europe between 1820 and 1914 literally provided the bodies required to build the industrial and agricultural sectors of the United States economy over that long period.

Investments

Foreigners began investing in business enterprises in the United States as soon as the new nation came into being. During the period 1790–1860 the export of capital to the United States most often took place through financial houses in London that specialized in business developments in and financial needs of the United States. Foreign investments in the United States approximated $100 million by 1808 and fluctuated around that level until 1830. In the decade of the 1830s foreign investments in the United States increased from a level of $100 million to $300 million. Foreign investments in the United States dipped sharply in the 1840s and then rose almost steadily throughout the remainder of the century to well over $3 billion by 1900.

Foreign investments in the pre-Civil War period, particularly those of the British, tended to be concentrated in canals, railroads, and cotton plantations. In the post-Civil War period, foreign investments tended to become more diversified, but with respect to agricultural development it is interesting to note that large amounts of British capital were invested in, and often lost in, large ranching enterprises in the Far West. The significance of foreign-invested capital in the development of the United States economy is open to debate. Professor Douglass North argues that foreign capital was important in the

1830s — in canal and railroad building — but thereafter the proportion of foreign capital in total capital formation dwindles in amount and importance, although in absolute terms it grows substantially throughout the nineteenth century.[3] This would seem to be a reasonable assessment.

From the viewpoint of American agricultural development, however, it will be recalled that the development of an effective rail and water transport system during the period 1820–60 was of critical importance in transforming a pioneer type of agriculture into a commercial type of agriculture. Thus it can be logically argued that because foreign investments in canal building and railroad construction in the 1830s made a significant contribution to the building of that critically important infrastructural element, they also contributed importantly to the development of American agriculture at a critically important time. Stated somewhat differently, foreign capital investments may have played a minor role in the overall development of the United States economy. But at one critically important time in the development of American agriculture, these investments probably played a decisive role; the transformation of a pioneer type of agriculture to a commercial type of agriculture in the Ohio and Mississippi river valleys after 1820 was absolutely dependent upon the development of an effective transport system.

Trade

The foreign trade of the United States in 1790 was well below the levels achieved in the pre-Revolutionary War years. Furthermore, the future of the new nation in the international market did not look bright. Great Britain applied the navigation laws to the United States and excluded it from the domestic British market and the British West Indies. The Napoleonic wars at times worked to the advantage of American traders and exports, but generally speaking they did not provide an economic climate in which international trade could flourish. During the War of 1812, United States exports fell off to almost nothing. Thus the foreign trade of the United States went through a long period, 1785–1815, of uncertainty and slow growth.

With the return of world peace in 1815, the foreign trade of the United States began a long and significant upward climb. Although the level of trade fluctuated with business conditions over the period 1815–60, the trend was persistently upward. The value of merchandise exports, for example, increased from $53 million in 1815 to $334 million in 1860. During this period, however, the value of imported merchandise exceeded the value of exports almost every year. This resulted from relatively large imports of manufactured goods that were in strong demand in the rapidly developing young nation. The chronic trade deficit was closed in two principal ways: (1) by loans provided by British investors and (2) by earnings received by American merchantmen for shipping services provided.

As might be guessed, the exports of the United States in the long period 1815–60 were primarily agricultural. In 1800, tobacco was the principal export commodity of the United States. But by 1820 cotton had moved into the number-one position. By 1820, the export of raw cotton amounted to 42 percent of total exports, and cotton, tobacco, and wheat and wheat flour together amounted to 67 percent of total exports. By 1840, cotton had assumed an even more dominant position in the export trade; in that year cotton exports amounted to 57 percent of total exports, and cotton, tobacco, and wheat and wheat flour together amounted to 77 percent of total exports. Cotton continued to be the leading export commodity of the United States up to the Civil War; in 1860 cotton amounted to 61 percent of total exports, and cotton, tobacco, and wheat and wheat flour combined amounted to 72 percent of total exports.

Not only was cotton "king" in the Deep South, it was "king" in international trade. Cotton linked the United States to the North Atlantic economy and acted to strengthen the economic bonds between England and the United States. But of even greater importance, the provision of the services required in the transporting, financing, insuring, and marketing of the cotton produced in the South by trading centers in the New England and Middle Atlantic states served to stimulate the urbanization and economic development of those states.

The rapid expansion in the export of raw cotton, primarily to the cotton mills of the English Midlands, supported the rapid expansion of the cotton plantation system across the Deep South. A strong worldwide demand for cotton cloth, improved technologies in the ginning, spinning, and weaving of cotton, slavery, and the opening of new lands favorable to cotton production all coalesced to create in a few years a cotton industry that stretched from the plantations of the Deep South through the trading centers of New York and New England to the cotton mills of England to market outlets around the world. In this favorable developmental setting the southern planters used their relatively large earnings to further expand that industry and to enrich their way of life. With their earnings from the sale of cotton they imported luxury goods, traveled abroad, purchased the services necessary for exporting their cotton, bought much of the food required by their slaves from the Upper South, purchased surplus slaves from the Upper South, and invested in new lands farther west. Southern planters for the most part did not invest in physical or social infrastructure, in merchandising operations, or in complementary industrial enterprises. Since returns from cotton production were high, perhaps higher than for any readily existing alternative, this economic behavior was perhaps rational for the short run. But for the long run it doomed the South to a process of development based upon one crop, primitive production technologies, and an antiquated social system. In the long run it led to a low productivity type of agriculture and a slow rate of economic growth.

In the post-Civil War period, 1865–1900, cotton immediately resumed its dominant position in the export trade of the United States. And it maintained that dominant position through the period 1866–79. But in 1880, the value of wheat and wheat flour exports exceeded the value of cotton exports for the first time, and manufactured goods were on their way to becoming an important element in the export trade of the United States. By 1900 the composition of merchandise exports from the United States had changed significantly. The value of manufactured goods now amounted to approximately 35 percent of total exports and was about double the value of either raw cotton, or wheat and wheat flour.

Several important developments occurred in the international trade of the United States in the period 1866–1900. First, the volume of trade, as measured by merchandise exports, increased about four times. Second, the United States moved into a trade position in which the value of its merchandise exports regularly exceeded the value of its imports. Third, cotton ceased to be the predominant commodity in the export trade of the United States. Fourth, total agricultural exports in quantity terms increased over five times. Fifth, and reflecting the new position of the United States as the leading producer of manufactured goods in the world, the composition of merchandise exports had shifted heavily in the direction of manufactured products by 1900.

The absolute expansion in the exports of agricultural products, particularly in the grains, between 1866 and 1900 contributed importantly to the development of American agriculture during that period. Without this expansion in agricultural exports, the farm depressions of the 1870s and the 1890s would certainly have been more severe and the economic consequences for farm people more devastating than they were. Nonetheless, it was clear by 1900 that exports of agricultural products would never again dominate the export trade of the United States as completely as they had in the nineteenth century. By 1910, the United States was producing 35 percent of all the manufactured goods produced in the world, and manufactured goods (not counting manufactured foodstuffs) accounted for about 45 percent of total exports of the United States.

Exports of raw food products trended upward over the long period 1900–1977; exports of raw cotton reached a peak in the late 1920s and have trended downward since then. But perhaps of greater importance, exports of both raw food and fiber products from the United States have fluctuated widely in the twentieth century. Exports of raw food products drifted downward in the first decade of the 1900s, then increased by more than four times between 1910 and 1921. From 1921 to 1936 exports of raw food products declined persistently and importantly; the value of food exports from the United States was lower in 1933 than in any year since 1870. In quantity terms, exports of raw food products increased about twelve times between the mid-1930s and 1951; in value terms, exports of raw food products increased about twenty-three times during the same period. With the end of the Korean hostilities, exports of raw food products declined sharply, falling some 42 percent between 1951 and 1954. First with government assistance and second with world economic recovery, exports of raw food products increased persistently between 1954 and 1972; then with some poor grain crops around the world in 1972 and 1974, exports of raw food products from the United States shot skyward during the period 1972–74. Between 1974 and 1990 exports of raw food products fluctuated in an extreme fashion. First, they continued to rise between 1974 and 1981; second, they fell sharply between 1981 and 1986; and third, they rose once again between 1986 and 1990. Cotton exports fluctuated in a random fashion over the same period.

The relative importance of four major U.S. crops in international trade may be seen in Figure 13.1. Note that for wheat, between 60 and 75 percent of domestic production is exported in most years, and those exports account for 30 to 40 percent of the total world trade in wheat. Coarse grains exports, on the other hand, account for only about 25 percent of domestic production but for about 60 percent of world trade in those grains. Soybean export share of both domestic production and world trade approximates 50 percent.

271

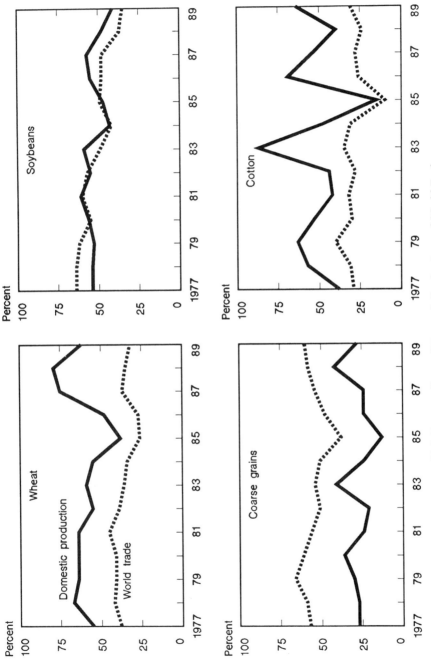

Fig. 13.1. U.S. Exports: Share of Domestic Production and World Trade

Exports of all agricultural products from the United States in the twentieth century, measured in quantity terms, have moved up and down as if they were riding a roller coaster (figure 13.2). These swings — some short, some long and wide — have been associated with world wars and their aftermath, economic depressions and recoveries, and good and bad cycles of weather. But whatever the cause of those fluctuations in agricultural exports, those movements have had a significant influence on the development of American agriculture. This is clear from a study of figure 13.2. For almost every period in which exports are increasing importantly, gross farm incomes are

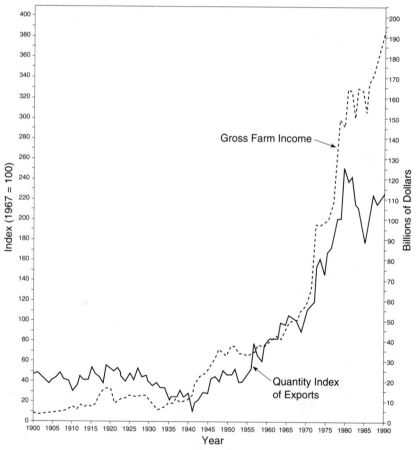

Fig. 13.2. Agricultural exports and gross farm income, United States, 1900–1990

rising, and whenever exports are falling importantly, so also are farm incomes. Since the expansions and contractions in quantities exported act to expand or contract the aggregate demand for agricultural products, it is reasonable to argue that those expansions and contractions in exports contributed to, or caused in part, the movements in farm incomes. Exactly how much those fluctuations in the volume of agricultural exports contributed to the fluctuations in farm incomes may have varied from period to period, but fluctuations in the export component of aggregate demand were an important causal element throughout the twentieth century, and they were the dominant causal element in the great upward movement of farm prices and incomes in the 1970s and 1980s.

Imports of agricultural products have increased on a trend basis over the long period 1900–1990, but the increase has been less rapid than that for exports and the fluctuations have been less extreme. These imports have not seriously impeded agricultural development in the United States for two reasons. First, nearly half of the agricultural imports into the United States over the years have not been competitive with commodities produced in the United States; they have involved such commodities as rubber, coffee, cocoa beans, bananas, tea, spices, and wool for carpeting. Second, the United States has such a great comparative advantage in the production of grains and oilseeds, and the livestock products produced from those grains, that competition from foreign producers has been limited in the main to various specialty commodities. The only two important agricultural industries that would be seriously hurt from foreign competition if import restrictions were lifted would be the dairy industry and the sugar industry. And since the production of sugar is highly uneconomic in most areas of the United States, foreign competition would create difficult problems for only one critically important agricultural commodity in the United States, namely, dairy.

In sum and in short, the export trade of the United States in agricultural products in the second half of the twentieth century has once again assumed the important role that it played in the seventeenth and eighteenth centuries. But it no longer dominates the export trade of the United States as it did throughout much of the nineteenth century. Total exports from the United States in 1989 amounted to $342 billion; of this total, agricultural exports accounted for some $40 billion, or about 12 percent. Imports of agricultural products offer no serious challenge to American agriculture except for certain specialty crops and dairy.

International trade in agricultural products has played both a positive and a dominant role in the development of American agriculture in the second half of the twentieth century. This role could be expanded if the United States were to move to a policy position of free trade. But such a policy position could lead to other problems — some of which were explored in chapter 8 and some of which will be explored in the next section.

The Modern Condition of Interdependence

In an average year in the 1980s the output from about 30 percent of the harvested acres in the United States moved into export. In 1988 the output of nearly two-fifths of the harvested acreage was exported. The ten leading markets for U.S. agricultural exports in fiscal 1988 are shown in table 13.1.

Stated differently, the United States has reached that stage in its development where it must sell approximately 30 percent of its annual crop production abroad or be confronted with a contraction in the aggregate demand for its farm products, a downward pressure on farm prices, and the need to reduce the size of its agricultural plant. Conversely, countries like Japan and S. Korea have become critically dependent upon the United States for supplies of grains and other foodstuffs. This basic interdependency is complicated by the fact that many countries with variable weather and unstable production (e.g., the republics of the former Soviet Union, India, and more recently the People's Republic of China) have come to depend upon the United States as supplier of grains and other basic food commodities when they experience a bad harvest or a crop failure. The United States has, thus, on top of its large and regular trade, become the residual supplier of basic commodities to much of the world, rich and poor, since 1960.

It is a fact then that the agricultural sector of the United States economy is highly dependent upon the world economy and the individual country parts of that world economy for its growth and well-being. Such growth and well-being are dependent upon two world conditions: (1) a reasonable rate of growth in the world economy and (2) a reasonable degree of stability in the demand for agricultural products emanating from that economy. Unfortunately, for reasons of weather, politics, and economics the above conditions cannot be satisfied. Thus the agricultural sector of the United States, because it has become so completely integrated into the world economy, is now subject to the infinite uncertainties of the world economy.

Table 13.1. Ten Leading Country Markets for U.S. Agricultural Exports, Millions of Dollars, Fiscal Year 1988

	Total	1	2	3	4	5	6	7	8	9	10
Total Agricultural Exports	35,341	Japan 7,274	S.Korea 2,250	Neth. 2,087	Canada 1,973	USSR 1,934	Mexico 1,726	Taiwan 1,577	Germany 1,306	Spain 848	U.K. 819
Feed Grains and Products	5,209	Japan 1,712	USSR 541	Taiwan 431	S.Korea 428	Mexico 394	Spain 194	Algeria 158	S.Arabia 153	Egypt 108	Israel 90
Wheat Unmilled	4,674	USSR 822	PRC 525	Japan 353	Egypt 314	S.Korea 264	Algeria 187	India 154	Morocco 133	Taiwan 123	Poland 122
Soybeans	5,015	Japan 958	Neth. 902	Taiwan 457	Spain 341	Germany 305	S.Korea 270	Mexico 261	USSR 172	U.K. 144	Portugal 132
Animal Products	6,058	Japan 1,844	S.Korea 748	Mexico 621	Canada 388	Taiwan 223	U.K. 205	France 178	Hong Kong 106	Iraq 105	Germany 85
Fruits and Vegetables	2,744	Japan 734	Canada 633	Hong Kong 168	U.K. 145	Taiwan 86	France 65	Neth. 63	Mexico 47	Singapore 44	Sweden 43

Source: U.S. Department of Agriculture, Economic Research Service; FATUS: Foreign Agricultural Trade of the United States. November/December 1988.

If India, the republics of the former Soviet Union, and the People's Republic of China have a series of good crops in a row, their demand for grains from the United States could be expected to fall off, and the level of prices received by farmers in the United States would decline. If a war should break out in the Middle East, nations around the world could be expected to build stockpiles of grains and other basic commodities, the demand for farm commodities in the United States would rise, and the level of farm prices would also rise. Or if the OPEC countries should act in concert to reduce oil exports and thereby drive up the price of petroleum still further, farm production costs in the United States would take another upward jump at the same time that imports of grain into Japan and Western Europe were being curtailed; in this situation American farmers would be squeezed between rising production costs and falling product prices.

These are the kinds of uncertainties that will confront American farmers in the years to come, where they have become one part, and an important part, of an interdependent economic and political world. It is not a situation that is conducive to stable economic growth at home. Neither is there any way for Americans to disengage themselves from the world market. They are locked into the world market, as one interdependent part. The American farm economy would collapse in the absence of the international market. As was suggested in chapter 8, the task confronting American farmers, farm leaders, and political leaders is to find ways of introducing stability into the unruly, unstable, uncertain interdependent world market. Such policy actions will involve costs — perhaps large costs in holding large reserves. But what are the alternatives? They are for American farmers and consumers to be buffeted around by unpredictable climatic, political, and economic forces arising at unpredictable points in an interdependent world society.

Suggested Readings

Hughes, J. R. T.; Rosenberg, Nathan; and Gallman, Robert E. "American Economic Growth: Imported or Indigenous?" Papers and Proceedings of the Eighty-Ninth Annual Meeting of the American Economic Association, Atlantic City, N.J., September 16–18, 1976. *The American Review*, 67 (February 1977), pp. 15–31.

Jones, Maldwyn Allen. *American Immigration*. Chicago: University of Chicago Press, 1960.

Leyburn, James G. *The Scotch-Irish: A Social History*, Chapel Hill, N.C.: University of North Carolina Press, 1962. Pt. III.

North, Douglass C. *Growth and Welfare in the American Past: A New Economic History,* 2nd ed. Englewood Cliffs, N.J.: Prentice Hall, 1974. Chap. III.

U.S. Department of Commerce. Bureau of the Census. *Historical Statistics of the United States: Colonial Times to 1957.* 1960. Pp. 39–47 and 529–66.

U.S. Department of Agriculture. Foreign Agricultural Service. *Quantity Indexes of U.S. Agricultural Exports and Imports.* FAS-M-76, Revised January 1960.

United States Trade: Performance in 1988, International Trade Administration, U.S. Department of Commerce, September 1989.

Williamson, Harold F., ed. *The Growth of the American Economy.* New York: Prentice-Hall, 1951. Chaps. 3, 12, 14, 27, and 41.

CHAPTER 14

ENVIRONMENTAL POLICY

The Resource Base

The West Europeans who came to North America in the sixteenth and seventeenth centuries, first as explorers and then as colonists, found a continent rich in resources, climatically hospitable to human beings, and of extraordinary physical diversity. That part of the continent that was to become the United States stretched some three thousand miles from the Atlantic to the Pacific and some twelve hundred miles from the Gulf of Mexico to the Canadian border. Traveling east across the U.S. portion of the continent one encounters first a coastal plain, narrow in the North and wider in the South, and then the Appalachian uplift, which reaches about 3,000 feet above sea level. From there one moves into the great interior lowlands stretching from central Ohio to eastern Kansas. The lowlands merge into the Great Plains, and at the western edge of the High Plains the Southern Rockies rise to 14,000 feet; continuing west one encounters first the high Colorado plateau and then the southern end of the Northern Rockies, the Wasatch range, and then one ridge after another across the Great Basin. Finally one must cross the 14,000-foot-high Sierra Nevada range, which extends north into Oregon and Washington as the Cascades; after this the traveler drops down into the fertile coastal valleys over the

Fig. 14.1. Physiographic Map of the Continental United States

low coastal ranges and then reaches the Pacific Ocean (see figure 14.1). It is a land of unparalleled beauty, diversity, and fertility.

Although all of this land mass lies within the temperate zone, climate and precipitation vary widely over the land because of different degrees of latitude, differences in elevation, and the height and direction of the mountain ranges. In the eastern half of the continental United States, where the average precipitation exceeds 30 inches per year, except for the tall grass country of central Illinois and Iowa, the land was covered with a dense forest of mixed broad-leafed and pine trees. In the West, where average precipitation falls below 20 inches per year, coniferous forests were limited to the rainy slopes of the mountain ranges (see figure 14.2). Between the forests were grasslands, tall and luxuriant east of the hundredth meridian but short and sturdy west of it. In the arid areas of the intermountain region and the Southwest, sage brush, bunch grass, and cacti made up the land cover. In this rich and varied vegetation cover animal wildlife was abundant. Species of deer were to be found everywhere, and elk, moose, and antelope in more restricted areas. These and smaller species were a part of the food chain for bears, big cats, wolves, and foxes. Beaver, muskrats, and otter populated the rivers and streams from east to west. Game birds — ducks, cranes, grouse, will geese, and passenger pigeons — existed in the millions. The streams and rivers were brimming with fish, and the coastal waters abounded with shellfish. And perhaps as many as 60,000,000 buffalo roamed the Great Plains and intruded in smaller herds into the eastern forest lands.

The water resources were providential; navigable rivers and lakes provided ready-made transport routes into the interior; rushing rivers and streams provided power; and the annual precipitation of 20 inches or more east of the hundredth meridian could and eventually did sustain a highly productive agriculture. Complimenting this favorable precipitation pattern were deep, rich soils in most of the interior lowlands. And the minerals were there, too, that would eventually underwrite a great industrial development: coal and iron, gold and silver, oil and gas, and many lesser but important minerals (copper, lead, and zinc).

When the Europeans arrived in North America there were perhaps 10,000,000 native Americans living north of the Rio Grande. For the most part these people were hunters and gatherers, but some practiced a primitive slash-and-burn kind of crop farming, and in the Southwest a few practiced a sophisticated kind of irrigated crop farming. As hunters and gatherers these native Americans lived reason-

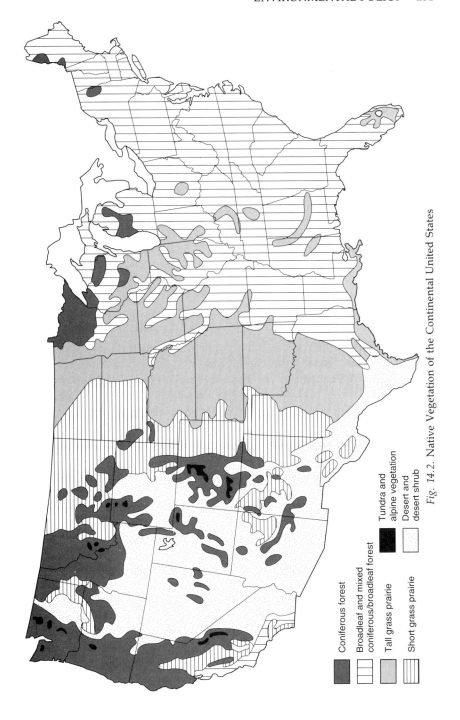

Fig. 14.2. Native Vegetation of the Continental United States

Coniferous forest

Broadleaf and mixed
coniferous/broadleaf forest

Tall grass prairie

Short grass prairie

Tundra and
alpine vegetation

Desert and
desert shrub

ably well off the rich bounty of the land, but like any primitive society with limited reserves and inadequate transport, individual tribes occasionally faced and suffered through starving times. These people lived in clans and tribes and had established, but not well-demarcated, living, farming, and hunting areas. Hence, the various clans and tribes feuded and fought much of the time over the boundaries of their established areas. In this context the Europeans arrived with superior hard (iron and steel) technologies and organizational skills as well as an insatiable appetite for acquiring and controlling these many and wonderful resources. Over a three-hundred-year period the Europeans, now known as white Americans, slowly pushed aside the native Americans and took title to all the land, as well as the resources above it and below it, in the continental United States.[1] By 1900 the resource base, or what was left of it, was firmly in the control of white Americans, under either private or government ownership.

Taming Nature

It is probably the case that no one talked about or wrote about the need for an environmental policy in the sixteenth and seventeenth centuries in the thirteen English colonies that were to become the United States; if the need was discussed in the eighteenth century, as it was in the latter part of that century in the United States, it was discussed under the heading of resource conservation. In fact, Victor Scheffer makes the point that the word *environmentalism* was seldom used before the appearance of Rachel Carson's book *Silent Spring* in 1962.[2] But white Americans certainly had an environmental policy over that three-hundred-year period, and it was probably more generally agreed to than any that has been articulated in the late 1980s or early 1990s. It was a policy to "tame nature" and to do so as rapidly as possible.

According to Clayton Koppes three beliefs held by white Americans with regard to the use of natural resources gave rise to the implicit environmental policy of "taming nature."[3] First, it was believed that there was an abundance of *unclaimed* natural resources. Indians used the land, but not in ways that white Americans felt bound to respect. The Indians often were migratory and had a concept of communal ownership that was foreign to white Americans. Thus, white Americans pushed the native Americans aside and took title to their lands, under English law, on the assumption that unused land could properly be appropriated by whites. Lewis Cass, governor of Michigan Territory, stated the white frontiersman's position clearly when he said that "red men were a 'provisional race' entitled to hold the land only until another group appeared who could make better use of God's blessings."[4] President Monroe, after being briefed by Governor Cass in Detroit in 1817, stated this hypothesis to Congress in his first annual message in December of that year: "The hunter state can exist in only the vast, uncultivated desert. It yields to the . . . greater force of civilized population and ought to yield, for the earth is given to mankind to support the greatest number which it is capable, and no tribe or people have a right to withhold from the wants of others more than is necessary for their own support and comfort."[5]

Second, white Americans believed that the natural resources of the North American continent were *inexhaustible.* And so they appeared to be up until the late 1800s. Lacking either a philosophical or an economic incentive to conserve the vast resources that lay "unclaimed" before them, white Americans exploited those resources in a reckless fashion — in reality, they plundered them.

Third, and related to the belief in the *inexhaustibility* of the continent's natural resources, was the belief that *immediate* use was best. The dominant mood of white Americans was that the people who did the backbreaking work of converting the wilderness' usable resources should reap the benefit of their labor as soon as possible.

Undergirding these beliefs was a judicial system that sanctioned the capture and "creative use" of "unclaimed" resources, a political philosophy that humans should have as wide a range of freedom as possible, and an economic view that an unfettered market should be the final determinant of resource use. In this social and political context white Americans set out to conquer the vast wilderness extending from the Atlantic to the Pacific and tame nature in the process. And, with some minor exceptions, they had completed this task by 1890.

First, the fur traders, hunters, and trappers moved into the wilderness to acquire the furs — beaver and muskrat — in high demand, and the skins — mostly deer skins — that were used in many utilitarian ways. In the area lying east of the ninety-sixth meridian (or what is now the western border of the state of Iowa) the business practice typically followed had the native Americans doing the trapping and hunting and the white Americans trading beads, blankets, cooking pots, whiskey, and firearms for the pelts and skins. West of the ninety-sixth meridian the native Americans were less cooperative and more hostile; hence white Americans had to do more of the actual hunting and trapping themselves. But the results were the same. The beaver had been trapped almost to extinction by 1840; but then the animal received a reprieve as beaver hats went out of style at about that time. Thereafter beavers were killed simply for making a nuisance of themselves by clogging up streams. The buffalo had been hunted almost to extinction in the continental United States by 1880. The slaughter of the great herds resulted from the demand for buffalo robes around the world and the policy of the U.S. government to starve the Plains Indians onto reservations set aside for them. Somehow the deer species survived the slaughter; the antelope, moose, and wolf survived by the slenderest of margins.

Behind the fur traders, trappers, and hunters came the land speculators and the settlers eager to own a piece of land of their own. Prior to the American Revolution the British Crown held the land speculators and settlers at bay east of the Allegheny Mountains, but after the Revolution the new government opened the flood gates and the whites poured into the interior lowlands of the Ohio and Mississippi river valleys (see the discussion in chapter 3). The new federal government of the United States was anxious to dispose of these interior lands for two reasons: (1) to fill the land with its own people to guard against British encroachment in the North and Spanish encroachment in the South and (2) to earn needed revenue through the sale of these lands. The land rush by speculators and settlers into the Ohio and Mississippi river valleys thus had the blessing of the federal government and more. The federal government aided and abetted the rush by defeating the Indian tribes in battle and removing them from their homelands and resettling them in reservations in so-called Indian lands farther west.

Dense forests covered most of the land east of the Mississippi River. Consequently, the first thing a pioneering settler did upon reaching the piece of land he had purchased, either from a speculator or from the government, was to begin cutting down trees or killing trees by girdling them. From the felled trees he would build a log house or lean-to, or he might sell logs to a sawmill if there was one nearby; if there was a stream or river nearby he would float the logs to a sawmill, or later, with the advent of the railroads, he might sell logs out of which to make railway ties or more probably as fuel to power the steam engines. The girdled trees he might let stand until they fell over and rotted on the ground, or he might cut them down for his own firewood or simply burn them in the field to get rid of them. But one way or another the pioneering settlers cleared most of the deciduous trees, both hardwoods and softwoods, from any land east of the Mississippi that looked like it might make good cropland.

In the North the settlers used their cleared land to produce corn and wheat and later meat animals. In the border states the settlers produced tobacco and corn on their cleared land and later slaves and mules for sale. In the South the settlers, large and small, produced cotton, cotton, and more cotton, as well as some corn, on their cleared land. All the settlers produced corn — partly for home consumption, partly to feed animals, and partly for making whiskey.

The conquest of nature did not end at the edge of the eastern forests. Upon reaching the tall grass country of central Illinois and Iowa the settlers, with help from the blacksmiths, developed steel-edged plows that could turn the heavy sod of that region. Once the Indians were subdued and removed, the tall grass country was quickly settled and converted into highly productive farms — producing all of the grains, cattle, and hogs. Given the humid climate, the deep rich soil, the absence of trees that had to be removed, and the arrival of the railroads, the settlers quickly moved from pioneering subsistence farmers to commercial farmers with surplus products for sale.

The Great Plains were next. With the passage of the Homestead Act in 1862 and the end of the Civil War, thousands of land-hungry people from the eastern part of the United States and northern Europe tried their luck on the plains. The land was free or cheap and the short grass sod was easy to work and prepare for seeding — most often to wheat. But the climate of the plains was harsh and hostile, and most of the newcomers from humid climates failed and gave up. Most of the first homesteaders in the 1870s knew how to farm where the annual rainfall exceeded 30 inches, but grain farming with less than 20 inches of precipitation per year required a whole new set of farming practices. It took seventy-five years to learn how to farm the Great Plains successfully, and it remains a high-risk business in the 1990s. In the meantime, the short hardy grass, on which the "buffalo roamed," was turned under and generation after generation tried to produce grain in its place. A few learned the ways of the plains, hung on, and became successful farmers.

To build the farm houses and barns, towns and cities, on the treeless tall grass country of central Illinois to the bunch grass country of eastern Colorado and north to the Canadian border and south to the Mexican border, required vast amounts of wood. For the most part it was supplied from marvelous stands of white pine in northern Michigan, Wisconsin, and Minnesota. Logging the white pine forests of those states was the principal enterprise in those areas from 1840 to 1920. By 1920 the white pine were mostly gone, leaving mile after mile of tree stumps — "the cutover." Some lesser species survived, jackpine and birch, and some of the land has been reforested with successful species like the Norway pine. But the great white pine forests were gone — gone to build the farmsteads and the towns and cities of mid-America.

The great coniferous forests of Oregon and Washington were too far from market in the 1800s and were hardly touched in that century. But the growing population of California needed lumber to build. Thus, the cutting of redwoods along the coast became commonplace, and the logging of pine and fir species on the western slopes of the Sierra Nevada became big business. But because of transport difficulties in the mountains and the limited market on the West Coast the stands of redwood, pine, and fir were never logged bare as was the case in the Great Lakes region.

Cattlemen and sheepmen were pushed into the drier rougher regions of the Far West by the advancing farmers on the Great Plains. By 1890 the large cattle and sheep ranches tended to be located in mountain valleys of the Rockies, the intermountain region between the Sierra Nevada and the Rockies, Wyoming, the Southwest, and unique grazing land like the Flint Hills of Kansas and the Sand Hills of Nebraska. But wherever the ranchers were located, they treated the unoccupied public domain as their private domain. They grazed their cattle and sheep on it free of charge, and often overgrazed it because it was a free good. What was left of the public domain — the mountains, the Bad Lands, and the desert — as it existed adjacent to these ranches, they felt they had the right to use as they saw fit, and use it they did. Cattlemen and sheepmen as of 1890 were inclined to treat what was left of the wilderness the same as white Americans had been treating it since 1607 in Virginia.

But as we shall see conditions and attitudes regarding resource use were changing in the 1890s.

Conservation in the Progressive Era

Concern about the deplorable state of agricultural practices in America and the reckless exploitation of natural resources, particularly the wanton destruction of the forests, increased in the second half of the nineteenth century. George Perkins Marsh, a lawyer, a self-trained scientist, and a keen observer of soil erosion and the destruction of hill-sides of the Green Mountains of Vermont from overgrazing and tim-ber cutting, in 1864 published a book entitled *Man and Nature,* which caught the attention of the growing scientific community and some politicians. In this volume Marsh explored "the fragile balance of inter-relationships between plants and animals" and went on to argue that "whenever man domesticates plants or clears a forest, or diverts streams, or interferes with some aspect of natural activity, the effects extend to a far wider sphere of the natural environment."[6] Here was the beginning of the science of ecology, and it was something solid on which conservation leaders could base their arguments.

In 1873 Dr. Franklin B. Hough, a Civil War surgeon and director of the National Census, as well as a follower of George Marsh, convinced the American Association for the Advancement of Science to lobby the federal government for legislation to protect and preserve the American forests. In a typical American political response Congress in 1875 created the Division of Forestry in the Department of Agriculture to *study* the problem. But it was a beginning, and more and more writers and professional and scientific groups were calling for legislation to provide protection for the remaining American forests. As a part of this growing interest in conserving the nation's forests and wilderness areas, Congress in 1872 established Yellowstone Park as "a national park and pleasuring ground."

The first important step by the federal government to conserve the nation's natural resources, particularly forest resources, occurred in 1891 with the passage of the General Revision Act (see chapter 5). This act repealed the Timber Cutting Act of 1878 and the Preemption Act of 1841, which had given individuals and business firms the opportunity to acquire prize timberland either free of charge or at the low price of $1.25 an acre. The act also gave the president, in this case Benjamin Harrison, the authority to establish "forest reservations." President Harrison created fifteen forest reserves, totaling 16,000,000 acres, on which the sale of timber was forbidden, during his term of office. But Congress *did not appropriate any funds* to manage or protect these reserves. President Cleveland created thirteen new forest reserves in 1897, but still there were no funds appropriated to manage these reserves. Congress did attach an amendment to the appropriation bill of 1897 that placed limits on the presidential authority to create forest reserves and altered the direction of the conservation movement away from preservation by directing the secretary of the interior to permit the cutting of trees on reserves and the use of waters within the reserves for mining, milling, and irrigation. This act did a number of things: it blunted and redirected the efforts of the conservationists; it illustrated the political power of the western mining, timber, and ranching interests in the Congress to protect their traditional right to exploit the nation's resources; it reestablished commercial access to the national forests; and it paved the way for the Roosevelt-Pinchot multiple-use policy of grazing, lumbering, and hydroelectric power generation in the national forests.

The stage was now set for the Progressive Era in conservation. Theodore Roosevelt became president in 1901 upon the assassination of President McKinley, and he brought to the nation a new, aggressive agenda of resource conservation. Koppes argues that there were three idea strands, or organizing principles, to the Progressive Era conservation movement: efficiency, equity, and aesthetics (often called preservation).[7] Theodore Roosevelt and his chief conservation lieutenant, Gifford Pinchot, believed that resources should be used but that they should be used efficiently. They also believed that the resources of this nation had been wasted in the past and that this waste resulted in large measure from the corrupting pressures of politics. Since resource matters were basically technical, Roosevelt and Pinchot argued, technicians rather than politicians should deal with them. Foresters should determine the annual timber cut; hydraulic engineers should determine the location of reservoirs and the feasibility of multiple-purpose river development; and agronomists should decide which forage areas could remain open to grazing, and for how long, without undue damage to those areas. For Roosevelt, Pinchot, and their followers conservation was, above all, a scientific movement. The essence of conservation in their view was rational planning to promote the efficient use of all natural resources.

For Pinchot and his followers conservation was not only a battle for efficiency but also a struggle for political liberty. They believed that efficient development and resource use would result in greater social equity. Public ownership and control were essential, they believed, to prevent further monopolization and waste of resources. But in the political battles that ensued for the management and control of the natural resources of the nation by Pinchot and his technician followers, this equity goal was often lost.

The third organizing principle of the conservation movement in the Progressive Era was aesthetic or preservationist. The goal of the people in this group, of which John Muir was a leading figure, was the preservation of natural areas of scenic beauty or scientific importance. But within this overall goal there were the divergent interests of love of beauty and love of wilderness. Beauty and wilderness shared the same need; namely, each had to be protected to continue to exist, but the rationales for the preservation of each were very different. Beauty in nature has many meanings, but whatever the meaning, beauty offers an easily grasped and widely shared impulse. Almost everyone wants to view the Grand Canyon, to cite but one example.

The human desire to protect the wilderness is more difficult to understand. For some, a wilderness experience may be necessary for psychological rejuvenation; this was obviously the case for John Muir. Others at the turn of the twentieth century feared the complete triumph of the then modern industrial civilization, and wanted to retain wilderness areas as exceptions to it. In the later twentieth century preservation of wilderness is generally cast in terms of protection of biological diversity or the defense of the earth itself.

But in the first decade of the 1900s Roosevelt, Pinchot, and their efficiency expert followers took a dim view of the preservationists and their unscientific love of beauty and wilderness in nature. Sometimes the two groups worked together, but more often they feuded. Despite this the preservationist school won some victories, the most notable being the creation of the National Park Service in 1916. But this victory carried with it problems for the preservationists. The organic act creating the Park Service directed it both to preserve natural areas and to provide for the public enjoyment of them. Thus, throughout the twentieth century there has been a running battle between those who seek to expand tourism in the parks through the building of access roads, camp grounds, and sumptuous hotels and those who seek to preserve sensitive ecosystems by maintaining the parks as close to the wilderness ideal as possible. The struggle continues in the 1990s.

The gospel of efficiency, with Roosevelt behind it, was the driving force of the conservation movement in the Progressive Era. Let us see how it played out in one important resource area, forestry. As of 1898 the newly created forest reserves were administered by the General Land Office of the Department of the Interior. Most of the officials of that office were law clerks trained in the legal aspects of land disposal, and they knew little or nothing about forestry or the problems of the arid West. Further, most officials of the General Land Office were political appointees with no interest in effective forest management. Pinchot, who was chief of the Bureau of Forestry in the Department of Agriculture, which did research on forestry problems but had no control over the reserves, began to lobby for the transfer of the management of the reserves to the Department of Agriculture, which he argued, dealt with biological science, of which forestry was a logical part.

From 1898 to 1905, Pinchot worked for the transfer. In the process he won over western Congressmen and cattle and sheep ranchers by arguing that the forest reserves, increasingly called national forests, should be opened to grazing under scientific management. Up to 1901 grazing in the forest reserves had been prohibited by the General Land Office, although the prohibition was not enforced because of a lack of funds. But Pinchot's position that the forest reserves should be *used* to produce a sustained flow of lumber as well as providing forage for cattle and sheep, all under scientific management, won him the enmity of the preservationists. The issue was joined in a speech by Pinchot before the Society of American Foresters in 1903 when he argued that the government's policy "is not to preserve the forests because they are beautiful . . . or because they are refuges for the wild creatures of the wilderness . . . but . . . [to make] prosperous homes. . . . Every other consideration comes as secondary."[8]

Pinchot, with the support of the president, won the political war, and the administration of the forest reserves was transferred in 1905 to the Bureau of Forestry. The Bureau of Forestry was renamed the Forest Service in 1905, and Pinchot immediately began expanding its staff and its responsibilities. From a staff of 123 in the Bureau of Forestry in 1898 he built the Forest Service with a staff of 1,500 people by 1908 — a staff of trained foresters with a spirit of public responsibility. When Roosevelt became president in 1901 there were 41 forest reserves totaling 46,000,000 acres; when he left office in 1909 there were 159 national forests totaling 151,000,000 acres.

More important, these 159 national forests were now managed forests, providing a sustained yield of lumber, watershed protection, and control over the number of cattle and sheep, and length of time, that they were permitted to graze in the national forests.[9] All this did not come easy. Local governments and politicians did not like the idea of losing control over the use of forest resources in their area; cattle and sheep ranchers did not want to pay to run their animals in the national forests, which heretofore they had done free of charge; the homesteaders and lumber companies did not want to pay for the logs they took from the national forests; and the preservationists, working mostly through eastern legislators, never stopped fighting Pinchot and his gospel of efficient use of the forests.

President Taft did not approve of the freewheeling political methods that Pinchot employed to gain his conservation objectives. Further, Taft believed in the strict construction of the Constitution, and he did not approve of Pinchot's liberal interpretation of his legislative authority to control and manage the nation's resources. Thus, late in 1909 President Taft fired Chief Forester Gifford Pinchot. But Pinchot did not drop out of sight. He was, for many years, active in national conservation policy and politics working through the National Conservation Association, which he had organized in 1909.

During the Taft presidency the momentum of the Progressive Era conservation movement ebbed away. Considerable action in the areas of water reclamation for irrigation and the development of hydroelectric power continued, however, through the Wilson administrations.

Conservation and the New Deal

Franklin Roosevelt had a personal interest in conservation problems that predated by many years his ascendancy to the presidency in 1933. While serving in the New York State Senate he was chairman of the fish and game committee and later while serving on the agricultural committee he became familiar with the problems of farmers and soil erosion in his state. While serving as assistant secretary of the navy in the Wilson administration he made it a point to develop a friendly and working relationship with Gifford Pinchot and the water conservationists; on one occasion, while visiting the lower Mississippi region during a severe flood, he suggested that reforestation would be a better and more permanent solution to the problem than building levees. And while sidelined by polio from 1920 to 1928 he worked at the reforestation of his Hyde Park estate and promoted private sustained-yield forest farming.

With this background Franklin Roosevelt reinvigorated the conservation movement during his presidency. But events during this period gave an additional push to the conservation movement and support for specific government actions. The economic depression was so deep and so all-encompassing by 1933 that public support for government action programs to protect the environment overrode the opposition of private firms engaged in exploiting the nation's natural resources (e.g., private hydroelectric power generation). The duststorms of 1933–35, which originated in the Great Plains, destroyed thousands of acres of farmland in that area, and were of such ferocity as to endanger lives in the plains region and spread dust as far east as the Atlantic seaboard. The duststorms of the 1930s literally frightened Americans into taking action to protect the environment.

Some of the first actions taken in 1933 included paying farmers for taking land out of production in highly erodible areas under the Agricultural Adjustment Administration and the initiation of erosion control terracing projects under the Public Works Administration. In

1935 the Congress created and funded the Soil Conservation Service in the Department of Agriculture under the leadership of Hugh Bennett. Bennett was known as the father of soil conservation who had the ear of President Roosevelt, and it was said that when he went up to Capitol Hill, the legislators simply asked, "How much money do you need, Mr. Bennett?" It was not quite that easy, but under Bennett's dynamic leadership, the Soil Conservation Service had 147 demonstration projects operating within one year, with 25,000 to 30,000 acres in each project. To back up this work Bennett established soil conservation nurseries and research stations and made liberal use of Civilian Conservation Corps personnel to get the work done. The Soil Conservation Service became a permanent part of the Department of Agriculture and was one of the more successful agencies spawned by the New Deal; in 1990 the service was working with farmers and landowners in nearly 3,000 soil conservation districts covering over two billion acres.

As the result of overgrazing on the public domain, erosion became a severe problem in the late 1920s and early 1930s. Conditions became so bad in the public domain that even cattle and sheep ranchers asked for help in regulating its use. Thus in the summer of 1934, triggered by the duststorms, the Congress passed the Taylor Grazing Act, which gave the secretary of the interior the power to create grazing districts on the public domain, issue permits to graze, and collect fees. The act also required the secretary of the interior to cooperate with "local associations of stockmen" to solve area problems. The Grazing Service, which was reorganized into the Bureau of Land Management in 1946, certainly moderated the pressure on grazing lands of the public domain, but it was not able to solve the problems of those lands. Overgrazing continues to be a problem, and grazing fees remain well below their true worth. Political pressure from western stockmen and congressional representatives to relax grazing regulations and to hold down grazing fees to uneconomic levels has been too great for the Bureau of Land Management to withstand.

Roosevelt's interest in wildlife, trees, and wilderness found expression in an expansion of preserved areas and a change in their orientation. The areas set aside as national parks and monuments grew from 14.7 million acres in 1933 to 20.3 million acres in 1946. The Forest Service and the Bureau of Indian Affairs designated large areas as wilderness zones and a host of wildlife refuges were added. But perhaps more important was the changed orientation of the National Park Service. Five new parks were added — Olympic, Kings Canyon, Big

Bend, Isle Royale, and Everglades — all with a wilderness orientation and all with boundaries drawn with newfound attention to ecological principles.

But even closer to the heart of Franklin Roosevelt was the establishment of the Civilian Conservation Corps. Within two years after its implementation there were 500,000 young men in the corps in 2,600 camps. Another two million would enroll before 1941. They built fire trails, lookout towers, roads, and fire breaks in the national forests. They stocked streams and lakes with a billion or more fish, set up 30,000 wildlife shelters, and restored old battlefield sites. *But mostly they planted trees.* They planted hundreds of thousands of them on the plains, on eroded hillsides, in cut-over regions, and in burned-out forests. They also formed brigades to fight fires.

Wildlife was not forgotten. The Pittman-Robertson Federal Aid in Wildlife Restoration Act of 1937 reallocated the excise tax on sporting arms and ammunition to the states in proportion to the number of their licensed hunters; these funds were to be applied to wildlife research, land acquisition, and other approved projects. The law also required the states to designate their own hunting license fees to fish and wildlife programs. Then, in 1939, the Bureau of Biological Survey from the Department of Agriculture and the Bureau of Fisheries from the Department of Commerce were consolidated into the new Fish and Wildlife Service of the Department of the Interior. This agency then became the principal unit within the federal government to do research on wildlife, protect endangered species, and negotiate treaties regarding migratory birds.

Secretary of Interior Harold Ickes and his water resource people believed that dams — big dams and lots of them — could do many wonderful things for the depressed economy of the 1930s. First, they would provide jobs in the construction phase; second, they would provide cheap hydroelectric power — public power — to serve consumers and new industries; and third, they would provide the basis for regional development involving an expanded irrigated agriculture as well as new industries.

The conservation movement of the 1930s did not view dams as ecological disasters. On the contrary, it saw them as an efficient way of using the important water resources of the nation for the benefit of everyone in society as well as an important way of combating economic depression. The Tennessee Valley Authority was viewed as the savior of the Tennessee Valley, and Valley authorities with dams as their centerpieces, it was argued, could bring economic and ecological progress to the developing world.

These visionaries of public hydroelectric power were right in part. The Tennessee Valley was rescued in the 1930s, and the Pacific Northwest did experience strong economic growth as a result of the multiple-purpose dams built on the Columbia River. Moreover, the generating capacity of the Bureau of Reclamation hydroelectric plants increased from an insignificant 30,000 kilowatts in 1933 to 2.2 million kilowatts in 1945, making it the largest generator of electrical power in the world.

The steam went out of the conservation movement following World War II and the great economic prosperity that followed in the late 1940s and the 1950s. New initiatives in reforestation, soil conservation, and wildlife protection were not undertaken. Dam construction continued and reclamation projects became even larger (e.g., the Central Valley project in California), but the dam builders became primarily interested in generating electric power and selling it to the highest bidder, public or private, which turned out to be increasingly private. The reclamation project developers disregarded entirely the 160-acre limitation, and dam building and federally supported irrigation became strictly business.

One final point needs to be made about a factor that had an important impact on post-World War II conservation developments. Aesthetic conservation underwent a crucial transformation in the late 1930s as it gained the support of the emerging science of ecology. The merging of the aesthetic and ecological rationales laid the foundation for a new and stronger preservationist philosophy in the 1960s and 1970s. This new philosophy, energized by the science of ecology, helped defeat the building of a dam at Echo Park in the heart of Dinosaur National Monument, and more important, drove from the drawing boards plans by the Bureau of Reclamation to build dams for Big Bend, Kings Canyon, and Grand Canyon national parks. Glen Canyon was lost to a big dam, but the other scenic areas were saved.

Silent Spring: **Environmental Awakening**

Environmentalism as a movement took shape in the United States in the period 1960–80. It grew out of the preservationist strand of conservation on one hand and the science of ecology, the study of the relationship between living organisms and their surroundings, on the other. The publication of Rachel Carson's *Silent Spring* in 1962 signaled the beginning of the movement; some people have described Carson as the midwife of the movement. She took the scientific evidence that had been accumulating in scientific journals and other obscure places, added her indignation to what was happening to the planet Earth, and exposed in a best-selling book the destructive side effects of the pesticide DDT as well as the subtle cumulative effects of modern technology.

As might be expected the book met with a storm of abuse. Scientists from the hard and agricultural sciences at first claimed that her charges had no scientific validity and that she was simply a hysterical woman from the lunatic fringe. But her charges stood up, her attackers retreated, and DDT was banned from use in the United States within a few years.

The movement gained momentum, and ecology became a household word in the 1960s. The ecologist Marston Bates in his book *The Forest and the Sea* (1960) argued that "man's destiny is tied to nature's destiny. . . . Man may be a very peculiar animal, but he is still a part of the system of nature."[10] And career ecologists were insisting both in popular and technical publications that respect for the biosphere, like respect for justice, must have an established place in law and government. They maintained that all human beings are entitled to clean and beautiful surroundings. They further argued that the protection of the environment, nature, is nonnegotiable. The science of ecology thus provided basic knowledge, logical relationships, and a sense of moral urgency to the environmental movement.

As a result, things began to happen. The Nature Conservancy, which began as a committee, within the new Ecological Society of America, to preserve endangered wildlands, had grown, with generous assistance from Carson's estate (she died in 1964), to the point in 1967 where it could afford a paid staff. In that year it received a major grant from the Ford Foundation, and by 1970 it had reached a state of financial security with a revolving fund of $4.5 million. In pursuit of its long-time goal of protecting plant and animal species through the purchase and management of wildlands, the Nature Conservancy had by 1990 saved over three million acres of land. Citizens were on the march, too, through old-time conservation organizations such as the National Audubon Society, the National Parks and Conservation Association, the National Wildlife Federation, and the Sierra Club to alert the public to various environmental threats and to mobilize support for wilderness protection and the 1967 Air Quality Act. Citizens were joining new action-oriented groups like Friends of the Earth and

Defenders of Wildlife and providing funding support for environmental law groups: the Environmental Defense Fund and the Natural Resources Defense Council. College activists organized a nationwide Earth Day in 1970 to call attention to the environmental degradation of the earth. As a part of this organizational activity by citizens, the major environmental organizations either established or strengthened their Washington offices and hired full-time staffs to lobby Congress and work with the relevant bureaucracies to further their environmental interests.

In 1971 there appeared another important book dealing with what was then called the environmental crisis; it was *The Closing Circle: Man, Nature, and Technology* by Barry Commoner. In this volume Commoner sets forth the ecological argument for protecting the global ecosystem. He begins by describing how the global ecosystem has evolved over billions of years and continues to evolve today as its various parts interact over time. Then he discusses at length how modern technological processes operate to pollute and degrade the ecosystem; from there he goes on to address the political and social issues involved in seeking solutions to the environmental crisis. In a later chapter he raises an interesting question: is it possible for a capitalistic system like the United States to continue to grow, based on technological developments such as occurred between 1940 and 1970 without doing irreparable damage to the global ecosystem? If not, then what must be the final result? Commoner gives his answer in the final chapter of the book: "We are in an environmental crisis because the means by which we use the ecosphere to produce wealth are destructive of the ecosphere itself. The present system of production is self-destructive; the present course of human civilization is suicidal."[11]

But all was not doom and gloom. The federal government began to take action in the 1960s to protect the environment. The Senate ratified the Treaty Banning Nuclear Weapons Testing in the Atmosphere, in Outer Space, and Under Water in 1963. The Clean Air Act, passed in 1963, greatly expanded the authority of the Public Health Service to control air pollution. This act was amended and strengthened in 1970 and 1977. A series of acts designed to improve the quality of water available for human consumption was passed in 1965, 1966, 1970, and 1972; the last of these came to be known as the Clean Water Act and was described by the Natural Resources Defense Council as "one of the strongest environmental laws ever written." The Solid Waste Disposal Act of 1965 recognized that waste disposal had become a nationwide problem. This act called for research and assistance to the states.

Congress took up the problem again in 1970 in the Resource Recovery Act, which emphasized improved disposal methods and the recovery of usable materials and energy. In these, and a flood of environmental bills that were not passed prior to 1969, Congress and the president were beginning to feel their way into a problem area that by 1970 Barry Commoner was calling an environmental crisis.

The National Environmental Policy Act (NEPA) passed by Congress in 1969 was certainly the most important piece of environmental legislation enacted into law up to that time, and perhaps that can still be said as of 1992. The NEPA did at least three important things:

First, it required each federal agency to prepare an environmental impact statement (EIS) before taking major action that might do harm to the environment. It did not forbid harmful actions, but it did require an assessment by the agency taking the action of the ultimate costs and benefits to the environment.

Second, it authorized the establishment in the executive branch of the government of the Council on Environmental Quality, which was to set long-term policy, advise the president, and monitor the EIS process.

Third, it created the Environmental Protection Agency (EPA) and invested it with the responsibility of protecting and improving the natural and human environment of the United States. The authorizing legislation directed the EPA to report directly to the president and to take over the environmental responsibilities of all existing federal agencies — some sixty-three in total. It began operations in 1970 with an annual budget of $1.28 billion; by 1980 its budget had increased to $5.6 billion, and this latter budget would soon prove to be inadequate to deal with the cleanup of thousands of leaking toxic waste dumps discovered in the early 1980s.

The political scientist Geoffrey Wandesforde-Smith identifies two compelling reasons for the NEPA. First, the management of programs to deal with environmental problems had grown too complex to be handled effectively by the compartmentalized structure of federal agencies that existed prior to 1969. Second, the federal government as the agent of all the people carried the ethical responsibility of managing the environment in the role of steward or protective custodian for posterity.[12] Certainly this was the logic behind the passage of the NEPA. But the political power to win the passage of the NEPA sprang from the increasing public awareness of the widespread pollution and degradation of the environment. The record of the NEPA in protecting the environment in the 1970s was uneven and depended to an important degree on the support given to it by the president. The NEPA forced the managers of each governmental agency that proposed to take an action that would have an impact on the environment to prepare an EIS. Program managers hated this. It was time-consuming and costly. And the law provided for public hearings to review the impact statements, a process that often brought to light pieces of information that the program managers would have preferred be kept secret. The results were mixed; sometimes the information provided in the EISs initiated actions that protected the environment and sometimes the filing of EISs became simply a *pro forma* nuisance. But on balance the statements became a means for making environmental information public and forcing government agencies to accept accountability for their program actions.

The EPA had an uneven and stormy history in the 1970s, which was to become even more mixed and stormy in the 1980s. With regard to the prevention and control of air pollution the EPA's regulations have been alternately weak and strong, obeyed and ignored. First, the EPA required new cars to have catalytic converters to break down dangerous compound emissions. As a result emissions of carbon monoxide, hydrocarbons, and nitrogen oxides began to decline in the early 1970s. But in 1976 the EPA set aside its emission standards and controls because of auto industry complaints, and exhaust pollution began to rise again. The EPA's record in controlling the pollutants from industrial firms — utilities, metal producers, and oil refineries — was also highly uneven.

Government action was taking place on other fronts in the 1970s. Some of the more important actions are described below. In the autumn of 1970, the Congress established the National Commission on Materials Policy. The commission made numerous useful recommendations, three of which are mentioned here:

1. Environmental costs should be taken into account in any cost-benefit analysis of materials extraction and use.
2. Market forces, rather than government subsidies, should determine the mix of imports and domestic production.
3. A single department of natural resources should be established. The interactions of materials, energy, and the environment are too numerous, too subtle, and too complex to be managed effectively in a decentralized manner.

"We have concluded," the commission stated, "that it is impossible to understand, much less solve, problems in one part of the interlocking materials-energy-environment system without recognizing that all parts of the system are interrelated." This last statement of the commission could have been taken out of a textbook on ecology.

The Safe Drinking Water Act of 1974 set health standards for toxic contaminants in drinking water. The Federal Environmental Pesticides Act of 1972 required all producers of pesticides to register these products with the EPA, and the Federal Pesticides Act of 1978 extended and tightened the loopholes in the original Federal Insecticide, Fungicide, and Rodenticide Act. The Toxic Substances Control Act of 1976 represented the first comprehensive effort by the federal government to regulate the chemical industry. The Surface Mining Control and Reclamation Act of 1977 established environmental controls on strip mining and required the restoration of land to its original contours. The Federal Water Pollution Control Act of 1977 dealt with the problem of sewage disposal by requiring most cities to build sewage treatment plants and by offering federal grants for plant construction. The National Parks and Recreation Act of 1978 tripled the wilderness area within the national park system. The Federal Land Policy and Management Act of 1976, a compromise act that emerged after six years of congressional wrangling, was supposed to set new standards in the management of public lands. Whether it provides more or less environmental protection remains to be seen. The Endangered Species Act of 1973 and amendments to it in 1978 and 1979 reaffirmed the importance of wildlife habitat, but the amendments gave greater consideration to economic, as against biological, factors and as a result weakened the protection for certain endangered species. The Fish and Wildlife Conservation Act of 1980 signaled an important shift in public thinking, namely, that wild animals are more than pests or game to be hunted; they are a universal good. It was the first federal law specifically to protect animals that are neither hunted nor endangered. The Comprehensive Environmental Response, Compensation, and Liability Act of 1980 authorized the federal government to respond to hazardous waste emergencies and created a superfund of $1.6 billion to be used for cleaning up chemical dump sites. In one of the last acts of his administration, President Jimmy Carter signed the Alaska Lands Act on December 2, 1980, which added some 104 million acres to the nation's dedicated lands in the form of national parks and monuments, wildlife refuges, national forests, and wild and scenic rivers in the state of Alaska.

The federal government made a strong effort in many directions to protect the environment in the 1970s. The knowledge base was there on which to take corrective action, and the will was there on the part of much of the electorate, but the opposition was also there in the form of polluting chemical and manufacturing industries, mining and timber companies, and Americans with their love of the automobile. As a result some of the actions taken by the federal government to protect the environment were bold and successful, but others were weak and vacillating.

Environmentalism in the 1980s and Beyond

By the end of the 1970s, and in spite of the many corrective actions taken by the federal government described in the preceding section, problems of environmental degradation and pollution in the United States appeared to be increasing. A whole new set of problems that had their origin in the massive and careless disposal of industrial chemicals and wastes were beginning to show up across the nation. These second-generation problems, with their largely unknown health and environmental consequences, first horrified and then frightened the general public. The first response, as we know, was the passage of the "Superfund Act" of 1980. But the magnitude of these problems soon overwhelmed the first efforts to deal with them. As the decade of the 1980s wore on a third generation of problems came into the scene, even larger in their consequences than those the nation had been trying to deal with before. These ecological issues, largely international in scope, include the greenhouse effect and global warming, thinning of the ozone layer, acid rain, massive tropical deforestation, extinction of species, and ocean and coastal pollution. Add to these the ticking of the worldwide population time bomb, and the national and international environmental agenda plate is full to overflowing for the decade of the 1990s and beyond.

The forward momentum of the environmental movement came to an abrupt halt with the ascendancy of Ronald Reagan to the presidency in 1981. Under his leadership all of the environmental protection and resource policies and programs enacted in the 1970s were reevaluated on the assumption that their enforcement had an adverse effect on the economy. Thus, to the extent the environmental laws permitted, the Reagan administration pursued a policy of deregulation. It further effected budget cutbacks on environmental programs wherever possible. For example, in 1981 the Reagan administration cut the U.S. contribution to the United Nations Environment Program from $10 to $2 million (Congress later restored it to $7.85 million). President Reagan ended Jimmy Carter's Young Adult Conservation Corps, and in 1984 he vetoed an act that would have created an American conservation corps.

But perhaps more than his antienvironmental policy, President Reagan's appointees to key governmental posts infuriated members of the environmental movement. James Watt, appointed to head the Department of the Interior, held a philosophy similar to that of nineteenth-century frontier Americans, namely, that the natural resources of the nation existed to be exploited and plundered by whoever got to them first. And as secretary of the interior he would help the private sector do just that in the 1980s. Thus, he favored oil drilling along the scenic California coast; he endorsed the so-called Sagebrush Rebellion against the federal control and management of public lands; and he made "sweetheart," if not illegal, leasing deals with private coal mining companies in Wyoming and Montana that cost the U.S. Treasury up to $132 million. It was policy positions and business practices such as these that forced Watt to resign in late 1983.

Anne Gorsuch, later Anne Burford, a lawyer from Colorado and a friend of James Watt's, was appointed by President Reagan to head the Environmental Protection Agency. As a friend of big business, not the environment, she attacked the EPA's important Division of Law Enforcement as a way of telling her agency to go easy on business firms polluting the environment. Because of her high-handed antienvironmental actions, she was called before Congress to explain those actions, and was eventually cited for contempt for failing to turn over files on 160 toxic waste dumps where her agency was allegedly not enforcing the "Superfund Act." She resigned as head of the EPA in the spring of 1983.

Budget cuts and the weakening of the enforcement of environmental laws took their toll in the 1980s; the environmental problems of acid rain, hazardous dump sites, and sewage disposal were mounting. Yet even the determined efforts of a popular president did not halt, or slow down, the environmental movement. On the contrary, public support for stronger antipollution and environmental protection laws grew. Membership in the Sierra Club, for example, increased from 180,000 in 1980 to 496,000 in 1989, membership in the Wilderness Society increased from 45,000 to 317,000 over the same period, and membership in the Environmental Defense Fund increased from 45,000 to 100,000. The largest organization, the National Wildlife Federation, had almost six million members in 1989. These organizations had political clout by 1989, and treasuries to match their greatly expanded memberships.

Mindful of these grass-roots political developments, Congress, which at first went along with President Reagan in his budget cutting of environmental programs, and deregulation actions, soon shifted its position and became a defender of existing environmental policies and programs. As a result the president and the Congress were often at odds over environmental policy in the 1980s. In spite of this conflict some noticeable pieces of environmental legislation were passed between 1981 and 1988. The Nuclear Waste Policy Act of 1982 established a national plan for the permanent disposal of highly radioactive nuclear waste. The Conservation and Recovery Act of 1984 revised and strengthened EPA procedures for regulating hazardous waste facilities. The Food Security Act of 1985 for the first time limited program benefits to farmers who produced commodities on highly erodible land or converted wetlands (this effort was rather ineffective but it was a beginning). The Safe Drinking Water Act of 1986 reauthorized the act of 1974 and revised and strengthened the EPA's safe drinking water programs. The Superfund Reauthorization Act of 1986 provided $8.5 billion through 1991 to clean up the nation's most dangerous abandoned chemical dumps and set strict standards and timetables for cleaning up such sites. The Clean Water Act of 1987 amended the Federal Water Pollution Control Act of 1972 and extended and strengthened the EPA's water control programs. The Global Climate Protection Act of 1987 authorized the State Department to develop an approach to the problems of global climate change. This was only a tentative step, but it was a beginning, and it did recognize that this was an international problem. The Ocean Dumping Act of 1988 amended the marine Protection, Research, and Sanctuaries Act of 1972 to end all ocean disposal of sewage sludge and industrial wastes by December 31, 1991.

George Bush during his campaign for the presidency in 1988 proclaimed, "I am an environmentalist." And during the 1988 campaign he tried to distance himself from the negative environmental image of Ronald Reagan; his rhetoric dealing with the environment was of a "kinder and gentler" tone. Bush began his administration with a strong proposal for revising the Clean Air Act; and he does deserve credit for working with Congress to enact the Clean Air Act of 1990. In the legislative process, however, opponents of the legislation within his administration gained strength and the final act was seriously weakened and compromised by administration-sponsored amendments.

Bush's underlying environmental philosophy is not much different from that of his predecessor, Ronald Reagan. In his view the free market can solve environmental problems better than government regulations, and no major changes are needed in American life-style to save the environment. His "environmental ethic," like the "conservation ethic" of Teddy Roosevelt and Gifford Pinchot of the Progressive Era, is based on a concept of wise management and efficient use of resources rather than the preservation of nature for its own sake. Thus, he was slow to respond to the environmental catastrophe that resulted when the *Exxon Valdez* ran aground in Prince William Sound in Alaska in 1989 causing the worst oil spill in U.S. history. He has been slow to develop an energy policy other than more oil drilling on the nation's dedicated land such as the Arctic National Wildlife Refuge. He has been slow to recognize the possibility of global warming due to the greenhouse effect in spite of the rapid buildup of carbon dioxide (CO_2) in the atmosphere since 1960. He has been slow to recognize the problem of a vanishing ozone layer in the atmosphere. And he seems totally unconcerned about the population explosion around the world. This position will no longer do, as we shall now argue, if the planet Earth and the people on it are to survive in living conditions somewhat similar to those of the past several decades.

The people of the United States and the world enter the decade of the 1990s and the twenty-first century in an environmental context totally new to man. The natural world, nature, has been exploited and plundered to the point where it can no longer heal itself. It is no longer an independent thing. Bill McKibben has argued that nature is dead.[13] By this he does not mean that trees will no longer grow, or the flowers will no longer bloom, or that we can no longer enjoy a walk on the beach. But he does mean that we have so altered the natural world that it can no longer respond independent of man. Man from now on must manage nature, if that nature is to provide hospitable environmental surroundings for man.

How did this come about? It came about through the developmental activities of man. It came about through centuries of cutting down the forests and pushing crop production onto increasingly fragile and erodible lands. It came about through three centuries of industrial production in which we have been pouring carbon dioxide into the atmosphere at an increasing rate, raising the concentration of such chemicals by 20 to 25 percent since 1860. The release of chlorofluorocarbons into the atmosphere over the past forty years has reduced the ozone layer over parts of Antarctica by as much as 50 percent, and now we learn in February 1992 that a similar development is occurring over the northern atmosphere and a reduction by as much as 40 percent is possible in the ozone layer over parts of North America and Europe. The development of nuclear power creates the possibility and increases the probability of nuclear power plant accidents, such as occurred at Chernobyl in the Soviet Union in 1986, an event that exposed thousands of people to high levels of radiation and spread radioactive fallout across northern Europe (worse still, it creates the possibility of a comparable catastrophe through the purposeful detonation of a nuclear bomb). And then there is the widespread failure of governments in nations and communities to come to grips with the burgeoning problem of waste disposal, particularly toxic wastes, that are generated by modern industrialized societies.

The consequences of these activities may be listed as follows: (1) the increased incidence of flooding in settled areas of the earth; (2) relatively rapid and unpredictable changes in the climate of the earth; (3) the increased exposure of broad segments of the world's plant and animal populations, including human beings, to hazardous ultraviolet rays; (4) the increased possibility of thousands, perhaps millions, of people dying from exposure to high levels of radiation, as well as the destruction of the flora and fauna of the areas affected; and (5) the increased possibility of humans, as well as plant and animal life on both land and sea, being poisoned and otherwise adversely affected by contamination from undisclosed or improperly constructed and managed waste dump sites.

In short, we have fouled and plundered nature to the point where we have endangered both ourselves and the natural world. Now we must learn to manage nature to save ourselves and the natural world. Can we do it?[14] Who knows?

Sustainable Agriculture

One management approach to protecting the natural world in the agricultural sector goes under the name of sustainable agriculture. The concept of sustainable agriculture in broad terms is straightforward: it is a system of agriculture that can be maintained indefinitely without impacting negatively on the environmental system. But when the investigator tries to be more specific, or make the concept operational, he or she immediately runs into difficulty; hence, definitions of sustainable agriculture vary with the background and purpose of the investigator.[15] An environmental purist might subscribe to the following definition: a system that can be maintained indefinitely on the same site area, that over the long term enhances the ecosystem surrounding the site area as well as the quality of life of the farmers and society involved, *and that does not import any resources* (e.g., energy) *from outside the site area*. This, however, is not a tenable concept for agriculture in the United States. Almost certainly the pursuit of policies to effectuate the concept would cause agricultural production to fall and life-styles to decline — perhaps to the point of severe food shortages.

A more acceptable concept might take the following form: a system that can be maintained indefinitely on the same site area, that over the long term enhances the ecosystem surrounding the site area as well as the quality of the farmers and society involved, and that seeks to make *minimal* use of imported resources. Admittedly this concept suffers from vagueness. But the environmental goal remains uncompromised, and the final part of the concept lends itself to the formulation and execution of policies by farmers, scientists, and politicians who have the management responsibility for achieving the goals stated in the concept.

If we can accept the last concept of sustainable agriculture as a realistic approach to protecting the natural world in the agricultural sector, then resource management must occur at three levels. First, at the production level farmers must adopt practices, given the state of technology, that protect and enhance the quality of their cropland, their ground and surface water, and their pasture and forestlands. This they can do by adopting such practices as minimum tillage, crop-residue covers, terracing hilly land, and substituting, to the extent possible, crop rotations and organic fertilizers for chemical fertilizers.

Second, at the research level, scientists must take full account of the environmental impact of each new scientific finding and technology developed, and make this information available to environmental control agencies such as the EPA, as well as the general public. But equally important, the managers of research funds and personnel must direct those research resources toward the development of production and processing practices that enhance the ecosystem rather than degrade it. The scientific community in the food and agricultural area must reorient itself in the direction of environmental enhancement rather than increased production regardless of the environmental consequences.

Third, politicians at the national and international levels must take *effective* steps to reduce acid rain, stop the depletion of the ozone layer, and halt the pouring of billions and billions of tons of CO_2 into the atmosphere each year, which is certain to alter climate patterns around the earth — only as of 1992 scientists cannot agree on where and how those patterns will be altered. A commonly accepted scenario is that if we, the world, permit emission rates of CO_2 to continue at these present levels global temperature will increase by 3 to 5° C by about 2030. There is much less agreement, however, about where the rains will increase and where they will diminish. All of this means that if we experience climatic changes of the magnitude and uncertainty described here, those changes and thus consequences for agricultural production could overwhelm any of the management initiatives taken at the two previous levels to protect and enhance the environment.

The future of the sustainable agricultural management approach to protecting and enhancing the environment, along with every other approach to protecting and enhancing the environment, is thus dependent on politicians in the United States, and in the rest of the developed world, taking *effective* action to significantly slow down the pouring of CO_2 pollutants into the atmosphere. It is probably too late to prevent any climatic change from occurring. But if the current annual emissions rate of 20 billion tons of CO_2 into the atmosphere continues, then the climatic changes are going to be large, perhaps devastating. Making adjustments to such changes could turn the modern, highly specialized agriculture upside down, and with it the present-day life-styles of both farm and urban people.

The environmental crisis that Barry Commoner first described in 1971 has the possibility of becoming an ecological nightmare by 2030. Will this happen? Who knows? The future of the environment worldwide, and the health and well-being of plant and animal life, is in the hands of the national and international political leaders.

Suggested Readings

Carson, Rachel. *Silent Spring*. New York: Fawcett World Library, 1962.

Commoner, Barry. *The Closing Circle: Nature, Man, and Technology*. New York: Knopf, 1971.

Gore, Al. *Earth in the Balance: Ecology and the Human Spirit*. New York: Houghton Mifflin, 1992.

Grove, Richard H. "Origins of Western Environmentalism." *Scientific American* 261, no. 1 (July 1992), pp. 42–47.

Hays, Samuel P. *Conservation and the Gospel of Efficiency: The Progressive Conservation Movement, 1890–1920*. Cambridge, Mass: Harvard University Press, 1959.

Meadows, Donella H., Dennis L. Meadows, Jørgen Randers. *Beyond the Limits: Confronting Global Collapse, Envisioning a Sustainable Future*. Post Mills, Vt.: Chelsea Green Publishing, 1992.

Petulla, Joseph M. *American Environmental History: The Exploitation and Conservation of Natural Resources*. San Francisco: Boyd and Fraser, 1977.

Scheffer, Victor B. *The Shaping of Environmentalism in America*. Seattle: University of Washington Press, 1991.

Vig, Norman J., and Michael E. Kraft, eds. *Environmental Policy in the 1990s*. Washington, D.C.: Congressional Quarterly, Inc., 1990.

CHAPTER 15

THE ROLE OF GOVERNMENT

Government has been involved in almost every aspect of agricultural development discussed in part III up to this point: in the development and execution of land policies, in the support of technological advance through research and development, in the building of social and physical infrastructure, and in the formulation and execution of immigration and trade policies. Thus one might argue that government, like the air we breathe, is a ubiquitous aspect of social and economic life. Nonetheless, in the nineteenth century governments in much of the Western world, and in the English-speaking nations in particular, sought as a matter of political philosophy to interfere in the economic and social life of individual citizens as little as possible. In this connection, the United States is said to have pursued a positive policy of *laissez-faire*.

The purpose of this chapter is twofold: first, to recall for the reader the vital role that government plays in providing services that are essential to the effective functioning of society and to its economic development; second, to describe and to appraise specific governmental interventions into the agricultural sector of the developing United States economy. These interventions have conflicted and continue to conflict with a philosophy of government that seeks to maximize the freedom of the individual. But this has not deterred farmers from seeking assistance from their government, nor the government from seeking to provide that assistance by taking intervening actions. As a result, governmental intervention in the agricultural sector of the economy in the second half of the twentieth century has become commonplace, as it has in many other sectors of the economy.

Farmers have on occasion turned to their state governments for economic assistance, as the Grangers did in the 1870s with respect to the regulation of the railroads and as California farmers have done with respect to orders regulating the marketing of their specialty crops. But farmers have correctly perceived that in most instances the problems plaguing them are market-wide and that the solutions to those problems must also be market-wide. Since at least 1850 the market for most agricultural commodities has been as wide as the national market, and for some commodities (e.g., wheat, cotton) the market has been worldwide. Hence farmers have typically turned to the federal government for intervening actions at the national and/or international levels. This being the case, the discussion in this chapter will focus on the actions and activities of the federal government. The many and varied regulatory activities of the state and local governments with respect to the food and agricultural sector will not be discussed.

Security and Essential Services

According to Adam Smith, writing in 1776, the sovereign government has three, and only three, duties or responsibilities to its citizens. They are

First, the duty of protecting the society from the violence and invasion of other independent societies; secondly, the duty of protecting, as far as possible, every member of the society from the injustice or oppression of every other member of it, or the duty of establishing an exact administration of justice; and thirdly, the duty of erecting and maintaining certain public works and certain public institutions, which it can never be for the interest of any individual, or small number of individuals, to erect and maintain . . . [1]

Given the successful discharge of these duties by the sovereign government, economic development naturally follows from the initiative and industry of individual private citizens. The body politic of the new nation accepted the Smith argument about the proper role of government as a general operating principle.

Except on the western frontier, in the Confederate South during the Civil War, and perhaps in the inner cities of the large cities since 1960, the various levels of government — federal, state, and local — have provided the physical security required by the average citizen in his or her everyday life throughout the history of the nation. The average citizen could go about his or her daily work — producing a product, improving property, saving and investing and raising a family — without undue fear of bodily harm to himself, or herself, or to members of his, or her, family, or undue fear that his, or her, property would be destroyed or stolen. In this context, members of society did work, save, and build, and make the economy grow. Lawlessness and strife (riots, rebellion, invasion), except on rare occasions, have not plagued the economy and the society of the United States. The three levels of government have held those social evils to an acceptable minimum.

The rights and duties of individual members of United States society have been set down in the Constitution, in enacted legislation, and in the common law. Lawful contractual relations between and among individuals have been spelled out in enacted legislation and in the common law, and a legal system has been developed to protect the rights of individuals and to enforce contractual obligations. Thus members of United States society live and act under the rule of law; they have not been and are not subject to the arbitrary and capricious acts of a personalized government (e.g., an absolute monarch, a despotic overlord, or a modern military dictator). From education and experience the average citizen usually knows which of his or her acts will be upheld in a court of law and which are likely to result in some kind of punishment. Thus the average citizen can go about his or her business of earning a living, saving and investing, and conducting family affairs with confidence that these actions will be sustained and rewarded by society — not be negated by some unknown and capricious act of government.

The federal government of the United States has undertaken to provide its citizens with an acceptable, stable currency. In this connection, its efforts have not always met with success. During wartime commodity prices have typically risen and the currency has depreciated (i.e., the value of the dollar has fallen), and in periods of economic depression commodity prices have fallen and the currency has appreciated. In the 1970s the nation was subjected to chronic commodity price inflation and a depreciation of the currency. In part these developments have been due to political weakness. But in part they have been, and still are, due to imperfect knowledge of the operation of the monetary and fiscal systems. With economists arguing among themselves about the causes of price inflation and deflation, it becomes next to impossible for the political decision makers to take actions designed to provide a currency that is stable in value over time. But despite all these monetary and fiscal shortcomings, it should be recognized that the federal government has never yielded to a runaway price inflation, and most of the time it has provided its people with a currency that has facilitated the exchange of goods and services and the assumption of contractual obligations over time. The management of the currency has been far from perfect, but it has been sufficiently adequate most of the time to support and promote a satisfactory rate of economic growth.

The different levels of government in the United States — federal, state, and local — have provided members of society with a variety of basic services. We have already considered certain of these services in some depth — transport and education, for example. Other important services include a secure and reasonably efficient postal service and the provision of telegraphic and telephone services through the institution of public utilities. In metropolitan areas it is common practice for government to provide such services as a safe water supply, sewage and waste disposal, fire protection, and police protection.

In the twentieth century the different levels of government have become involved in providing a set of social services which were highly controversial at their inception but which now are widely accepted. These social services include: retirement plans, economic assistance for the poor and the aged, and the provision of food for the poor. With each passing year, more and more people accept the view that the state should provide health care for all its citizens, just as it provides everyone with an education, and that the state should ensure some minimum level of living for all its citizens (i.e., minimum levels of consumption in such important areas as food, shelter, medical care, education, and clothing.) Slowly but surely, the United States is moving to a policy position wherein the basic welfare of each member of society is ensured.

Since its inception in 1789, the federal government and the state and local governments as well have been progress-oriented governments. Whether the actions of these governments have always been in the best interests of their citizens, present and future, is open to debate, and certainly the actions of these governments have not always been consistent with constitutional constraints, scientific laws and relationships, and moral and ethical precepts. But on balance the actions of these governments have been taken with the *purpose* of settling the country, increasing the productivity of its citizens, facilitating trade and commerce, maintaining a tolerable degree of equity among its citizens, and protecting the basic rights of its citizens. In this sense the different levels of government in the United States have been progress-oriented governments.

Economic Intervention in the Nineteenth Century

Although the body politic of the United States accepted the Adam Smith argument about the proper role of government as a guiding principle, *in practice* various segments of the body politic have repeatedly called upon government to intervene in the operating economy in their behalf. Farm people and their elected representatives have tried in various ways to use the power of government to protect and enhance their economic position over the years, *as have other economic interest groups.* Sometimes farmers have been successful in such efforts: first, in getting government to intervene in their behalf and second, in achieving the purposes of that intervention. But more often farmers have been unsuccessful, or they have lent their support to ill-conceived, foolish ventures. And on some occasions intervening actions taken on behalf of nonfarm interests (e.g., manufacturing and commercial interests) have had adverse effects on farmers. The record, as we shall see, has been uneven and has produced some strange results.

Over the years, interventions into the operating economy by the federal government that have affected the agricultural sector, either directly or indirectly, have fallen into four principal categories: (1) actions that sought to increase farm prices through some kind of supply management; (2) actions concerned with money, banking, and credit; (3) actions designed to change the structure of markets (e.g., to give farmers monopoly power, or to curb the monopoly power of others); and (4) changes in trade policy primarily involving actions to raise or lower tariff duties and/or to impose or withdraw import controls.

Increasing Farm Prices

In the nineteenth century farmers and their leaders talked a great deal about farm prices and the need to raise them — particularly between 1870 and 1897. Sockless Jerry Simpson and his fellow Populist party campaigner Mary Ellen Lease told Kansas farmers in the summer of 1890 to "raise less corn and more hell." But during the nineteenth century neither the state governments nor the federal government developed any programs, or took any actions, aimed at raising farm prices through the management of domestic supplies. The dominant economic philosophy of *laissez-faire* made such a course of action unthinkable.

Money, Banking, and Credit

Under the Constitution, the federal government was given the exclusive right "to coin money, regulate the value thereof, and of foreign coins." A mint was established in 1791, and a year later Congress, acting on the recommendation of Alexander Hamilton, established a coinage system. But the federal government pursued inconsistent policies — backed and filled — throughout the nineteenth century with regard to the establishment of a central bank to manage the money supply, to charter and regulate local banks, and to assist the federal government in the management of its fiscal operations. The federal government created the Bank of the United States in 1791 to assist the government with its fiscal operations and to serve as a central bank to the private economy by providing credit and influencing the money supply. This bank was not rechartered in 1811, but problems encountered by the federal government demonstrated the need for a central bank and the Second Bank of the United States was chartered in 1816 for a period of twenty years. The conservative credit policies of the Second Bank incurred the wrath and the opposition of westerners, primarily farmers, who favored cheap and easy credit, and President Jackson vetoed a bill rechartering the Second Bank in 1832. From that date until 1913, when legislation creating the Federal Reserve System was passed, the banking system of the United States was not supervised by a central bank and the money supply was not managed by a central bank. Before 1864, paper money and credit were issued by local banks chartered by state governments; bank regulations were weak, and local banks often overextended credit and failed when holders of their notes sought to redeem them in a harder currency (e.g., gold). The creation of the National Banking System in 1864 limited the issuance of bank notes to national banks, which were subject to closer regulation and surveillance than state banks. The money supply was further and accidentally influenced by the fiscal operations of the federal government (e.g., the issuance of Greenbacks during the Civil War), the discovery and production of gold, and government policy regarding the coinage of gold and silver.

In all this maneuvering with respect to monetary policy, banking systems and regulation, and government fiscal policy, farmers were

consistently on the side of liberal banking laws, weak banking regulations, an expanded money supply, and easy credit. Farmers generally
believed that cheap money and easy credit worked to their advantage,
and in this they were correct. They needed credit to develop their
farms, and they found it easier to pay off their debts with inflated
product prices than with constant or falling product prices. With the
demise of the Second Bank of the United States in 1832, the liberal
money and banking views of farmers generally prevailed through 1864
and resulted in an upward trend in farm prices irregularly interspersed with price booms and money panics. In the period after the
Civil War the banking system began to develop along orthodox lines,
with a conservative approach to the supply of money based on the
gold standard and with increased governmental regulation of banks.
This orthodox trend culminated in the Federal Reserve System in 1913,
which was established to oversee the banking system and manage the
money supply. In this trend toward orthodoxy in the latter half of the
nineteenth century, farmers found that the former policy of cheap
money and easy credit was transformed into one of hard money and
expensive credit. In this changed situation farmers called for the free
and unlimited coinage of silver as a means of expanding the money
supply, but this they were unable to achieve. Further, and more important, no special credit programs tailored to the longer-term production and development needs of farmers were established by the
government to assist them during this period. Thus farm credit for developing farms and expanding production was in short supply and expensive in the last decades of the nineteenth century and the first decades of the twentieth.

Changing the Structure of Markets

Regarding the altering of market structures, farmers took some actions and had some limited successes in the post-Civil War years. The
Grange succeeded in passing legislation in several states for regulating
the railroads with respect to passenger and freight rates and to prevent
discrimination. The first laws were declared unconstitutional in the
state courts, but later and more carefully drawn laws were upheld by
those courts. Further, the efforts of the Grange culminated in the passage of the federal Interstate Commerce Act of 1887, which provided
the basis for controlling passenger and freight rates across the nation.
The Grange and other farmers' organizations tried in the post-Civil
War period to establish centralized organizations for purchasing farm

supplies — organizations that would give farmers some monopoly power in the market. But these ventures met with little success. Farmers found that it was easy to talk about gaining monopoly power in the market but that it was extremely difficult to achieve positions of monopoly power in practice. This was especially true where the government was not inclined to intercede with legislation to assist farmers to gain monopoly powers in the market. Government, the captive of big business and great industries during this period, was not about to help farmers or laborers develop any countervailing power in the marketplace.

Trade Policy

Except for the on-again, off-again efforts to establish an effective banking system, economic intervention by government in the nineteenth century was most generally concerned with the formulation and reformulation of a trade policy. Actions in the trade area typically were not taken on behalf of farmers and did not operate to the advantage of farmers. But those actions had important consequences for farmers and the development of agriculture. Thus we will consider them in some detail.

The federal government tinkered endlessly with the tariff structure during the nineteenth century. The first tariff act, the Tariff Act of 1789, was imposed to raise revenue for a new government urgently in need of revenue; protection was only nominal under this act, with rates averaging about 5 percent of the value of the products imported. As a result of strong competition from English manufacturers, and the dislocations of developing American industries caused first by the Napoleonic Wars and second by the War of 1812, the first truly protective tariff for the United States was passed in 1816; under this act, tariff duties ran as high as 20 percent of the value of some imported products. With help from farmers in the northern and western states, industrialists from New England and the Middle Atlantic states succeeded in passing a tariff act with even higher duties in 1828; under this act, tariff duties on imported items subject to duty averaged between 50 and 60 percent of the value of those products. The Tariff Act of 1828, "The Tariff of Abominations," marked the highest level of trade protectionism for the United States between Independence and the Civil War.

Southern planters who were interested in expanding their exports of tobacco, rice, and cotton — particularly cotton — and in importing low-priced manufactured goods from abroad fought the tariff hikes of 1816 and 1828 unsuccessfully. But under the leadership of President Jackson and with some help from western farmers, who were beginning to get interested in foreign markets, the Tariff Act of 1833 was passed by Congress. It provided for tariff duty reductions over a nine-year period. Tariff duties were further reduced in legislation passed in 1846 and 1857. The changing level of tariff protection from 1820 to 1974, as measured by the value of tariff duties expressed as a percentage of the value of all dutiable product imports, is portrayed in figure 15.1. (With tariff duty rates fixed in any piece of legislation, the level of tariff protection in any year, as measured by the percentage that duties collected are of the value of dutiable products imported, varies with the composition of product imports.)

When the South seceded from the Union in 1861 and representatives from the southern states withdrew from the Congress, northern industrialists were immediately successful in passing through the Congress a highly protectionist tariff act. The average level of tariff

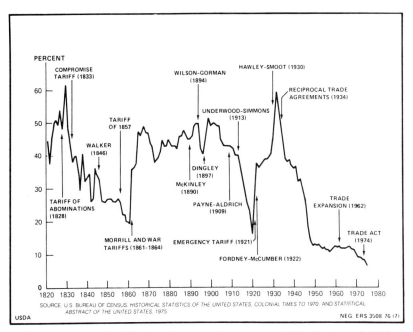

Fig. 15.1. Selected tariff and trade acts and percentage of U.S. duties on dutiable imports before and after passage

duties on protected (dutiable) products was pushed back up to almost 50 percent of the value of dutiable imports. And there, with the help of western farmers, eastern industrialists were able to hold tariff duty rates until the first decade of the twentieth century.

Throughout the nineteenth century, the struggle over trade policy and levels of protectionism was essentially a struggle between the emerging industrial North and the expanding plantation South. The northern industrialists wanted protection from the more technologically advanced industrialists of England and the European continent. The southern planters sought a policy of free trade in which they might expand their exports of cotton, and thus expand the plantation economy of the South, and then import low-priced manufactured goods from England and the Continent. Northern and western farmers were not sure what they wanted; hence they came down first on one side of the issue and then on the other.

But the plantation economy of the South, based on slavery, was destroyed by the Union victory in the Civil War, and the industrial North became one of the dominant industrial areas of the world as a result of the Civil War. Thus trade policy was settled in favor of the industrial North for a period of forty years or more. Whether western grain farmers acting in their own best interests could have modified the protectionist trade policy that emerged may be debated. But western grain farmers did not try. They relived their victorious battles, sang the marching songs of the Grand Army of the Republic, and waved the bloody shirt of secession whenever they came together in a meeting. As the western grain farmers became important exporters of grains in the period 1870–1900, they did not join with the ex-Confederate cotton farmers in seeking a policy of free trade, or freer trade — they did not because pride and passion stemming from the "War of the Rebellion" would not let them.

Economic Intervention in the Twentieth Century

Increasing Farm Prices

From time to time throughout the history of the nation farmers have tried to increase farm prices by controlling production or withholding supply. Before the 1920s these efforts were usually limited in scope, were undertaken without the blessing of the government, and failed to achieve farmers' goals. But in the 1920s farmers sought to develop a national plan, called Equality for Agriculture, which would manage the supply of each commodity involved so that only a specified amount would be fed onto the domestic market; this would yield prices that would in turn produce an *equality for agriculture.* The remainder of the supply of each commodity would be sold in the foreign market for whatever price it would bring. The losses on foreign sales were to be handled in various ways depending upon the version of the plan. This plan was incorporated into a McNary-Haugen bill and introduced into the Congress five times. The fourth and fifth versions were passed by Congress in 1927 and 1928 but were vetoed each time by the president.[2] Thus the first national effort to enhance farm prices through the management of supplies failed to become law. But farmers came close and they would be back and try again within a few years.

With the passage of the Agricultural Adjustment Act of 1933, farmers gained their first comprehensive supply management program backed by the power of the national government. The original AAA had many features: [3]

1. Payments to farmers
2. A processing tax to raise revenue
3. Commodity programs aimed at reducing production
4. Marketing orders directed at managing supplies of milk and specialty crops
5. Price support to farmers through the use of nonrecourse loans
6. Commodity storage.

The central objective of all these features was to raise prices to farmers by limiting in some way the flow of products onto the market. These first efforts at controlling production and managing supplies were sometimes crude, involving such actions as plowing under cotton, killing little pigs, and burning potatoes. And these first efforts were relatively unsophisticated: acres diverted from the production of one crop were left free to be planted to other crops, and price support was offered to farmers on occasion without effective production control measures. Thus the effectiveness of the production control programs under the AAA in reducing supplies coming onto the market was a much debated subject in the 1930s. In retrospect it would appear that except for the commodities cotton and tobacco, the control programs were relatively ineffective. The severe droughts of 1934 and 1936 did much more to reduce production in the 1930s than did the control programs under the AAA.[4]

During World War II and the postwar reconstruction period,

1940–52, farm prices soared and programs of production control and supply management became inoperative. But farm prices declined during the period 1952–54 and came to rest on the statutory levels of price support. By law this brought certain control programs back into operation — primarily acreage control programs for the important commodities of wheat, corn, and cotton. It also raised the issue of the social desirability of raising farm prices and holding them above equilibrium levels through production control and supply management. During the period 1955–65 there was a continuous struggle between those who advocated holding farm prices above their equilibrium levels through the employment of production controls and supply management and those who wanted to eliminate production controls and supply management devices and let farm prices fall to their market clearing levels.[5] This struggle came to an end in a compromise solution which became the Food and Agriculture Act of 1965. The principal features of that compromise solution were:

1. Voluntary acreage control programs for most important crops where farmers were paid not to produce
2. Price support for farmers participating in the control programs at or near world market levels
3. Income payments to farmers participating in the control programs as a means of protecting farm income
4. Foreign and domestic disposal of surplus agricultural products.

This solution, which lowered levels of price support to world market levels, took the pressure off production control and supply management as a means of supporting farm income and transferred the pressure to the federal treasury. Price support under this compromise became a vehicle for stabilizing the farm economy. Income support for farmers in any one year was to be determined by the size of the federal budget earmarked for farm income support — was to be determined by the generosity of the federal government. Production control and supply management in this scheme of things became the mechanism for holding down the costs of the farm programs of storage and surplus disposal, and of income payments themselves, by limiting the volume of the products on which payments had to be made.

The compromise solution of 1965 held together through 1972, at which time the programs once again became inoperative. They became inoperative as farm prices and incomes shot skyward as a result of the poor world grain harvests in 1972 and 1974. Between 1974 and 1977 farm product prices moved sideward or declined, and input prices rose dramatically. Thus in 1977, when the Act of 1973 expired and new food and agricultural legislation was before Congress, the leading question was not whether production control and supply management should be an integral part of the act; it was a foregone conclusion that they would be. The leading question to be answered was, How generous would the federal government be in supporting farm incomes by making income payments to farmers? In other words, How much was the federal government willing to spend on income payments to farmers? Programs of production control and supply management had become auxiliary types of programs to ensure that the cost of the income support programs did not get out of hand. The role of production control and supply management programs in the late 1970s was no longer that of limiting the flow of products into the market and thereby forcing up prices in the marketplace.

Money, Banking, and Credit

In the first decades of the twentieth century there was a growing demand by farmers for more relevant agricultural credit. The lack of long-term mortgage credit had been a sore subject with them for many, many years. The fast-growing western farm areas were continuously short of loan funds, interest rates were high — running to 10 to 15 percent — and many abuses existed, such as excessive charges for the renewal of short-term loans. The Country Life Commission, appointed by President Theodore Roosevelt in 1908, listed among the causes contributing to the deficiencies of country life "a lack of any adequate system of agricultural credit whereby the farmer may readily secure loans on fair terms." Two commissions, one private and one appointed by President Wilson, went to Europe in 1913 to study agricultural credit and cooperation in Northern Europe. The reports of these commissions plus continuous agitation from farmers resulted in the passage of a bill in 1916 that created a Federal Land Bank system to make long-term mortgage credit available to farmers on realistic terms.[6] The farm credit structure was further developed in 1923 when the Intermediate Credit Act was passed. This act created twelve intermediate credit banks, which were intended to make loans to farmers' cooperatives and farmers' associations, which in turn were expected to make intermediate or production loans to farmers. This operation got off to a slow start in the 1920s, since links between the intermediate credit banks and farmers had to be forged, and experience with this kind of credit had to be gained. But over the years, and with the development of some new credit institutions in the 1930s, this form of credit has become an important source of operating capital for farmers.

The desperate financial straits in which thousands of farmers found themselves in 1933 compelled the new Democratic administration to take immediate action to help them with their financial problems. The administration in cooperation with the Congress took three important steps with regard to credit in 1933. First, the president by proclamation on March 27 abolished the Federal Farm Board, reassigned its powers and duties to the governor of a new agency, the Farm Credit Administration, and brought together all federal farm credit activities into this agency. Second, under Title II, the Emergency Farm Mortgage Act, part of a general agricultural act passed in May 1933, the government stood ready to refinance farm mortgages held by mortgagees other than the Federal Land Banks, to reduce the rate of interest on all Land Bank loans, to extend the due date time for loans held by the Land Banks, to create a fund of $200 million to make "rescue" loans to farmers, and to take various other credit actions to assist farmers. Third, the Farm Credit Act passed in June 1933 cleared away some obsolete and unworkable aspects of earlier credit legislation and established two new types of credit agencies: (1) a central bank and twelve regional banks for making loans to cooperatives and (2) a system of twelve regional production credit corporations that would organize, supervise, and finance local production credit associations to enable cooperating groups of farmers to borrow from the intermediate credit banks. The farm credit system created in 1933 and unified within the Farm Credit Administration thus consisted of four major elements: (1) twelve Land Banks for making mortgage loans, (2) twelve intermediate credit banks for making production loans, (3) thirteen banks for cooperatives for making loans to farmers' cooperative associations, and (4) twelve production credit corporations for creating the necessary local institutions whereby the intermediate credit banks could reach out and serve the individual farmer.

This farm credit system grew and served the larger, commercial farmers of America extremely well up through 1980. As of 1976 this farm credit system obtained all its loan funds by selling securities to investors. It was completely owned by its users — farmers and their cooperatives. The net worth of these users was more than $3.3 billion. The total credit extended by all units of the farm credit system to farmers and cooperatives in 1976 amounted to $34.5 billion. This total extension of credit amounted to approximately 25 percent of the credit used by farmers and their cooperatives in that year. But farmer borrowers from other credit institutions benefit from the system because it serves as a pacesetter for all institutions making credit available to farmers.

The Farm Credit Land Banks and many, many private banks in rural areas ran into trouble in the farm depression of the 1980s. Farm land prices rose dramatically in the 1970s; in this land boom the federal Land Banks and many private banks made loans to farmers to enlarge their operations based on the inflated land prices. When farm prices sagged in the 1980s and interest rates rose as the result of a tightened monetary policy, many highly leveraged farm operators defaulted on their loans. As a result a rural financial panic set in: many private banks in rural areas went bankrupt; to stave off bankruptcy private banks and the federal Land Banks terminated loans rather than extending them, forcing more farm foreclosures and more defaulted loans. In this context some of the federal Land Banks faced insolvency. At this point in the credit crisis the federal government stepped in with the Agricultural Credit Act of 1987. This act did two important things: (1) it provided the Land Bank system with the funds (up to $4 billion) to meet its financial obligations and remain solvent, and (2) it required a complete reorganization of the Farm Credit system and gave new regulatory powers and responsibilities to the overall Farm Credit Administration.

The Congress could not in 1987 permit the Farm Credit system to fail — the economic survival of too many farmers was at stake. The 1987 legislation gave the Farm Credit system a new lease on life, but whether it reestablished the system on a viable basis remains to be seen.

The federal government has tried since 1935 through a succession of agencies — the Resettlement Administration, the Farm Security Administration, and the Farmers Home Administration — to help low-income farm families on low-production farms become viable commercial operators. The principal instrument of help has been supervised loans — supervised loans to purchase a farm, or additional land to enlarge a farm, and to purchase livestock and machinery. Some farm families, aided by this supervised credit, have fought their way into the productive, commercial category of farm operators. But relatively speaking, only a few have met with success. It is generally agreed that these credit programs for aiding the small farmer have achieved far less than was expected of them. Why should this be? There are at least two reasons. First, Congress has never supported the credit programs for the rural poor as generously as it has supported programs to aid commercial farmers; congressional representatives from rural areas have not represented the needs of the rural poor in legislative battles over appropriations in the same effective ways as they have the needs of commercial farmers. The downtrodden in rural areas have traditionally been poorly represented in Congress. Second, improving the management skills of poorly educated adult farmers, who have already been branded by society as losers, turns out to be a very time-consuming, costly business. Providing the amounts and kinds of financial and technological supervision that most of the clients of the Farmers Home Administration, and its predecessor agencies, have required to pull themselves up into the category of successful commercial farmers costs more than the budgets of those agencies would permit. Thus the farmer clients of these agencies typically have not received the amount of supervision that they required, and the process of transforming low-production farmers into high-production farmers has slowed down or broken down.

Commercial farmers, however, were much more successful in the twentieth century than in the nineteenth in solving their credit problems. This was true for at least two reasons. First, farmers and their leaders better understood the workings of the monetary and credit systems in the twentieth century than they had in the nineteenth. Hence they were able to act more intelligently in their own behalf in the twentieth century. Second, and stemming from the first point, farmers and their leaders gave up trying to build an entire money and banking system that operated to their economic advantage and redirected their efforts to the building of credit institutions and to creating those credit instruments (e.g., long-term mortgage credit, intermediate production credit) that fit their particular needs. In these efforts, the federal government became a willing partner, and the government and farmers working together built a farm credit system that worked reasonably well until both borrowers and lenders got carried away by the land boom of the late 1970s.

Changing the Structure of Markets

A longtime dream of farmers has been that of altering the atomistic structure of the markets in which they buy and sell by gaining some, preferably a great deal, of monopoly power in the purchasing of their supplies and in the marketing of their products. In the purchasing of nonfarm-produced inputs farmers have gained some monopoly power through the development of large-scale purchasing cooperatives. These cooperatives, exempted from the antitrust laws by the Clayton Antitrust Act and the Capper-Volstead Cooperative Marketing Act and benefiting from favorable treatment in income tax legislation, have become major suppliers of feeds, fertilizers, and petroleum products to farmers and have passed along important savings to their farmer patrons. But these cooperatives and their farmer patrons have also learned that great monopoly gains were not to be made in these enterprises. The better-managed large-scale purchasing cooperatives have made an important contribution to the financial operation of many, many commercial farmers; they have not, however, made those farmers rich.

It is on the other side of the market where the hopes of farmers have soared the highest and where the reality has been the most depressing. Exempted specifically from the antitrust laws by the Capper-Volstead Cooperative Marketing Act of 1922 and under the eloquent leadership of the cooperative organizer Aaron Sapiro, farmers in the 1920s sought through nationwide cooperative marketing associations that made binding delivery agreements with their members to gain control of enough of the supply of certain commodities (e.g., the grains) to enable the cooperative to set, or determine, the price of the products in the market. Farmers were to gain a "fair" price in the market by achieving monopoly control over supply. But Sapiro and his farmer friends were not able to sign up enough farmers to binding delivery contracts to gain control, a monopoly control, over a significant portion of the supply. When it came down to signing a binding delivery contract, most farmers were unwilling to sign. Farmers in the 1920s dreamed of gaining a monopoly position in the market, but most were not ready to take the steps required to "close their shop."

Farmers turned directly to government in the late 1920s and the 1930s for economic assistance, as we have seen. They had tried altering the structure of the market through collective action and found that course of action wanting. But in the 1950s and 1960s farmers once again turned to collective action as a means of gaining a monopoly position in the market. This time they called it "bargaining power for farmers." The conservative farmers' organization, the American Farm Bureau Federation, talked about farmers' need for increased bargaining power and suggested the formation of bargaining associations in certain specialty crops to enable the farmers involved to realize higher prices and more favorable conditions of sale. But the Farm Bureau did little more than talk about bargaining power. A new radical farm organization, the National Farm Organization (NFO), took the position that farmers would get higher prices if, and only if, they gained a monopoly control over supply, withheld that supply from the market, and forced prices upward in the market. NFO leadership argued that government would not take the actions required to increase significantly the prices received by farmers; thus, if farmers wanted higher prices, they would have to take collective action to raise their prices. On the basis of this argument the NFO conducted drives to increase its membership, and it carried out several withholding operations in an effort to drive up prices in regional livestock markets. Once again it became clear that the farmers who refused to participate in the withholding operations — the "free riders" — defeated those who joined the operations. The NFO withholding operations had a modest influence on livestock deliveries to the regional markets involved but no perceptible effect on price. The NFO was unable to gain control over and withhold a large enough portion of the supply moving to market to have a significant effect on price. The NFO failed in its objective of raising farm prices through the gaining of a monopoly position in the market.

In the winter of 1977–78 another new farm organization, the American Agricultural Movement, called a farm strike without attempting to sign up members. The leaders of the AAM simply called upon all farmers not to market their products. The results of this effort were similar to those of earlier efforts. The striking action had no perceptible influence on marketings, hence upon farm prices. Except for a few militant farmers in each succeeding generation, farmers seem unwilling to take those actions necessary to gain a monopoly position in the market with respect to supply; hence they are unable to set, or fix, or determine, or even influence significantly, prices in the market. The dream of farmers to gain a monopoly position in the market remains just a dream.

Trade Policy

Trade policy in general, and for agriculture in particular, is complex and confusing in the twentieth century. As can be seen in figure 14.1, levels of tariff protection declined importantly in the first two decades of the twentieth century. But with the onset of the farm depression in 1921 and the Great Depression in 1929, farmers joined with industrialists in demanding increased tariff protection, and tariff duties were raised in 1922 and again in 1930. These actions quickly brought on retaliatory action abroad, and American farmers and industrialists saw their exports decline precipitously in the early 1930s. High tariff walls no longer served to protect American industry, and they could not help or protect an export-oriented agriculture in the 1920s and 1930s, just as they had not been able to do so in the 1870s and 1880s. Thus a major shift in United States trade policy — a shift toward liberalization — took place in the 1930s. (The effect on tariff duties may be seen in figure 15.1.)

This shift in trade policy is well described by Robert Tontz:

> To implement the new trade policy, President Roosevelt, following the recommendation of Secretary of State Cordell Hull, requested that Congress authorize executive commercial agreements with foreign nations within carefully guarded limits to modify the existing duties and import restrictions in such a way as would benefit American agriculture and industry.
>
> Congress passed the Hull inspired Reciprocal Trade Agreements Act of 1934 as an amendment to the Hawley-Smoot Tariff Act of 1930. The Trade Agreements Act was designed to attain a reduction in the excessive duties set in the 1930 Act and thus expand foreign markets for U.S. products. This and consequent legislation were successful in contributing to a significant expansion of U.S. exports.
>
> The Trade Agreements Act was based on the premise that, in order to obtain and develop foreign markets for U.S. products, corresponding market opportunities in the United States had to be afforded also to other countries.
>
> Under the Trade Agreements legislation, the President was empowered to enter into reciprocal trade agreements with other countries through executive proclamation and without ratification of the Senate. The Act also provided that the unconditional most-favored nation treatment (that is, equality of treatment to all nations) would be continued, except in the case of nations discriminating against American commerce. The law required that every trade agreement was to contain a provision to permit its termination at the end of not more than three years after coming into effect. The President's tariff-reducing power was limited to 50 percent of duties existing on January 1, 1934.
>
> In previous tariff adjusting, presidential authority had been dependent upon the findings of the Tariff Commission, whereas in the future there was to be no such inhibition on the new authority. Tariff rate adjustment was shifted from the Tariff Commission to the State Department.
>
> Congress extended the authority to make trade agreements in 1937, 1940, and 1943 without significant amendments, and in 1945 it extended the authority and gave the President the further authority to lower rates by 50 percent of the existing duties as of January 1, 1945. Any item which had been reduced by 50 percent in the period 1934–45 was subject to another possible reduction of 50 percent — or a 75-percent reduction in all — for concessions from other countries. The year 1945 marked the legislative highpoint of the program. Since then, amendments have tended to restrict, rather than to expand, the power of the President.[7]

The United States, as a matter of principle, continued to press for trade liberalization in the post-World War II period. A charter for an international trade organization was drawn up in 1948; it specified rules for the reduction of tariffs, the elimination of quotas, and the creation of the conditions for the expansion of multilateral trade on equal terms. But this charter was too advanced, or too radical, for the United States Congress, and the treaty died in committee. In addition, most European and Asian countries were more concerned with postwar reconstruction than they were with liberalizing their trade policies. But out of this effort emerged a modest agreement, the General Agreement on Tariffs and Trade (GATT). The GATT has become a permanent agreement, and a permanent international agency has been built around the agreement. Nations belonging to the GATT, of which the United States has been a leader, have developed working rules and procedures for negotiating tariff reductions and for holding trade consultations and settling trade disputes without setting in motion a series of trade retaliations.

But, although the GATT has proved to be a useful international agency for discussing trade problems, it has not, on balance, met with success in reducing barriers to trade in agricultural products around the world. *This is the case because trade policy has become in country after country the external shield of domestic agricultural policy.* The United States, plagued by low farm prices and agricultural surpluses in the 1950s and 1960s, employed import controls to keep wheat and cotton from flowing into the United States when it supported the prices of those products above the world level. And import barriers form the cornerstone of the domestic policies for dairy and sugar in the United States. Other countries have developed comparable trade barrier shields. The agricultural importing nations of the European Economic Community (EEC) employ a variable levy system to protect the prices and incomes of their producers. Japan employs a national trading corporation to import most of its agricultural products. Canada and Australia make use of marketing boards, governmentally created monopolies, to sell their more important agricultural products abroad. Each important importer and exporter of agricultural products has developed a set of trade policies and programs designed to implement its domestic agricultural policies and programs.

In this context the United States and other trading nations of the world can no longer come together and negotiate, under the most-favored nation clause, say, a 10 percent or 20 percent reduction in the tariff duties on agricultural products imported into their countries. Such reductions would play havoc with their domestic agricultural policies and programs. The community of nations has reached the

stage in its economic development in which an international conference called to negotiate a lowering of trade barriers on agricultural
products involves much more than negotiations on tariff duties or the
extent of import controls — in reality it involves negotiations on the
internal domestic agricultural policies of the countries involved, of
which the trade barriers are only the external reflection.

In the United States, as in almost every developed country, the national government has worked with farmers and their leaders to create
a set of interrelated programs to protect farm prices and incomes that
stretch from the individual farm plant to the most distant foreign market around the world. These programs are integrally related; change
one program and there are repercussions throughout the system.
Thus domestic production policy, domestic price and income policy,
and foreign trade policy with respect to food and agriculture must be
viewed as a whole and treated as a whole, since these policy pieces fit
together as a whole. In this sense the distinction made earlier in this
chapter between governmental actions designed to increase farm
prices through the management of supplies and governmental actions
affecting foreign trade has disappeared. Similarly, independent actions by government to change or modify trade policies for agricultural
products are likely to be counterproductive. Trade policy has become
one part of a seamless policy web with respect to food and agriculture.

This is not to suggest that the export trade in agricultural products
has declined or will decline as a result of the maze of trade barriers currently in existence. We know from the discussions in chapter 13 that
exports of agricultural products from the United States have increased
greatly in the 1960s and 1970s. But it is to suggest that the type of trade
agreements employed so successfully in the late 1930s, or the general
rounds of trade negotiations attempted in the 1950s and 1960s, will not
prove successful in the late 1970s and 1980s with respect to lowering
trade restrictions on agricultural products. Ways must be found,
which have not yet been discovered, to enable countries to negotiate
trade agreements with one another that take account of each other's
domestic agricultural goals, policies, and programs.

But the above conclusion has not stopped the United States from
trying to negotiate a general lowering of trade barriers and with that
action a general lowering of domestic subsidies to agriculture. Reagan
administration officials who had been defeated, by the agricultural
committees of the Congress and their farm lobby allies, in their efforts
to introduce reform measures that would have reduced farm price and
income support in the agricultural acts of 1981 and 1985, were looking

for ways to realize their farm policy reform goals outside conventional legislative channels. In the Uruguay Round of GATT trade negotiations Reagan administration officials sensed that they had found the opportunity they had been looking for, namely, to pursue their domestic farm policy objectives through international negotiations. Consequently, U.S. trade negotiators took an early lead in the Uruguay Round in insisting that agricultural trade policy reform, including domestic farm policy reform, should become a key component of those negotiations. Accordingly, the ministerial conference in Punta del Este, which launched the Uruguay Round in September 1986, declared in a written pronouncement that agricultural trade issues, *including the internal "structural surpluses" that were distorting agricultural trade*, would be given a high priority in the forthcoming negotiations.

The first official U.S. negotiating proposal on agriculture presented in July 1987 came straight out of the Reagan administration's free market ideology; it proposed to eliminate over ten years *all* agricultural subsidies in all trading nations (including the U.S.) that distort domestic production and hence trade. This became known as the Zero Option proposal and was fought over in one form or another for the next three years. The high-protectionist countries — EC countries and Japan — would have none of it. The low-protectionist countries — the Cairns groups led by Australia — favored some variation of the Zero Option proposal. Some American farm groups came to support the Zero Option proposal for domestic political reasons, knowing full well that the EC and Japan would block it in the negotiating process. In the meantime, using the disarmament analogy, they moved to *increase* export subsidy programs for U.S. farm products to be used as bargaining chips in further trade negotiations. And that is how matters turned out. At the ministerial meeting in Brussels in December 1990, the entire Uruguay Round of trade negotiations collapsed because nothing could be agreed upon in the area of agriculture. But American farm groups succeeded in getting some provisions in the Budget Reconciliation Act of the "1990 Farm Bill" that would increase export subsidies on agricultural products in the event of the failure of the Uruguay Round trade negotiations. In sum, and to the dismay of trade policy reformers, American farm interests, with the help of farm interests in the EC and Japan, succeeded, first, in blocking any internationally negotiated trade reforms and, second, in using those negotiations to boost agricultural export subsidies at home.

It is clear that the Reagan free market ideological approach to agricultural trade reform in a multinational GATT negotiating setting does not work. There are those who believe, including the author of this volume, that reforms that open up agriculture trade must be negotiated between pairs of important trading partners in which (1) the domestic farm programs of each country are fully taken into account, and (2) opportunities for expanding trade are "discovered" through negotiations that are advantageous to each country. Trade between two individuals, or two countries, can only occur, and only be expanded, when both parties to the transaction feel that they have gained from doing so.

The Winter of 1977–78

Almost all cash crop farmers were squeezed severely between falling product prices and rising input prices during the period 1975–77. A certain proportion of those farmers were pushed to the edge and into bankruptcy in 1977. These were typically younger farmers who had purchased high-priced land during the boom years 1973–75, who had bought large and expensive lines of machinery, and some of whom had experienced drought conditions in 1977. Many of these crop farmers in financial difficulty banded together in the American Agricultural Movement. Members of this loosely formed organization at first took the position that they did not want a "government handout," and as discussed earlier they called for a nationwide farm strike — all farmers were asked to withhold their products from the market. But this strike did not create a ripple on the flow of farm products to market.

It is interesting to speculate why this group of aggressive young farmers called for a strike in the first instance rather than turned to the government for help. It is hypothesized here that these farmers had come to the conclusion that the government of the United States was willing to place a price and income floor under their industry but not willing to give them the tools, the monopoly power, to force prices in the marketplace up to the levels that they deemed fair. Thus they tried to forge the necessary monopoly power through farm group, or collective, action. But in this effort they failed completely. Hence they turned once again to the government for help in the winter of 1977–78.

The program that farmers in the American Agricultural Movement (AAM) asked the Congress to legislate is outlined below:

1. Prices of all farm commodities would be protected at price levels between 100 and 115 percent of parity — livestock as well as grains, fibers, fruits, and vegetables. Unlike current programs, AAM's proposal would not rely

on Government loans, purchases, or set-aside programs to achieve desired prices. Instead, legislation would be passed making the sale, purchase, or trading of any agricultural commodity illegal at less than the established level.

2. Under AAM's plan, Congress would legislate a requirement that all farm goods must sell at 100 percent of parity starting October 1, 1978. Thereafter, prices would be adjusted in response to changes in a modified version of the Prices Paid Index. Feed, seed, and feeder cattle — three items usually included in that Index — would be omitted. . . .

3. Farmers would be permitted to produce unlimited quantities of any agricultural commodity. But actual sales would be controlled through the use of marketing quotas and certificates. Farmers would be responsible for storing, unsubsidized, any surplus production.

4. Quotas would be based upon anticipated demand as projected by a National Agricultural Board of producer representatives.

5. Farmers would be allocated marketing quotas on the basis of their production histories, with quotas tied to the land or farm.

6. Marketing quotas could be filled with either current or stored production.

7. No farm good would be exported at less than parity prices.

8. Agricultural imports that compete with domestically produced farm goods would not be sold for less than 110 percent of the parity price.

9. To protect consumers, prices would not be permitted to rise above 115 percent of parity.

10. The Government could acquire strategic reserves through purchases on the open market, but would not be permitted to sell these reserves for less than 115 percent of parity.[8]

In support of this program proposal AAM farmers descended on Washington in droves. They tramped the halls of the Congressional Office Buildings; they occupied the Administration Building of the Department of Agriculture; and they drove tractors up and down the busy streets of Washington. It was a new experience for congressmen and bureaucrats to meet dirt farmers in their offices and meeting rooms. And in this effort the farmers did have some success — or at least they scared some senators for a brief period.

On March 21, 1978, the Senate, in response to the militant pleas of farmers, passed a bill that did three important things. First, it required the secretary of agriculture to set aside at least 31 million acres of cropland in addition to the 15-million-acre set-aside already announced for 1978, for which farmers would be paid an average of $75 per acre. Second, it raised wheat, corn, and cotton target prices and loan levels as follows:

1. Wheat target price to $3.55 a bushel, from $3–$3.05; wheat loan to $2.85 per bushel, from $2.25–$2.35.

2. Corn target price to $2.50 a bushel, from $2.10; corn loan to $2.25 a bushel, from $2.
3. Cotton target price to 70 cents per pound, from 52 cents; cotton loan to 50 cents per pound, from 44 cents.

Third, it created a sliding scale of target prices for the crop year and linked it to the set-aside program. Each participating farmer would establish his own target price, depending upon the amount of land that he set aside. For example, the bill established seven wheat target prices ranging from $3 per bushel for farmers who set aside 20 percent of their cropland to $5.04 per bushel for those who set aside 50 percent of their cropland. The $5.04 figure represented 100 percent of parity. A comparable sliding scale was established for corn and a new set-aside provision established for cotton.

Firm estimates of the price and cost consequences of these Senate bill provisions were never made, but Senator Edmund Muskie of Maine argued on the floor of the Senate that this "three-headed monster" would add billions to the federal budget. A few weeks earlier the Department of Agriculture had released a statement saying that the original AAM proposal would raise food prices in the fourth quarter of 1978 by 20 percent, compared with the projected rise of 4 to 6 percent. The same release stated that retail beef, pork, and poultry prices would increase by 50, 40, and 30 percent respectively from 1977 to 1979 if the AAM proposed program were to take effect.

On the basis of this information President Carter let it be known that he would veto legislation containing the three Senate provisions. Thus the stage was set for the defeat of the Senate bill in the House of Representatives. When a Conference Committee report containing most of the Senate provisions was submitted to the House of Representatives for a vote, the Conference Committee report was badly beaten. The House of Representatives, with its strong urban orientation, would have nothing to do with the emergency farm legislation passed by the Senate. The House was not prepared to pass legislation that could raise food prices to urban consumers by 20 percent or more.

From the actions taken by farmers and the actions taken by the government during the winter of 1977–78, certain propositions became evident. Perceptive observers have been aware of these propositions for some time, and it was hypothesized earlier that farmers too had come to perceive them. Proposition (1): The government of the United States stands willing to provide farmers with a price-income support floor — a floor to keep the farming industry from falling into a deep economic depression. Proposition (2): The government of the United States stands willing to provide all farm operators, except the great corporate enterprises, with a modest income supplement and many and varied kinds of technical and financial assistance. Proposition (3): The government of the United States will not grant farmers the program devices, the monopoly power in the marketplace, to enable them to push up farm product prices significantly and hence increase retail food prices significantly. This latter action the government of the United States cannot take. Food prices represent the cutting edge of the general price inflation, and to give farmers the programs and the power to push food prices upward by a significant amount would be to exacerbate the general price inflation and to infuriate millions of urban consumers.

The 1980s and Beyond

The agricultural acts of 1981, 1985, and 1990 were consistent, in broad terms, with the general propositions set forth in the previous section. The president and the Congress did not grant any farm commodity group the monopoly power to drive its product prices upward in the market place to monopolistic levels. The various acts continued to provide commercial farmers with price and income support. And the acts continued to provide commercial farmers with various kinds of financial and technical assistance (e.g., crop disaster payments, export subsidies). These various forms of assistance, it turned out, played an all-important role during the farm depression of the 1980s.

In the Agricultural Act of 1981, the farm interests in Congress outmaneuvered the new president, Ronald Reagan, and his advisers and actually succeeded in raising the level of price and income support for farmers (i.e., loan rates and target prices). In the next year, 1982, agricultural exports began to fall, and fell steadily through 1986. This caused farm product prices to sag, farmers to place more wheat and corn under loan, the government to acquire more stocks as farmers turned over their wheat and corn to the government under the nonrecourse loan provision, and costs of government programs to soar to nearly $19 billion in 1983. In the Agricultural Act of 1985, loan rates were lowered, but target prices were maintained at the high levels established in the 1981 act. Market prices of the grains declined with the lowering of price support levels; this contributed to the increase in exports in the second half of 1980 as was noted in chapter 8. But with lower product prices, deficiency payments per farmer increased in amount; and with high farmer participation in the commodity pro- grams total payment costs rose. The results were predictable. The government costs of price and income support rose to the un- precedented levels of almost $26 billion in 1986 and $22 billion in 1987. With an increase in agricultural exports after 1986, farm product prices rose and the pressure on the support programs declined, as did the to- tal costs of the programs. But one thing is clear from the experience of the 1980s: since the programs provide a fixed level of price and in- come support, the costs of those programs must vary inversely with the prosperity of the farm sector. When farm prices and incomes are good the programs tend to become inoperative and their costs decline, but when farm prices and incomes sag, the programs become opera- tive and government costs increase. This, of course, is the way they are supposed to work. But their working, and the magnitude of their working, places an unpredictable burden on the federal budget.

The structure of the "1991 Farm Bill" is supposed to reduce the bur- den on the federal budget (see Chapter 8). But this is by no means cer- tain. First, if the U.S. economic recession of 1991 and 1992 becomes worldwide (and in 1992 there are indications that it might), then agricultural exports from the United States could begin to fall once again with the consequence that domestic farm prices start down once again and the costs of price and income support start to rise once again. Further, the "GATT trigger" provision in the Budget Reconcilia- tion Act of 1990 could come into play, if the Uruguay Round negotia- tions are still stalled by June 1992. This provision obliges the secretary of agriculture to spend an additional $1 billion on export subsidies, adopt a marketing loan subsidy program for wheat and feed grains, and waive all planting reductions. If the negotiations are still a failure in June 1993, the secretary would then be permitted to reverse all, or part, of the $13.5 billion in domestic farm budget cuts (over five years) that were an integral part of the budget reconciliation package of 1990. Whether all or a part of these provisions become operational remains to be seen. But if some part, or all, of these provisions should become operational in addition to a possible decline in U.S. farm exports in the first half of the 1990s, then costs of government programs of price and income support for farmers would soar once again. This is not a prediction, but given the way farm price and income support pro- grams are structured, plus the possibility of the "GATT trigger" provi- sions becoming operational, then a replay of huge farm program costs in the 1990s is a possibility.

There is, of course, always the possibility of significant farm policy reforms taking place, which would obviate much or all of the above reasoning. Or the world economy may, in 1992, be only a step away from taking off in another great decade of growth and prosperity. But neither would seem to be a realistic possibility. Thus, the reader is encouraged to study the developments of the 1990s to discover what happened and why.

Suggested Readings

Benedict, Murray R. *Farm Policies of the United States, 1790–1950.* New York: Twentieth Century Fund, 1953.

Cochrane, Willard W., and Ryan, Mary E. *American Farm Policy, 1948–1973.* Minneapolis: University of Minnesota Press, 1976.

Hadwiger, Don F., and Talbot, Ross B. *Pressures and Protests: The Kennedy Farm Program and the Wheat Referendum of 1963.* San Francisco: Chandler Publishing, 1965.

Paarlberg, Robert L. "How Agriculture Blocked the Uruguay Round." *SAIS Review,* 12, no. 1 (Winter/Spring, 1992), pp. 27–42.

Smith, Adam. *An Inquiry into the Nature and Causes of the Wealth of Nations,* edited by Edwin Cannan. New York: Modern Library edition by Random House, 1937.

Tontz, Robert L. *Foreign Agricultural Trade Policy of the United States, 1776–1976.* U.S. Department of Agriculture. Economic Research Service. ERS-662. January 10, 1977.

U.S. Department of Agriculture. Economics, Statistics, and Cooperatives Service. "An Analysis of American Agricultural Movement Proposal." *Issue Briefing Paper.* March 3, 1978.

CHAPTER 16

THE FORCES IN REVIEW

We have identified and discussed seven forces that have influenced importantly the development of American agriculture: (1) Abundant Land, (2) Farm Mechanization and Technological Advance, (3) Physical Infrastructure, (4) Social Infrastructure, (5) International Inputs, (6) Environmental Policy, and (7) Government. And within each of these broad categories are to be found numerous specific influencing forces. For example, under "physical infrastructure" we identified roads and highways, canals and waterways, railroads and water management systems, electric power grids, input supply systems, and product marketing systems. And under "international inputs" we identified the legal system, economic institutions, immigration, foreign capital, and foreign trade. In short, many, many forces, or factors, have been involved in the development of American agriculture.

We have perhaps identified the more important forces contributing to the development of American agriculture. But have we identified all of them? Certainly not. Three additional forces come immediately to mind. They are (1) Prosperity and Depression, (2) Belief and Value Systems, and (3) Energy Availability. Other observers of the process of agricultural development in the United States might well identify still additional forces, and they almost certainly would categorize those forces somewhat differently from the way it was done in this volume. But the discussion in this chapter will focus on the three additional forces noted above.

Prosperity and Depression

Whether the category "prosperity and depression" should be viewed as a force influencing agricultural development or a resultant condition is perhaps debatable. But whatever the view, it is certainly true that the process of agricultural development underwent change as the nation moved from periods of depression to prosperity and back to depression. During the nineteenth century sales of western land increased, immigration to these shores accelerated, and the whole process of western settlement and transformation of pioneer farms into commercial farms was speeded up during periods of national prosperity. In such periods credit to farmers was more readily available, new markets for their products opened up, and more families were willing to accept the risks of pioneering. But in periods of depression, or money panics, the whole process of westward settlement and the development of the hinterland ground to a halt. Thus the process of westward settlement and agricultural development in the nineteenth century tended to move in waves — the waves rolling forward in periods of prosperity and receding in periods of depression.

The process of agricultural development changed dramatically in the twentieth century. The age of pioneering and westward settlement was over. Farmers in the twentieth century have been concerned with increasing the productivity of their limited acres through the application of all kinds of new and improved techniques, producer goods (e.g., mixed feeds, fertilizer), and capital items to those acres. In this changed developmental situation the influence of general economic prosperity and depression has not lessened; if anything, it has become greater. When farm prices decline, credit becomes tight and the financial position of farmers becomes weak (as during a business recession or depression), farmers curtail their purchases of producer goods, and their investment in capital items can decline to negative levels as depreciation exceeds new acquisitions. But given a condition of international prosperity, farm exports expand, farm prices rise, the financial position of farmers generally strengthens, and farmers immediately expand their purchases of producer goods and are likely to expand greatly their investments in capital items. A capital-intensive, export-oriented agriculture, such as we now have in the United States, is influenced importantly by international economic conditions. International prosperity leads to a widening of agricultural product markets and a deepening of capital[1] on American farms; an international recession has the opposite effect.

Belief and Value Systems[2]

Beliefs, according to John Brewster, are *concepts of ways of life and work which people feel obliged to follow for the sake of proving their worth. Values are the relative weights that people assign to their various beliefs.* Beliefs and values are thus as interdependent as the two sides of a coin; neither can exist without the other. But although beliefs and values are interdependent, they are not identical. Often people share the same beliefs yet have different values because they attach different weights to those beliefs.

In the belief systems of nineteenth-century Americans, the brightest star was a sense of destiny, often described as the American Dream. This dream had three components: (1) a vision of government based on the voice of the plain people, (2) a vision of an economic realm of peace and plenty based upon the diligent industry of its people, and (3) a vision of a world realm of law and justice. Accompanying this sense of destiny was a compelling belief that the best of all possible national economic organizations is a proprietary form of organization in which a democratic government (1) provides its citizens with the services they cannot provide themselves but require in order to become increasingly successful proprietors (e.g., roads, agricultural colleges), (2) abstains from taxing those with high incomes more heavily than those with low incomes because the high incomes were proof of industriousness and (3) abstains from passing laws that limit the powers of proprietors by preventing them from running their businesses as they see fit. This overriding commitment to a proprietary form of political economy rested upon a three-cornered belief system: (1) a democratic belief system, (2) a work belief system, and (3) an enterprise belief system.

The central components of the democratic belief system were (1) that all men are equal in dignity and worth, (2) that none, however wise or good, is wise or good enough to have a controlling power over any other, and (3) that each person is entitled to a voice in making the rules that govern all.

The central components of the work belief system were (1) that striving for excellence in any employment is the proper way to earn respect for oneself and the respect and esteem of others and (2) that no employment is any "higher" or any "lower" than any other as a means for a man to prove his worth. The work of a shoemaker or a farmer was just as "high" as the work of a clergyman or physician as a way of proving one's worth.

The central conviction of the enterprise belief system was that capital accumulation through an increasingly successful proprietorship is the correct and proper test of a man's worth to society. The achievement of excellence in any form of employment is best measured by the amount of capital accumulated by the persons involved. In this belief system the most desirable form of economic organization is one of individual proprietorships; the businessman's highest social responsibility is maximizing the profits of his business; and if he is to win the badge of high distinction he must reinvest those profits in his business and thereby cause it to grow.

Given the above belief systems in which the enterprise belief system was the most highly valued, or prized, of the three, the whole pattern of agricultural development in the United States in the nineteenth century unfolds in a logical scenario. The body politic pushed for the distribution of the public domain in small, family-sized parcels. Individual families acquired those parcels and became independent proprietors — freeholders. The farm proprietor drove himself and his family to clear the land of trees, to improve the homestead, and to convert a clearing in the forest into a commercial operation. Through hard work and individual deprivation the family accumulated capital and over time built highly productive farms across the continent from the Atlantic Ocean to the Pacific. The successful builders earned the respect and esteem of their peers, earned the badge of highest distinction in a society of small, individual proprietors, and in so doing were participants in a rapid and successful process of national agricultural development. This was the way that the belief and value systems of Americans in the nineteenth century motivated — drove — the process of agricultural development.

In the twentieth century the value, or weight, given to the enterprise belief system in the national society and among farm people has declined somewhat, and the value, or weight, given to the democratic belief system has increased relatively. Thus we have individual farmers participating in the political process to establish rules for directing the use of resources on individual farms. Witness the efforts to pass the McNary-Haugen legislation, the operation of the AAA programs, the succession of farm programs during the 1950s and 1960s, and the efforts of farmers in the American Agricultural Movement during the winter of 1977–78 to achieve 100 percent parity for their product prices. The weights given to the three belief systems — democratic, work, and enterprise — have slowly changed in the twentieth century, and with this change has come a change in farm policies. This change has not come about easily; the long and fierce conflicts over farm policy from 1920 to 1990 attest to this. The triad of democratic, work, and enterprise belief systems still, however, serves to guide, direct, and motivate farmers to produce and accumulate, and thereby produce increasing amounts in succeeding periods in a system of individual proprietorships. The average size of these proprietorships increases every year, and the number of them decreases every year, but American farmers still pursue the nineteenth-century dream so eloquently conceptualized and described by John Brewster.

Energy Availability

During the nineteenth century farmers searched continuously for a convenient and efficient source of power. In the early part of the century in the North and West, and during much of the century in the South, farmers were dependent upon the human back for power, with the energy required to work the human back coming from the food supply. Later in the century farmers turned to machines powered by horses and mules, with the energy coming from farm-produced feed. Late in the century farmers in certain situations turned to steam tractors for power, with coal providing the energy required. But none of these sources of power were convenient, and in most instances they were highly inefficient. Thus the search for a convenient and efficient source of farm power continued.

In the early part of the twentieth century the gasoline-engined tractor was developed. By the 1920s this source of power had been developed to the point where it was highly convenient: it started easily; it handled easily; it moved at desirable speeds; and it had the power to perform the field tasks required of it. It was also a highly efficient source of power at the going market prices of gasoline from 1920 to 1970. Petroleum was plentiful in the United States and the price of gasoline was cheap — in nineteenth-century terminology, "dirt cheap." Cheap energy based upon plentiful petroleum supplies also made the production of nitrogen fertilizer inexpensive. Thus an entire technological strategy based upon cheap petroleum energy was developed and pursued over the period 1920–70. Gasoline-engined tractors and their machine hookups were substituted for human labor and horse power; plants were developed that made efficient use of soil nutrients; plant populations per acre were increased; and low-priced commercial fertilizers were applied to the land in increased amounts to provide the nutrients required by the plants. Also, on the central and southern Plains and in the Southwest, vast acreages were irrigated using cheap sources of energy, including natural gas. As a result, yields per acre, output per worker, output per unit of input, and aggregate farm output all increased. The strategy was highly successful; the income consequences for the aggressive and innovative farmers were reasonably good, and the food price consequences for American consumers were great. And all for one reason: the price of energy, petroleum in particular, was cheap — dirt cheap.

By the early 1970s it had become clear that supplies of petroleum in the United States were not inexhaustible. Annual imports of petroleum into the United States increased from 372 million barrels in 1960 to 1,184 million barrels by 1973, and to 2,058 million barrels by 1990. In the latter year the United States imported 42 percent of its petroleum. Over the period 1960–90, imports of petroleum peaked at 47 percent of domestic utilization in 1977 and fell as low as 27 percent in 1985; over the same period prices of crude oil rose from around $3.00 a barrel in 1960 to roughly $7.00 in 1974 to close to $36.00 in 1981 and then declined irregularly to about $21 a barrel in 1990. Under a moderate-level economic growth assumption, crude oil prices per barrel are projected to increase to about $33 in the year 2010, or about 50 percent above the 1990 price level. Developments in the petroleum industry, worldwide, after 2010 are anyone's guess. But given the known reserves of crude oil, as of 1990, and the rate of production in that year, the world would run out of petroleum in forty-five to fifty years, if production continued at the 1990 level.[3] Of course it can be argued that the "known reserves" will increase over time with further exploration. Offsetting that development could be a significant increase in annual crude oil production; after all, crude oil production, worldwide, tripled between 1960 and 1990. A reasonable scenario would run as follows: crude oil prices will rise substantially, perhaps by 50 percent, between 1990 and 2010; after 2010, barring any dramatic technological development such as the development of commercial fusion, the market for crude oil should tighten in the extreme and the price of crude oil skyrocket.

What does this mean for the development of agriculture in the United States and around the world in the years to come? It means that a strategy of agricultural development based upon technological developments that are dependent upon very cheap energy is no longer a viable strategy. The price developments that occurred for petroleum-based energy products during the period 1970–90, and seem likely to occur between 1900 and 2010, mean that farmers in the 1990s and beyond must be prepared to deal, first, with rising energy costs and, second, with dramatic and unpredictable fluctuations in energy costs. This means in turn that farmers must develop production strategies that minimize the purchase of energy-using products (e.g., fuel oil, nitrogen fertilizer) and financial strategies that enable them to cope with sudden and dramatic increases in energy costs. These kinds of adjustments will not be easy, but they are manageable in terms of existing technologies.

In the longer run, if the world begins to run out of petroleum, and this development is complicated by significant changes in the climate, the production and financial adjustments farmers are forced to make may not be manageable for the individual farmer. At this point the production of the food and fiber in the amounts required by a modern civilized society seems likely to become dependent on the development of new technologies by the research establishment to substitute in some way for the vanishing energy provided by petroleum. And locational shifts in production, as well as massive water management projects, seem likely to become dependent on an expanding role of government in supporting such adjustments. The long-run future of food and fiber production in the United States and the world is clouded with great uncertainty as the result of (1) the depletion of critical natural resources and (2) the pollution of the environment, which could lead to significant climatic changes. Our capacity to cope effectively with these two developments rests entirely on our ability to create through research the technologies that can counteract those developments.

Ordering the Forces: The Nineteenth Century

It would be nice in a work such as this to rank the various forces of agricultural development in their order of importance. The author will not do this, however, and for one important reason: he does not know how to do it. Some of the forces discussed have been pervasive in their effects. Others have been specific with respect to time and place. Some are highly intangible. Still others have done their work in an indirect fashion. But all the forces discussed in part III have, in the opinion of the author, had an important influence on the development of agriculture in the United States.

In the nineteenth century, however, one force towers over all the others. It is "Abundant Land." The settlement of the vast hinterland from the Appalachian Mountains to the Pacific slope was the great achievement of the American people during the nineteenth century. The promise of cheap or free land drew millions of immigrants to these shores during the nineteenth century and pulled millions more into the wilderness and across the continent in one century. Abundant land dictated the nature of the settlement process and the extensive nature of the agricultural process. Land was used by the government to support three wars, to help finance the building of an effective transport system, to help support a system of primary education, and to help create and support a system of higher education, including agricultural research and education. Abundant land, cheap or free, motivated, shaped, and drove the entire process of agricultural development in the United States in the nineteenth century.

The frontier environmental philosophy of "taming nature" of the seventeenth, eighteenth, and nineteenth centuries does not stand alone as an important force of agricultural development. It should be viewed as a complementary force to "Abundant Land." The land was there to be acquired, cheap or free. The philosophy that nature existed to be tamed provided the moral imperative for the frontiersman, or pioneer, to go forth and wrest that land from the native Americans and then from nature itself. So the force "Taming Nature" assumes importance as a facilitating force; in the nineteenth century it provided the justification for turning the wilderness of an entire continent into one great commercial farm plant.

It is difficult, if not impossible, to say which force had the second greatest influence on the agricultural development process. The development of the transport system — the canals and railroads — during the period 1820–60 was all-important in developing markets for the western farmers during that period. But without the immigrants the western settlements could not have been made in the first place. And without the development of the various kinds of laborsaving machinery, the pioneer farms could not have been transformed into commercial farms. The belief and value systems of the pioneers motivated them to work, as persons driven, and to save and accumulate. The physical security and system of justice provided by the federal and state governments facilitated the accumulation of property and trade and commerce. Finally, education freed the farmer from the dead hand of the past and made it possible for him to behave like a rational businessman — to adopt and effectively employ new technologies, and to become an informed citizen acting in his best interests.

Who can say, after "Abundant Land," which of the above named forces was most important? All were important. A set of forces, auxiliary to "Abundant Land," emerged and interacted during the nineteenth century, almost as if they were orchestrated, to support a rapid rate of agricultural development during that century. That is the lesson to be learned from a review of the forces in the nineteenth century.

Ordering the Forces: The Twentieth Century

The forces of agricultural development identified as being at work in the nineteenth century carry over into the twentieth century but with differing degrees of importance. Farmers continue to use land in the production of food and fiber products, but "Abundant Land," cheap or free, ceases to play a dynamic role in the agricultural development process. Land becomes one of several conventional factors of production in the twentieth century. Immigration also ceases to play a dynamic role in the development of the American economy in the twentieth century. And primary education becomes institutionalized in a complete system of education, so that its unique role as a contributing force of agricultural development is lost from sight.

The content of certain forces changes. The force "Building Physical Infrastructure," which during the nineteenth century was concerned primarily with the building of canals and railroads, is concerned in the twentieth century with the building of highways, irrigation systems, electric power grids, and input supply and product marketing systems. And the content of the force "Government" changes radically in the twentieth century — changing from the provision of security and essential services to widespread intervention into the operating economy on the behalf of farmers.

The negative environmental force, "Taming Nature," of the nineteenth century does a complete turnabout in the twentieth century. Environmental policy first becomes concerned with the conservation of natural resources (e.g., the forests) primarily to gain efficient use of those resources; then the preservation strand gains momentum (e.g., the establishment of national parks and wilderness areas); and finally, the science of ecology provides the scientific basis for protecting the total environment. The emergence of a positive environmental policy had a marginal influence on the development of agriculture (e.g., the establishment of the Soil Conservation Service in 1935) in the first half of the twentieth century. But in the second half it has played a more important role—in the regulation of toxic chemicals and in protecting the entire ecosystem of farming areas.

Some forces play increasingly dynamic roles in the twentieth century. Fluctuations in business conditions, prosperity and depression, and fluctuations in farm product exports influence importantly rates of growth in the agricultural industry. But the force that has had the greatest direct and observable influence on agricultural development in this century is "Farm Mechanization and Technological Advance"; this force lifted agricultural production to a completely new and highly productive plane; this force gave American agriculture its essential and unique character in the twentieth century. It was responsible for the intensive use of machines and mechanical power on farms and the concomitant dramatic decline in labor requirements. It resulted in important increases in yields per acre, in output per worker, and in output per unit of input. It made possible the sustained increases in aggregate farm output from 1935 to 1975. It was the vehicle of agricultural modernization.

This force does not, however, stand alone. It is only as effective at the farm level as the research, technological development, and extension activities that stand behind it. Technological advances can occur at the farm level only to the extent that new and improved technologies have been developed in public and private institutions, and have been made available to and extended to farmers. And the development of new and improved technologies can take place only to the extent that disciplined research has revealed the basic properties of and the relevant relationships among the natural phenomena involved. But as we know, the requisite research did take place, the new and improved technologies were developed in both public and private institutions, those new and improved technologies were carried forth, were extended, to farmers, and technological advances at the farm level did occur.

It can thus be argued that two closely related forces — (1) farm technological advance and (2) research, development, and extension — stand out as the dominant forces of agricultural development in the twentieth century. Many other forces, as has been noted, revolve around these twin forces and make their contribution to agricultural development. But for the twentieth century, as was true for the nineteenth century, it is not possible to assign a rank order of importance to the numerous other forces. They act and interact in many and varied ways and do not lend themselves to quantitative specification.

The great and dominating forces stand out, and the specific developmental roles of numerous other forces can be noted in certain time periods and geographic locations. But the interaction of the numerous forces that have been identified in the development process becomes as complex as society itself; hence the contribution of the numerous forces to the development of agriculture cannot be weighed and assigned specific numbers.

Forces of the Twenty-First Century

As agricultural development in the United States moves into the 1990s and edges toward the twenty-first century, several aspects of that development become clear. First, increases in food and fiber production must come about through farm technological advance (i.e., increases in output per unit of input). And this can only occur through increased investments in research and technological development. Second, as a part of this development process, the production and processing of food are becoming increasingly specialized with respect to location and technical complexity. The successful operation of such specialized, complex production processes will require high-quality management. Third, continuous specialized, complex production on the same site will require that much attention be paid to the protection of the soil and water resources of each site. And should the climate begin to change, or become more variable, as a result of the greenhouse effect, the management of these food production units will become increasingly demanding. The adjustments that may have to be made on these units, in the event of significant climatic changes, are beyond the comprehension of most agricultural experts as of 1992.

This means that four critically important forces that we have explored in this volume — farm technological advance, research and development, the availability of energy, and environmental policy — are going to be intertwined in some as yet unknown, but necessarily effective, fashion if the agricultural sector is to continue to produce bountifully in the twenty-first century to meet the needs of an expanding U.S. and world population. Technological advances must continue to occur at the farm level to enable increased output in essentially the same space. The scientists and engineers must continue to develop the new and improved technologies to be adopted at the production level. The energy must be available to power the specialized, complex food production units either from petroleum pools still being discovered or from forms of energy that have yet to be developed through scientific research and advanced engineering. Finally, farmers, scientists, engineers, and national and international politicians must work toward the same goal, namely, a *managed environment* in which changes in that environment are sufficiently benign to permit food production units, as well as human beings, to adjust to those changes without undue hardship. Can it be done? Some readers of this volume may find out.

A Multidimensional Process

As was stated in chapter 1, the concept of agricultural development is multidimensional. The many dimensions include: improvement in the real incomes of farm people, the provision of adequate supplies of food for all members of society, the eradication of poverty among farm people, changes in the organization and location of production activities resulting in increased output, changes in technological arrangements leading to increased output, changes in social institutions leading to improvements in the production and distribution of food and fiber products, and changes in the human agent — physical, mental, and attitudinal — employed in agricultural pursuits resulting in increased worker productivity. In part III we have discovered that many forces have been involved in supporting and fostering agricultural development in its many dimensions. In certain periods certain forces tended to dominate the development scene of agriculture. But — and this is the important point for this discussion — each force had an important role to play, perhaps a vital role to play, at a particular time or place. Take away the flow of immigrants into the United States during the nineteenth century, and the continent could not have been spanned and settled in one century. Take away the security and essential services provided by the government, and the development process would certainly have been greatly slowed, perhaps halted. Take away the belief and value systems that existed, and family units of the new society would not have chosen to become pioneers seeking land on the frontier, enduring the hardships of the frontier, and driving themselves to the breaking point to develop farms of their own. Take away the development of laborsaving machinery in the nineteenth century, and the process of transforming pioneer farms into commercial farms would have been slowed substantially. Take away the development of an effective transportation system during the period 1820–60, and the area of the Ohio and Mississippi river valleys could not have become a great surplus-producing and exporting region for agricultural products. Take away the research, development, and extension effort, when the supply of undeveloped land came to an end around 1900, and the aggregate output of agriculture in the twentieth century could have been increased only through the intensive use of labor in agricultural production and an increase in the real cost of food. Take away the intervening efforts of government during the Great Depression of 1929–39, and the entire economy, including the agricultural sector, could have collapsed.

"Abundant Land" may have dominated the process of agricultural development during the nineteenth century, and the twin forces of farm technological advance and research, development, and extension may have dominated that process in the twentieth century. But neither operating alone could have promoted and sustained the process of agricultural development. In fact, by the very nature of the interdependent development process neither could have stood alone or operated alone. The multidimensional process of agricultural development in the United States has been promoted and sustained by a broad set of interdependent forces, the absence of any one of which would have certainly slowed the development process and perhaps halted it for extended periods.

It is then a mistake to view the process of agricultural development in the United States as the product of a single, or monistic, cause, or force. To take such a view is to misread historical developments in the United States and is certain to lead to faulty policy prescriptions. A set of interdependent forces, interacting through time in response to physical and social conditions, promoted and sustained the process of agricultural development in the United States. This is not to say that the set of forces identified in this volume is perfectly identified or was ideally suited to deal with the development problems encountered in the historical process of development. It is to say first that the forces of development identified in this work promoted and sustained a rapid rate of agricultural development for two centuries and second that those forces interacted through various stages of historical development in such a way that the absence of any one of them would have operated to slow or cripple the process of agricultural development.

Coordinating the Forces

Over the past twenty-five years the complexity of national economic development, together with the need for a multiple approach to the promotion and support of that development, has become well appreciated. Unfortunately, this is not always the case with regard to agricultural development, where monistic theories of agricultural development continue to command attention in the less-developed world. But whatever the state of affairs regarding an understanding of the development process, whether overall or agricultural, many, if not most, less-developed countries have turned to national economic planning as a mechanism for coordinating the policies, programs, and projects aimed at promoting and supporting economic development.[4] Some countries have turned to "comprehensive planning" whereby the national government seeks to control and direct the use of all resources employed in the economy; others have turned to a concept of "holistic planning" whereby the government takes account of the operation of the *whole* economy in its formulation and execution of policies, programs, and projects, but it does not attempt to direct the use of each and every resource; still others have turned to an *ad hoc* concept of planning whereby the government plays a leading role in the formulation and execution of policies, programs, and projects, but it does not seek to integrate them into an internally consistent national plan.

Spokesmen for the less-developed countries give many and varied reasons for this emphasis on national development planning. It is argued that an economy motivated and directed by private self-interest, where not controlled by the state, will not develop along lines consistent with the goals and needs of most members of the society involved. To avoid policy errors and miscalculations, and thus speed the process of development, it is commonly argued that an overall authority must coordinate the policies, programs, and projects aimed at promoting and supporting economic development. Or sometimes it is argued that the development process has become so complex and so involved in modern times that coordination through national planning is necessary to keep the overall process from collapsing. But whatever the reason given, national development planning, of which agricultural development planning is an integral part, has become throughout the less-developed world a widely accepted institutional form for coordinating the forces of development.

This, however, is not the way agricultural development occurred in the United States. The various forces that have promoted and supported agricultural development in the United States from 1775 to 1990 have taken shape and become operational in response to a felt need on the part of some or all of the citizens of the Republic (although the need for a holistic national development plan to coordinate the policies, programs, and projects aimed at promoting and supporting economic development has received increased attention in recent years). In some cases an activity became a significant force for promoting and supporting agricultural development as a result of individual private decisions, as when immigrants came to America, families joined the westward migration and became pioneer farmers, and tinkerers — blacksmiths and mechanics — developed laborsaving machinery for the use of farmers in the nineteenth century. In some cases farm people joined in loose or formal associations to undertake activities that operated to promote and support agricultural development; the establishment of primary country schools by farm people in the nineteenth century and the development of purchasing and marketing cooperatives in the twentieth century are good illustrations of this. In other cases individual entrepreneurs with the aid and backing of government undertook activities that operated to promote and support agricultural development; a prime example of this was the building of a railroad system in the nineteenth century. It is also the case with regard to large speculators in western land, which may or may not have made a positive contribution to agricultural development in the United States. In still other cases the federal or state governments undertook activities that operated to promote and support agricultural development; such activities included building canals in the 1820s and 1830s, establishing a national highway system in the twentieth century, agricultural research, adult education for farmers, and programs of price and income support. In each of these cases a felt need induced or motivated some unit, or combination of units, in American society to undertake an activity that usually, but not always, operated to promote and support the development of the agricultural sector in the United States.

Now it can be argued that permitting individual units of American society to take action in response to a felt need did not always contribute to agricultural development. This was certainly the case with respect to protective tariff actions of the federal government, which were supported by western grain farmers throughout much of the nineteenth century; this action reduced their export opportunities and increased the price of inputs to them. Although the hopes and aspirations of most Americans have always been to become independent freeholders, the federal government in the first seventy years of nationhood was slow in making land available to them in reasonable-sized parcels with a minimum cash outlay. The federal government was extremely slow in fashioning a credit system tailored to needs of farm producers. As a final example, the state and federal levels of government were also extremely slow in developing a national highway system in the twentieth century to complement the rapid developments in truck transportation. In sum and in short, the implicit development policy of a spontaneous response to a felt need did not always produce the desired response in the optimum period of time.

But this implicit and spontaneous development policy, it is argued here, did work extremely well for the United States. The activities, which we have called forces, undertaken in response to a felt need by certain units of society, did come along in most instances in the form and at the time required by the process of agricultural development. As a result, the agricultural sector of the United States economy developed at a satisfactory pace and on a sustained basis over a two-hundred-year period. Given the human and social adjustments involved in agricultural development, it is questionable whether a more rapid rate of growth would have been acceptable to the individuals involved. Further, once the period of pioneering was past, the quality of life for the average white American living in rural areas compared favorably with that of urban white Americans.

Viewing the issue somewhat differently, one shudders to think what the agricultural development process in the United States would have looked like had that development process been defined and directed by a comprehensive plan of development in 1790. The social and economic goals of the new nation were too obscure, the knowledge base on which to plan too restricted, and the march of events too dynamic between 1790 and 1860 to have permitted any series of development plans to direct and coordinate the agricultural development process along lines consistent with the goals and aspirations of that emerging society and in harmony with the changing geographical and physical parameters. In short, rational national economic planning, given the conflicting social and economic goals of the North, South, and West, the huge territorial acquisitions, and the momentous westward migration, would have been impossible. In this highly dynamic context, the general and implicit development policy of permitting certain units, and certain combinations of those units, of society to respond spontaneously to felt needs was a highly successful policy, and perhaps the only policy that could have proved successful in that dynamic context.

Basically this is still the development policy of the United States for the economy as a whole, and for the agricultural sector, as of 1990. But with the increased intervention of the federal government into the operation of the economy, and the increased likelihood that the policies, programs, and projects of the federal government will make contact and conflict with one another, the following question is raised more often and with greater intellectual force — Should not these diverse intervening activities of the federal government be coordinated in some form of a national development plan? Some people in the political campaign of 1992 have argued that the nation needs an "industrial policy" to guide and direct the development of certain industries and to eliminate others. Other people maintain that we have too much government intervention in the economy, as of 1992, and that the real need is to privatize certain public activities such as education.

The answers to these questions will not be attempted here. That is the proper subject of another book. But this historical study should remind us that physical conditions and institutional situations are constantly changing, so that the implicit and spontaneous general development policy pursued so successfully for 200 years may need to be changed at some future time.

Suggested Readings

Brewster, John M. *A Philosopher among Economists: Selected Works of John M. Brewster.* Philadelphia: Murphy, 1970.

U.S. Department of Agriculture. Economic Research Service. *Agriculture and Economic Growth.* Agricultural Economic Report No. 28, March 1963.

U.S. Department of Agriculture. Economic Research Service. *How the United States Improved Its Agriculture.* Foreign-76, May 1964.

U.S. Department of Energy, Energy Information Administration. *Annual Energy Outlook 1992, with Projections to 2010,* DOE/EIA-0382(92), 1992.

Worster, Donald. "Transformations of the Earth: Toward an Agroecological Perspective in History." *Journal of American History,* 76 (March 1990); pp. 1087–1106.

CHAPTER 17

CHANGES IN STRUCTURE, ORGANIZATION, AND PRODUCTIVITY

From the discussion in part II, we know that agricultural development in the nineteenth century was extensive. It was extensive in two senses. First, the nation added one farm after another across the continent. Second, the cultivated area of individual farms grew in size. The first development resulted from the westward movement and settlement. The second resulted from the adoption of horse-powered, laborsaving machinery. In this extensive development, yields per acre did not increase, nor did average output per unit of input. But output per worker increased dramatically.

With the closing of the frontier, the extensive phase of agricultural development came to an end. In the twentieth century, farmers have continued to adopt laborsaving machinery — but they have done more. They have participated in a technological revolution with three principal strands: (1) mechanical, (2) biological, and (3) chemical. As a direct result of this technological revolution on farms, the input of capital per farm, in all forms, has increased greatly; the size of farm measured in terms of area, or aggregate output, has increased; and the total number of farms has decreased. As a further result, yield per acre, output per unit of input, and output per worker have all increased importantly. In the twentieth century, agricultural development has been intensive.

In this chapter we plan to explore the changes in farm organization in more detail and to describe the development with greater precision. Next we will describe and analyze changes in farm productivity during the twentieth century, for which good data are available. Finally, we will compare the process of agricultural development in the United States with that of another country that experienced rapid agricultural development but which developed very differently, namely, Japan.

Basic Changes in Farm Organization and Structure: 1775–1990

The basic social objective of organizing agricultural production into family-managed and family-operated units has not changed over the long period 1775–1990. And the basic family objective of seeking to maximize its total wealth has not changed. But the organization of resources on family farm proprietorships for maximizing the wealth position of the families involved has changed importantly over this period.

During the period 1775–1825, individual families sought to improve their wealth position by moving west and acquiring as much land as possible, either through the illegal process of squatting on land not authorized for settlement or by the purchase of land, directly or indirectly, from the government at a low price of $1 to $2 per acre. The years immediately succeeding settlement were spent clearing and developing the land. In the South this was accomplished to an important degree through the human back power of black slaves; in the North it was accomplished through the human back power of family members. The improved "farm" was commonly sold to settlers in a later wave of westward migration who might in turn resell it or remain on it and develop it into a commercial farm.

This phase of speculative farm development drew to a close earlier in the Deep South, perhaps before 1825, with the opening up and development of markets for raw cotton in England and the European continent. And it drew to a close later in the Northwest Territory, perhaps between 1825 and 1850, with the opening up of markets for grain and animal products on the East Coast, the Deep South, and abroad. A surplus of grain and animal products was produced for sale on northern farms first by expanding the area under cultivation on existing farms and second by adding new farms to the national farm plant. Given the high cost of human labor, this increase in the area under cultivation was achieved by the continuous adoption of horse-powered, laborsaving machinery on northern farms. This machinery substituted for scarce human labor in the production of grain crops. The size of the surplus for sale on individual farms and in the aggregate was slowly increased throughout the nineteenth century as a result of increased area specialization in the production of crops in the North.

In the Deep South the cotton surplus for sale was increased by an expansion in the black slave population, which permitted an increase in the area under cotton cultivation. This process of expansion in cotton production under black slavery continued until the Civil War. After the Civil War cotton production continued to expand through a great increase in the area of cotton under cultivation. But in the post-Civil War period this was made possible by the slow adoption of improved machines in established areas and the rapid expansion of the area under cotton production west of the Mississippi River, particularly in Texas, on family-managed and family-operated farms.

In the period, then, roughly from 1825 to 1900, and excluding the special case of cotton production in the pre-Civil War period, a surplus of agricultural products was produced in the United States by expanding the total area under cultivation, with constant yields per acre. This was made possible in a period of scarce human labor by the continuous adoption on farms of new and improved units of machinery that substituted for human labor. In this context, the number of farms increased, as did the area under cultivation on existing farms, and farms became increasingly specialized in the production process.

Since the frontier was closed by 1900 and new land could be brought into production (except in Montana and Wyoming) only through expensive projects of reclamation or drainage, if agricultural production in the aggregate was to be increased in the twentieth century, it had to come about through an expansion of cultivated land on existing farms or through increased yields in existing cultivated acres. The number of acres of cropland harvested increased modestly in the first two decades of the twentieth century, but fewer acres were harvested in the United States in the 1960s and early 1970s than were harvested in 1910. Thus the great expansion in production that occurred in the twentieth century did not come about through an expansion in the area cultivated. It came about through a great increase in crop yields per acre. It also occurred at a time when the amount of human labor employed on farms declined precipitously.

What has occurred on American farms over the period 1900–1980 is, then, the following. New and improved forms of machinery have continued to substitute for expensive human labor. The convenient gasoline-engined tractor has replaced horses and mules as a source of power. At the same time that machines and tractors were substituting for human labor and animal power, new and improved forms of biological capital (e.g., hybrid seed corn) were substituting for land, and new and improved forms of chemical capital (e.g., commercial nitrogenous fertilizer) were substituting for land. The result was greatly increased crop yields per acre concurrent with reduced labor inputs per acre and increased capital inputs per acre. The agricultural production process has become increasingly productive during the twentieth century in terms of yields per acre, output per worker, and output per unit of input.

This could and did occur because it was cheaper in terms of the farm profit and loss statement to substitute relatively cheap tractor power and machinery for relatively expensive human labor and to substitute relatively cheap farm chemicals for increasingly expensive land. Mechanical capital and chemical capital were cheap over most of the period 1900–1980 because they were produced by, and/or implemented by, an extremely cheap and convenient form of energy, petroleum. In a general sense, then, what occurred during this period was the substitution of petroleum for human labor and land in the farming operation. A technological strategy, based on cheap petroleum energy, had a great and successful payoff in American agriculture.

The implications of this technological strategy for the structure of American farming were far-reaching. The new and improved forms of capital — mechanical, biological, and chemical — both induced and enabled farms to grow in size. Thus, with the total number of acres cultivated in the national plant holding constant, the number of operating farms had to decline. And the decline in the twentieth century has been monumental. The number of farms rose modestly from 6.4 million in 1910–14 to 6.8 million in the mid-1930s, and then declined to 2.4 million in 1980. Concurrent with the decline in the number of farms, the bulk of commercial production has tended to concentrate on a relatively small number of very large farms. In 1980 some 271,000 farms, each grossing $100,000 or more, produced and marketed approximately 68 percent of the total product moving to market (see table 8.4). Technological advances and capital formation on American farms have resulted in some dramatic changes in the organization of American farms in the twentieth century. These changes in turn have resulted in a very great change in the structure of American farming.

The shape of the development process in American agriculture from the close of the Civil War to 1970 may be viewed in summary form in table 17.1. We see that the input of labor increases steadily from 1870

Table 17.1. Major Farm Input Groups, United States, 1870–1970 (1967 = 100)

Year	Labor	Real Estate	All Forms of Capital	Total Inputs
1870	190	43	8	43
1880	238	59	12	55
1890	276	70	15	66
1900	302	83	20	77
1910	321	98	25	86
1915	331	102	29	92
1920	341	102	34	98
1925	338	99	36	99
1930	326	101	40	101
1935	299	99	34	91
1940	293	103	44	100
1945	271	98	55	103
1950	217	105	70	104
1955	185	105	81	105
1960	145	100	87	101
1965	110	99	94	98
1970	96	98	103	99

Source: Prepared for the author by the U.S. Department of Agriculture, Economics, Statistics, and Cooperatives Service, July 10, 1978.

to 1920 and then decreases just as persistently from 1920 to 1970. The input of land increases dramatically from 1870 to 1910 and then holds almost constant from 1910 to 1960. The input of capital in farming in 1870 was relatively unimportant, but the input of capital increased by almost thirteen times between 1870 and 1970. In this period American agriculture moved from a land-extensive form of agriculture to a capital-intensive form of agriculture.

The long-run trends in farm inputs noted above continue through the 1970s: inputs of human labor continue to decline, inputs of farm real estate hold about constant, and inputs of mechanical power, machinery, and agricultural chemicals continue their long upward climb (see table 17.2). *But the organization of American agriculture begins to change after 1980.* For the first time in over 100 years the input of farm machinery declines over a ten-year period, 1979–89 (see table 17.2). And the input of agricultural chemicals for the first time since World War II stops its strong upward movement — first declining, then leveling off, and finally increasing sharply in 1989. The input of real estate also declines over the period 1979–89. Only one category of inputs, Miscellaneous, increases substantially in the decade of the 1980s. As a

Table 17.2. Indexes of Total Farm Input and Major Input Subgroups, United States, 1970-89 (1977 = 100)

Year	Total Input All	Nonpurchased[a]	Purchased[b]	Farm Labor[c]	Farm Real Estate[d]	Mechanical Power and Machinery[e]	Agricultural Chemicals[f]	Feed, Seed, & Livestock Purchases[g]	Taxes and Interest[h]	Miscellaneous[i]
1970	96	106	87	112	105	85	75	96	102	89
1971	97	103	90	108	103	87	81	102	101	89
1972	97	103	91	110	102	86	86	104	102	92
1973	98	103	93	109	100	90	90	107	102	90
1974	98	103	93	109	99	92	92	99	103	87
1975	97	103	90	106	97	96	83	93	100	82
1976	98	100	96	100	98	98	96	101	102	90
1977	100	100	100	100	100	100	100	100	100	100
1978	102	100	105	100	100	104	107	108	99	103
1979	105	100	111	99	103	104	123	115	103	113
1980	103	100	106	96	103	101	123	114	100	96
1981	102	98	106	96	104	98	129	108	99	108
1982	99	96	102	93	102	92	118	107	95	116
1983	96	93	101	97	101	89	102	103	99	101
1984	96	91	101	92	99	86	120	106	93	110
1985	92	87	97	85	97	80	115	102	96	116
1986	89	84	94	80	96	77	109	110	97	110
1987	89	82	95	78	95	73	111	117	100	122
1988	87	80	94	75	94	72	111	110	97	119
1989[j]	88	79	98	76	93	73	122	119	94	123

Source: U.S. Department of Agriculture, Economic Research Service, *Production and Efficiency Statistics, 1989*, ECIFS9-4, April 1991.
a Includes operator and unpaid family labor, and operator-owned real estate and other capital inputs.
b Includes all inputs other than nonpurchased inputs.
c Includes hired, operator, and unpaid family labor.
d Includes all land in farms, service buildings, grazing fees, and repairs on service buildings.
e Includes interest and depreciation on mechanical power and machinery repairs.
f Includes fertilizer, lime, and pesticides.
g Includes nonfarm value of feed, seed, and livestock purchases.
h Includes real estate and personal property taxes, and interest on livestock and crop inventory.
i Includes such things as insurances, telephone, veterinary fees, containers, and binding materials.
j Preliminary.

Table 17.3. Number of Farms, Net Cash Income, Off-farm Cash Income, and Farm Balance Sheet by Value of Sales Class, 1990

Item	$1,000,000 and over	$500,000 to $999,999	$250,000 to $499,999	$100,000 to $249,999	$40,000 to $99,999	$20,000 to $39,999	Less than $20,000
				Thousands			
Number of Farms	16	27	64	214	306	259	1,254
				Dollars			
Per farm operation:							
Gross cash income	3,708,945	777,624	401,468	183,937	78,565	34,749	7,216
Cash receipts from marketings	3,627,349	727,763	360,125	162,726	68,623	29,958	5,713
Direct government payment commodities	178,029	115,158	82,351	42,585	17,151	6,928	804
Price-support-only commodities	363,458	139,212	89,344	53,523	23,619	7,840	1,059
Nonsupported commodities	3,085,862	473,393	188,430	66,618	27,853	15,191	3,850
Government payments	28,096	36,056	33,174	15,055	5,749	2,024	192
Farm-related income	53,501	13,804	8,168	6,156	4,193	2,767	1,311
Cash expenses	2,464,395	504,645	243,201	113,559	52,664	25,557	7,586
Net cash income	1,244,550	272,978	158,267	70,378	25,901	9,192	−370
Per family off-farm income	28,472	25,916	27,629	18,096	25,335	31,916	35,206
				Thousand dollars			
Per farm balance-sheet							
Farm assets	4,915	2,092	1,264	815	494	330	167
Real estate	3,201	1,412	853	584	364	254	135
Livestock and poultry	867	200	110	63	38	24	9
Machinery and motor vehicles	423	187	140	95	58	34	16
Crops stored	136	85	59	34	12	5	1
Purchased inputs	29	15	8	3	1	1	0
Investments in cooperatives	221	176	81	28	14	6	2
Other financial	40	18	13	8	7	6	3
Debt	1,051	447	275	147	78	42	19
Real estate	337	205	129	77	43	27	14
Nonreal estate	714	242	146	70	35	15	5
Equity	3,864	1,646	989	668	416	288	148

Source: U.S. Department of Agriculture, Economic Research Service, *National Financial Summary, 1990*, ECIFS10-1, November 1991.

result of these developments, total inputs in the American farm plant decline by 16 percent between 1979 and 1989. (We will discuss the implications of this organizational development in the next chapter.)

The Modern American Farm

There is, of course, no single type of modern American farm. There are many different types with regard to size, products, and financial status. As of 1990, we categorize the 2.1 million American farms into four basic types: very large farms grossing over $250,000 per year, large farms grossing between $100,000 and $249,999 per year, medium-sized farms grossing between $40,000 and $99,999 per year, and part-time farms grossing less than $39,999 per year (see table 17.3). There are 107,000 very large farms, which produce and sell 56 percent of the total national farm product. The assets of these farms range from $1.2 million to nearly $5 million, with their equity ranging from nearly $1 million to $4 million. These very large farms on average are important recipients of direct government payments under the commodity programs. But we note that the very largest (those grossing over $1 million per year) produced only a small percentage of commodities eligible for price support (see table 17.3). The yearly net cash incomes of these farms are, on average, positive and range from $158,267 to $1,244,550. By modern industrial standards these farms are still small, but by historical farm standards they have become large-scale operations.

There are 214,000 large farms, which produce and sell 21 percent of the total national farm product. The assets of these farms average $815,000 with an equity position of $668,000. Direct government payments under the commodity programs average $42,585 per farm, and we note that receipts from commodities eligible for price support on these farms are almost equal to the receipts from nonsupported commodities. The net cash income from farming for this group averages $70,378 per year. In terms of number of farms this is a large group, and the net income position of the average farm in this group is reasonably good, but the contribution of this group to the total national farm product is less than half that of the very large farm group.

There are 306,000 farms in the medium-sized group, and they produce and sell only about 13 percent of the total national farm product. The assets of these farms average only $494,000, but their equity position on average is good at $416,000 per farm. The role of government in providing income and price support for this group of farms is small. But off-farm income becomes a major factor for farms in this group; it averages $25,335 per farm per year in comparison with net cash income from farming of only $25,901. When people refer to the small family farmer, they must be referring to farmers in this group. But it is important to recognize that the average family in this grouping, which we have defined as medium-sized farms, as of 1990, was earning one-half of its income from nonfarm endeavors.

There are 1,513,000 farms in the part-time farming group. But this large group of farms produces and sells only about 10 percent of the total national farm product. The assets of farms in this group are, as would be expected, small, and the contributions of government in the form of income and price support are negligible. The net cash farm income in this group ranges from −$370 to $9,192. The major source of income for families in this group is off-farm income, ranging from $35,206 per year for the smallest of these farms to $31,916 per year for the next larger-size group. These are not farms in the traditional sense. These are family enterprises in which the major and sustaining source of income comes from nonfarm activities, and farming is a sideline.

The modern American farm that produces the bulk of product moving to market is thus by historical standards a very large enterprise. And each year farms in this grouping become larger. Modern large-scale machinery and equipment support the trend toward bigness; with large-scale modern machinery a farmer and his son, and perhaps a hired hand or two, can operate one of these farms. Business failures among the less aggressive, poorer managers make the trend toward bigness a reality. The productive assets, particularly the land, of those going out of business are immediately gobbled up by the more aggressive, better farm managers, and as a result the average size of the large commercial farms increases each year. As of 1990, the end of this cannibalistic process is not in sight, although the process is slowing down simply because the universe of farms is declining in size. There are fewer farms to be gobbled up. Technological advances in machinery and equipment, the competitive process, and governmental price and income support interact to drive out the weak and enable the strong to become even larger.

Changes in Farm Productivity, 1870–1990

The record of American agricultural development can to an important degree be read from table 17.4.[1] Total farm output increased significantly between 1870 and 1900. It increased primarily through the adding of farm inputs — land and labor — but not exclusively. The

Table 17.4. Indexes of Farm Output, Input, and Productivity,
United States, 1870–1990 (1967 = 100)

Year	Output	Input	Produc-tivity	Year	Output	Input	Produc-tivity
1870	17	43	40	1949	74	105	71
1880	26	56	47	1950	74	104	71
1890	31	66	43	1951	76	107	71
1900	40	77	53	1952	79	107	74
1910	43	86	50	1953	79	106	75
1911	42	88	48	1954	80	105	76
1912	47	90	53	1955	82	105	78
1913	43	90	47	1956	82	103	80
1914	47	92	51	1957	81	101	80
1915	49	92	53	1958	87	100	87
1916	44	92	48	1959	88	102	87
1917	47	93	51	1960	91	101	90
1918	47	95	49	1961	91	100	91
1919	47	95	50	1962	92	100	92
1920	50	98	52	1963	96	100	96
1921	45	95	47	1964	95	100	95
1922	49	96	51	1965	98	98	100
1923	50	97	51	1966	95	98	97
1924	49	99	50	1967	100	100	100
1925	41	99	51	1968	102	100	102
1926	52	101	52	1969	102	99	103
1927	52	99	52	1970	101	100	102
1928	54	101	53	1971	110	100	110
1929	53	102	52	1972	110	100	110
1930	52	101	51	1973	112	101	111
1931	57	101	56	1974	106	100	106
1932	55	97	57	1975	114	99	116
1933	51	96	53	1976	117	100	117
1934	43	90	48	1977	120	102	118
1935	52	91	57	1978	125	104	120
1936	47	93	50	1979	134	107	125
1937	57	98	59	1980	125	105	119
1938	57	96	60	1981	142	104	137
1939	58	98	59	1982	140	100	140
1940	60	100	60	1983	116	98	118
1941	62	100	62	1984	135	97	139
1942	70	103	68	1985	142	93	153
1943	69	104	66	1986	134	90	148
1944	71	105	67	1987	132	90	147
1945	70	103	68	1988	123	89	138
1946	71	101	71	1989	137	89	155
1947	69	101	68	1990	143	90	160
1948	76	103	74				

Source: U.S. Department of Agriculture, Economic Research Service.

increase in output in percentage terms was greater than the increase in inputs; there was some increase in productivity during this period; output per unit of input increased from an index value of 40 in 1870 to 53 in 1900. This increase in productivity resulted primarily from the substitution of new and improved machines for human labor, since we know that yields per acre did not increase during this period.

Total farm output increased slowly from 1900 to 1930. The frontier was closed, and new land could be brought into production only through heavy investments in reclamation and drainage. Increases in farm output during this period had to occur through either the increased application of human labor or farm technological advance. But the input of human labor in agricultural production did not increase between 1900 and 1930; it held almost constant. And from table 17.4 we see that agricultural productivity — output per unit of input — did not increase during this period. Total farm output increased slowly during this period as modest amounts of land and capital were added to the national farm plant, and agricultural productivity held almost constant.

The period 1930–37 was a period of uncertainty and instability. The new and improved technologies were available during this period to support widespread technological advance on farms and a sustained increase in agricultural productivity. But this development did not occur for two reasons — deep depression and severe drought. Deep depression kept farmers from investing in the available technologies, and the severe droughts of 1934 and 1936 negated farmers' efforts to increase output through the use of new and improved technologies.

The technological payoff began in 1937 and continued for nearly thirty years. Output per unit of input increased irregularly but persistently from 1937 to 1965, as farmers adopted one new and improved technology after another. This is the way that total farm output increased over the long period, 1937–65. Over this period the input of productive resources held almost constant. In fact, the loss of human labor inputs was almost exactly balanced by the addition of capital inputs. Farmers increased their total output year after year by adopting new and more productive technologies, embodied in capital, year after year.

Between the years 1965 and 1975 the productivity index in table 17.4 behaves rather strangely. It sputters and it moves upward in discrete jumps. The productivity index holds almost constant between 1965 and 1970, as the indexes of both total output and total inputs hold almost constant. The productivity index takes a large upward jump between 1970 and 1971, in response to a large increase in the index of total output. Once again the productivity index holds almost constant between 1971 and 1974, as does the index of inputs. Between 1974 and 1975 the productivity index takes a second discrete upward jump in response to an increase in the output index and a modest decline in the input index.

Perhaps the technological revolution in America moved in fits and starts over the period 1965–75, as the productivity index in table 17.4 suggests. But the author and most experts are inclined to doubt such a staircase process of development. It is more likely that this staircase pattern of increase in the output and productivity data simply represent statistical aberrations. Further, variations in the weather and crop growing conditions often produce unplanned and substantial variations in output.

Following 1975, total farm output increases substantially on a trend basis through 1990 (see table 17.4). There are, however, some drastic annual fluctuations in output due to the weather; note the sharp decline in 1983 due to bad weather. But something else was happening. As noted earlier total inputs employed in farming declined 16 percent between 1979 and 1989. This decline in inputs employed did not, as we know, cause total output to decline; total output increased on a trend basis over this period. As a consequence the productivity index increases by 38 percent between 1975 and 1990. This then is our measure of farm technological advance over the period 1975–90. The measure tells us that in terms of farm technological advance it was one of the most dynamic periods in the history of American agriculture.

The Japanese Comparison

Agricultural development in the United States over the long period 1800–1990 was arduous and difficult for the farmer participants, and it involved continuous and painful adjustments to the changing physical and economic environments. But by the criteria of (1) growth in production, (2) accumulation of wealth by the surviving participants, and (3) the provision of an adequate food supply, agricultural development in the United States must be judged a success. The process of agricultural development in Japan from the time of the Meiji Restoration in 1867 has been just as successful as that which took place in the United States, but the process was very different. The achievements of the two countries and the differences in the development routes taken by them emerge from a comparative study of agricultural de-

Table 17.5. Changes in Output, Input, and Productivity in United States and Japanese Agriculture, 1880–1960

	Annual Compound Rate of Change				
	1880 to 1900	1900 to 1920	1920 to 1940	1940 to 1960	1880 to 1960
United States					
Output (net of seeds and feed)	2.2	0.8	1.3	1.9	1.5
Total input	1.6	1.1	0.3	0.2	0.8
Total productivity (output/input)	0.6	-0.3	1.0	1.7	0.7
Number of male workers	1.1	0.2	-0.9	-3.9	-0.9
Output per male worker	1.1	0.6	2.2	5.8	2.4
Arable land area	2.7	1.9	-0.1	-0.2	1.1
Output per ha. of arable land	-0.5	-1.1	1.4	2.1	0.4
Japan					
Output (net of seeds and feed)	2.1	2.2	0.7	1.5	1.6
Total input	0.2	0.6	0.3	1.0	0.6
Total productivity (output/input)	1.9	1.6	0.4	0.5	1.0
Number of male workers	-0.1	0	-0.9	-0.1	-0.3
Output per male worker	2.2	2.2	1.6	1.6	1.9
Arable land area	0.5	0.7	0.1	0	0.3
Output per ha. of arable land	1.6	1.5	0.6	1.5	1.3

Source: Adapted from Table 6.2, chapter 6, in *Agricultural Development: An International Perspective*, by Yujiro Hayami and Vernon W. Ruttan (Baltimore: Johns Hopkins Press, 1971).

velopment in the two countries from 1880 to 1960 by Professors Yujiro Hayami and Vernon Ruttan.[2]

Total farm output in the United States increased 1.5 percent per year, on an annual compounded basis, over the period 1880–1960; total farm output in Japan increased 1.6 percent per year over the same period. (See table 17.5.) Agricultural productivity (output per unit of input) in the United States increased by 0.7 percent per year over the period 1880–1960; agricultural productivity in Japan increased by 1.0 percent over the same period. In gains in productive efficiency over this eighty-year period, Japan had the edge.

But the patterns of development by time periods for the two countries are markedly different. (See table 17.5 and figure 17.1.) Total output in the United States increases from 1880 to 1930 primarily through the employment of more conventional resources. As a result, productivity rises modestly between 1880 and 1900, and then holds almost constant from 1900 to 1930. In Japan the total input of productive resources increases only modestly over the long period 1880–1940. Total agricultural output increases over this period primarily as a result of increased resource productivity. Farm technological advance was the principal source of increased output in Japan over the period 1880–1940. After 1935, output in the United States increases almost exclusively as a result of increased resource productivity. World War II raises havoc with the agricultural development process in Japan, but following the war output in Japan increases partly because of an increased in-

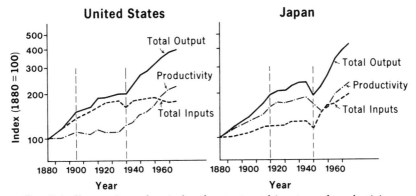

Fig. 17.1. Changes in total agricultural output, total inputs, and productivity, United States and Japan, 1880–1969 (log scale). Employing revised data, this figure is adapted from figure 6.1 in chapter 6 of Yujiro Hayami and Vernon W. Ruttan, *Agricultural Development: An International Perspective* (Baltimore: Johns Hopkins University Press, 1971), p. 116.

Table 17.6. Land and Labor Endowments and Relative Prices in Agriculture: United States and Japan, 1880–1960

	1880	1900	1920	1940	1960
United States					
(1) Arable land area (million ha.)	76	129	189	187	181
(2) Number of male farm workers (thousand)	7959	9880	10221	8487	3973
(3) (1)/(2) (ha./worker)	10	13	18	22	46
(4) Value of arable land ($/ha.)	163	129	352	180	711
(5) Farm wage rate ($/day)	0.90	1.00	3.30	1.60	6.60
(6) (4)/(5)	181	129	107	113	108
Japan					
(7) Arable land area (thousand ha.)	4748	5200	5997	6121	6071
(8) Number of male farm workers (thousand)	7842	7680	7593	6365	6230
(9) (7)/(8) (ha./worker)	0.61	0.68	0.79	0.96	0.97
(10) Value of arable land (*Yen*/ha.)	343	917	3882	4709	1415000
(11) Farm wage rate (*Yen*/day)	0.22	0.31	1.39	1.90	440
(12) (10)/(11)	1559	2958	2793	2478	3216

Source: Adapted from table 6.1, chapter 6, in *Agricultural Development: An International Perspective*, by Yujiro Hayami and Vernon W. Ruttan (Baltimore: Johns Hopkins Press, 1971).

put of resources and partly because of increased productivity. Farm technological advance does not play the same dominant role in Japan in the post-World War II period that it does in the United States.

Why is the shape of the development process, or the pattern of the development process, for the agricultural sector so different for these two countries? Hayami and Ruttan argue that the different patterns of development for the two countries are to be explained by the different resource endowments, hence different relative prices of the factors of production of the two countries (as we have argued earlier with respect to the pattern of agricultural development in the United States). The United States was richly endowed with good arable land in a favorable climate: 10 hectares of arable land per worker in 1880, and 46 hectares of arable land per worker in 1960. Japan was poorly endowed with arable land: .61 hectares of arable land per worker in 1880, and .97 hectares of arable land per worker in 1960 (see table 17.6). Further, labor was plentiful in Japan and wage rates were low, whereas exactly the opposite obtained in the United States. Thus the ratio of land prices to wage rates was relatively low in the United States and relatively high in Japan. (Compare lines 6 and 12 in table 17.6.) Stated differently, a farm worker in Japan in 1880 had to work approximately nine times as many days (1559 ÷ 181 = 8.61) as a farm worker in the United States to buy a hectare of land.

Given these resource endowments and relative factor prices, land was used abundantly in the production process in the United States in the nineteenth century. Research and development focused on the production of efficient mechanical technologies that could be substituted for human labor on farms throughout the period 1880–1960, thus enabling the land operated per worker to increase from 10 hectares in 1880 to 46 hectares in 1960. As land became scarce in the United States in the twentieth century, and consequently high-priced, the emphasis in research and development shifted toward the production of biological and chemical technologies. As a result of this shift in emphasis, yields per hectare of land have increased importantly in the United States since 1935, as have total output and resource productivity.

In Japan agricultural development followed a different track from the beginning. Because land was scarce and high-priced and labor was plentiful and low-priced, a development strategy was sought and found which would take advantage of the abundant supply of human labor and which would produce new technologies that could substitute for land. The strategy emphasized the development of new and improved biological and chemical technologies. The application of such technologies on farms involved (1) the substitution of new and improved plant varieties and commercial fertilizers for land, and (2) the heavy use of human labor in the preparation of seedbeds, in weeding, and in the application and management of irrigation water. This approach greatly increased yields per hectare over the period 1880–1940, as well as output per unit of input and total output. During this period the Japanese followed a strategy of agricultural development almost the direct opposite of that followed in the United States. And it was highly successful because it was *rational* in terms of the resource endowments of Japan and the consequent relative factor prices.

In the language of Hayami and Ruttan, relatively high land prices in Japan *induced* a quest through the disciplined process of research and development for new and improved technologies that could substitute for the factor land. In the economically rational, work-oriented society of Japan, that quest was successful. The new and improved biological and chemical technologies that were developed, when used in combination with the abundant supplies of human labor, resulted in a rapid rate of agricultural development between 1880 and 1940. Relatively high labor prices in the United States *induced* a quest through the disciplined process of research and development, first, for new and improved technologies that could be substituted for the factor labor and, second, for new and improved technologies that could be substituted for that increasingly scarce factor, land. In the tolerably rational and performance-oriented society of twentieth-century America, those quests too were successful. The new and improved technologies that were forthcoming in the United States, at first largely mechanical and then increasingly biological, have resulted in an ever-growing and bountiful supply of food for domestic consumers and for sale in overseas markets.

Conclusion

There is no one royal road to successful agricultural development. What might be a desirable approach, or strategy, for one country could be the wrong approach for another. And what might be the proper approach, or strategy, at one time in the history of a country could be the wrong approach at another time. In this connection it will be interesting to see how the agricultural economies of the United States and Japan adjust to rising energy prices during the long-run future, 1990–2010. Resource adjustments in the farm production process to rising energy prices were slow to occur in the United States in the short period 1974–78.

As a guiding principle, it might be argued that a nation should always seek to maximize its rate of increase in agricultural productivity. But such a principle says little more than that a nation should always seek to produce and distribute its agricultural product as efficiently as possible. Such a principle offers little in the way of guidance with respect to dividing up the national research and development budget among competing claimants. Such a principle has little to say regarding the choice of resource-allocating mechanisms: whether to rely on the market or turn to development planning. Further, and perhaps of greater importance, efficiency is not the sole criterion used by most societies in making decisions regarding the development of agriculture. Society is concerned about the distribution of farm incomes and assets. Society is interested in food security. Society is interested in the rates of human resource adjustments (i.e., occupational mobility, geographical mobility), and on and on.

Once again we are forced to recognize that agricultural development is multidimensional. Society has many goals, some major, some minor, within the agricultural development process. And in seeking to achieve those different goals, which are often conflicting goals, a society is likely to pursue policies that do not contribute to a maximum rate of increase in agricultural productivity.

But perhaps one general conclusion can be advanced. If a nation has the goal of increasing the real incomes of its producers and consumers of food, it cannot in the name of equity, or in the name of security, *always* choose to produce and distribute its food supply by a less, rather than by a more, efficient method. Rather, it must continuously seek to increase the productivity of the resources employed in producing and distributing its food supply. To a tolerable degree both the United States and Japan did that over the period 1880–1960. Both employed their conventional resources and their research and development resources in ways such that the total productivity of agriculture either increased or held constant over the long period 1880–1960 and in the years since 1960 as well. Thus despite whatever else those countries did in the way of fighting wars, redressing inequities among their citizens, and achieving various forms of social security, the food and agricultural policies pursued by those countries had the effect of increasing the real incomes of producers and consumers of food.

Suggested Readings

Hayami, Yujiro, and Ruttan, Vernon W. *Agricultural Development: An International Perspective*. Baltimore: Johns Hopkins Press, 1971.

Ruttan, Vernon W. *Induced Innovation and Agricultural Development*. Staff Paper 77-1. New York: Agricultural Development Council, 1977.

Sundquist, W. B. "Agriculture and Economic Development: The Minnesota Case." Staff Paper P77-9. Department of Agricultural and Applied Economics, University of Minnesota, April 1977.

U.S. Department of Agriculture. Economic Research Service. *Changes in Farm Production and Efficiency, Special Issue Featuring Historical Series*. Statistical Bulletin No. 561, September 1976.

U.S. Department of Agriculture. Economic Research Service. *Production and Efficiency Statistics, 1989*, ECIFS9-4, April 1991.

Wilcox, Walter W.; Cochrane, Willard W.; and Herdt, Robert W. *Economics of American Agriculture*, 3rd ed. Englewood Cliffs, N.J.: Prentice Hall, 1974. Chaps. 1–4.

CHAPTER 18

THE WATERSHEDS OF DEVELOPMENT

On at least two occasions in the history of the American nation the course of agricultural development underwent a significant change. In our terminology, agriculture in its process of development crossed two major watersheds.[1] The first occurred during the period 1763–85, when important changes in land settlement policy could have changed, and briefly did change, the direction of agricultural development. The second occurred during the period 1900–1920, when agriculture made the transition from an essentially extensive form of production to an intensive form. The first we will consider from the perspective of contrasting development alternatives — comparing what might have been and what actually occurred. The second we will consider as an important demonstration of how the structure of agricultural production must and does change when the resource base changes.

We will also take a close look in this chapter at various resource and developmental changes that have occurred in American agriculture during the 1980s in the context of an unpredictable World Market. It is difficult to make sense out of the many and varied developments — some domestic, some foreign — that are occurring with respect to American agriculture. But some profound changes appear to be taking place in the production and distribution of food. It is possible that American agriculture is crossing another major watershed in its development. We will take a careful look at the developments of the 1980s to see if we can ascertain the contours, or shape, of this watershed, if indeed a watershed is discernible, and the new direction in which it may be leading. If it is not possible to describe accurately the developments of the 1980s because of our close proximity to them, as well as our involvement in them, it should be possible to identify the key forces and relationships to be watched as the process of agricultural development continues to unfold in the future.

The Period 1763–85

A royal proclamation of 1763 forbade the surveying and disposition of any land west of the divide of the Appalachian Mountains and reserved for the exclusive use of the Indians all land lying west of that line and east of the Mississippi River. In response to the demand of English and colonial land speculators, the line of settlement was shifted westward in 1768. Thus it appeared that the new settlement policy adopted by the British government in 1763 might be crumbling. But in 1774 the British Crown took two actions that reaffirmed and made permanent the conservative land settlement policy of 1763. It tightened the terms on which land east of the proclamation line could pass into private hands; grants were no longer to be free; all land was to be sold at auction and in minimum parcels of 100 acres. But more important, the Quebec Act of 1774 moved the boundaries of the Province of Quebec south to the Ohio River, thus negating the claims of Virginia and Massachusetts for lands lying west of the proclamation line and north of the Ohio River. Most of the land lying south of the Ohio River was again reserved for the exclusive use of the Indians. The fur trade with the Indians was to be regulated by the governor of Quebec. In short, by the conservative land and settlement policies adopted by the British government between 1763 and 1774, the development of the Eastern Seaboard colonies was to be restricted to the Eastern Seaboard.[2]

To frontiersmen engaged in hunting and trapping, poor pioneer families seeking small parcels of cheap land, and southern planters looking for large tracts of land to take the place of their worn-out tobacco land, this conservative land and settlement policy was an anathema. As stated in chapter 2, this land policy turned the frontiersman, pioneer farmer, and southern planter against the mother country and ultimately led to their strong support of the American Revolution. But not everyone in the colonies suffered from the new land policy. Large holders of virgin land east of the mountains, like the Penns, and rich land speculators who held large tracts of land already granted, but not yet settled upon, stood to gain from rising land values caused by the embargo on settlement west of the Appalachian Mountains. And farmers in the established agricultural areas of the colonies would certainly have gained in two ways had the new land and settlement policy continued over a long period of time: (1) competition from the produce of the new and richer lands in the Ohio and Mississippi river valleys would have been less severe; and (2) it would have been more difficult for surplus agricultural labor to get farms of their own; hence farm labor would have been more plentiful and cheaper.

The above conclusion rests upon an important and profound proposition. Had the new land and settlement policy continued for a long period of time, say fifty to 100 years, agricultural development along the Atlantic Seaboard in the area of the original thirteen colonies would have been altogether different from what it was. With an increase in the demand for food and lower wage rates, the production of food would have been increased by applying more labor to the available land; agriculture would have become labor intensive. Land values would have risen. Farmers would have been forced to protect and conserve their expensive resource, land. Farmers in the area of the original thirteen colonies would have been forced to adopt some type of conservation model, perhaps the Norfolk rotation which was being adopted in England, to preserve and enhance the fertility of their land. With land in short supply and labor in long supply, relatively speaking, agricultural development in the area of the thirteen original colonies would have moved in a direction 180 degrees different from the course it did take.

But the new land and settlement policy of the British government did not hold over a long period of time. The Americans won the Revolutionary War, and in the land ordinances of 1785 and 1787 the public domain of the new nation west of the Appalachian Mountains and extending to the Mississippi River was thrown open to settlement. By war, purchase, and astute treaty making, the public domain was extended west to the Pacific Ocean during the nineteenth century. The Indians who lived in that vast area had to be subdued and removed to reservations. This was achieved with relative ease by white Americans as a result of their insatiable demand for land, their great numbers, and their superiority in military arms and organization. Thus the American victory in the Revolutionary War turned the process of agricultural development away from an inward, intensive development in the area of the thirteen original colonies and toward an expansive, extensive development that spread across the continent in one century.

The expansive, extensive development of American agriculture that did in fact take place is described in chapters 3 through 5 of this volume and will not be repeated here. The point to be stressed here is that the way agriculture developed in the area that now comprises the United States could have been much different, and almost certainly would have been much different, had Great Britain won the Revolutionary War. The territorial rights of the Indian tribes would have been protected and guaranteed for a longer period of time, fur trade with the Indians would have been an important determinant of settlement policy for a longer period of time, and the agriculture along the Atlantic Seaboard would have become more labor intensive and land conserving than it was. And since the outcome of the Revolutionary War was in doubt for at least seven years, the alternative course of agricultural development sketched above does not represent a flight of fantasy. It is the course that would have obtained had the British won the Revolutionary War and had they continued the land and settlement policy originated in 1763, which seems highly likely since those land policies were one of the reasons why the war was fought in the first place. In this sense, then, the period 1763–85 constituted a watershed in the development of American agriculture. Acts of the British government from 1763 to 1774 turned the process of agricultural development in one direction; acts of the new American government beginning in 1785 turned it in the opposite direction.

The Period 1900–1920

The statistical evidence that American agriculture crossed a major watershed during the period 1900–1920 is unmistakable. (See table 18.1.) Farm employment increases in every decade from 1870 to 1910, but it increases at a decreasing rate. During the decade 1910–20 farm employment decreases modestly; from 1920 to 1970 employment in farming decreases at an increasing rate. Before 1910–20 farming as part of the agricultural complex was an expanding industry in terms of employment opportunities; after 1910–20 it was a contracting industry in terms of employment opportunities.

Farm output follows the same general pattern as farm employment. In the great decade of homesteading, 1870–80, farm output increased 53 percent. Thereafter farm output continues to grow until 1910, but

Table 18.1. Changes in Farm Employment, Farm Output, Output per Worker, Output per Unit of Input, and Total Population, 1870–1970 (1870 = 100 for all indexes)

Year	Farm Employment		Farm Output		Output per Worker		Output per Unit of Input		Total Population	
	Number[a] (Millions)	Percentage Change	Index[b]	Percentage Change	Index	Percentage Change	Index[b]	Percentage Change	Number[c] (Millions)	Percentage Change
1870	8.0	. . .	100	. . .	100	. . .	100	. . .	39.9	. . .
1880	10.1	26	153	53	121	21	118	18	50.3	26
1890	11.1	16	182	19	125	3	108	-08	63.1	25
1900	12.8	10	235	29	147	18	133	23	76.1	21
1910	13.6	6	253	8	149	1	125	-06	92.4	21
1920	13.4	-1	276	9	164	10	123	-02	106.5	15
1930	12.5	-7	318	15	204	24	133	08	123.1	16
1940	11.0	-12	353	11	256	25	153	15	132.1	7
1950	9.9	-10	441	25	353	38	181	16	151.7	15
1960	7.1	-28	529	20	594	68	225	24	180.7	19
1970	4.5	-37	614	16	1,104	86	265	18	205.4	14

[a]1870 to 1900 based on data from U.S. Bureau of Census, Population Series P-9, No. 11. From 1910 to 1960 the figures are from Average Annual Farm Employment, U.S. Department of Agriculture, Agricultural Marketing Services. Projection for 1980 based on trends.

[b]Three-year averages centered on the year. Estimates for 1870–1900 made by the Agricultural Adjustment Research Branch, Farm Production Economics Division, USDA, Agricultural Research Service. Production data from 1910 to 1970 are from the annual series Changes in Farm Production and Efficiency, USDA, Economic Research Service.

[c]Population July 1, Bureau of Census Population Reports.

it increases at a decreasing rate over the entire period 1870–1910. During the decade 1910–20, farm output increases, but at almost the identical rate of the previous decade, 1900–1910. Over the period 1920–60, the rate of increase in farm output trends upward. A clear change in the direction of the rate of growth in farm output occurs in the period 1910–20, or possibly the longer period 1900–1920.

Changes in the productivity index, output per unit of input, are irregular during the period 1870–1900, but on a trend basis the rate of change is positive. During the period 1900–1920 changes in the productivity index are negative. From 1920 to 1960 agricultural productivity increases dramatically — increases at an increasing rate. Output per worker follows a similar but not identical pattern. Worker productivity declines irregularly over the period 1870–1910 and then increases miraculously over the period 1910–70.

Can these statistical indicators of a watershed in the development of American agriculture be supported by a logical argument? We think they can. Farm output increased greatly between 1870 and 1880 because this was the great decade of extensive development in American agriculture. Land in farms increased by 31 percent in one decade, and for the most part the land added to the national farm plant during this decade was good farmland. Employment in farming increased by 26 percent in the decade of the 1870s. But farm output increased more. Why? This was also the period in which horse and mule power in conjunction with land preparation machines and harvesting machines were rapidly substituting for human back power in the form of the man with the hoe and the man with the scythe. As a result, both total productivity (output per unit of input) and labor productivity increased rapidly during the decade 1870–80. Thus a great extensive development in combination with the widespread adoption of horse- and mule-powered machines produced a great burst in the outturn of agricultural products — an increase of 53 percent in one decade.

This basic form of agricultural development continued throughout the remainder of the nineteenth century: bringing new and additional land into production, adding more workers to the expanded land area, and substituting horse-powered machines for human labor. But the best agricultural land was gone by 1880; the land added to the national plant after 1880 tended to have a lower production potential; much of it was located in the arid West or was in hilly regions of the Midwest or South. Technological developments on farms in the 1880s and 1890s constituted more of the same: the substitution of larger, and sometimes more efficient, horse-drawn machines for the farm worker. This form of agricultural development resulted in an increase in farm output *but an increase at a decreasing rate.* And when the cheap land with a good to fair production potential was gone as of 1900, this form of agricultural development lost its capacity to increase total output either in an efficient manner or at a rate equal to the rate of population growth. For practical purposes the great period of extensive growth in American agriculture which began in 1785 had come to an end by 1900.

During the period 1900–1920, total output in the United States increased slowly as land of low quality was added to the national plant, high-cost land involving irrigation and drainage was added to the national plant, and farmers experimented with new sources of power. Worker productivity leveled off and initiated an absolute decline in the number of people employed in farming beginning in 1910. Most important, the index of agricultural productivity turned down, and in terms of percentage change became negative, indicating that new and additional resources employed in farming in this period produced less product than resources similarly employed in earlier periods. Technologically speaking, American agriculture was in the doldrums in the years 1900–1920. Although it was probably not visible to the participants at the time, American agriculture was marking time during this period — marking time between the end of one stage of development and the beginning of another.

By 1920 the gasoline-engined tractor had been developed to the point where it was both efficient and convenient, and farmers began to substitute this form of power for horses and mules on a widespread basis. New and improved biological technologies began to flow to farmers for adoption on a regular basis in the 1930s, and crop yields began to increase. The use of commercial fertilizer in combination with new plant varieties became an important source of increased yields in the late 1930s. The new mechanical developments built around the gasoline engine, the new biological developments with the potential for greatly increasing yields, and the new chemical developments that made the increased yields a reality interacted to produce an upward trend in the rate of growth in total farm output between 1920 and 1960. Overall agricultural productivity became positive again in the 1920s and on a trend basis increased at an increasing rate over the period 1920–70. With the increase in total output and the absolute decline in the farm labor force, worker productivity increased miraculously between 1920 and 1970. The technological revolution in American agriculture during the period 1920–70 produced a form of agricultural development that was completely different from that which came to an end in 1900. The development process during the years 1920–70 was science-based; it involved the intensified use of capital on farms; and the total output of agriculture increased as a result of the increased productivity of the resources employed, where the total input of resources employed held almost constant. The agricultural development process from 1920 to 1970 was the product of science and technology.

The Period 1970–1990

As we learned in chapter 7, farm prices were relatively stable during the period 1950–70 (see figure 7.1). This period of relative farm price stability may be observed again in the accompanying figure 18.1. For much of this period farm prices rode on the commodity programs of price support, and farm incomes were suspended somewhere between economic prosperity and depression. American agriculture underwent a tremendous shake-up during this period. New technologies were adopted on farms at a rapid pace, crop yields increased dramatically, the less efficient, less aggressive farmers went out of business in

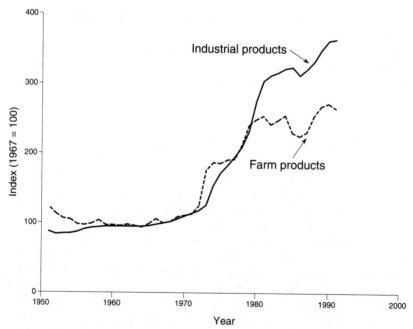

Fig. 18.1. Farm Product and Industrial Product Prices, United States, 1950–1991

droves, and the productive resources from the failed farms were recombined in larger, more productive farms.

Farm product prices rose nearly 150 percent between 1970 and 1980 (see figure 18.1). Prices of industrial products lagged behind the farm price increases in the first half of the 1970s, and the average farmer experienced an income bonanza. Led by rising energy costs, industrial product prices caught up with farm product prices in the second half of the 1970s, farm incomes turned downward, and once again farmers called on government to assist them by raising the levels of price and income support. The restructuring of American agriculture continued in this period. Farm technological advance continued to drive agricultural production, crop yields continued to increase, the less efficient, less aggressive farmers continued to go out of business, and their resources continued to be recombined in larger and more productive farms.

The decade of the 1980s was, for farmers, a different story. The upward thrust in farm prices, driven by expanding exports, came to an end around 1981, as the export expansion boom also came to an end. Farm prices leveled off, declined, and then rebounded toward the end of the decade (see figure 18.1). But the terms of trade turned against agriculture as industrial prices continued to rise throughout the 1980s. Also, real interest rates climbed to terrifying levels for farmers. In this context highly credit leveraged farmers, large and small, went out of business in large numbers. In spite of the difficult economic times of the 1980s, however, farm technological advances continued to march on, crop yields continued to increase (but at a somewhat slower rate than in the two previous decades), the less efficient, less aggressive farmers joined the debt-ridden set of farmers in continuing to go out of business, and the productive resources of these discontinued farms were recombined in larger and more productive farms.

This line of argument is supported by work done by Lloyd Teigen of the Economic Research Service of the USDA. He writes: "This 'cannibalism' contributed to rising farm productivity; because — for the most part — bigger farmers are better farmers than small farmers. In the last three censuses, corn yield on the smallest Illinois farms was 30 bushels per acre less than corn yield on the largest farms. In Georgia the difference in corn yield was nearly 40 bushels per acre in those years. . . . Dairy farms show a pattern similar to corn."[3]

The growth of farm output, input use, and factor productivity for selected periods — business cycle periods, 1948–89 — may be reviewed in table 18.2. The estimates in table 18.2 are derived from new productivity indexes constructed by the Economic Research Service to

Table 18.2. Growth in Output, Input Use, and Factor Productivity, Selected Periods, 1948–89

	Average Annual Growth Rates								
	1948–89	1948–53	1953–57	1957–60	1960–66	1966–69	1969–73	1973–79	1979–89
Output	.0203	.0143	.0140	.0378	.0142	.0308	.0311	.0254	.0136
Inputs	.0020	.0134	.0007	.0051	-.0054	.0163	-.0032	.0233	-.0149
Labor	-.0271	-.0266	-.0462	-.0381	-.0399	-.0150	-.0117	-.0147	-.0261
Land and buildings[a]	.0023	.0063	.0023	.0037	.0013	.0034	.0031	.0056	-.0020
Durable capital[a]	.0104	.0704	.0077	.0083	.0082	.0252	.0140	.0274	-.0327
Intermediate inputs[b]	.0194	.0249	.0379	.0384	.0125	.0397	-.0074	.0501	-.0062
Total factor productivity	.0184	.0094	.0134	.0327	.0196	.0145	.0344	.0021	.0285

Source: Prepared for the author by V. Eldon Ball, leader, Resource Measurement and Productivity Section, U.S. Department of Agriculture, Economic Research Service, 1992.

[a]Includes machinery and crop and livestock inventory as of January 1.
[b]Nondurable purchased inputs (e.g., fuel oil).

replace the old series presented in table 17.4. Although the estimates for individual years differ, the basic trends of the two sets of indexes are similar. Note that the estimates in the first column of table 18.2 for the period 1948–89 are consistent on a trend basis with the estimates in table 17.4. For the period 1948–89 in table 18.2 farm output grows at an annual rate of 2 percent per year, while total input use grows at only about two-tenths of 1 percent per year. Consequently, the annual rate of increase in total factor productivity over the entire period is almost 2 percent per year. But the new Economic Research Service productivity indexes indicate that the growth in output over the period was irregular, as was the case with input use. Hence, increases in total productivity vary from less than 1 percent per annum in the period 1948–53 to over 3 percent in the period 1957–60.

Perhaps the growth of American agriculture from 1948 to 1989 was as lumpy as the data in table 18.2 indicate, or perhaps the discontinuities in table 18.2 are statistical aberrations and the actual process was somewhat smoother. But the overall trends are clear: total output grows at an annual rate of 2 percent per year; the input of labor declines over the entire period, reaching a high of −4.6 percent in 1953–57; and the inputs of durable capital and intermediate inputs increase in most periods, with the net result that total factor productivity increases close to 2 percent per year. It is interesting to note that the input of durable capital increased by 7 percent per annum in the period 1948–53, right after World War II, but becomes a negative 3 percent per annum in the period 1979–89.

The key numbers in table 18.2 for this discussion are those in the last column, or for the period 1979–89. In that period, *inputs in all factor categories decline.* This is the only period in table 18.2 in which this occurs, and is probably the only period in which this occurred since the beginning of the technological revolution in American agriculture back in 1933. But note: output continues to increase on an annual basis. Consequently, the index of total productivity soars to a rate of increase of almost 3 percent per year. Stated differently, and most importantly, because of the increased productivity of the factors of production in the 1980s, farmers were able to increase output even though the total input of those factors declined.

The estimates for the period 1979–89 in table 18.2 provide empirical support for an argument that the author will now advance. The high rate of productivity on American farms in the 1980s did not result from the adoption of one or two highly visible and important, new and improved technologies (e.g., hybrid seed corn and a greatly increased usage of chemical fertilizers). To the contrary, it resulted from the controlled use of productive resources — controlled refinements in the use of productive resources — to gain increased efficiency in the productive processes of many different commodities. This is a development that has been going on for a long time; the estimates in table 18.2 for the long period 1948–89 are suggestive of this development. But it is our thesis that this development has progressed to the stage where production processes on the better commercial farms are sufficiently different from those processes, say, in the 1950s, that it can be argued that farming has entered a new age — the age of a mature industrialized agriculture. In our terminology, farming in America began to cross another watershed in the 1980s. We are too close to that happening to say whether this crossing will stand out in as bold relief as the watershed of 1910–20. But on the far side of this new watershed farming is going to have a factorylike appearance in which the steps in the production process are fully integrated and the entire process strictly controlled.

The essence of this mature industrial age of agriculture is *control* — control over the input of resources into established processes or into new and improved technological processes. To what purpose, it may be asked. To which we may respond: controls to determine the return to adding a particular input to an established process; controls to determine the return to the adoption of a new technology; or controls to determine the return to the refinement of an existing technology. Based on this information the manager is then in a position to further refine or adjust a given production process to squeeze the last ounce of efficiency out of the process. This, we reason, is what was happening in the 1980s, as indicated both by the decline of inputs employed in table 18.2 and by the increase in output.

Why now? Why in the 1980s? To repeat what was said earlier, this development did not first take shape on January 1, 1981. Every step in the intensive development of American agriculture since 1920 has pointed in this direction. But only recently have the technological tools been developed to give management the controls it required to achieve high levels of efficiency in production processes bedeviled with life-cycle problems and unpredictable variables (e.g., the weather). We suggest two that have been among the most important: (1) the technology of gathering and processing information involving electronic computers, and (2) new and improved technologies to effectively prepare seedbeds and to plant crops under variable conditions.

With reference to the second point, all sorts of programs have been developed to assist farmers to manage crop residue covers and minimum tillage operations. And numerous machines have been developed to ensure that seeds are planted at the proper depth on undulating land, and that each soil type receives the proper application of chemical fertilizer. Something called site-specific farming is under development in Illinois.[4] Using a computer, soil samples, and satellites, the software of the technology determines how much fertilizer, herbicide, and seed each acre requires. The satellite receiver sits on top of the tractor cab and tells the computer inside the tractor's exact location. The computer then tells the tractor hookup how much chemical fertilizer and herbicide to apply on that specific site. The technology allows farms to adjust crop inputs to the yield potential of a particular soil type. It is also a wonderful example of controlling and refining the use of resources in the farm production process.

The computer played a role in the preceding improved production technology, but it has a wider role to play in the information-gathering and -processing part of managing a large, modern commercial farm. Basically this tool enables the farm manager to *know* how each phase of the production process is functioning. If he is a large dairy farmer he can keep tabs on the productivity of *each* cow; if he is a large hog farmer he can follow the farrowing history of *each* sow; if he is a large crop farmer he can develop a production history of each parcel of land under different input combinations and practices. These and other farmers use this information technology to develop marketing strategies. And they use it to develop detailed cost and returns information on each farm enterprise as well as the return to input use at the margin. From this wealth of information that has become available to managers of large farm operations over the past twenty years, managers are able to control and direct each phase of their various production processes in a manner inconceivable fifty years ago. It is this control that has moved large-scale commercial farming toward a factorylike operation in recent years. And as indicated in table 18.2, this control has enabled farmers to increase total farm output in the 1980s even as the input of each category of inputs registers a decline.

We need to consider another form of control at this point: financial control of the enterprise. This type of control may not always rest in the hands of the individual we call the farmer. In the past banks have often exercised financial control over a farm, when they were carrying the mortgage or the production credit of that farm; but banks are not inclined to provide the innovative leadership that leads to a modern industrialized farm. Other business entities, however, are so inclined.

Feed companies, on one side of the farm production unit, and processing companies, on the other, have for years taken financial and operating control of poultry-producing units. This has happened to some extent in the production of vegetables for processing. It is beginning to happen in hog production. And there are examples of cattle feed lots being integrated into meat-processing enterprises.

There are two aspects of this financial control of farm producing units either by a feed-supplying company or a meat-processing company that need to be considered. First, if for whatever reason an economic surplus — a profit — is generated in the farm producing unit, that surplus (or profit) will be captured by the business firm in financial control of the unit. This is of critical importance to the people involved. Independent farmers do not like the idea of becoming paid employees of an outside firm and losing the opportunity of making a profit from their operations. But it has happened and it continues to happen in the poultry and livestock industries.

Second, the business firm exercising financial control over a farm production unit will in most cases exercise control over the production operations too. This is key to the line of argument being advanced here. A poultry-processing firm that takes control of a poultry-producing unit, or a meat-packing firm that takes control of a livestock-producing unit, will in the typical case modernize that unit, bringing in the most up-to-date production techniques, before integrating it into the operating schedule and the product requirements of the processing unit. In effect, by this integration two production lines, sequentially related, are joined to produce one product, meat. In so doing, all the management controls employed in the processing plant to maximize its efficiency will be adapted for use in the livestock-producing unit. The result is a streamlined process in which resources and improved technologies are combined in a controlled situation by management to achieve maximum efficiency. In the poultry and livestock industry the concept of an industrialized production organization has taken hold, and continues to take hold, as the old concept of an independent farming operation is disappearing.

The wonders of the new biotechnologies have not been mentioned in connection with this watershed in American agriculture. They may turn out to have a tremendous impact on the production of plants and animals. If so, we can be sure that these new and improved technologies will be incorporated into the industrialized production processes of modern crop farms and the new livestock enterprises just discussed. If this happens the productivity of those production processes will be further increased, provided management effectively controls their introduction and employment. But the new biotechnologies have not played a leading, or dominant, role in the watershed that American agriculture crossed in the 1980s, or is crossing in the 1990s.

This watershed involves refinements and adjustments in the use of many and varied inputs and the adoption of new and different improved technologies to create production processes that are far superior to, hence far more efficient than, older methods. What makes all this possible is the newfound control, based on electronic information systems, that management has gained over each phase of the farm production process. The control over the use of productive resources on the modern large-scale crop farm is not yet at the level achieved, say, on the assembly line of an automobile factory; but the control achieved in a modern large-scale poultry production unit is coming close. The level of control achieved on both types of farms is, however, much closer to the control level in an automobile assembly line than to that of a typical farm operation in the 1920s. The large-scale commercial farm of the 1990s is a part of a new age — a mature industrial age.

The Paradox of Agriculture

The decade of the 1870s was a decade of extraordinary agricultural development. (See table 18.1.) In that decade farm output increased 53 percent, output per worker 21 percent, and output per unit of input 18 percent. But it was also a decade of deep agricultural depression and severe economic distress. Perhaps only the early years of the 1930s rival it for severity of economic distress among farm people. The reason for this agricultural depression may be deduced from table 18.1; population growth as a measure of demand increased only 26 percent in the decade of the 1870s while total output increased 53 percent. Rising per capita incomes and an increase in farm exports, as elements of increased demand, had to absorb approximately one-half of the increased output if the level of farm prices were to hold constant; and they could not come close to doing so.

In the first two decades of the twentieth century the agricultural development process in America almost ground to a halt. Total farm output increased only 8 percent between 1900 and 1910, and only 9 percent between 1910 and 1920. Output per worker increased only 1 percent between 1900 and 1910, and 10 percent between 1910 and 1920. Output per unit of input, our measure of agricultural productivity, actually decreased over the twenty-year period 1900–1920. In terms of technical development, this period was a failure. But in economic terms it was a glorious period. Because the terms of trade were favorable for agriculture, the period 1910–14 has become known as the "golden age of American agriculture." But the golden age lasted longer than four years. Secretary of Agriculture James Wilson, in his annual report to the president in 1910, wrote "year after year it has been my privilege to record 'another prosperous year in agriculture.' "[5]

The reason for this peacetime prosperity in American agriculture, year after year, from 1900 to 1914, can be deduced from table 18.1. We see that population, as a measure of the aggregate demand for farm products, rose 21 percent between 1900 and 1910. But farm output increased only 8 percent during that decade. Thus, unless agricultural imports increased greatly during the decade 1900–1910, farm prices had to rise; demand was pressing on supply. As a matter of fact, agricultural imports did increase significantly in both the first and second decades of the twentieth century. But not by enough to enable the increases in supply to keep pace with the increases in demand. Hence, farm prices rose during fifteen years of peace and the five years of war and immediate postwar emergencies.

Agricultural development, technologically speaking, was a huge success in the decade of the 1950s. Output increased 20 percent during that decade, in spite of halfhearted governmental efforts to control production. This increase in farm output resulted exclusively from increases in agricultural productivity, which resulted in turn from a successful research and development effort. The process of agricultural development rolled along with great force in the 1950s, driven by the engine of farm technological advance.

The decade of the 1950s was, however, a time of hardship and heartbreak for many farm families. Farm product prices were falling, and input prices were rising. Caught in this squeeze, the weaker, less technically proficient and less commercially oriented farmers dropped out of farming in large numbers. Some went broke, some quit before they went broke, and some, particularly older farmers, sold out to their aggressive neighbors when they could still make a good deal for themselves. But regardless of the exact form of financial dissolution, the cost-price squeeze in the 1950s pushed, or induced, a million and a half farm families to give up farming in that decade. The strong, on the other hand, who could make the new technologies, the new commercial practices, and the government programs work to their advantage survived, became more productive, expanded their operations, and in the long run became wealthy.

The decade of the 1980s was somewhat similar to the 1950s. It was a period of rapid farm technological advance — the annual rate of increase in productivity reached almost 3 percent, as all categories of inputs declined (see table 18.2). But it was also a decade of economic hardship for American farmers. Farm product prices sagged, purchased input prices, including interest rates, soared, and many farmers went out of business, including some large-scale commercial operators. In terms of agricultural development for the national economy the decade of the 1980s was a huge success; in terms of the financial well-being of most farmers, it was an economic nightmare.

The above review makes it clear that periods of rapid agricultural development — periods of rapid technical improvement and development — are invariably periods of economic distress and hard times for farmers. This is because periods of rapid technical improvement and development invariably lead to bountiful supplies of farm products; and bountiful supplies invariably lead to low farm prices as those supplies press against demand. This being the case, it would seem that urban consumers, the agricultural production scientists, and developers of new and improved agricultural technologies are natural allies and that urban consumers would regularly pressure the state and federal legislatures to increase the appropriations for agricultural research and development. But since urban consumers are only dimly aware of these relationships and they have what appears to them to be more pressing needs (e.g., lowering their taxes and raising their social security benefits), they rarely if ever pay any attention to the level and content of agricultural appropriations for research and development. This they leave to persons more directly involved, namely, farmers.

It would seem from the foregoing discussion that farmers generally, or on the average, would oppose appropriations in support of agricultural research and development. Their economic interest would seem to be best served by little or no scientific research, a slow rate of technological advance, lagging supplies, and the consequent soaring prices, as was the situation between 1900 and 1915. But this is not what happens in agriculture, because there is no such thing as an average farmer. There are all kinds of farmers with different skills and interests. A relatively few are excellent farmers who are highly competent with respect to both production technology and commercial relations. Some are highly competent in the area of production technology but naive in commercial relations or *vice versa*. Some are traditionalists and do not like to change. Some are reckless in their financial dealings; others are prudent. Some are followers and move with the herd. Still others are incompetent with respect to technology, or commerce, or both.

In the spectrum of farm operators, some study technical reports and releases, visit the scientists at their state agricultural colleges, and regularly attend conferences and meetings dealing with technical subjects. Such farmers are quick to adopt new technologies, and they are the farmers who reap the economic gains of the new technologies.[6] These farmers are highly supportive of agricultural research and development and participate in the legislative process year after year, either directly or through paid representatives, to increase the appropriations for research and development activities. Thus it is the better farmers who know how to make use of the new and improved technologies and who gain economically from the early adoption of those technologies, who provide the leadership in and the support from, the agricultural community for agricultural research and development. The traditionalists, the followers, and the incompetents in the farming community pay little or no attention to what takes place in research and development. They either do not understand or do not want to understand the implications of research and development and of farm technological advance for themselves and their neighbors; hence they pay little or no attention to research and technological development and to the implications of these developments for their economic survival.

Thus it turns out that rapid and widespread technological advance in American agriculture from 1920 to 1990 worked to the advantage of two groups: (1) urban consumers and (2) the small, select group of farmers who were in the technological vanguard. For the rest, the agricultural development process based on rapid and widespread technological advance has been a nightmare. The process of agricultural development, which has worked so beautifully for society as a whole and which is so admired by developmental economists generally, has culled and reculled the farm population so that, as of 1990, some 321,000 farmers produced over 77 percent of the product. The process of agricultural development in the United States from 1920 to 1990 was not easy on the participants. And if the analysis presented in this chapter is correct, the future will not be easy on the participants, as agriculture crosses another major watershed in the 1980s and 1990s.

Suggested Readings

Brewster, John M. "Farm Technological Advance and Total Population Growth." *Journal of Farm Economics*, 27, no. 3 (August 1945), pp. 509–25.

Schertz, Lyle P., *et al. Another Revolution in U.S. Farming?* U.S. Department of Agriculture, Economics Statistics and Cooperative Services, Agricultural Economics Report No. 441, December 1979.

Technology, Public Policy and the Changing Structure of American Agriculture, Congress of the United States, Office of Technology Assessment, Washington, D.C., March 1986.

Teigen, Lloyd D. *Agricultural Policy, Technology Adoption, and Farm Structure*, U.S. Department of Agriculture, Economic Research Service, October 1988.

Wilcox, Walter W.; Cochrane, Willard W.; and Herdt, Robert W. *Economics of American Agriculture*. 3rd ed. Englewood Cliffs, N.J.: Prentice Hall, 1974. Chap. 16.

IV. A Conceptual Model of Agricultural Development: 1950–1990

CHAPTER 19

THE DEMAND AND
SUPPLY COMPONENTS

A great number of facts and various trends have been presented in this volume as part of a general description of agricultural development in the United States. But except for the watershed hypotheses presented in chapter 18, those facts and trends have not been organized into any kind of general explanation of agricultural development in the United States. What is needed now is a general theory that "explains" how those many facts came about, and the relationships among them, and why the various trends took the shape and the direction that they did. Such a general explanation for the post-World War II period is constructed in this part of the book. It takes the form of a theoretical politico-economic model.

It is thus the purpose of this and the following chapter to build a theoretical model that has the capacity to explain the unique development of American agriculture, or the food-producing sector of it, in the post-World War II period. This model is based upon historical fact and empirical measures and estimates, but it is not an econometric model. It is a conceptual model that takes account of social and political institutions as well as market forces. It seeks to explain behavior, not to predict it.

In point of fact, the conceptual model developed in this and the following chapter is constructed primarily, but not entirely, on facts, trends, and developments from the period 1950–70. The model is then used in chapter 21 to analyze and understand developments in the period 1970–90. Since no person, whether econometrician or poet, can know the future, and hence predict it, we do not try to use this model to predict the future. We use the model to try to understand better what took place in the agriculture sector in the recent past, 1970–90.

In the concluding chapter of this book, we employ all the knowledge packaged in the book, including the conceptual model, to explore possible future developments. Few, if any, predictions will be made in that chapter, but we will explore the future in terms of the past.

Food Consumption Patterns

In terms of major categories of food and individual food products, the food consumption patterns of American consumers have changed radically in the twentieth century. Between 1910 and 1970 the per capita consumption of red meat increased about 20 percent, but it began to fall in the 1970s, and in the 1980s it fell nearly 10 percent. The per capita consumption of poultry, on the other hand, increased by more than five times over the long period 1910–90. The per capita consumption of fruits and vegetables, overall, increased over the long period 1910–90, but within this broad category much happened. The consumption of both fresh fruits and vegetables fell significantly between 1910 and 1970, and then made spectacular gains in the 1970s and 1980s. And the consumption of processed fruits and vegetables, including frozen items, increased importantly throughout the period 1910–90. The per capita consumption of eggs rose steadily between 1910 and 1950, and has declined just as steadily since 1950. The per capita consumption of potatoes declined dramatically between 1910 and the late 1950s and has been increasing steadily since that time (french fries and chips turned the consumption of potatoes around). The per capita consumption of fats and oils in total held reasonably constant over the period 1910–70, and then for some reason increased sharply in the late 1970s and the 1980s; within this total, the consumption of animal fats, including butter, fell some 70 percent between 1910 and 1977 and then held constant on a trend basis between 1977 and 1990, while the consumption of vegetable fats and oils increased more than five times between 1910 and 1990. The per capita consumption of dairy products, excluding butter, rose steadily between 1910 and 1946, declined slowly between 1946 and 1970, and then has been increasing once again since 1970. The increase in the consumption of dairy products occurred primarily in lowfat milk and cheese consumption, as the consumption of whole milk continued to decline. The per capita consumption of flour and cereal products declined persistently between 1910 and 1960, held constant in the 1960s and 1970s, and increased sharply in the 1980s. The per capita consumption of beans and peas increased modestly between 1910 and 1942 and has fluctuated around an almost constant trend since that date. The per capita consumption of tree nuts and peanuts has increased about 30 percent between the middle 1960s and 1990. Finally, the per capita consumption of sugars and sweeteners nearly doubled between 1910 and 1970 and has held almost constant since 1970.

In these changing food consumption patterns, especially in the decades of the 1970s and 1980s, one can see the impact of nutrition education. But important for this discussion, the average American consumer is eating a very different basket of food products in 1990 than he or she was in 1910.

But the overall food consumption of the average American has changed very little. In terms of total calories, the average consumer reduced his or her intake from 3,550 calories per day in 1910 to 3,160 in 1951, and then increased his or her daily intake to 3,600 calories in 1988. In terms of pounds of food consumed, the average American consumed about 1,600 pounds of food in 1910 and approximately 1,750 pounds in 1989.

The best measure that we have of the resources embodied in the food consumed by the average American is the index of per capita food consumption. This index is price-weighted: meaning that a pound of meat is weighted into the index at perhaps $1.00 and a pound of flour at perhaps 10 cents. In this example, if a consumer increases his or her consumption of meat by one pound and reduces his or her consumption of flour by one pound, the value of the index will increase by a factor reflecting the ninefold increase in costs. The price weights thus reflect the differential cost of producing a pound of meat over a pound of flour, and in principle the larger quantity of resources embodied in the meat.

Using the index of per capita food consumption as the measure of the average consumer's total food consumption, we observe that total per capita food consumption held almost constant between 1910 and 1935, and increased significantly between 1935 and 1946. (See figure 19.1.) This was a time of economic recovery (1935–40) and great wartime prosperity (1940–46). And during the latter period there was little to buy in the way of consumer durables — automobiles and housing. The index again holds remarkably constant during the period 1946–65.

From 1965 to 1990 the index of per capita food consumption shows a slight upward trend (see figure 19.1). In that twenty-five-year period the index rose less than one-half of 1 percent per year. In sum, the average American consumes about the same total quantity of food, but not the same food items, year after year. But on occasions, when the consumer's real income is rising, he or she will increase his or her total consumption of food by substituting a high-valued product (e.g., beef) for a low-valued product (e.g., bread) in his or her diet. By this process, the average American consumer increased his or her total consumption of food significantly during the period 1935–46 and very modestly during the period 1965–90.

These per capita food consumption data tell us three important things about the demand for food in the United States.[1] First, changes in consumer incomes have little effect on per capita food consumption (i.e., the income effect is small). Second, and as a consequence of the first point, and except in the periods 1935–46 and 1965–90, the total domestic demand for food has varied directly with population. In the 1950s, the domestic demand for food grew at a rate of 1.9 percent per year (noncompounded) as a result of a comparable rate of population growth. In the 1970s, the rate of growth in the domestic demand slowed to about 1 percent per year (noncompounded) as the rate of population growth declined to that level. Third, the aggregate demand for food by consumers is highly unresponsive to price. In periods of rising food prices, consumers sometimes reduce their consumption of total food modestly, as happened in 1973–75, but they did not in 1965–72 and in 1935–46 — periods in which food prices were

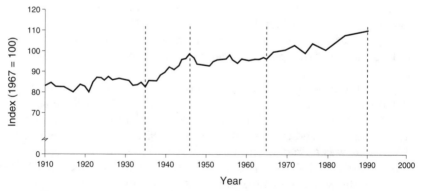

Fig. 19.1. The per capita consumption of food, United States, 1910–1990

increasing. In the short run consumers continue to eat about the same amounts of the same kinds of foods day after day. In the longer run they shift the product composition of their diet, but they continue to consume about the same total quantity of food whether measured in calories, or pounds, or an index of resources employed in producing the total basket of food.

The Nature of Consumer Demand for Food

The food consumption information presented in the previous section suggests, and numerous statistical studies confirm, that the aggregate domestic demand for food is highly inelastic. At the retail level the price elasticity of the aggregate domestic demand for food approximates − .25; at the farm level it is at least − .15 and perhaps as low as − .1.[2] These price elasticities have the following meaning: if the supply of food at the retail level declined by 2.5 percent, the price of food could be expected to rise by 10 percent; and if the supply of food products at the farm level declined by 2.5 percent, the price of farm food products could be expected to rise between 17 and 25 percent. The nature of the demand for total food by consumers is such that any small change in supply gives rise to a relatively large price response in the free market. This basic supply-price relationship for food colors all economic aspects of the food and agricultural sector and governs all considerations of food and agricultural policy.

The explanation for the severe price inelasticity of total food demand is not hard to find or to understand. The explanation has two parts. First, biological requirements — the size of the human stomach — determine the total amount of food that the consumer will ingest per day and dictate that he or she will ingest that amount of food day after day. Second, food has few close substitutes. The consumer may on occasion substitute a mineral tablet for a food product, but for the most part the human biological system renders it impossible to substitute theater tickets or jewelry or clothes for food on a sustained basis. The human consumer is forced by biological requirements to ingest *food products* in roughly the same total amount day after day. Thus the *total* demand for food by consumers has been and must continue to be highly inelastic.

What is true for food in the aggregate is not, however, necessarily true for individual food products. One individual may satisfy the protein requirements of his or her biological system by consuming relatively large amounts of red meats, another may choose fish, another dairy products, and another legumes. And the same individual may over time satisfy the protein requirements of his or her system by shifting from fish products to red meat or *vice versa*. The consumer may do this in response to a change in the price of the products or to a change in personal income, or to new nutritional information about the products. Thus we would expect the price elasticity of demand to be higher for individual food items than for food in total. This will be the case because individual food items will have more substitutes than food in the aggregate, and the greater the number of food item substitutes that a food product has, the greater will be its price elasticity.

The amount of an individual food item demanded, at a given price, varies with changes in personal incomes. The amount demanded of certain foods, e.g., red meats, typically increases with rising personal incomes, and the amount demanded of certain other foods, e.g., bread, typically decreases with rising personal incomes. And the amount demanded of certain products, e.g., dry cereals, may change drastically as a result of advertising, and the amount demanded of certain other products, e.g., animal fats, may change significantly with new nutritional information. In sum, the demand for individual food products by consumers is forever changing and for a variety of reasons.

These demand relationships are illustrated in figure 19.2. The total demand for food, DD in figure 19.2, for a single consumer, or for all domestic consumers, is drawn with a steep slope, suggesting severe price inelasticity. In the total demand for food, the price-quantity relationship is such that any small change in quantity gives rise to a relatively large price change.

The initial demand, say in 1910, for oranges, d_1d_1, is small and is drawn with a gentle slope, suggesting a relatively high price elasticity for oranges. Over time the demand for oranges increases to d_2d_2, and the slope of the demand curve becomes more steeply inclined, suggesting a decline in the price elasticity of oranges. It is hypothesized here that advertising and nutrition education interacted over the long period 1910–80 to expand the demand for oranges, especially in juice form, at any given price, p_1, and to decrease the price elasticity of demand.

The initial demand, say in 1910, for flour, d_1d_1, is large and is drawn with a steep slope, suggesting a relatively low price elasticity. Over time, the demand for flour, at any given price, p_1, contracts, but there is no significant change in the price elasticity of flour. It is hypothesized here that rising real incomes over the long period 1910–80 caused con-

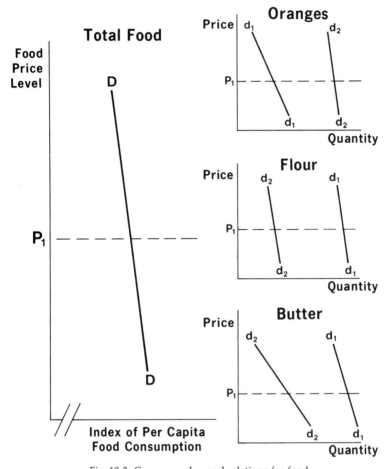

Fig. 19.2. Consumer demand relations for food

sumers to eat less bread and other cereal products, but this shift had no appreciable influence on the price elasticity of the demand for flour.

The initial demand, say in 1910, for butter, d_1d_1 is large and is drawn with a moderate slope, suggesting a moderate price elasticity for butter. Over time the demand for butter, at any given price, p_1, contracts, and the slope of the demand for butter becomes more gentle, suggesting that the price elasticity of butter increases. It is hypothesized here that nutrition education in conjunction with the increased availability of palatable low-priced vegetable oil substitutes over the long period

1910–80 caused the demand for butter both to contract and to become more elastic.

In sum, it is not possible to generalize about the behavior of demand for individual food products. Statements with regard to shifts in demand and changes in price elasticity for individual food products can be made only after each product has been analyzed.

The Aggregate Demand for Farm Food Products

The aggregate domestic demand for food products at the farm level may be conceptualized as the aggregate consumer demand curve for food, DD in figure 19.2, less the marketing and processing costs at each aggregate quantity. The domestic aggregate demand curve for food at the farm level is reproduced as D_dD_d in figure 19.3. The curve D_dD_d in this figure is hypothesized to have the same slope as curve DD in figure 19.2. But the mechanics of subtracting the marketing and

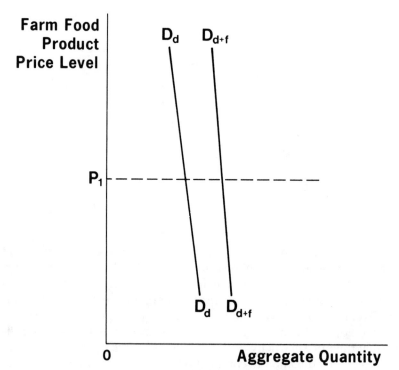

Fig. 19.3. The aggregate demand for farm food products

processing costs at each quantity causes the price elasticity of demand to be lower at the farm level than at the retail level for each quantity. The price elasticity of the aggregate domestic demand for food products at the farm level for the mean average price is estimated to fall between $-.1$ and $-.2$. In this connection, as long as the marketing margin does not change as the level of farm prices changes or the volume demanded changes, the price elasticity of demand will always be lower at the farm level than it is at the retail level, and in approximately the same proportion as the farm share is of the retail value. For example, if the price elasticity of demand for all foods at the retail level is $-.25$ and the farmer's share of the retail food dollar is 40 cents, the price elasticity of demand for all food products at the farm level is $-.1$, or $-.25 \times .40 = -.1$.

To the aggregate domestic demand for farm food products must be added the foreign demand. The foreign demand for American farm food products, it will be recalled, expanded rapidly during the 1970s. There were two principal causes of this rapid expansion in foreign demand: (1) the growth in world population and (2) rising real incomes in both the developed and less-developed world, but particularly in the developed world. It was once argued that the foreign demand for American farm food products was price elastic and hence this foreign demand operated to make the aggregate demand for American farm food products relatively more elastic. But this is no longer the situation. The largest importers of American farm food products — Japan, the European Community, and the USSR — have insulated themselves from the world market in such a way that their demand for imports is unresponsive to price over the customary range of prices. Stated differently, these important importers employ trading practices that make their demand for many, but not all, food product imports perfectly inelastic over wide ranges of prices. This behavior on the part of some of the principal importers of American food products must then operate to make the aggregate demand for food products confronting American farmers somewhat more inelastic than the aggregate domestic demand. The aggregate demand for farm food products, D_{d+f} D_{d+f}, is thus conceptualized in figure 19.3 with a slightly steeper slope than the aggregate domestic demand D_d D_d.[3]

The foreign component of the aggregate demand for farm food products is, however, highly unstable. It is unstable for at least three reasons, the first two of which are closely related. First, this foreign component varies inversely with crop growing conditions around the world. It contracts when the weather and other conditions are favorable, and it expands when they are unfavorable. Since the weather is unpredictable, these expansions and contractions in the foreign demand for American farm food products are unpredicatable. These variations in foreign demand are also sharp and wide.

Second, in years of bad weather and poor crops, such as 1972–74, when grain and other staple stocks are pulled down to the minimum and future food supplies are uncertain, nations confronted with that uncertainty invariably seek to build up their stocks of staples to guard against the uncertain future. They may be unsuccessful in their efforts, but the bidding for scarce supplies drives the aggregate demand farther to the right and acts to push up prices in the world market. In years of good weather and good crops the opposite results obtain. When national stocks become large and there is uncertainty in the world market with respect to the possible dumping of stocks, some nations and companies will seek to divest themselves of stocks, and this action contracts the foreign demand for food products and operates in the short run to drive farm product prices downward. The uncoordinated stocking policies of nations can thus serve to accentuate the short-run fluctuations in the foreign component of the aggregate demand for food products confronting American farmers.

Third, from time to time nations change their foreign trade policies as a result of changes in their domestic economic or social policies. This occurred in the Soviet Union in 1972–74 when it decided to import large quantities of feed grains to maintain its livestock herds when confronted with a poor domestic crop, rather than liquidate those herds as it had done in similar situations in the past. And the People's Republic of China would appear to be changing its foreign trade policies in the late 1970s and 1980s in response to changing domestic economic and social policies. Such changes in the foreign trade policies of large and important nations have had in the past and can have in the future an important effect on the export demand for agricultural commodities in the United States. Further, these changes in the trade policies of foreign nations are largely unpredictable. A case in point is the on-again, off-again state of negotiations in the Uruguay Round of the GATT trade negotiations. Further, the trade policy positions of countries often change in response to economic conditions in those countries.

What we have then is an aggregate domestic demand for farm food products that is increasing in the 1970s and 1980s at about 1 percent per year as a result of population growth in the United States; this expansion is steady and for the short to intermediate run it is certain.

This expansion is augmented by increased foreign demands resulting from population growth in the less-developed world and raising real incomes in the developed world; this expansion, too, is reasonably steady and certain. But the foreign component of aggregate demand is highly unstable owing to variable and unpredicatable crop growing conditions around the world and changing foreign trade policies. As a result of these weather-induced and trade-policy-induced phenomena, the aggregate demand for farm food products confronting American farmers grows at an uneven pace — grows in a "herky-jerky" fashion. This uneven growth in aggregate demand, where that demand is severely price inelastic, can and does in free market situations give rise to wide, sharp, and unpredictable farm food price level fluctuations.

The Supply Curve of the Individual Farm Firm

The cost structure of a single enterprise is illustrated in figure 19.4.[4] This firm is in short-run equilibrium; the minimum point of the aver-

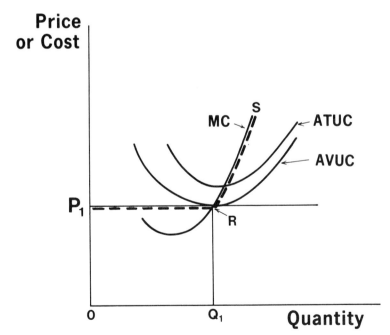

Fig. 19.4. Supply curve of a single enterprise farm firm

age variable unit cost curve, AVUC, is tangent to the price line P_1. At price P_1 this firm stands ready to offer quantity Q_1 on the market; it is prepared to do so because its variable costs, or out-of-pocket costs, of production are being covered at quantity Q_1 by the price P_1. At prices higher than P_1 the marginal cost curve, MC, describes how much product this firm will offer on the market; at prices below P_1 this firm will not offer any product on the market because at such prices its variable costs will not be met. The supply curve of this firm is thus described by the heavy dashed line P_1RS in figure 19.4. That line describes the quantities of product that the firm is prepared to offer on the market at varying prices, and that is our definition of supply.

The cost structure of the firm, hence the supply curve of the firm, can shift for any one of several reasons. First, the firm can for any given state of technology move along its long-run average variable cost curve — or long-run planning curve — and experience falling, or possibly rising, costs by so doing. Second, it can adopt a new and cost-reducing technology — experience a technological advance. Third, input prices to the firm may rise or fall and as a result push up or drive down the cost structure of the firm. Let us consider these possibilities in more detail.

As a firm moves along its long-run planning curve by expanding in size, its unit costs of production typically decline in the early stages of expansion as it experiences increasing returns to size;[5] this is illustrated in chart A of figure 19.5 by the movement of the firm from position $AVUC_1$ to $AVUC_2$. In this stage of expansion per unit costs decline as the firm is able to combine its lumpy resources (e.g., a grain combine) more efficiently and increase its output per unit of input. But, as the size of the firm continues to expand, a stage is reached in which per unit costs of product cease to fall as it experiences constant returns to size; this is illustrated by the movement of the firm from position $AVUC_2$ to position $AVUC_3$ in chart A of figure 19.5. And should the firm continue to expand in size, it must ultimately reach a stage in which its per unit costs of production rise as it experiences decreasing returns to size. Thus the cost structure of the firm, and the supply curve of the firm, can be and are influenced by size or scale, and the long-run planning curve provides a general description of the results of that influence.

The adoption of a new technology, which represents a farm technological advance, increases the output per unit of input of the farm firm and in turn lowers the cost structure of that firm. This phenomenon is illustrated in chart B of figure 19.5. The adoption of the new and *im-*

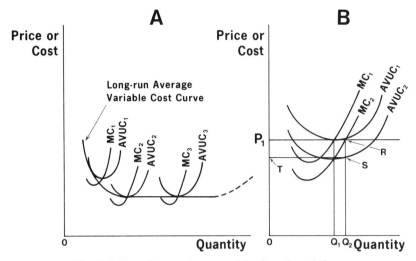

Fig. 19.5. How the supply curve of the farm firm shifts

proved technology raises the production function and lowers the cost structure of the firm from $AVUC_1$ to $AVUC_2$. This development shifts the marginal cost curve of the firm, which above the minimum point of the average variable unit cost curve is the supply curve of the firm, to the right from MC_1 to MC_2. This development expands the supply curve of the firm; at price P_1 the firm is prepared to offer on the market $0Q_2$ amount of product after the technological advance, as compared with $0Q_1$ amount before. A farm technological advance simultaneously lowers the per unit costs of production of the firm and expands the supply curve of the firm. And the profits of the firm are increased (or its losses reduced) by the rectangle P_1RST in chart B of figure 19.5, so long as the price of the product remains at P_1.[6]

The effects of a change in input prices on the cost structure of the firm, hence on its supply curve, can also be illustrated in chart B of figure 19.5. If all input prices should fall proportionately, so there is no tendency for the farm operator to substitute one resource for another, the cost structure of the firm would simply fall in the manner illustrated in chart B of figure 19.5. The cost structure of the firm would fall from position $AVUC_1$ to $AVUC_2$, and the supply curve of the firm would shift to the right from MC_1 to MC_2. A decline in input prices thus has the effect of increasing the supply of the firm, and a rise in input prices of decreasing the supply of the firm. (It turns out, then, that a decline in input prices has the same effect on the cost structure of the firm, hence upon the supply curve of the firm, as a farm technological advance. It should be recognized, however, that a farm technological advance shifts the production function upward, whereas the decline in input prices has no direct effect on the production function.)

We know that over the period 1950–70 farm input prices were not falling; in general they were rising. Thus a general decline in input prices cannot explain the rightward shifting of the supply curve of many, if not most, farms during the period 1950–70. The basic explanation is to be found in the general and widespread process of farm technological advance during this period. Farm after farm, year after year, experienced a lowering of its cost structure, and the consequent expansion in supply, as a result of its adopting one new and improved technology after another — a phenomenon illustrated in chart B of figure 19.5. But farms were also becoming larger during this period. Thus many must have experienced increased returns to size that resulted in a lowering of their cost structures and an expansion in their firm supply curves. In this view, then, widespread farm technological advance in combination with increased returns to size on some farms operated to override the effects of rising input prices and propelled the supply curves of most, but not all, farms rightward in an expanding action. The result was a sustained increase in the supply of farm products in spite of the rising input prices and falling to constant product prices of the period.

Some further technical, but important, points must be made. Although the movement along the long-run planning curve from position $AVUC_2$ to $AVUC_3$ in chart A of figure 19.5 represents an expansion in supply for the firm, or firms, involved, that movement does not necessarily represent a net gain to society. Output per unit of input does not increase as a firm moves from position $AVUC_2$ to $AVUC_3$ and the aggregate supply of the industry will not have increased if the firm expanding from position $AVUC_2$ to $AVUC_3$ did so by acquiring the productive resources of firms going out of business with the same or similar long-run average variable cost structures. But if the firm expanded from position $AVUC_2$ to $AVUC_3$ by acquiring the productive resources of smaller high-cost firms, such as are represented by $AVUC_1$, then the average productivity of factors of production for the industry will have increased, as well as the total output of the industry. And to some degree this is what happened over the period 1950–70.

But in the real world two processes were occurring simultaneously. One aggressive, innovative operator might reduce his unit costs of production by adopting one or a series of new and unproved technologies and then expand along his new long-run planning curve by acquiring the productive resources of a smaller, high-cost farmer neighbor. Another, aggressive, innovative operator might expand from position $AVUC_2$ to $AVUC_3$ along the long-run average variable cost curve shown in chart A of figure 19.5 by acquiring the productive resources of smaller, high-cost farmers going out of business, and then upon reaching position $AVUC_3$ adopt one or a series of new and improved technologies, which lowers both his long-run and short-run cost structures. Both operators increased the average factor productivity of the industry, as well as the total output of the industry, in two different ways but in different sequences. In more general terms, part of the increased supply of farm food products over the period 1950–70 resulted from technological advances on specific farms, and part from a restructuring of the industry involving fewer total farms in which the resources of the smaller, high-cost farms were recombined with the resources of ever-expanding larger, low-cost farms.

The Aggregate Supply Curve of the Agricultural Food Industry

The aggregate supply curve of the agricultural food industry may be defined as the sum of all farm enterprise marginal cost curves for all farms where product prices rise and fall together and proportionately. We know in fact that all food product prices do not rise and fall together and proportionately, but through the ubiquitous process of resource substitution *they tend to do so*. Thus the above definition is relevant, even though it is a bit contrived. Where the prices of all food products rise and fall together and proportionately, it must be the case that these different products are close substitutes for one another; hence it is possible to assume that these various products constitute one great product, food. In this event each farm firm produces one product, food.

This assumption is important in explaining the aggregate supply response behavior of farm firms. Without such an assumption the analysis goes awry. Farm firms can and do substitute resources among enterprises where the price of one product varies relative to another. Where this occurs, the marginal cost curve (i.e., the supply curve) of each enterprise on the farm can be, and may well be, relatively elastic. The summation of such a set of enterprise marginal cost curves would yield an aggregate industry supply curve that is relatively elastic — a result that does not accord with the facts. The input of most productive resources of the *representative farm firm* in the short run is fixed. For the farm as a whole the input of land is fixed, much of the labor input is fixed, and the input of heavy machines and equipment is largely fixed. The inputs that can be varied for the farm as a whole include such items as nonfarm-produced power, fertilizer, and pesticides. Given this situation, the marginal cost curve of the farm firm in the production of the one commodity, food, must be relatively inelastic.[7] This concept is illustrated in chart A, The Firm, in figure 19.6. The marginal cost curve of the firm exhibits some elasticity at low levels of prices, but at high levels of prices the marginal cost curve becomes severely inelastic. This is because adding additional amounts of nonfarm-produced power, fertilizer, and pesticides to a fixed land and labor base *with no change in the state of technology* yields little in the way of increased output. The firm is approaching the stage of total diminishing returns.

The aggregate supply curve for the industry is the horizontal sum-

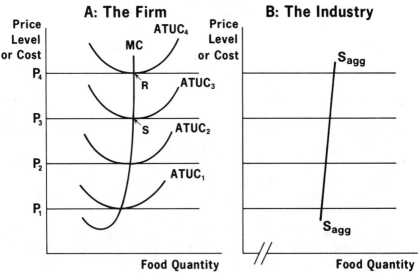

Fig. 19.6. The aggregate supply curve of the farm firm and the agricultural food industry

mation of the marginal cost curves for all firms in the production of the commodity, food. This concept is presented graphically in chart B, The Industry, in figure 19.6; the aggregate supply curve of the industry is drawn with a steep slope to illustrate the severe inelasticity of that relationship. Such an inelastic aggregate supply concept is in accord with numerous statistical studies which have found that the elasticity of the short-run aggregate supply curve for the agricultural industry ranges between .0 and .3. The aggregate supply curve for the agricultural industry is highly inelastic, but economists argue endlessly about exactly how inelastic it is.

A related concept is represented in chart A of figure 19.6, which should be noted. As the price level rises from P_1 to P_4 the average total unit cost curve, $ATUC_1$, which includes the fixed costs of the firm, rides up the marginal cost curve and becomes tangent to each succeeding higher price level. The tangency at each succeeding price level illustrates the general case wherein, after a period of adjustment, the cost structure of the representative firm rises to the new level of product prices, and the firm is once again in a no-profit, no-loss situation. This occurs because the profits that result from the increased product price level are capitalized into the fixed assets of the farm, primarily land, through the competitive process, and the value of those fixed assets rises until the per unit costs of the farm firm are once again equal to the product price level. Competition for the fixed assets drives the cost structure upward until the profits have been wiped out. This position is illustrated in chart A of figure 19.6 at point R.

The difficult situation in which farm operators find themselves when the farm price level falls is apparent from chart A, figure 19.6. When the farm price level falls, the only option open to the farmer is to move back along his marginal cost curve for the aggregate, food. But because the supply curve of the firm is inelastic, this action reduces the total supply of food on the market only slightly. Thus no quick brake to the falling price level is provided in the way of a significant reduction in the aggregate supply. In the meantime, the unit costs of production of the representative farmer remain at the level $ATUC_4$. If the price level falls to P_3, for example, the representative farmer will be sustaining losses equal to P_4RSP_3. In sum, the representative farmer has no place to hide when the farm price level falls; he must stand and take his losses until the price level rises again or he goes through the wringing-out process of deflating his asset values, which means, primarily, his land values.[8]

Aggregate Demand and Supply in Interaction

We now have an aggregate demand relation and an aggregate supply relation for the agricultural food industry. Both relations are highly inelastic in terms of price. Those relations are presented graphically in figure 19.7; the curves intersect at an arbitrarily determined price level of 100. Now let it be assumed that the aggregate demand for food increases by 5 percent. Given the extreme price inelasticities of both demand and supply, the 5 percent increase in demand generates a 25 percent increase in the farm food product price level (figure 19.7). And it is readily seen that a contraction in demand of 5 percent would result in a comparable decline in price level.

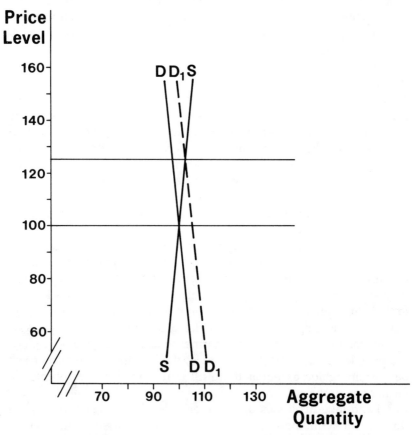

Fig. 19.7. Price level solutions for the agricultural food industry

The price level solutions of figure 19.7 lead to an inescapable conclusion: the food-producing sector of agriculture, which is most of the industry, is basically an unstable industry. In a free market situation, any small change in demand relative to supply, or in supply relative to demand, must produce wide swings in the farm food product price level and as a consequence give rise to large fluctuations in the gross returns to the producers of food. In historical fact, the rates of growth of these aggregate relations in the twentieth century have not been equal. The aggregate demand for farm food products powered primarily by slowly changing rates of population growth in the United States and secondarily by a wildly fluctuating export demand has expanded rapidly in some periods, 1900–1920 and 1972–80, and slowly in other periods, 1920–35 and 1955–65. Aggregate supply powered primarily by farm technological advances has also increased unevenly. Aggregate supply increased slowly in the period 1900–1920 and increased rapidly in the period 1950–65. The price level and gross income consequences of the unequal rates of growth of an inelastic aggregate demand and an inelastic aggregate supply may be reviewed in figure 7.1.

Possible and actual price level solutions for the period 1950–70 are portrayed in figure 19.8. The aggregate demand for farm food products is assumed to increase throughout that twenty-year period at the rate that population grew in the United States in the 1950s; such a projection implicitly assumes that domestic per capita food consumption was constant over the period and that export demand was also constant. The aggregate supply of farm food products is assumed to increase throughout the twenty-year period at the rate of increase in agricultural productivity achieved in the 1950s. The projection of aggregate demand and aggregate supply under these assumptions results in a sense in the worst of all possible worlds for the food-producing sector of American agriculture: a long period of moderate population growth, large increases in productivity, and no increase in exports. The line ABC in figure 19.8 traces the price level solutions for such a set of assumptions. The farm food product price level falls by nearly 70 percent over the twenty-year period.

The line ABDT traces a less extreme set of price level solutions. The price level solutions along this line are based on the assumptions that farm food product prices fall by some 30 percent and remain at that level for a period of years (the BD segment of the line). As a result of financial losses at that level of product prices, farm operators reduce their investment in capital items embodying new and improved technologies, as well as their purchases of new forms of operating capital;

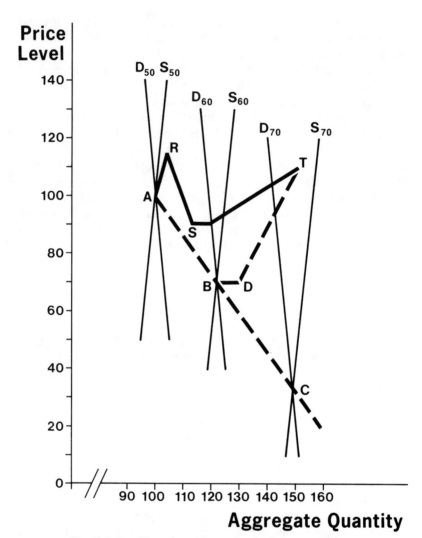

Fig. 19.8. Possible and actual price level solutions, 1950–70

rates of increase in productivity slow down, and hence the rate of increase in aggregate output slows down. With this latter development
the level of farm food product prices begins to rise, as is shown by the
segment of the line DT in figure 19.8.[9]

But the farm price level during the twenty-year period 1950–70 did
not in actuality move along either of the lines described above. The

farm price level moved along the line ARST in figure 19.8. The farm price level shot up sharply during the Korean War in the early 1950s (to point R); next it declined sharply in the early to mid-1950s (to point S); there it came to rest on the government mechanism of farm price supports; it rode on the mechanism of farm price support throughout the remainder of the period, rising slowly as the level of support was increased and as export demands increased (reaching point T in 1970). The farm price level did not decline to the levels portrayed by lines ABC, or ABDT, for one important reason: the federal government of the United States intervened to support the prices received by farmers. This the government did in response to the pleas and supplications of farmers for help.

Price level solutions other than the ones portrayed in figure 19.8 for the period 1950–70 were, of course, a possibility. One possible solution is of particular interest. *If* the farm product export boom of the 1970s had occurred in the 1960s, the aggregate demand curve in figure 19.8 would have shifted to the right more rapidly than is shown in that figure, and the farm price level would have been driven far above the solid line ARST. But that did not happen, as we know. The price level reality of the period 1950–70 is that portrayed by the line ARST.

Thus it turns out that a free market model of aggregate demand and supply cannot explain the behavior of the food-producing sector of American agriculture in the post-World War II period. Governmental intervention must be included in the general conceptual model. This will be done in the next chapter.

Two Levels of Price Instability

Up to this point in this chapter we have been discussing price level and industry-wide instability — the great price and income swings in American agriculture. But within the food-producing industry there is a great deal of individual commodity action. All farm food product prices do not in fact move up and down together in perfect rhythm. They tend to do so as a result of the ubiquitous process of substitution on both the supply side and the demand side. But they do not do so. This commodity variability is best described by the cobweb theory.[10]

The cobweb theory of farm commodity price behavior is illustrated in figure 19.9. This cobweb theory is based on two conditions unique to the agricultural industry. First, crop production extends over a season and is not repeated until the next season. Second, the production at the end of the season flows to market in a rush, making for a per-

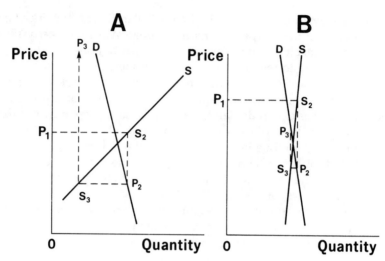

Fig. 19.9. Cobweb price-quantity interactions

fectly, or nearly perfectly, inelastic short-run supply curve. Bearing in mind these two conditions, we can trace the cobweb price-quantity interaction for two assumed commodities in figure 19.9. Let us begin with price P_1 of season 1 in chart A. Price P_1 induces farmers to produce quantity S_2 in season 2. At the end of the crop season all of S_2 comes to market and is sold in the market for price P_2. Price P_2 induces farmers to produce quantity S_3 in season 3. At the end of the crop season the quantity S_3 comes to market in a rush and sells for some very high price, P_3, which is off the chart.

The price-quantity behavior in chart A explodes. This will happen for any commodity in which the slope of the demand curve is more steeply inclined than the slope of the supply curve. Commodities characterized by this type of a demand-supply relationship will experience extreme price instability. Potatoes are a good example of such a commodity.

The price-quantity observations in chart B dampen down, or converge on the equilibrium point, through time. In chart B the slope of the demand curve is slightly less steeply inclined than the slope of the supply curve. Although milk is not a crop and does not satisfy perfectly all the conditions of the cobweb theory, milk production is seasonal, and once produced it does come to market in a rush. The cobweb interaction in chart B may thus be thought to represent milk, in which price behavior is relatively stable over time.

Individual farm food product prices, as a result of this cobweb type of interaction, fluctuate through time, with commodities such as potatoes and onions exhibiting the greatest price instability, the grains exhibiting somewhat less instability in the whole spectrum of commodity price instability, the red meats still less instability, and finally milk the least instability. But these food product prices do not zip and zoom about completely at random. They zigzag around the moving farm food product price level as illustrated in figure 19.10. The process of substitution forces this result. When the price, say, of potatoes shoots above the farm food product price level, farmers who are able to do so plant more potatoes to reap the relatively higher price, and consumers who are able to do so reduce their purchases of potatoes and eat more bread or rice; as a result the price of potatoes falls at the end of the next growing season. This process of substitution goes on continuously for each and every commodity, operating to pull any commodity price that moves far from the general level back toward that level. The force of substitution, like the force of gravity, works continuously to pull individual food commodity prices toward the food commodity price level. But it never succeeds completely, as is explained by the cobweb interaction. Hence individual farm product prices fluctuate in varying degrees around the moving farm food product price level.

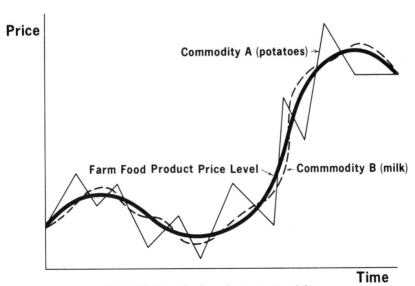

Fig. 19.10. Farm food product price instability

What we have in the food-producing sector of the agricultural industry in a free market situation are two forms of price instability, hence two kinds of price problems: (1) price level instability and (2) commodity price instability. The former can make many farmers rich, as it did during the period 1940–51, or force great numbers of farmers into bankruptcy, as happened during the period 1920–33. The latter leads to nagging resource allocation problems and product inefficiency. The former leads to the intervention of government into the operation and management of the farm economy, as occurred in 1933.

The latter seems to tantalize economists and command their almost complete attention, to the neglect of the consequences of the former.

Suggested Readings

Cochrane, Willard W. *Farm Prices: Myth and Reality.* Minneapolis: University of Minnesota Press, 1958. Chaps. 1, 2, 3, and 4.

Johnson, Glenn L., and Quance, C. Leroy, eds. *The Overproduction Trap in U.S. Agriculture.* Baltimore, Md.: Johns Hopkins University Press, 1972.

Schultz, Theodore W. *Agriculture in an Unstable Economy.* New York: McGraw-Hill, 1945, Pt. II.

Teigen, Lloyd D. *Agricultural Policy, Technology Adoption, and Farm Structure.* U.S. Department of Agriculture, Economic Research Service, Staff Report No. AGES880810, October 1988.

Tomek, William G., and Robinson, Kenneth L. *Agricultural Product Prices.* Ithaca, N.Y.: Cornell University Press, 1972. Chaps. 3, 4, 5, and 10.

Wilcox, Walter W.; Cochrane, Willard W., and Herdt, Robert W. *Economics of American Agriculture,* 3rd ed. Englewood Cliffs, N.J.: Prentice-Hall, 1974. Chaps. 4, 5, 13, and 14.

CHAPTER 20

GOVERNMENT INTERVENTION, CANNIBALISM, AND THE TREADMILL

Government Intervention in the Farm Economy

Farmers, as businessmen, do not like price instability. Great downswings in the level of farm prices, such as occurred in 1929–32, can break and have broken thousands of farmers financially. Commodity price variability operates to create price and income uncertainty in the minds of farmers, hence acts to dampen their price expectations, and as a result they restrict their investments in the farm enterprise.

As we are aware from the discussions in chapters 6, 7, and 15, farmers began in the 1920s to call upon government to stabilize their industry — to put a price-income support floor under it. In 1933, a full set of price- and income-stabilizing measures was enacted into law and made operational in the farm economy. Since 1933, those measures have evolved with respect to concept, method of application, and emphasis; hence the set of specific measures employed in any one year has differed somewhat from the set employed in another year. But the basic intervening measures employed by government are four in number.

First, the government makes a commitment to support the price of certain commodities during the forthcoming year. This commitment is typically made for all the more important crops and some of the livestock products. For the storable commodities, the price support commitment is effectuated through the use of nonrecourse loans.[1] Consequently, the level of price support for a specific commodity is often described as the loan rate. Price uncertainty is thus replaced by price certainty in the minds of farmers for the commodities involved, and increased overall price level stability is achieved through the process of product substitution.

Second, the government provides farmers with programs of production control for certain commodities. Such programs have operated to contract the supply of a commodity, or to slow its rate of expansion. On occasion these programs have been mandatory for all producers of the commodity involved,[2] but usually farmers have been paid by the government to reduce their production of a given commodity. Such reductions in production have been realized, or attempted, by withdrawing some specific acreage on each participating farm from the production of that crop. This is a slippery, inefficient way of reducing production, since it is relatively easy for farmers to substitute capital inputs (e.g., fertilizer) for land, but it is the technique of production control employed by government in most cases.

Third, the government acquires and removes surplus products from the market, thereby expanding the demand for the commodities involved. These surplus removal operations have sometimes taken the form of government purchases of the product in the market at the support price (e.g., dairy products have been acquired in this way), with the disposal of the product through such programs as domestic school lunches and foreign food aid. But over the years perhaps the largest acquisitions of surplus products by government have occurred through farmers opting to turn over their commodity to the government under the nonrecourse loan device. This has been true particularly for the grains and cotton.

Fourth, since 1965 the government has increasingly substituted programs of income payments to farmers for the support of commodity prices above market equilibrium levels as a means of supporting farm incomes. Under this type of program, the government establishes a target price (some concept of a fair price) for each commodity and makes a payment to the farmer on all, or some portion, of his production of a crop equal to the difference between the target price and the market price. By this device, the government is able, when all is working right, to support the incomes of farmers, allow prices to fall to market clearing levels,[3] and to avoid the acquisition of unwanted surplus stocks. These payment programs do, however, have one great drawback; that drawback is their high cost to the government.[4] Americans learned in the 1980s just how expensive these income payment programs could become (see chapter 8).

The intervening actions by government to provide farmers with price and income support and stability have by and large operated on individual commodities — have been commodity programs. As such, they have broken the cobweb interaction for the commodities involved and have provided a substantial degree of price stability for those commodities. But in the early years of these commodity programs, the aggregate effects of such programs were largely ignored. Land taken out of wheat production, for example, simply flowed into the production of sorghum or barley. Beginning with the Soil Bank program in 1956, the aggregate effects of these programs were taken into account by requiring that land taken out of a crop that was in surplus production be held idle in a nonproducing, soil-conserving use. Thus government intervention in the farm economy to provide price and income support and stability typically operates through individual commodity programs, with the specifics of each program tailored to the unique characteristics of the commodity involved. The aggregate effects of the programs are taken into account by the requirement that the land taken out of the production of a specific crop remain idle.

The economic implications of these various commodity stabilization programs are illustrated in figure 20.1. In chart A, we have the example of price support through an expansion in demand resulting from increased government purchases of the commodity; this is illustrative of the commodity milk and various nonstorable commodities. Government determines that the price of commodity A be supported at P_s. The government enters the market to make purchases of the commodity; this has the effect of expanding the demand for this commodity from $D_1 D_1$ to $D_2 D_2$.[5] With a demand of $D_2 D_2$, the market clears 0C amount of this commodity at price P_s The price of the commodity is supported in the market at P_s by the purchase operations of the government. As a result, the government acquires AC amount of this product which it must now dispose of outside the commercial market. Private buyers of this commodity must pay the price P_s for it rather than the price P_M, which would obtain in a free market.

In chart B of figure 20.1, we have the example of price support through a contraction in supply resulting from a production control program. This could be illustrative of the commodity wheat when the control program was working perfectly. The government determines that the price of commodity B is to be supported at price P_S. The operation of the government program of production control has the effect

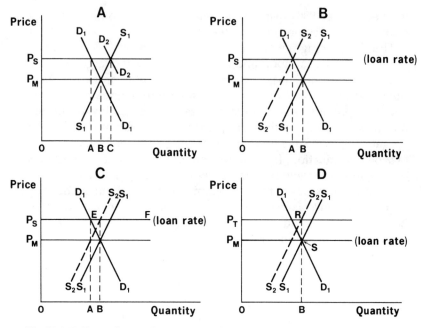

Fig. 20.1. Different forms of governmental intervention in the farm economy

of reducing the supply of commodity B from S_1S_1 to S_2S_2. With a supply of S_2S_2, the market clears at 0A amount and the price is supported in the market at P_S. In this situation, the government acquires no commodity. But the supply coming on the market is less, by AB amount, than it would be in a free market, and purchasers of the commodity must pay the price P_S rather than the price P_M, which would obtain in a free market.

In chart C, we have the example of price support through an expansion in demand and a contraction in supply, owing to the operation of government programs. This is illustrative of the commodity wheat in the typical year prior to 1965. Government determines that the price of commodity C be supported at price P_S. The operation of the government program of production control has the effect of reducing supply from S_1S_1 to S_2S_2. At the price P_S, farmers stand ready to offer on the market 0B amount; this amount will not clear the market at P_S with a demand of D_1D_1. Market price comes to rest on the loan rate which is equal to P_S. The government acquires AB amount as farmers exercise their option of turning over their commodity to the government under the nonrecourse loan device. In effect, the demand for the commodity becomes D_1EF and the price of the commodity is supported at P_S, or the loan rate. Private purchasers of the commodity must pay the price P_S for this commodity rather than the price P_M, which would have obtained in the free market. The government must find a way of disposing of AB amount of the commodity outside the commercial market.

In chart D, we have the example of income support for farmers in conjunction with production control and price support for the commodity at or near the equilibrium level. This is illustrative of wheat under the Food and Agricultural Act of 1977 as well as later acts. Government determines that the target price for calculating income payments to producers of this commodity be set at price P_T. The operation of the production control program by the government has the effect of reducing the supply of this commodity from S_1S_1 to S_2S_2. At the target price P_T, farmers stand ready to offer on the market 0B amount; this amount clears the market at price P_M, which is equal to the loan rate. The price of the commodity is thus supported in the market at the price P_M. Farmers receive a payment on each unit of product produced by them eligible for payment equal to $P_T - P_M$. If under the program farmers were eligible for payment on all units of the product produced by them, all farmers producing this product would receive total payments equal to the rectangle P_TRSP_M in chart D.

It should be recognized that the price-quantity solutions presented in the four illustrative cases in figure 20.1 assume that the programs in each case were working perfectly, which in practice was not the case. The programs worked imperfectly, producing all manner of unexpected results for numerous reasons: imperfect knowledge on the part of the program planners, variations in crop growing conditions, ill-conceived programs in the first place, and wrongdoing on the part of some farmer participants and program administrators. Thus, the programs were forever changing to take account of, and to correct, past mistakes, and forever becoming more complex, with increased options, to take account of variations in farming conditions and variations in farm size and cost structure.

The "Farm Acts" of the 1980s and 1990 continue to rely heavily on the program devices of income payments and acreage controls, but they contain so many program options with respect to payment arrangements and acreage retirement schemes that a simple graph like that presented in chart D of figure 20.1 can no longer be said to describe the operations of such a commodity program. To an important degree each farm operator can construct a government program to fit the requirements of his or her farm from the available program options with respect to amount of acreage to retire, the proportion of a program crop on which to receive payments, and the relation of program features among crops on the farm. This process at the local level now has a name; it is called "farming the government." But chart D of figure 20.1 describes in conceptual terms the operation of a commodity program at the national level, as of 1990, that relies on income payments and acreage controls as a means of supporting farm income, even though it does not come close to describing the operation of such a program at the local level.

The operation of the government programs described above kept individual commodity prices and the level of farm prices from falling to those depths in the 1950s and 1960s, which numerous studies have suggested would have occurred in the absence of those programs,[6] and which is suggested by the dashed trend lines in figure 19.8. The operation of the government programs described above put a floor under farm prices and incomes in the 1950s and 1960s and held those prices and incomes relatively stable. For an indication of the relative stability of farm food product prices during the period 1950–70, observe the full, heavy line ARST in figure 19.8. The commodity programs supported directly the prices of the commodities for which there were programs. These included all the important crops and certain livestock products. And through the ubiquitous process of substitution on both the demand and supply sides, the individual commodity programs supported and stabilized the general level of farm food product prices.

This is not to suggest that farmers were satisfied with the levels of price and income support that were realized in the 1950s and 1960s — most certainly they were not. In general, farmers felt that the government could have, and should have, provided higher levels of price and income support than it in fact did. But it is to say that the intervening actions of the federal government in the farm economy in the 1950s and 1960s held the level of farm food product prices well above the level that would have been realized in a free market situation. This was the meaning of government intervention in the historical period 1950–70, and it is the meaning for the theoretical politico-economic model under construction.

The Politics of Intervention

The programs of price and income support described in the previous section did not come into being automatically or easily; they were forged in political arenas through the complex political process of compromise, group pressures, and vote trading. As such, those programs often failed to meet the goals of the sponsors of the price and income support legislation (i.e., farmers and their organizations), and the programs were often encumbered with provisions that were inefficient or unworkable or unacceptable or all three. In sum, the farm commodity programs of price and income support were, and continue to be, the product of political markets. Thus, to appreciate the product of those political markets, one must have some understanding of the markets themselves.

Farmers and their organizational spokesmen knew what they wanted in the way of price support in the 1950s and 1960s. They wanted price support at "full parity." (Parity is defined as that price of a unit of farm product for the period in question which will give that unit a purchasing power equal to the purchasing power that it had in 1910–14.) In the late 1950s and early 1960s, the parity prices of agricultural commodities ranged from 20 to 40 percent above the actual prices of those commodities. So to have supported farm commodity prices in that period at full parity would have meant supporting farm commodity prices at 20 to 40 percent above their existing levels. Urban congressmen, union leaders, and industrial leaders were opposed to such an increase in farm food product prices because of the impact that price increases at the farm level would have had on retail food prices. Presidential administrations were opposed to such high levels of price support since (1) they would entail increased program costs and (2) they would have adverse implications for agricultural exports. Thus the levels of commodity price support that emerged from the political markets of the 1950s and 1960s represented a compromise — a compromise between the demands of farmers for full parity and urban pressures to hold down food costs and federal expenditures. During this period, most farm food product prices were supported by government programs somewhere between 75 percent and 90 percent of full parity. This was high enough to hold farm food product prices reasonably stable (refer to figure 19.8), but low enough to keep the commodity programs from giving a significant upward thrust to retail food prices, and low enough to hold government expenditures on farm commodity programs to a tolerable level. Generally speaking, no one was happy with the compromised price support programs adopted and employed by government to support farm commodity prices in the 1950s and the first half of the 1960s; certainly the farmers were not. But in a tolerable sense they worked and were accepted.

If farmers were unhappy with the level of price support in the government programs, they were even more unhappy with the production control provisions. As a general proposition, farmers dislike holding their productive resources idle; they want to produce to the maximum capacity of their resources at all times. Consequently, farmers and their congressional spokesmen in the drafting of the price and income support legislation continuously introduced provisions enabling them to escape the stringent production control provisions of the legislation; and they were often successful in keeping such loopholes in the legislation. For example, farmers would seek provisions to graze their "idle" acres, or they would seek permission to plant "exotic" crops, such as sunflowers, on their "idle" acres. But the greatest loophole was the provision that production was to be controlled at the farm level by withdrawing acres of land from production. Under this production control device, farmers could and did farm their uncontrolled acres more intensively, add capital to those acres, and increase the outturn of agricultural production on them. Government programs thus tended to induce an increased capital intensification of agriculture in the 1950s and 1960s, and the control features of the programs were continuously one step, or more, behind the increases in per-acre yields during the period.

The insistence of farmers to employ acreage controls rather than, say, marketing quotas measured in pounds or bushels or bales thus resulted in a slippery, inefficient form of production control. Rarely did this form of production control result in the neat solution portrayed in chart B of figure 20.1. In most instances, reliance on acreage controls led to the type of solution portrayed in chart C, where the government had to acquire AB amount of product to hold market prices at the support price level, P_S.

The typical price-quantity consequences of intervening actions by government to support farm prices and incomes in the 1930s, the 1950s, and the first half of the 1960s are illustrated in figure 20.2. Government determines that the price of the commodity in question shall be supported at price P_S. At that price, the government acquires a certain volume of product to meet its commitments to a domestic feeding program, a foreign food aid program, or to the armed forces; as a result, demand expands from D_1D_1 to D_2D_2. A program of acreage production control is implemented; as a result, the supply of this commodity is reduced from S_1S_1 to S_2S_2. But at support price P_S, the actions described above do not clear the market. At this price farmers stand ready to offer on the market AB amount of product for which

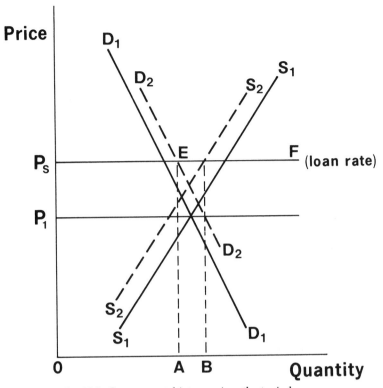

Fig. 20.2. Governmental intervention: the typical case

there is no immediate use. To hold the market price of this commodity at the committed level of price support P_s, the government in this instance is required to take over AB amount of this commodity and add that amount to its surplus stock of that commodity. In effect, the demand for the farm food product under consideration becomes, through the price support operation, D_2EF. This kind of operation, modified to fit the specific requirements of individual commodities, the government undertook year after year in the 1950s to support the prices of milk, wheat, feed grains, and cotton. As a result, the value of government inventories of agricultural products rose from slightly over $1 billion in 1952 to slightly under $8 billion in 1959. Government intervention to support farm prices and incomes in the 1950s resulted in a continuous buildup of government-owned stocks. In the 1960s, with a more stringent application of production control, a significant increase in foreign exports, and a shift to an income payments approach (chart D, figure 20.1), the volume of government inventories of agricultural products slowly declined.

Two secretaries of agriculture have tried to provide a rationale for the buildup of stocks under government programs. Secretary of Agriculture Henry A. Wallace, drawing upon the biblical story of the seven good years and the seven lean years in Egypt, argued that the buildup of stocks in an "ever-normal granary" could serve to insure the nation and the world against the shortfalls in production that would result from a prolonged period of bad weather and poor crops. Secretary of Agriculture Orville L. Freeman believed that government-owned stocks of agricultural commodities should be viewed as a resource to be used to help new nations of the developing world build social and physical infrastructure. The views of these two secretaries of agriculture gained some converts, but the prevailing view in the body politic was that the buildup of stocks in the hands of government was an indicator of the weakness in, or the failure of, government programs of price and income support. The stocks themselves were thus viewed as an unnecessary cost to government and a price-depressing factor in the market; hence they should be sold off, or be given away, at the first convenient opportunity. That opportunity came in 1973, following the poor world grain crop of 1972. Secretary of Agriculture Earl L. Butz reduced the stock holdings of the United States government in agricultural products to the maximum extent possible. But then, as food prices continued to soar and a world food crisis developed in 1973–74, urban consumers and national political leaders discovered belatedly that large stocks of farm food products in government hands to serve as a security reserve against unforeseen contingencies did constitute a valuable national asset.

Since 1973, the body politic has sought to define, without too much success, a legitimate role for a government-owned and government-managed reserve stock of staple farm food products. Despite the lack of success in writing and passing legislation that defines the legitimate role of reserve stock programs for agricultural products, the Carter administration in 1977–78 moved to establish a limited grain reserve of some 30 to 40 million tons with the expressed goal of reducing price fluctuation of farm food products, *both on the down side and on the up side.* Farmers, at the time, were not sure that they liked this policy step, but they have come to welcome this reserve idea, operated on a voluntary basis, as another program option available to them. Urban consumers for the most part have been unaware of the operation of this limited reserve program. The idea of a grain reserve program to help stabilize the prices of farm food products for both farmers and consumers remains a viable idea in the 1990s; Cochrane and Runge in a recent farm policy book argue once again for the need of a major grain reserve program in the volatile, uncertain world of the 1990s.[7]

Theory of the Treadmill

The role of farm technological advance in reducing unit costs and expanding supply was discussed in chapters 10 and 19. But the process of economic adjustment to a farm technological advance has not yet been elaborated. That process will be developed in this section in the theory of the treadmill.[8]

The "early-bird" farmer, who adopts a new and improved technology, finds that his unit costs of production are reduced; this is illustrated in chart A of figure 20.3 by the decline of the farm-firm cost structure from $ATUC_1$, to $ATUC_2$. As a result of the adoption of the new and improved technology, Mr. "Early-Bird" (1) increases the output of his firm, and (2) earns a profit for his innovative action. These consequences are illustrated in chart A of figure 20.3. At price P_1, Mr. "Early-Bird" stands ready to offer on the market 0B amount after the adoption as compared with 0A amount before. And he earns a profit equal to the rectangle P_1RST as a reward for his innovative action.

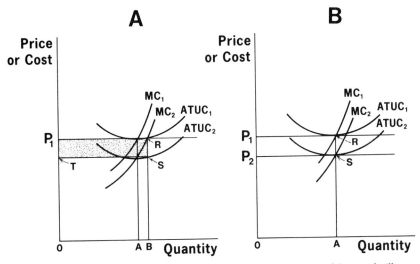

Fig. 20.3. Firm and industry solutions in a free market: the theory of the treadmill

Mr. "Early-Bird" will continue to earn a profit equal to P_1RST so long as the price of the product holds at P_1. The price P_1 will hold for Mr. "Early-Bird," the first adopter, because in the atomistic situation of American agriculture, the increased output of this one farmer will have an infinitesimal influence on total market supply. And this will be the profit consequences for all the early adopters of this new and improved technology. But as more and more farmers adopt the improved technology, total market supply will increase. In a free market situation, other things remaining unchanged, this increase in supply will cause the price of the product to fall.

With increased information regarding the improved technology and a falling product price, a situation is created wherein Mr. "Average-Farmer" will want to adopt the technology. The widespread adoption of the technology by the average farmer will further increase supply and that will cause the price of the product to decline still more. It is also likely that marketable supplies of the commodity involved will be augmented by the entry of new firms into the commodity enterprise, attracted by the increased profitability of the enterprise given the availability of the new and improved technology.

The final solution for the adopters of the improved technology in a free market situation is illustrated in chart B of figure 20.3. Price falls from P_1 to P_2 and the economic gains to all the adopters of this technology are wiped out.[9] The firms are once again in long-run equilibrium where each firm produces $0A$ amount at the lower price P_2, and each firm is in a no-profit/no-loss situation. In this situation, the costs of all the factors of production are being covered, including a wage to the operator for his labor and management. But there is no entrepreneurial profit.

In the long run, the gainers from farm technological advance in a free-market situation are the consumers; they are going to receive the same amount of product, or more, at a lower price.

The losers from farm technological advance are the laggard farmers who do not adopt the improved technology. If the cost structure of a laggard farmer is $ATUC_1$ in chart B of figure 20.3, then after the fall in the product price to P_2, the laggard farmer would be sustaining losses equal to the rectangle P_1RSP_2. But in all probability the cost structure of the laggard farmer would be well above the structure $ATUC_1$ shown in chart B of figure 20.3, and he would be sustaining losses even at the price P_1. The widespread adoption of the new technology and the fall in the product price from P_1 to P_2 thus has the effect of further widening his losses, and in the long run he must fail and go out of business.

To sum up, the aggressive, innovative farmer is on a treadmill with regard to the adoption of new and improved technologies on his farm. As he rushes to adopt a new and improved technology when it first becomes available, he at first reaps a gain. But, as others after him run to adopt the technology, the treadmill speeds up and grinds out an increased supply of the product. The increased supply of the product drives the price of the product down to where the early adopter and all his fellow adopters are back in a no-profit situation. Farm technological advance in a free market situation forces the participants to run on a treadmill.

For the laggards who never got on the treadmill, the consequences of farm technological advance are more devastating. Farm technological advance either forces them into a situation of economic loss or further widens their existing losses. In the long run, such sustained losses must force them into bankruptcy and out of the business of farming.

As these laggard farmers have been forced out of business by the process of farm technological advance, their productive assets have typically been acquired by the better, more aggressive farmers — by the "early-bird" farmers who prospered from the temporary gains of the early adoption of the new and improved production technologies. The acquisition of the productive resources of their less fortunate and less able neighbors does not have the effect of increasing the unit costs of production to these more aggressive and more innovative farmers, since they typically experience constant returns from increasing the size of their operations. In terms of chart A, figure 19.5, each of these farmers, by the acquisition of his neighbor's productive assets, moves out along his long-run planning curve from cost structure $AVUC_2$ to cost structure $AVUC_3$.[10] In this way, the better, more aggressive farmers improved their wealth positions even if they did not improve their immediate profit positions.

Not only did the process of farm technological advance force the participants in the process onto a treadmill, but it created a condition in which the strong and aggressive farmers gobbled up the weak and inefficient. The process of farm technological advance has contributed importantly to the redistribution of productive assets in American agriculture in which commercial production has been, and continues to be, concentrated on the larger farms. The process of farm technological advance has resulted in widespread cannibalism in American agriculture.[11]

The Treadmill with Government Intervention
and Producer Cannibalism

Falling product prices are the logical result of farm technological advance in a free market situation. But falling product prices are not consistent with an agricultural industry with a price support floor under it. Farm food product prices fell from the post-World War II highs in the early 1950s. But those prices leveled off in the mid-1950s and held almost constant from 1955 to 1965 as farm market prices rode on the commodity prices support mechanisms. In the late 1960s, farm food product prices trended modestly upward as the level of price support was increased and export sales expanded. The question may thus be asked, Does the treadmill argument hold where government places a price-income support floor under the farming industry? Is it logical to expect farm technological advance to fuel the development process in agriculture and lead to a treadmill type of solution where government price support programs are in operation?

The answer is yes, although we get some slightly different theoretical price-cost results; these results are, however, in accord with the price-cost facts of the period 1950–70.

The operation of the treadmill with fixed price supports provided by government is described below. Mr. "Early-Bird" adopts a new and improved technology and the cost structure of his firm declines. In figure 20.4, the cost structure of the "Early-Bird" declines from position

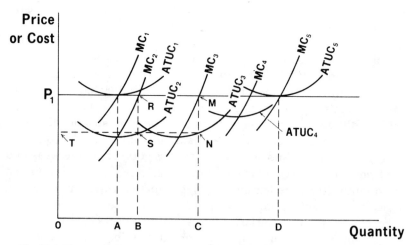

Fig. 20.4. The treadmill solution with governmental intervention and cannibalism

ATUC₁ to position ATUC₂. The price of the product holds constant at P_1, and Mr. "Early-Bird" earns profits equal to the rectangle P_1RST as a reward for his innovative act. Other farmers follow the lead of Mr. "Early-Bird" and adopt the improved technology. The cost structure of each of those adopters declines, and each earns a profit equal to the rectangle P_1RST in figure 20.4. But as more and more farmers adopt the new technology and as they increase the aggregate supply of the product involved, *the price of the product does not fall.* The price-supporting action of the government holds the market price of the product at P_1.

In this situation, Mr. "Early-Bird," and each of the farmers who followed him in the adoption of the improved technology, continues to earn a profit equal to the rectangle P_1RST in figure 20.4. Each adopting farmer is pleased with the per unit profits in this situation and wants to increase his production and sell more units. Thus each sets out to expand the size of his operation. Under constant returns to size, the unit costs of production of these expanding farmers do not rise as they purchase more land and equipment and expand their output. This output expansion by the better, more aggressive farmers is illustrated in figure 20.4. The cost structure of each of the farms involved expands from position ATUC₂ to position ATUC₃. With price holding constant at P_1 through government action, the profit position of each of these farm firms expands to the new and larger rectangle P_1MNT.

As more and more farmers adopt the improved technology — as Mr. "Average-Farmer" adopts — and each seeks to expand his operation through the process of buying land from his laggard neighbors, the price of farmland begins to rise. In terms of figure 20.4, the average total unit costs of the farm firm begin to ride up the marginal cost curve MC₃ as profits (1) are used to purchase the scarce input, land, from laggard neighbors and (2) are capitalized into the price of land already owned. The new cost structure position for each expanding firm is illustrated by structure ATUC₄ in figure 20.4. Each firm involved has grown larger and expanded its output. But unit costs of production have risen for each firm as a result of rising land values.

Not shown in figure 20.4 are the cost structures of the less aggressive, laggard farm firms that have gone out of business. Since the arable land base in the United States in the second half of the twentieth century is relatively fixed, the expansion of the aggressive firms illustrated in figure 20.4 could only take place as those firms acquired the land resources of the less aggressive, laggard farmers. Thus we see that cannibalism is an integral, and indeed a necessary, part of farm technological advance with fixed prices (i.e., product prices riding on government price supports). The profits created through the adoption of improved technologies by the aggressive and more efficient farmers drive them to expand their operations, which they can do only by acquiring the scarce land assets of their laggard neighbors.[12] Consequently, competition for the scarce land assets drives up the price of land.

The solution is not complete at cost structure position $ATUC_4$ in figure 20.4. Each of the firms in that position is still earning a profit as the direct result of having adopted the improved technology, where the price of the product is held constant at P_1 through government action. Thus each of these firms strives to expand its operation still further, and as a result expand its profit position. But this competitive striving to become still larger in size further increases the price of the limiting factor, land. In their quest for additional land, these aggressive farmers simply bid up the price of land. The final solution is illustrated by cost structure position $ATUC_5$ in figure 20.4. At that position, each of the innovative, aggressive firms is back in a no-profit position as a result of the competitive process in which the price of land has been driven up to that level where the minimum point of the short-run cost curve is tangent to the fixed price line. It could be said that a "land market" treadmill has replaced the "product market" treadmill.

In this solution, the scale of operations for the better, more aggressive farmers has increased. The total number of farms has declined as many of the smaller, less efficient farms have gone out of business. The price of the product has held constant owing to government price-supporting operations. And the reductions in the unit costs of production resulting from the initial farm technological advance have been wiped out by the increase in the price of land. Significantly, these logical conclusions are consistent with the economic facts and trends in American agriculture during the period 1950–70. (See chapter 7.) Thus it may be argued that the theory of the treadmill with government intervention to support the price of farm commodities holds, not only in a logical sense, but in a relevant sense as well.

The Hard Lesson from History

We know now why farmers adopt new and improved technologies and expand their output even though they complain of low product prices and rising input prices. They do so because each farmer sees the adoption of a new and improved technology as a means of either increasing his profits or reducing his losses. But in a competitive situation, with many producers, there is no way that an individual farmer can hold onto himself the short-run income gains from the adoption of the new and improved technology. Such income gains are lost to him in the longer run through the competitive process. They are lost in a free-market situation through falling product prices. They are lost in a price-supported situation through rising prices of the fixed factors — typically land.

The question may be asked, Cannot the farmer get off the treadmill if he receives income support in the form of payments rather than price support? The answer is no, if those payments are linked to his volume of production and there is a free market in land. In this situation, the innovative farmer will adopt the new and improved technology for the same reason that he did in a free market situation; the adoption of the new and improved technology reduces his unit costs of production. As more farmers adopt the technology, industry supply increases and the price of the product falls. But the income of the adopting farmers is maintained, partly at least, by the receipt of income payments. Such farmers will then seek to expand their output by acquiring the productive assets of their smaller and less successful neighbors. In this process, the price of the scarce factor, land, will be bid upward until the profits created by the receipt of the government income payments are wiped out.

The above analysis further suggests the fallacy of trying to raise, or support, the incomes of farmers through government actions designed to support product prices above equilibrium levels or through government payments to farmers based on their volume of production. The income gains to farmers resulting from such governmental activities will be used by the larger, more efficient, more aggressive farmers to expand their operations through the purchase and acquisition of the productive assets of their smaller, less efficient neighbors. In this cannibalistic process, the price of land is bid upward, the cost structures of all farm firms are raised, and the income assistance provided by government is wiped out. Income gains to farmers from governmental programs of price and income support have, in the long run, been bid into increased land values and have increased the wealth position of landowners. In the main, the landowners who have benefited from government programs of price and income support have been the larger, aggressive, innovative farmers in each farming community who have used the income assistance from government to acquire additional land. In the process, these farmers have bid up the price of all farmland, including their original land, and have made themselves wealthy landowners.

"Escape from the Treadmill: Is It Possible?"

The farmer, as a farmer, is on a treadmill, from which, history tells us, he cannot escape. Any gain in income to American farmers, whether it emanates from technological advancements that serve to develop the farm economy, or from a rapid increase in demand, or from government programs of price and income assistance, or from some combination of all of these, must be dissipated in the competitive process through falling product prices and/or rising prices of the scarce factor of production (i.e., land). But this does not keep farmers from seeking a means of escape. Many farmers and their economic advisers in the 1970s thought they had found the avenue of escape in the form of a *continuously* expanding export market. But the export boom came to an end in 1982, and with it the upward surge in farm prices. The competitive struggle in its fiercest form resumed in the 1980s.

Other farmers looked to the government as a way to escape from the treadmill. And for a brief time it looked as if they had found it. The target price for the grains increased in a stair-step fashion from 1971 to 1985 with loan rates following close behind. But the huge increases in the costs of government programs of price and income support brought this development to an end in the middle 1980s. Since that time levels of price and income support have been declining. And as of 1992, there is strong support in the body politic to reduce government subsidies to commercial agriculture even more.

There are a talented few who have been able to stay ahead of the competitive results of the treadmill by continuously adopting new and improved technologies. For such an operator the short-run profits from the adoption of a particular improved technology must be computed away over time. But if he adopts productivity-increasing technologies in an endless succession, he should produce a stream, or flow, of economic gains for himself. And this we hypothesize is what a talented few farm operators have been able to do over the years. For each new and improved technology that the innovative operator adopts the treadmill grinds on, but he is able to stay ahead of his competitors by staying ahead of them in adopting one new and improved technology after another.

There is, perhaps, another way for the owner-managers of certain modern farm operations to escape from the competitive results of the treadmill. The data in table 18.2 and the arguments advanced with respect to the watershed of the 1980s and 1990s suggest an avenue of escape. If the principal means of expansion ceases to be adding acres of land to the farm operation, which appears to have happened in the 1980s, and the expansion of output on an individual farm occurs through the skillful combination of resources and technologies by management, all of which are truly variable and their prices do not rise in response to their use in that enterprise, then the resulting profits should accrue to the skilled management that brought the superior production process into being. In this situation the new fixed factor is management. And with government intervention to support the price of the product involved the economic gains should be "capitalized" into the new fixed factor, management. This line of reasoning is absolutely dependent upon two assumptions: (1) all resources are truly variable to the enterprise and any development within the enterprise does not cause the prices of the resources employed to rise, and (2) government continues to support the price of the product produced by the firms involved.

Then, does it follow that, if the farming situation reverts to a free market, profits of our skilled manager who put together the superior production process will be competed away via the treadmill? The answer is yes, if that production process can be readily copied, and there is no barrier to the entry of new firms into this product line. But if the superior production process developed by the management of a particular farm has unique aspects that cannot be readily copied, then management should be able to hold on to the economic gains flowing from that production process. And we see some of this happening in the 1980s — management is combining new and improved technologies with existing resources to create increasingly productive processes that are unique to the particular large-scale farming operation involved. In this situation management has developed something of a production monopoly, and competition via the treadmill is less effective in draining away the profits from this particular enterprise. Entry may occur into the product line, output increase, and the price of the product begin to fall, but it is reasonable to argue that entry will cease and the price of the product stop falling, as the result of entry by firms *not blessed with the uniquely superior production process*, before the product price falls to the level of the minimum cost position of our firm with the uniquely superior production process. In this case the superior producer with the unique production process escapes from the treadmill, in part at least, by becoming a quasi monopolist. In a true free market with no monopoly elements there is no escape from the treadmill in the long run.

Suggested Readings

Brown, William P. *Private Interests, Public Policy, and American Agriculture.* Lawrence: University of Kansas Press, 1988, particularly chaps. 11 and 12.

Cochrane, Willard W. *Farm Prices: Myth and Reality.* Minneapolis: University of Minnesota Press, 1958. Chap. 5.

Herdt, Robert W., and Cochrane, Willard W. "Farm Land Prices and Farm Technological Advance." *Journal of Farm Economics*, 48, no. 2 (May 1966), pp. 243–63.

Raup, Philip M. "Some Questions of Value and Scale in American Agriculture." *American Journal of Agricultural Economics*, 60, no. 2 (May 1978), pp. 303–8.

Schumpeter, Joseph A. *The Theory of Economic Development.* Cambridge: Harvard University Press, 1936. Chaps. I, II, III, and IV.

U.S. Congress. Congressional Budget Office. *Public Policy and the Changing Structure of American Agriculture.* Background Paper, September 1978. Chaps. I, II, and III.

CHAPTER 21

USING THE MODEL TO
UNDERSTAND THE 1970s AND 1980s

In this chapter we will look at the development of American agriculture over the period 1970–90 — a period of extraordinary price and income gyrations — with the help of the economic model conceptualized in the preceding two chapters. We are aware of most of the facts, trends, and developments of this period from the presentations in chapters 8, 17, and 18; thus it is not our purpose to present any new information in this chapter.[1] It is our purpose to organize the facts, trends and developments of this period in accordance with the conceptual model as a way of explaining the volatile behavior of the farm sector during the 1970s and 1980s. But first let us be clear about the model; a general formulation is presented below.

The Conceptual Model

The structure of the market in which agricultural development occurred during the period 1950–70 was atomistic. The market was composed of many producer-sellers and, usually, many buyers. There were so many producer-sellers in the market that no single producer could have any perceptible influence on supply, hence upon the product price, by his individual actions. Occasionally, the fewness of buyers in the market gave rise to various forms of monopolistic behavior. But a high degree of substitution among farm food products sustained the dominant market characteristic of atomicity in farm food product markets.

The aggregate demand for farm food products (i.e., the aggregate commodity, food) was, and remains, highly inelastic with respect to price. The domestic component of this aggregate has become unresponsive to changes in income; on the average, Americans have reached that stage of opulence in which rising per capita incomes increase the per capita consumption of food little, if at all. This being the case, the domestic component of aggregate demand was increasing, as of 1970, only insofar as the domestic population was increasing. And since the rate of population increase in the United States had fallen to something close to 1 percent per year, the domestic component of the aggregate demand for farm food products could be increasing no faster than approximately 1 percent per year.

The foreign component of aggregate demand, as of 1970, was highly responsive to increasing per capita incomes in the developed world and to rising per capita incomes and rapid rates of population growth in the less developed world. The rapid rate of increase in the export demand for American farm food products was, however, interrupted and destabilized by unpredictable variations in the weather, hence in growing conditions around the world in the 1960s and early 1970s, and by unpredictable changes in the foreign trade policy of important trading nations. The insulation of domestic markets by large importers of American grain and other farm food products further operated to make the foreign component of aggregate demand severely inelastic and contributed to an increased inelasticity of the aggregate demand confronting American farmers. The result of these diverse forces in the late 1960s and early 1970s was that American producers of food products were confronted with a severely inelastic aggregate demand that expanded unevenly and unpredictably — sometimes moving ahead of the growth in supply, sometimes lagging behind it. The behavior of this aggregate demand relation generated wide, sharp, and unpredictable swings in the farm food product price level.

The aggregate supply of farm food products is also highly inelastic with respect to price. Logic suggests that the aggregate supply relation should become relatively more elastic with the passage of time as farmers employ more and more nonfarm-produced inputs. But the best statistical evidence, as of 1970, continued to indicate that the aggregate supply relation for farm food products was highly inelastic.

The source of expansion in the aggregate supply of farm food products during the period 1950–70 was farm technological advance.

The continuous and widespread adoption of new and improved technologies increased the productivity of the resources employed in farming significantly in the fourteen-year period 1951–65; the aggregate supply of farm food products rose by close to 30 percent in that period as a result of greater resource productivity. During the period 1965–70, the rate of increase in resource productivity fell to almost zero, and since the national farm plant did not expand, the aggregate supply of farm food products increased very little.

The promise of lower unit costs of production and increased profits induced farmers to adopt the new and improved technologies on a widespread basis as they became available. The early adopters of each new and improved technology reaped a temporary profit for their innovative acts. But the operation of the treadmill slowly but surely wiped out the income gains of these early adopters and eventually pushed each one toward or into a no-profit position.

Given the operation of these forces, the aggregate supply of farm food products pressed against aggregate demand during the period 1951–65. And given the price elasticities of aggregate supply and demand, the pressure of supply on demand could have resulted in a precipitous decline in the level of farm food product prices with great losses in ownership equity, widespread bankruptcy, and a general financial wringing-out process in American agriculture.

But this did not happen. It did not happen because of the intervention by government. That intervention in the form of price support in the 1950s, price support and income payments in the 1960s, production control and land retirement throughout the period, and domestic and foreign demand expansion operated to put a price and income floor under the farming sector. As a result, the prices received by farmers for food products held relatively constant between 1955 and 1965, and rose modestly between 1965 and 1970.

Agricultural development with governmental intervention did not result in a general financial wringing-out process. But it did result in a selective wringing-out process in which the strong consumed the weak — it resulted in cannibalism. The innovative, aggressive farmers who adopted the new and improved technologies early in the competitive game under a situation of governmental price and income support used their resultant income gains to further expand their operations and their total profits. They accomplished this by buying out their less able, less innovative, less aggressive neighbors. In sum, farm technological advance in conjunction with governmental programs of price and income support operated in the period 1950–70 to speed up the process of farm enlargement as the strong consumed the weak.

Without question, the pressure of aggregate supply on demand was abated in the period 1965–70 as increases in resource productivity on American farms tapered off to nearly zero and the volume of agricultural exports increased significantly. It even seems reasonable to hypothesize that, as the twenty-year period of extraordinary technological advance drew to a close in 1970, the expanding forces of aggregate demand and aggregate supply for farm food products were approximately equal at the level of prices existing in 1970. Stated differently, if the forces of aggregate demand and aggregate supply had held constant at the magnitudes that existed in 1969–70, it is reasonable to hypothesize that the level of prices that existed in 1969–70 would have held constant without governmental intervention. Partly by management, but mostly by accident, the forces, aggregate demand and aggregate supply, in the dynamic process of development came into rough balance in 1969–70.

The Price Response

But the rough balance described above did not last long. Export demand increased strongly in 1970 and 1971 and increased dramatically between 1972 and 1973. Concurrently, the rate of farm technological advance speeded up in the early 1970s; the rate of increase in factor productivity between 1969 and 1973 was highest for any period between the end of World War II and 1989 (see table 18.2). The early 1970s was thus a highly dynamic period with surging exports and widespread adoption of new and improved technologies.

We will look first at the price response. We will use the commodity corn as a proxy for the aggregate of all farm food products. We do this because we want to relate market prices to government program prices, and this can only be done for individual commodities. Corn, however, is a good proxy for the aggregate of all farm food products, because it is by far the most important farm product in terms of cash receipts, and it serves as the feed base for the whole livestock industry.

The market price for corn rose, in response to the surge in export demand, from $1.03 per bushel in the first quarter of 1971 to $3.36 in the first quarter of 1974 (see figure 21.1). Then the price of corn fell back to $1.72 in the first quarter of 1977. What could generate such dramatic price movements? The answer is clear. The interaction of a severely inelastic demand with a severely inelastic supply can explain a large part

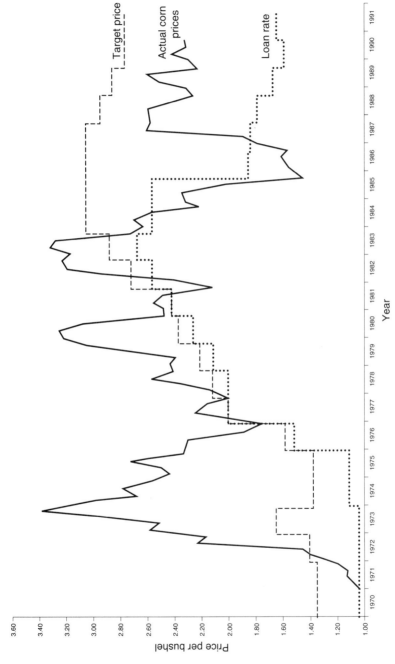

Fig. 21.1. Corn prices, actual (quarterly averages), target, and loan rates, United States, 1970–1991

of the price increase for corn in 1973 and 1974; then when reserve stocks ran low in 1973, panic buying set in, forcing all grain prices, including corn, to unprecedented levels in 1973–74. With a good corn crop in 1975 and an easing in export demand in 1975, the price of corn came tumbling down to $1.72 in the first quarter of 1977. As we learned in chapter 19, when the demand and supply relations are highly inelastic, it takes only a small shift in one or the other to produce a dramatic price response.

The market price for corn continued its roller-coaster-like movements from 1977 to 1990 (see figure 21.1). Part of this price oscillation is a result of surges and contractions in export demand, and part is attributable to poor corn crops in 1983 and 1988. It is no wonder that farmer-businessmen operating in a world of price instability such as is exhibited in figure 21.1 regularly call on government to help bring price stability into that world.

The Political Response

The pleas of farmers to their government, as we know, have not gone unanswered. The loan rates for corn from 1970 to 1990, on which participating farmers may obtain price-supporting nonrecourse loans, are shown in figure 21.1, as are the target prices from which deficiency payments for participating farmers are computed. In the early 1970s the loan rates and target prices for corn were so low, relative to the market prices of corn, that they became nonoperational. And a few people, including Secretary of Agriculture Earl Butz, began to talk about the government programs as a thing of the past. But many farm leaders were not of that mind, and with help from their congressional representatives, they were able to raise the level of the loan rates and target prices in the second half of the 1970s to levels that once again were operational (see figure 21.1). In the early 1980s, compliments of the Agricultural Act of 1981, loan rates and target prices were pushed up to still higher levels. As this was occurring, agricultural exports, particularly grain exports, began to fall, and fall sharply. As a result the bottom fell out of the corn market: prices fell from $3.29 per bushel in the third quarter of 1983 to $1.44 per bushel in the first quarter of 1986. But this time the full brunt of the price decline did not come to bear on farmers; with target prices for corn fixed at $3.03 per bushel (see figure 21.1), support payments to corn producers approximated $6.2 billion in 1986 and $5.9 billion in 1987. Under the provisions of the Agricultural Act of 1985, target prices began to decline in 1988, and,

Table 21.1. Corn Production and Commodity Credit Corporation Operations, 1970–90

Year	Production	CCC Operations		
		Reserve[a]	Inventory[b]	Loans Outstanding[c]
		Million bushels		
1970	4,152		30	105
1971	5,646		47	160
1972	5,580		40	79
1973	5,671		4	7
1974	4,701		3	0
1975	5,841		0	32
1976	6,289		0	143
1977	6,505	212	4	480
1978	7,268	585	101	158
1979	7,928	670	260	116
1980	6,639	0	242	350
1981	8,119	1,276	280	442
1982	8,235	1,890	1,143	129
1983	4,174	447	202	45
1984	7,672	389	225	657
1985	8,875	711	546	2,589
1986	8,226	1,498	1,443	2,102
1987	7,131	1,127	835	928
1988	4,929	724	362	337
1989	7,525	387	233	112
1990	7,933	0	371	209

Source: U.S. Department of Agriculture, Agricultural Stabilization and Conservation Service.
[a]Corn under loan under the provisions of the Farmer Owned Grain Reserve Program.
[b]Corn owned by the CCC.
[c]Corn under standard nonrecourse loan provisions.

buoyed by an expanding export demand, the market price of corn moved up above $2.50 per bushel at the same time. As a result of these two developments the cost hemorrhaging of the governmental corn program did not end, but it was reduced to more manageable proportions (i.e., to the $2 billion $3 billion range).

Another aspect of the corn program may be observed in table 21.1. The Commodity Credit Corporation operations reported in table 21.1 emanate from the use made of nonrecourse loans by farmers. Note that in the early 1970s, when corn prices far exceeded the loan rate, farmers placed very little corn under the loan, and government pulled its inventory of corn down to zero in 1975 and 1976. But when corn prices were at or below the loan rate in 1985 and 1986, farmers made heavy use of the nonrecourse loan device as a means of supporting the price of their product. In 1986 farmers had sealed nearly 1.5 billion bushels of corn in the Farmer Owned Reserve, had placed 2.1 billion bushels under the traditional loan program, and the government had acquired 1.4 billion bushels from loan takeovers. During the 1980s the government loan program played a major role in supporting the price of corn.

The role of government in supporting farm prices and incomes is made abundantly clear in figure 21.1. With price gyrations as pronounced as those shown in figure 21.1 it is understandable that producers of such a commodity would seek some kind of price and income protection from their government. But if that government is foolish enough to provide price guarantees to its producers at historical peak levels, as the U.S. government did for corn growers in 1984 through 1987, then it must expect to bear a heavy cost burden, which the federal government did in 1986 and 1987.

Farm Firm Actors: Four Vignettes

The graphic illustration in figure 21.2, and in figures 21.3–21.5, represents developments in four different situations and the behavior of farm firms in each of those situations. To each of those situations we give a name — a name involving a specific year (e.g., the 1971 vignette). The pricing parameters of each situation are precisely those of the year in the title of the figure. But the behavior of the farm firms in each situation is timeless. This time distinction is important, as is the recognition that the behavior of the actors — the farm firms — is not tied to a specific dated time sequence.

As the development process opens in the 1971 vignette (figure 21.2)

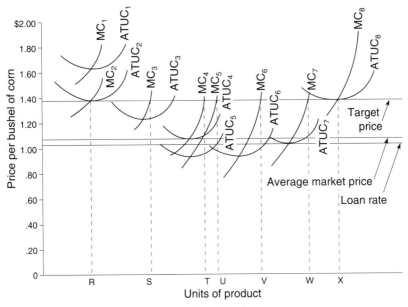

Fig. 21.2. The 1971 vignette

we postulate that there are corn producers in four different positions: small high-cost producers in positions 1 and 2; medium-sized, medium-cost producers in position 3; and large-sized, low-cost producers in position 4. Producers in position 1 are losing money, and producers in position 2 are breaking even, thanks to a relatively high target price provided by government; producers in position 3 are making a profit given the target price, but relative to the actual market price they are not covering their costs; and producers in position 4 are breaking even relative to the actual market price, and are making a substantial profit given the target price provided by government. It will be observed that firms in positions 1, 2, 3, and 4 are arranged so as to conform to the configuration of the long-run planning curve (see figure 19.5, chart A). And it is assumed that all corn producers in positions 2 through 8 are participants in the corn program, which is close to reality.

Now we hypothesize that one firm, or perhaps a few, in position 4 adopt an important set of new and improved technologies. This action by these innovative firms shifts their production functions upward and consequently lowers their average total unit cost (ATUC) functions as illustrated by the firms in new position 5. The firms in position

5 have by this action expanded their individual profit positions (all the necessary lines to indicate this expanded profit position are not shown in figure 21.2, but the result can be easily deduced, from the MC and ATUC curves of the firms in position 5). The operators of these firms are pleased with their enhanced profit positions and seek to increase their profits even more. This each can do by expanding to position 6 along their respective long-run planning curves. How do they accomplish this? They accomplish it by purchasing the land and other resources of the small, high-cost producers in position 1. As this cannibalistic process proceeds, the obvious occurs. The number of small high-cost producers dwindles, and in the competition for the land resources of the dwindling number of farmer-losers, the price of land for those seeking to expand their operations is bid to higher and higher levels. In the final solution shown in figure 21.2 some, or all, of the aggressive, innovative farmers arrive at position 8 with their average total unit costs increased as a result of the higher prices they have paid for land in the expansion process. At position 8, those firms have, through the competitive process, driven their costs up to a break-even, no-profit position. This is the classic treadmill with government intervention.

Two further points need to be made with respect to figure 21.2. First, all of the aggressive, innovative firms need not have pushed their expansion to position 8; some could have stopped at position 6, for example. These firms will show a handsome profit, as indicated in figure 21.2, until the higher land prices in the land market are capitalized into their particular pieces of land; at that point in time the imputed costs of firms in position 6 (based on the increased market price of land) will also approach the target price level. Second, at that point in time all of the producers from position 2 to position 8 will be petitioning their government to raise the target price level to enable them once again to make a profit from their farming operations. Given the operation of the treadmill, government intervention to support the price of a product above the market level turns out to be a self-defeating policy.

In the 1974 vignette (figure 21.3), the average market price for corn is shown at its average 1974 level of $3.02 per bushel. This high price resulted from some poor crops around the world in 1973 and 1974, the former Soviet Union entering the world grain market in a large way, and the United States depleting its grain reserves to unprecedented levels. In this context all corn producers from position 2 to position 8 try to increase their output to benefit from the bonanza price of $3.02 per bushel. Producers in each position from 2 to 8 are able to increase

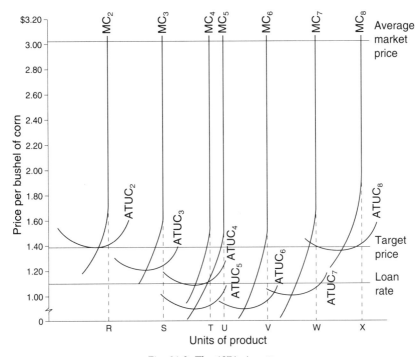

Fig. 21.3. The 1974 vignette

their output modestly, as indicated by the marginal cost curves of those firms, through the addition of readily available variable inputs (e.g., fertilizer). But land, heavy machinery, and family labor are fixed in amount on each of these farms in the short run. Adding variable inputs to these fixed factors would quickly lead, if pursued, to a leveling off of total output, and to total diminishing returns if pursued to any length. Thus, as shown in figure 21.3, the marginal cost curve for the firms in each position becomes perfectly vertical, indicating that firms in each position have reached their output maximum in the short run in response to the market price of $3.02 per bushel.

The question may be asked in respect to figure 21.3: What became of the small, high-cost firms in position 1. They are not shown in figure 21.3 because it is postulated that they had ceased to exist by 1974 as full-time commercial farms. We suggest that a few improved their production methods, reduced their unit costs, and moved into position 2, or even possibly position 3, if they were also able to expand the size of their operations. In line with the argument presented in the

1971 vignette, many, probably most, sold out to farmers bent on expanding the size of their operations. Another segment of this group of small, high-cost farmers found steady jobs in town and became part-time farmers; increasingly farming became a sideline enterprise for them. Thus, in one way or another, we postulate that the small, high-cost farms in position 1 in the 1971 vignette had ceased to exist by 1974.

In the 1974 vignette all firms are making extraordinary profits, and hence there is no incentive in the short run for a firm in position 2 to sell out to a firm in position 5, 6, 7, or 8 that is seeking to expand. But in the longer run the gobbling up of the smaller firms by larger ones would certainly continue. This is evident from figure 21.3. Although the per unit profit of a firm in position 2 is only slightly less than that for a firm in, say, position 7 or 8, the total profits from the higher volume of sales of a firm in either position 7 or 8 greatly exceed the total profits of a firm in position 2. Hence, there would be an incentive for producers in positions 3 through 8 to try to purchase the land and other resources of producers in position 2. As this process proceeds, the competition for the scarce resource, land, held by producers in position 2 would once again start pushing land prices upward. And this is what happened throughout the 1970s — producers in position 2 were cannibalized and land prices rose.

As Boulding pointed out years ago, when the price of the fixed factor rises industrywide, the ATUC curves of firms in the industry simply ride up their respective marginal cost curves.[2] This is the result that we observe in the 1981 vignette (figure 21.4.) Soaring land prices throughout the 1970s drove the cost structures of all firms in positions 3 through 8 to a level at or near the market price for corn. (Incidentally, the market price for corn in 1981 had declined by more than 50 cents from the high of $3.02 per bushel in 1974.) Further we note that the firms in position 2 have disappeared in figure 21.4; the explanation for the disappearance of this group of firms is the same as that given for the lost firms in position 1.

What is not shown in figure 21.4 is the shift of an increasing number of firms out of positions 3, 4, and 5 and into positions 6, 7, and 8 during the 1970s, which had the twin effects of cannibalizing the firms in position 2 and driving up land prices. The latter effect, as we know, pushed the cost structures of all remaining firms close to the market price level for corn. The former effect (not shown in figure 21.4) resulted in an increasing proportion of the total farm output of the na-

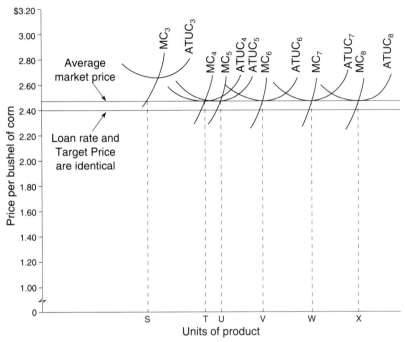

Fig. 21.4. The 1981 vignette

tion being produced, as of 1981, on a relatively few large to very large farms (see table 8.4).

The increase in the levels of price and income support — the loan rate and target prices — to match the increase in the market price of corn is also illustrated in figure 21.4. Farmers, and their lobbyists and legislative representatives in Washington, worked from 1974 on to raise these support levels so that, if there were a significant downturn in market prices, those prices would come to rest on the enhanced support levels. As we see from figure 21.4 both the loan rate and the target price for corn had been raised to $2.40 per bushel, just slightly below the market price, by 1981. And, as we shall argue later, that would have been a good place to leave the target price.

As we see from the 1988 vignette (figure 21.5), that advice was not taken. The target price for corn was raised to $3.03 per bushel for much of the 1980s, and was fixed at $2.93 for the year 1988. The loan rate was first raised and then lowered to $1.77 in 1988 (see figure 21.1). But the cost structures of firms in positions 3 through 8 were not pushed up

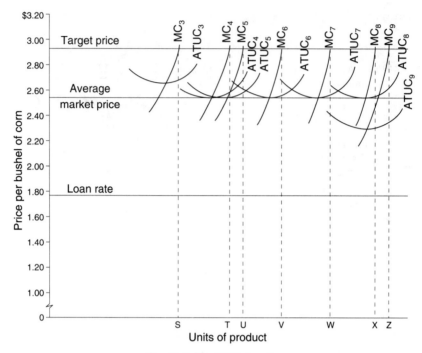

Fig. 21.5. The 1988 vignette

to the target price level through rising land prices for two important reasons. First, the farm sector fell on hard times, in which corn and other grain prices fell substantially between 1981 and 1986 before rebounding to $2.54 in 1988. In this context a good number of aggressive farmers, who had overextended themselves financially in the 1970s to expand their operations, could not meet their credit obligations and were forced out of business. In this atmosphere there was no upward pressure on land prices; on the contrary, land prices fell through the early and middle 1980s; the competitive bidding for the scarce factor, land, fell silent in the middle 1980s, as most farmers struggled to remain solvent.

Second, as we discussed in chapter 18, owner-managers of large-scale farming operations are increasingly getting their costs down and increasing their output, not by adopting a particular new technology (e.g., a new plant variety) or by acquiring additional crop acres, but rather by developing unique and specialized production processes, carefully controlled to squeeze the last ounce of efficiency out of such production processes. This development emphasizes the employment of resources and technologies purchased from the nonfarm sector, the prices of which would not necessarily rise with increased use in the farm sector, and it downplays the role of land in the production process. The goal of such industrialized farming is increased output through increased total factor productivity, which in turn leads to a decrease in total inputs. This is precisely what happened to the commercial farm plant of the United States in the period 1979–89 as reported in table 18.2. The name of the new game in farming is tight control over the use of resources in every aspect of the production process.

This development is illustrated in figure 21.5 by the large commercial farms in position 9. Farms in this position increase both the output and the profits of those operations without increasing their size, which to this point has most often been measured in terms of acres farmed. In the industrialized farm of the 1980s emphasis is on the development of efficient production processes, not the farming of additional acres. In this industrialized orientation the continuous upward pressure on land prices should be reduced.

Whether the cost structures of firms in positions 3 through 9 will, through some form of the treadmill, rise to the target price level in figure 21.5 remains to be seen. One reason why this may not occur is, of course, because the political market, as of 1992, is in the process of lowering levels of income support (i.e., target prices) throughout agriculture. Another reason is that the development of a unique production process on a particular farm by an innovative owner-manager, a process that cannot be readily copied and applied to another particular farm, means that originator of that production process should be able to hold on to the profits from such a process for an extended period of time. But one would be foolish to predict that the profits indicated for a firm in position 9 could be held indefinitely. Those profits will attract competition in some form, and the treadmill will reappear in a new form.

Economic and Political Realities

We do not in the four vignettes attempt a full and complete description of all that happened in the American farm sector in the 1970s and 1980s. We attempted to represent in these vignettes the major developments in the commercial agriculture of the United States in the 1970s and 1980s. Some critics might say that the vignettes represent the imagination of the author. Imagination was involved in creating those representative pictures, but it is our position that those representations are in accord both with the economic factors of the period and with economic theory.

First, the vignettes were produced within the actual pricing parameters of the period, both market and government. Second, while total farm numbers declined, the number of large and very large farms increased. Third, land transactions — the sale and purchase of land — for the most part took place between persons living in the same county, indicating that most farmland sold during this period was acquired by neighbors. Fourth, the vignettes take account of and reflect the land boom of the 1970s and farm depression of the 1980s.

With respect to economic theory the firm cost functions, although not constructed from actual data, are consistent with traditional theory in their shape and behavior. The shifting of the firm cost structures to the right along an essentially flat long-run planning curve is consistent with much empirical information about the economics of farm size in agriculture. And the treadmill itself is an adaptation to the farm scene of Professor Schumpeter's theory of economic development.[3] The vignettes put all these facts and theory together to "explain" the development of American agriculture in the 1970s and 1980s.

It is clear from the material presented in this chapter that the profit, or loss, position of a farm firm at any particular time is dependent on three largely unrelated developments. The first is the skill a manager exhibits in reducing the unit costs of the firm, as well as expanding its scale of operations. The second development, for the grains in particular, is what happens in the world market for those grains, and hence to the market price confronting the individual grain producer in the United States. The third is what actions the government takes, or does not take, in providing price and income support to the individual farm producer.

As we observed in the 1971 vignette, the skill of the manager in reducing his or her costs and expanding the size of the operation played the dominant role. In the 1974 vignette, the dramatic rise in the market price of corn overshadowed all other developments in that time period. The 1988 vignette makes two points: first, the importance of target prices and deficiency payments to the income position of most corn producers in that time period and, second, the emergence of the industrialized farm with tightly controlled and refined production processes.

The innovative, skilled manager thus controls only one aspect of his or her economic destiny, namely, improving the production efficiency of the firm. What happens in the world market and the national political market is beyond his or her control. Consequently commercial farmers have banded together in commodity associations to seek from their government price and income protection from the volatile world market in which they must operate (see figure 21.1). This is as it should be. But what is not as it should be, is the overgenerous response of the national government. It is one thing to provide commercial grain farmers with a safety net in the event of a precipitous price decline; it is another to guarantee grain farmers a generous economic return, as the government did in the setting of the target price above $3.00 per bushel for corn between 1984 and 1987 and only slightly below $3.00 in 1988 and 1989. In the judgment of this writer the government should have held to the target price of $2.40 per bushel, as of 1981, with a somewhat lower loan rate. This would have provided corn farmers with an important amount of income protection in the middle 1980s and reduced the horrendous cost of government programs during that period.

Another thing the federal government could and should do, to benefit both consumers and producers, is to operate a legitimate grain reserve program to even out the great swings in world grain prices. It would buy grain in periods of oversupply and falling prices, and sell grain in periods of short supply and rising prices — *not to raise the long-term level of grain prices*,[4] but to moderate market price swings such as those that took place in the 1970s and 1980s as shown in figure 21.1. In a world of moderate price swings the farm manager should be able to control his or her own economic destiny through improving the production methods and reducing the production costs of the enterprises involved. In a world of moderate price level movements, the industrial age in farming as discussed in chapter 18 can flourish; but when product prices are gyrating in an extreme and unpredictable fashion the farm entrepreneur must run for cover and wait for the price storm to blow over before investing in new and improved production processes.

Suggested Readings

Agricultural Outlook. U.S. Department of Agriculture, Economic Research Service, October 1991, pp. 32–39.

Breimyer, Harold F. "The Changing American Farm." *The New Rural American. The Annals of the American Academy of Political and Social Science*, 429 (January 1977), pp. 12–22.

Cochrane, Willard W., and Runge, C. Ford. *Reforming Farm Policy: Toward a National Agenda*. Ames: Iowa State Press, 1992.

Farm Futures: The Business Magazine for Agriculture. P.O. Box 11652, Des Moines, IA 50340; recent and current issues.

V. Summation

CHAPTER 22

SOME CONCLUDING THOUGHTS

What Have We Learned?

In the nearly two-hundred-year period from 1607 to 1775 agriculture in the thirteen colonies developed very slowly. As late as 1760 settlements still hugged the Atlantic coastline, except where they followed accessible rivers inland. Many of the first settlers were adventurers, not farmers; and all had to learn to farm in a strange new land with a dense forest cover, a thin, rocky soil for the most part, and unknown climatic patterns. The first settlers learned how to plant and raise tobacco and corn from the native American Indians. They also brought horses, cattle, and pigs from Europe. And slowly, very slowly, they learned, mostly by trial and error, to farm the Atlantic coastal plain and the river valleys running into it.

By the time of the American Revolution, 1775–83, a surplus of rice was being produced around Charleston, South Carolina, a major crop of tobacco for export in Maryland, Virginia, and North Carolina, a surplus of grain on the better farmland around Philadelphia, and New England had developed an important export trade in fish, lumber, and rum. The white settlers on the frontier raised a little corn for home consumption, turning any surplus into corn whiskey to trade, either with the Indians for furs and skins or with local merchants for salt, powder and shot, and simple tools and cloth. All this was occurring east of the Appalachian uplift.

During the Revolution and in the years immediately thereafter frontiersmen were pushing over the ridges, down the valleys, and through the gaps in the Appalachian uplift. By 1790 the trails and pathways through and around this mountainous barrier were well known and established; thus the gates into the great interior lowlands were open. Through these gates poured a flood of emigrants seeking new fertile lands on which to settle. At first they came principally from the Eastern seaboard, then from the British Isles, then from all over Northern Europe — all pulled by the lure of abundant land, cheap or free, that they could make their own. Prior to the Civil War they could purchase this land at public auction at one to three dollars an acre, or from a land speculator at a somewhat higher price, or if they had the nerve they could squat on Indian land free of charge, which many did. After the Civil War they could homestead 160 acres of land for a small filing fee (ten dollars in the first years), or they could purchase land, perhaps better located, from the railroads or from various state agencies. This great land rush lasted till about 1900; by then most of the public domain that could be farmed with any chance of success had been sold or given away to private parties.

The life of the pioneers both east and west of the Mississippi River was unbelievably hard. There were Indian attacks, credit crises, sickness and accidents, loneliness and homesickness, and sometimes starvation. There were no public services to fall back upon, except an occasional military fort. Many failed and stole away from their creditors in the night, some sold out to a new wave of settlers, but some succeeded and turned a log cabin in a clearing in the forest or a sodhouse on the open prairie into a commercial farm.

The pioneers in the great interior lowlands, from their experience east of the Appalachians, usually had a pretty fair idea what crops were suitable to that area; it was corn and livestock north of the Ohio River, tobacco and corn in the Upper South, and cotton and corn in the Deep South. The pioneer did, however, have a twofold problem: (1) how to increase the production of their farms to a point where there was a surplus for sale and (2) how or where to sell that surplus once it came into existence. The first part of the problem was resolved through backbreaking labor by the family abetted by a continuous stream of labor-saving machinery — efficient plows, horse-driven cultivators, and all sorts of harvesting equipment. The second part of the problem was resolved in the North, at least, by the coming of the railroads; in the South the steamboat on the inland rivers played a similar role. Out of these developments a great and highly productive national farm plant had taken shape by the end of the nineteenth century.

This was a period of extensive growth. The national farm plant became more productive through the adding of one farm after another. Crop yields did not increase in the nineteenth century, and livestock production efficiency increased very little. But the extensive growth was so great, and the expansion in total farm output so great, that farmers were confronted with low prices and hard times from 1870 to 1896.

There were, however, some dark sides to the nineteenth-century success story of agricultural development. The native American Indians were driven from their tribal homelands and relocated on small, inhospitable reservations. The expansion of the cotton industry in the Deep South was based on black slave labor. To make way for the farms in mid-America the great hardwood forests were cut down; to build the houses, barns, fences, and towns of mid-America the great white pine forests were cut down; and in the mad rush to bring all of mid-America under the plow, much of the fertile topsoil of that land was washed away and into the Gulf of Mexico. The pioneers tamed most of the continent in one century, but at a terrible cost to the environment and to the people involved.

As the great westward expansion and settlement came to a close around the turn of the twentieth century, the flow of human labor into agriculture slowed to a trickle between 1900 and 1910 and became negative between 1910 and 1920. Agriculture crossed a watershed between 1910 and 1920, shifting from an extensive form of development with expanding employment opportunities to an intensive form with contracting employment opportunities. And the decline in human labor employed in agriculture, which began in the decade 1910-20, continued throughout the twentieth century, even as it continues today (1992).

Farmers continued to invest in labor-saving machinery in the period 1900-1920; this was the period that tractors and trucks first made their appearance on American farms. But no major technological advances took place on American farms during this period, to substitute for the declining input of land and labor on farms. As a consequence factor productivity actually declined during this period, and total farm output increased only moderately. But this slowed economic development in agriculture did not hurt farmers; to the contrary, with total farm output lagging behind demand, farm prices rose steadily between 1896 and 1914, and soared between 1914 and 1920. The period 1910–14 is often described as the "golden age" of American agriculture.

American farmers entered into a depression in 1921 from which they did not recover until the advent of World War II. But two important developments occurred in this twenty-year period. First, new and improved technologies began to flow forth from the Land Grant colleges and agribusiness firms. The Land Grant colleges that were inaugurated way back in the 1860s began their technological payoff in the period 1920–40; but the farm depression of the period kept farmers from taking full advantage of the flow of new and improved technologies in the period 1920–1940. Second, the federal government intervened in the farm economy in an important way to provide price and income support for farmers. Those commodity programs of price and income support, in somewhat revised form, are still with us in 1992.

With the end of World War II, the backlog of production technologies, and farmers generally in strong financial positions, farmers jammed these new and improved technologies into their farming operations and the decade of the 1950s turned into one of the most dynamic in the history of American agriculture. Farmers adopted the new technologies at a rapid pace, output per unit of input increased dramatically, total farm output increased significantly, farm prices and incomes declined, the commodity programs of price and income support became major operations and farmers went out of business in record numbers. The treadmill ground on in a relentless fashion.

This process of intensive development, with farmers adopting new and improved technologies, factor productivity increasing, total farm output increasing, and farmers going out of business, continued over the period 1960–90. But several points with regard to this thirty-year period need to be noted. First, the international export market became increasingly important to farmers during the period; but this export market is unpredictable and subject to large shifts in demand, with the consequence that it has given rise to large fluctuations in domestic farm prices and incomes. Second, the structure of American farming has changed dramatically; this has occurred as the assets of the smaller, less efficient producers, who went out of business, were gobbled up by their larger, more aggressive farmer neighbors. This, of course, has made these large, aggressive farmers even larger, so that by 1990 some 320,000 large to very large farms produced and sold 77 percent of the total national product. Third, this process of intensive development had progressed to the stage in the 1980s where, we argue, farming had crossed, or was crossing, another watershed. This new stage we call the "industrial age" of farming. The essence of this industrial age is control — control by management over the usage of resources and technologies in the production process to obtain maximum efficiency.

Just as in the extensive development of the nineteenth century, there has been a dark side to the intensive development of agriculture in the twentieth century. Literally millions of farm families have been forced off the land, as they failed in the tough competitive business of farming. And the intensive farming practices of the twentieth century involving continuous cropping and heavy applications of chemical fertilizers and pesticides have contributed to soil erosion, pollution of surface and ground waters, and the further destruction of wildlife. There were, however, signs in the 1980s that the degradation of the environment through intensive farming, at least in the United States, was slowing down. There is reason to hope, as of 1992, that after nearly four centuries of wantonly destroying our physical environment, we are, through more enlightened self-interest and more rational government policies, bringing the worst aspects of that destruction to an end in the agricultural sector.

From this entire volume, and this brief review, the reader should recognize that agricultural development is an unending, ever changing, process. Economic and physical conditions give rise to problems, the resolution of those problems gives rise to economic development, that development in the context of new conditions gives rise to new problems, and so it goes. A key point of this historical study, to which we will return later in this chapter, is that, if we understand the past, we have the best knowledge base that is available for dealing with new problems arising out of new sets of conditions. The best guide for anticipating the future, we argue, is an understanding of what has transpired in the past.

General Uses of Historical Analysis

First, it should be recognized that some people are interested in learning about, and coming to know about, some aspects of their historical background, not for the power that such knowledge may give them for dealing with the future, but for the sheer pleasure that coming to know and understand the past gives them. Readers of the works of Bruce Catton dealing with the American Civil War will understand this point, as well as the many, many readers of such popular historians as Bernard De Voto, Barbara W. Tuchman, and Arthur M. Schlesinger, Jr. For these people, coming to know and understand their historical background, or some aspect of social development, is important in and of itself; these people receive a deep sense of satisfaction from knowing how their family or their nation or their civilization evolved. And many people must also feel this way about the development of American agriculture, because that development process played a dominant role in American civilization for at least 300 years.

Second, knowing and understanding the various and relevant historical processes provides observers of, and actors in, current events and developments with a needed perspective on those events and developments. Those who know and understand the relevant historical processes will not see each current event as an independent episode. They will see each event as part of a process which they understand; hence they will have some understanding and appreciation of how that event came to pass, its potential magnitude, its duration, and its various implications. For observers or actors with historical perspectives, a current event does not stand out as an independent, or accidental, event; the event had a cause and it will have future implications; it is simply the current expression of a historical process.

Whether individuals with the knowledge of the relevant historical process, and the society of which they are a part, can control the event and direct it to their advantage is a different matter. For example, man and society cannot control the event of an earthquake. But an earthquake is no longer viewed as an independent, accidental event. It is part of an evolving process that is measured not in historical time but in geological time and a process that, as of 1990, is rapidly coming to be understood and appreciated. The event of a modern business recession is somewhat comparable to the event of an earthquake. Members of a capitalistic society have considerable perspective on a modern business recession. But the occurrence of a modern business recession cannot be predicted with any degree of reliability, and great confusion and controversy surround every corrective action taken to prevent or cope with such recessions.

Nonetheless, it is argued here that it is better to view the events noted above, and every other event, as part of a process through time rather than as independent accidents, or acts of God. As the more important historical processes come to be understood with greater clarity and incisiveness, actions taken to direct such processes to the advantage of society can be more effective and should be less controversial.

Third, historical description, historical analysis, and historical data series can and do provide the grist out of which to construct and test theories of economic development and rigorous economic models, conceptual or quantitative. Historical description can and does suggest the important, or key, variables to include in a theory, or a model. Historical analysis can and does provide hypotheses concerning the relationships among the variables included in a theory, or a model. And historical data series enable the model builders to estimate the parameters of the theoretical system under consideration.

Theories and models of development cannot and do not jump full-blown from the minds of theorists living in isolation. They emerge over time from the minds of individuals who have experienced development firsthand and who have carefully studied the historical record of countries undergoing development. Historical description provides the facts and data with regard to development. Historical analysis begins to order those facts and data and provide a description of the shape and direction of the development process. From this work the theorist can formulate hypotheses regarding the behavior of key variables and the interaction among those variables, and perhaps build a theory of development.[1] Later empiricists employing both the theory and the historical data series may build econometric or other types of quantitative models to provide estimates of the relationships among important variables in the development process.[2] This is the way the analytical process operates. Hundreds of historical studies involving data collection, historical description, and historical analysis provide the raw materials out of which first theories, or conceptual models, with increased explanatory power are formulated[3] and then second empirical models are constructed and estimated.

Fourth, decision makers in government, in business, and in various kinds of organizations often study the historical record — turn to past experience — for guidance in making current decisions. The historical record often provides hints regarding the causes of operational and policy errors made in the past that may be avoided in the future, as well as success stories that might be duplicated. Further, part of the virtue of historical analysis is that it provides a view of what may be reoccurring situations or processes. Hence a current situation or process or policy that has reoccurred can be appraised in terms of past experience.

Such a general procedure, however, has both its good and bad aspects. In making current policy decisions it is reasonable to review and study the decisions made by comparable units of society in *similar* situations in the past. The short- and long-run consequences of such historical decisions can be analyzed and appraised, and conclusions can be reached concerning the desirability or undesirability of such decisions. But such a procedure can result in ill-advised, or even false, guidance in making current policy decisions, *if* conclusions are drawn directly and without qualification from a study of past situations and decisions where the situations are not similar. In short, employing historical precedent to guide current policy decisions can produce disastrous results, where the current situation differs in certain important respects from the original historical situation.

Does this mean, then, that the historical record should never be used as a guide to current decision making, since the current situation will rarely, if ever, be exactly similar to some historical situation? Clearly, the answer is no. But in using the historical record, or historical precedent, in guiding current policy decision making, the decision makers must recognize that the drawing of direct and superficial analogies to some historical period or event can be misleading. In using the past as a guide to making a decision about a future course of action, the approach must involve a careful analysis, a comparative analysis, of the periods involved. Practitioners of this procedure must know and understand the historical period or event or process under consideration and know and understand the current period or event or process for which the policy decision applies. Similarities and dissimilarities between the historical and current situations can then be identified, and consideration given to their differences, in the formulation of a current decision. As a result, the current decision will almost certainly be modified, or take a somewhat different direction, from the policy decision in the historical situation. In this analytical procedure the lessons of history are brought to bear on current policy decision making but not in a rotelike way. Through comparative analysis only the elements of the historical situation that are relevant to the current situation, that have a bearing on the current decision process, are considered.

It may be argued that the above type of historical comparative analysis is not easily done in an unbiased manner. And such an argument has much validity. Different practitioners of historical analysis tend to produce different historical analyses with different conclusions, just as different builders of quantitative models produce different kinds of models that generate different quantitative answers. This happens because analysts of both persuasions differ in their training, creativeness, and beliefs and values.

Nonetheless, current policy decisions dealing with prospective developments are made, and must be made, all the time. And knowledge of the historical past, whether it be incorporated into a historical comparative analysis, as suggested here, or into a quantitative model that may be projected into the future, is our only firm or solid guide for making those policy decisions. Thus it seems appropriate to recognize here in an overt manner the use of historical analysis in the making of current policy decisions, since, in fact, it takes place all the time with more or less skill.

Specific Uses of This Historical Analysis

The historical analysis of the development of American agriculture presented in this volume is likely to find its greatest use among formal students of agriculture in American colleges and universities. It will provide them with the basic facts of that development, order those facts for them into a concept of a process, and indicate to them the unending nature of that process. Formal students of agriculture can learn whence the modern agriculture of the 1990s came and the direction in which it is trending; hence they can come to appreciate the transitory nature of the present state of American agriculture. In this sense formal students of agriculture can gain a perspective on current and prospective developments in American agriculture.

Students of agricultural development should gain additional insights from this historical analysis. The extreme complexity of the agricultural development process should be apparent from the analysis. The multidimensional aspects of agricultural development should become explicit in this analysis. Finally, the generalized model of agricultural development presented in part IV should help the formal student of agricultural development forge his or her own explanatory, conceptual model of agricultural development for the country and the period that is of interest to him or her.

Foreign students of agricultural development can gain the same insights into the agricultural development process as those described for this general category of students directly above. This historical analysis should make it clear to foreign students from the developing world how difficult the process of agricultural development has been even for a country as richly endowed with natural resources as the United States. Further, the analysis should dramatize for such students the unending character of the agricultural development process. The problems confronting American agriculture in the 1990s are very different from those that confronted it in the 1890s or the 1790s, but they are no less difficult and no more tractable. The process of agricultural development does not come to an end when a nation achieves the status of a developed nation, however defined. The economic problems confronting American farmers in 1990, in the uncertain and unstable world in which they find themselves, are just as difficult and perhaps more unmanageable than those that confronted American farmers in 1890. Agricultural development is an unending process.

Finally, there are few, if any, policy answers that farm leaders and farm politicians can lift directly from this historical analysis of American agricultural development for use in solving current farm problems. But farm leaders and farm politicians can gain from this analysis knowledge and understanding of the development process in American agriculture — how the process operates, the supply response of producers, the nature and growth of demand, the behavior of farm prices, the distribution of income and wealth, and on and on. And on the basis of this knowledge and understanding, it should become clear to farm leaders and farm politicians, if they are willing to listen, why certain past policies have produced unexpected results, why certain other policies have created more problems than they have solved, and why certain kinds of policies will be required in the future to cope with existing and emerging problems. But there are few, if any, pat answers.

In sum, this historical analysis cannot be used as a cookbook. It does, however, provide the basis for formulating policies that have the capacity to deal effectively with the emergent problems of the food and agricultural sector. It does this because it provides knowledge and understanding of the operation of the food and agricultural sector in a dynamic, developmental context.

A Look at the 1990s and Beyond

As we look into the immediate future and beyond with respect to American agriculture, based on historical facts, trends, and analysis, what might we expect? First, let us recognize that there will be some developments that, as of 1992, are clearly unexpected. After recovering from the surprise, or possibly even shock, of the unexpected it may well be that we can discover clues to the unexpected and how to deal with such developments by studying the historical past. But we cannot discuss in this volume what is unknown to us.

Based on the past there are four areas in which we can expect developments that merit discussion at this time: (1) the future development of farm firms in the industrial age; (2) the role of American agriculture in an increasingly global market; (3) the implication for American agriculture of rising energy costs — perhaps slowly at first and then more sharply; and (4) the implication for the world in general, and American agriculture in particular, of global warming and the unpredictable shifts in weather patterns that will accompany it.

Large-scale commercial farms did not move into the industrial age, with tightly controlled production processes, overnight. Farm firms have been trending in this direction since crossing the watershed of 1900–1920. The aggressive, innovative farmers have for seventy years reduced the costs of their operations through the continuous adoption of new and improved technologies and have expanded the size of their operations by gobbling up the resources of their laggard neighbors. But this trend had so changed the organization and operations of large-scale commercial farms by the 1980s and early 1990s, that the author believed it was proper to argue that such farms had entered a new age — a mature industrial age. The productivity data for the decade of the 1980s presented in table 18.2 signaled for the author the crossover of large-scale commercial farming into this new age. Total farm output increased in that decade, it will be recalled, through large increases in factor productivity as inputs in all factor lines declined. The production processes in farming had become so efficient by the decade of the 1980s that farmers could increase aggregate output even as they reduced their total input of productive resources.

There is no reason why the trends that carried commercial farming to and over the watershed of the 1980s and 1990s should not continue into the twenty-first century. The research and technological development base is in place and functioning well, although it could be improved through increased funding. The technology of electronic information systems, by which farm managers are able to gain effective control over the use of resources and technologies in the production process, is still in its infancy; farmers are still learning how to use this technology to their advantage. And owner-managers of large-scale commercial farms are coming into these positions better educated, with more management skills, than ever before. The way is open in the future for the development on commercial farms of highly productive production processes with probably less emphasis on the extensive factor, land, and more emphasis on new and improved biological, chemical, and mechanical technologies, all controlled by the more effective use of electronic information systems.

If they are to prosper, these highly productive large-scale commercial farms will require both an expanding and a stable export market. If the picture of commercial farming operations that we have described is the correct one, then a strong competitive position for American commercial farms in the export market is assured. The problem, or problems, for American farm producers will be, first, expanding the export market and, second, achieving more stability in it. The resolution of both of those problems extends far beyond the individual farm gate. Expanding the export market will require action by the federal government at two levels: (1) continuous negotiation both multilaterally and bilaterally to reduce trade barriers at home and abroad and (2) the pursuit of fiscal and monetary policies that contribute to economic prosperity worldwide and produce capital flows and exchange rates that are conducive to the increased export of American farm products. In the past the U.S. government has worked hard, but not always wisely, at reducing trade barriers through negotiations; but it has pursued domestic fiscal and monetary policies that have impacted negatively on its export of both farm and industrial products. We can only hope that the federal government will be more successful in the future than it has been in the past in reducing the trade barriers of individual countries to the international movement of farm products, and that eventually the government of the United States will start pursuing saner fiscal policies that are reflected in financial conditions more favorable to the export of agricultural commodities.

Whether the international market for agricultural products is stable or unstable depends to an important degree on factors outside the control of American farmers and the U.S. government. The two most destabilizing factors in the international market for agricultural products are (1) variable crop-growing conditions and (2) prosperity and depression. The United States could moderate the destabilizing effects of variable crop-growing conditions in important regions of the world by operating a grain reserve program with the capacity to stabilize (*not raise*) world grain prices. And the major industrial nations of the world could go a long way toward moderating international economic fluctuations by working in concert rather than by pursuing individual courses of action. Whether these market-stabilizing efforts will be made is impossible to say. But important to this discussion is the recognition, first, that the long-run prosperity of an American agriculture is absolutely dependent upon both an expanding and stable export market, and second, that the realization of those twin economic objectives rests to an important degree upon the policies pursued by the federal government in its domestic fiscal and monetary operations and in its trade negotiations with foreign nations.

If energy prices rise in the future as suggested in chapter 16 — perhaps by 50 percent by the year 2010 and then skyrocket thereafter — this will have a major impact on world economic development as well as on American agriculture. With regard to American agriculture, such a pricing development should provide a strong incentive for farmers to move toward a low-input, minimum tillage form of cultivation. This type of energy-economizing response by farmers, and similar responses in other sectors of the economy, could have the effect of slowing the price rise for energy, but would not stop it.

As farm production costs rose with rising energy prices, the costs of food products to consumers would, of course, rise. The extent of such production cost increases, and the accompanying food price increases, cannot be predicted here with any precision. But one thing is certain: if energy prices increase, the cost of producing food products will also increase, as well as the price of food to consumers. We are not discussing a U.S. phenomenon here; this will be a worldwide development. Finally, of course, the above line of reasoning rests on the assumption that there will be no miraculous breakthrough in energy creation, hence availability, in the next twenty years. As of 1992 that would appear to be a realistic assumption, but you never know.

Concentrations of CO_2 in the atmosphere have increased importantly in recent years — from 315 parts per million (PPM) in 1958 to about 355 PPM in 1990 — as the result of the increased burning of fossil fuel and the destruction of forests; this is an established set of facts. This increased concentration of CO_2 in the atmosphere creates a "greenhouse effect," which in turn operates to warm the global climate; this is a widely accepted theory. This global warming (the global atmospheric temperature has increased almost 1°C in the past 100 years), it is believed, will cause the earth's weather patterns to shift, but by how much and where remains open to question.

The climatic developments described above have important implications for American agriculture, as well as for the rest of the world. An important shift in weather patterns could force a relocation of crop and animal production, as well as a myriad of lesser production adjustments, in the United States. But equally, or perhaps more important, as of 1992, is that we do not know where, when, or by how much the relevant weather patterns may change. Consequently, individual farmers and responsible government agencies find it next to impossible to make plans to deal with the impending weather changes, if in fact they believe that such changes are likely to occur.

There are, however, some things that the political leaders of the nation, in collaboration with the scientific community, can do. First, and foremost, the political leaders of the United States in cooperation with the political leaders of all other nations should be taking steps, effective steps, to reduce the emission of CO_2 into the atmosphere. This would limit the greenhouse effect and moderate the global-warming process. It is just possible that the taking of such steps could save modern civilization as we know it.

Second, the policy leaders in the U.S. Department of Agriculture with the assistance of the scientists in the department should be monitoring the research efforts of the scientists concerned with global warming, atmospheric changes, and climatic changes. Leaders in agriculture, both policymakers and scientists, should keep abreast of the latest facts, theories, and state of knowledge regarding global warming and its implications for changes in weather patterns.

Third, as the knowledge regarding global warming and its implications for changes in weather patterns becomes firmer, policy leaders in the Department of Agriculture should establish a team, or teams, to make plans to deal with those climatic changes that appear to be a realistic possibility. If the expected climate changes are small, such a team could help with fine-tuning the adjustments that would be called for. But if the expected climate changes are large, adjustments to them are likely to be beyond the capabilities of a single farmer, even a very large farmer, and some kinds of government programs would be called for to assist with those adjustments: relocating farmers, for example. The team should have plans ready to deal with contingencies stemming from major climatic changes.

There are people who believe that all this talk and theorizing about global warming is a bunch of nonsense; it may turn out that they are correct. But for the author the evidence is too powerful, and the consequences too catastrophic, to be ignored.[4] It is possible that global warming and its climatic consequences could have a greater impact on American agriculture, and civilization itself, in the twenty-first century than anything discussed in this volume. Some of the readers of this volume will have the opportunity to learn the truth.

Notes

NOTES

Chapter 1

1. Ole E. Rölvaag, *Giants in the Earth* (New York: Harper and Brothers, 1929); John Steinbeck, *The Grapes of Wrath* (New York: Viking Press, 1939); and James A. Michener, *Centennial* (New York: Random House, 1974).

2. For a fuller discussion of these concepts the reader may wish to refer to Charles P. Kindleberger and Bruce Herrick, *Economic Development*, 3rd ed. (New York: McGraw-Hill, 1977), chaps. 1 and 2; and Douglass C. North, *Growth and Welfare in the American Past: A New Economic History*, 2nd ed. (Englewood Cliffs, N.J.: Prentice-Hall, 1974), chaps. 1 and 2.

3. See, for example, the studies by Daryll E. Ray and Earl O. Heady, *Simulated Effects of Alternative Policy and Economic Environments on U.S. Agriculture*, Center for Agricultural and Rural Development, Report 46T, Iowa State University, Ames, Iowa, March 1974; and Frederick J. Nelson and Willard W. Cochrane, "Economic Consequences of Federal Farm Commodity Programs, 1953–72," *Agricultural Economics Research*, 28 (April 1976), pp. 52–64.

4. Paul W. Gates, *The Farmer's Age: Agriculture 1815–1860*, vol. III of *The Economic History of the United States* (New York: Holt, Rinehart, and Winston, 1960); and Fred A. Shannon, *The Farmer's Last Frontier: Agriculture, 1860–1897*, vol. V of *The Economic History of the United States* (New York: Farrar and Rinehart, 1945).

5. Thomas N. Urban, "Agricultural Industrialization: It's Inevitable." *Choices: The Magazine of Food Farm and Resources Issues*, fourth quarter, 1991.

Chapter 2

1. A good brief description of the early settlements may be found in Peter N. Carroll and David W. Noble, *The Restless Centuries: A History of the American People* (Minneapolis: Burgess Publishing, 1973), chaps. 3 and 4. A fuller discussion may be found in John E.

Pomfret, *Founding of the American Colonies: 1583–1660* (New York: Harper and Row, 1970). But anyone who wants to explore the colonization period in depth must turn to Charles M. Andrews, *The Colonial Period of American History*, vols. I-IV (New Haven: Yale University Press, 1934).

2. See B. H. Slicher van Bath, *The Agrarian History of Western Europe, A.D. 500–1850* (London: Edward Arnold Publishers, 1963), pp. 239–62.

3. Yujiro Hayami and Vernon W. Ruttan, *Agricultural Development: An International Perspective* (Baltimore: Johns Hopkins Press, 1971), p. 28.

4. Ross M. Robertson, *History of the American Economy*, 2nd ed. (New York: Harcourt, Brace, and World, 1964), p. 47.

Chapter 3

1. Curtis P. Nettels, *The Emergence of a National Economy, 1775–1815*, vol. II of *The Economic History of the United States* (New York: Holt, Rinehart, and Winston, 1962), p. 140.

2. The specific provisions of the Ordinances of 1785 and 1787 may be conveniently reviewed in Ross M. Robertson and James L. Pate, eds., *Readings in United States Economic and Business History* (Boston: Houghton Mifflin, 1966), pp. 181–85.

3. Whitney was involved in litigation over patent rights to the cotton gin for many years, but most authorities agree that Whitney did in fact invent the cotton gin.

Chapter 4

1. Paul W. Gates, *The Farmer's Age: Agriculture 1815–1860*, vol. III of *The Economic History of the United States* (New York: Holt, Rinehart, and Winston, 1960), p. 72.

2. Robert E. Gallman, "Human Capital in the First 80 Years of the Republic: How Much Did America Owe the Rest of the World?" *The American Economic Review*, 67, no. 1 (February 1977), p. 31.

3. The Indian chief, Red Eagle, was part white, and his white man's name was Bill Weatherford.

4. The word "Ecunchate" means, or refers to, the "Holy Ground" on which the Creek Indian nation lived.

5. Gloria Jahoda, *The Trail of Tears* (New York: Holt, Rinehart, and Winston, 1975), pp. 15–18.

6. Grant Foreman, *Indian Removal, The Civilization of the American Indian* Series (Norman, Okla.: University of Oklahoma Press, 1953), preface.

7. The economics of slavery may be explored in two articles: Ulrich B. Phillips, "The Economic Cost of Slaveholding in the Cotton Belt," and Alfred H. Conrad and John R. Meyer, "The Economics of Slavery in the Ante Bellum South." Key portions of these writings are reprinted in Ross M. Robertson and James L. Pate, eds., *Readings in United States Economic and Business History* (Boston: Houghton Mifflin, 1966), pp. 195–207.

8. William Cronon, *Nature's Metropolis: Chicago and the Great West* (New York: W. W. Norton, 1991).

Chapter 5

1. Walter Prescott Webb, *The Great Plains* (New York: Houghton Mifflin, 1936), p. 156. And reprinted in the Webb volume by permission of the publisher Arthur H. Clark Co. from their Early Western Travels series, vol. XVII, pp. 147–48.

2. *Ibid.*, p. 17.

3. Fred A. Shannon, *The Farmer's Last Frontier: Agriculture, 1860–1897*, vol. V of *The Economic History of the United States* (New York: Farrar and Rinehart, 1945), p. 53.

4. Ross M. Robertson, *History of the American Economy*, 2nd ed. (New York: Harcourt, Brace, and World, 1964), p. 251.

5. Shannon, *The Farmer's Last Frontier*, p. 59.

6. For an evaluation of the Homestead Law see Paul Wallace Gates, "The Homestead Law in an Incongruous Land System," *The American Historical Review*, 41, no. 4 (July 1936), pp. 652–81.

7. As recounted by Gilbert C. Fite in his volume *The Farmers' Frontier, 1865–1900* (New York: Holt, Rinehart, and Winston, 1966), p. 38.

8. Douglass C. North, *Growth and Welfare in the American Past: A New Economic History*, 2nd ed. (Englewood Cliffs, N.J.: Prentice-Hall, 1974), pp. 130–31.

9. See the discussion by Everett E. Edwards, "American Agriculture — the First 300 Years," *Farmers in a Changing World, 1940 Yearbook of Agriculture.* Washington, D.C.: Government Printing Office, 1940, pp. 263–65.

Chapter 6

1. Walter Lord, *The Good Years: From 1900 to the First World War* (New York: Harper and Brothers, 1960), pp. 2–3.

2. Nicknamed after his county, Tama County, Iowa.

3. Murray R. Benedict, *Farm Policies of the United States, 1790–1950: A Study of Their Origins and Development* (New York: Twentieth Century Fund, 1953), p. 200.

4. *Ibid.*, pp. 200–201.

5. *Ibid.*, p. 201. All selections reprinted by permission.

Chapter 7

1. For a good analysis of the way in which the technology — hybrid corn — was generated and propagated in U.S. agriculture see Zvi Griliches, "Hybrid Corn: An Exploration in the Economics of Technical Change," *Econometrica*, 25, no. 4 (October 1957), pp. 501–22.

2. Commission on Food and Marketing, Report of the Commission, *Food from Farmer to Consumer* (Washington, D.C.: Government Printing Office, June 1966), p. 100.

3. *Ibid.*, p. 2.

4. See the studies by Daryll E. Ray and Earl O. Heady, *Simulated Effects of Alternative Policy and Economic Environments on U.S. Agriculture*, Center for Agricultural and Rural Development, Report 4GT, Iowa State University, Ames, Iowa, March 1974; and Frederick J. Nelson and Willard W. Cochrane, "Economic Consequences of Federal Farm Commodity Programs, 1953–72," *Agricultural Economics Research*, 28 (April 1976), pp. 52–64.

5. For detailed program expenditure and cost information see Willard W. Cochrane and Mary E. Ryan, *American Farm Policy, 1948–1973* (Minneapolis: University of Minnesota Press, 1976), chap. 8.

6. Edwin G. Nourse, Joseph S. Davis, and John D. Black, *Three Years of the Agricultural Adjustment Administration* (Washington, D.C.: Brookings Institution, 1937), p. 23.

7. U.S., Department of Agriculture, *The New Farm Act: A Short Summary of the Provisions of the Agricultural Adjustment Act of 1938*, General Information Series Pub. No. G-83, February 1938.

8. The historical detail of this struggle may be traced in Cochrane and Ryan, *American Farm Policy*, pts. I and II.

9. For a full discussion of rural poverty see *The People Left Behind*, A Report by the President's National Advisory Commission on Rural Poverty, Washington, D.C., September 1967.

Chapter 8

1. For a good, brief discussion of these causes, as well as the relevant trade data, see Donna U. Vogt, *Agricultural Exports: Overview and Selected Data*, CRS Report for Congress, Congressional Research Service, Library of Congress, January 12, 1990.

2. For a review of this period see Willard W. Cochrane, *Feast or Famine: The Uncertain World of Food and Agriculture and Its Policy Implications for the United States*, National Planning Association, Report No. 136, February 1974.

3. This and the following section of this chapter rely heavily on the historical input-output data presented in *Production and Efficiency Statistics 1989*, and earlier issues, U.S. Department of Agriculture, Economic Research Service, ECIFS9-4, April 1991.

4. The farm politics and policies of this period may be reviewed in Willard W. Cochrane and C. Ford Runge, *Reforming Farm Policy: Toward a National Agenda*, (Ames: Iowa State Press, 1992), Chaps. 3 and 5, and David Rapp, *How the U.S. Got into Agriculture: And Why It Can't Get Out*, Congressional Quarterly, Washington, D.C., 1988.

5. For definitions of these and other terms employed in the farm programs of the federal government see *National Food Review*, U.S. Department of Agriculture, Economic Research Service, January-March 1990, vol. 13, issue 1, Glossary; or Rapp, *How the U.S. Got into Agriculture: And Why It Can't Get Out*.

6. For a description of how the complicated commodity provisions will work in the "1990 Farm Bill" see *The 1990 Farm Act and the 1990 Budget Reconciliation Act: How U.S. Farm Policy Mechanisms Will Work under the New Legislation*, U.S. Department of Agriculture, Economic Research Service, November 1990.

7. For one version see Robert L. Paarlberg, "How Agriculture Blocked the Uruguay Round," *SAIS Review*, vol. 12, no. 1 (Winter-Spring 1992).

Chapter 9

1. For a description of the human suffering and personal triumphs read Mari Sandoz, *Old Jules* (Boston: Little, Brown, 1935).

2. This figure of 147 million acres is larger than the figure of 80 million acres cited in chapter 5 for two reasons. First, the definition used here is more inclusive than that used in chapter 5. Second, much land was homesteaded in Montana, Wyoming, and other Rocky Mountain states after 1900.

3. A description and discussion of the various land acts passed between 1800 and 1862 are to be found in chapters 3, 4, and 5.

4. Vernon Carstensen, ed., *The Public Lands: Studies in the History of the Public Domain* (Madison: University of Wisconsin Press, 1968), pp. xxii–xxiv.

5. *Ibid.*, p. xxv.

6. James Wilson, "The American Farmer of To-Day," in *The Making of America*, vol. V of *Agriculture*, ed. Robert M. La Follette (Chicago: De Bower, Chapline, 1907), pp. 14–15.

7. Douglass C. North, *Growth and Welfare in the American Past: A New Economic History*, 2nd ed. (Englewood Cliffs, N.J.: Prentice-Hall, 1974), p. 127.

Chapter 10

1. The resources employed will not be the same, or used in the same way. They must be employed in a new configuration unless a miracle has occurred. But to *measure* a technological advance, we must hold constant the volume of resources employed. And the only way that this can occur where different resources are employed is to hold their value constant.

2. For more information on the changing composition of physical assets in American farming see Alvin S. Tostlebe, *Capital in Agriculture: Its Formation and Financing since 1870* (Princeton, N.J.: Princeton University Press, 1957), chaps. 1 and 4.

3. This section is adapted from the section "How the Engine Works," in Willard W. Cochrane, *The City Man's Guide to the Farm Problem* (Minneapolis: University of Minnesota Press, 1965), pp. 53–58.

Chapter 11

1. As contrasted with *social* infrastructure in agricultural development, which is treated in chapter 12.

2. The term *surplus products,* as used here, and elsewhere in this volume in a developmental context, refers to supplies over and above the subsistence needs of the farm family; it is not used in a burdensome sense as the term was often used in the United States in the 1950s and 1960s.

3. George Rogers Taylor, *The Transportation Revolution, 1815–1860,* vol. IV of *The Economic History of the United States* (New York: Harper and Row, 1951), p. 31.

4. Robert W. Fogel, *Railroads and American Economic Growth* (Baltimore: Johns Hopkins Press, 1964).

5. Estimates of the amount of irrigated land in the United States vary between 40 and 50 million acres depending upon the definition of irrigation used and the year involved.

6. The 11.6 million consumers, as of 1990, include rural nonfarm residential consumers.

7. For an up-to-date look at this rapidly changing industry see the article by Dale C. Dahl and Richard J. Magnani entitled "Structural Changes in Minnesota Fertilizer Distribution," *Minnesota Agricultural Economist,* no. 602, Agricultural Extension Service, University of Minnesota, August–September 1978.

8. For a good discussion of the agricultural input industry in the 1980s see *Agricultural Input Industry Indicators in 1974–85,* U.S. Department of Agriculture, Economic Research Service, Agricultural Information Bulletin No. 534, November 1987.

9. A good description of total food system of the United States may be found in *Food Review: Focus on the Food System,* Year Book Issue, USDA, ERS, July–Sept 1991, Vol. 14, Issue 3.

Chapter 12

1. The philosophy of education and the exact text of the educational laws of 1642, 1647, and 1648 in the Massachusetts Bay Colony may be reviewed in David B. Tyack, ed., *Turning Points in American Educational History* (Waltham, Mass.: Blaisdell Publishing, 1967), chap. 1.

2. The contrasting philosophy of education in Virginia and elsewhere in the Old South is well described in Tyack, *Turning Points in American Educational History,* chap. 2.

3. Elsye Davey Larson, *Country Schoolhouse* (New York: Comet Press Books, 1958), pp. 3–5. Elsye Larson has written a lively and informative account of the role of the country schoolhouse in rural Minnesota to which persons interested in the history of rural education

may wish to turn. But I was unable to locate Elsye Larson to fully acknowledge the material quoted above.

4. Senator Morrill introduced a bill in March 1890 "to apply a portion of the proceeds of the public lands to the more complete endowment and support" of the land grant colleges. This bill was passed by Congress and signed into law by President Harrison on August 30, 1890. The 1890 law carried an annual provision of $15,000 to each state and territory and an annual increase of $1,000 for ten years, after which the annual provision would be $25,000. This law specifically stated that no distinction of race or color was to be made in the admission of students, but where separate colleges for white and black students were maintained, this would be considered in compliance with the law provided the funds were equitably divided between the two races. Thus the act of 1890 institutionalized the flow of funds into the black A & M colleges.

5. For a good account of the development of agricultural science in the United States see Margaret W. Rossiter, *The Emergence of Agricultural Science: Justus Liebig and the Americans, 1840–1880* (New Haven: Yale University Press, 1975).

6. Charles E. Rosenberg, *No Other Gods: On Science and American Social Thought* (Baltimore: Johns Hopkins University Press, 1961).

7. Many divide their time among teaching, research, and *extension*. But our discussion of the extension function falls in a later section of this chapter.

8. Carl E. Pray and Catherine Neumeyer, *Trends and Composition of Private Food and Agricultural R & D Expenditures in the United States,* Department of Agricultural Economics, Cook College, Rutgers University. February 1989, mimeograph.

9. See Alfred C. True, *A History of Agricultural Education in the United States, 1785–1925,* U.S. Department of Agriculture Miscellaneous Publication No. 36, July 1929, pp. 288–89.

10. The value of the inputs saved is assumed to run into perpetuity. However, because the rate of discount is high, the returns forthcoming far into the future do not significantly influence the computed internal rate of return.

11. Willis L. Peterson and Joseph C. Fitzharris, "The Organization and Productivity of the Federal-State Research System in the United States," Staff Paper P74-23, Dept. of Agricultural and Applied Economics, University of Minnesota, October 1974, p. 34.

12. R. G. Echeverria, "Assessing the Impact of Agricultural Research," in *Methods for Diagnosing Research System Constraints and Assessing the Impact of Agricultural Research,* vol. II, *Assessing the Impact of Agricultural Research,* ed. R. G. Echeverria (The Hague: ISNAR, 1990).

Chapter 13

1. J. R. T. Hughes, "American Economic Growth: Imported or Indigenous? What Difference Did the Beginning Make?" *The American Economic Review, Papers and Proceedings,* 67, no. 1 (February 1977), p. 16.

2. This does not include the flow of illegal immigrants into the United States in the 1970s and 1980s, which involved a high proportion of Mexicans.

3. Douglass C. North, *Growth and Welfare in the American Past,* 2nd ed. (Englewood Cliffs, N.J.: Prentice-Hall, 1974), pp. 37–39.

Chapter 14

1. It is true that the native Americans were left with some pitifully small reservations, usually on marginal land that the white Americans did not want or did not at the time think had any real value.

2. Victor Scheffer, *The Shaping of Environmentalism in America* (Seattle: University of Washington Press, 1991), page ix.

3. Clayton Koppes, "Efficiency/Equity/Esthetics: Towards a Reinterpretation of American Conservation," *Environmental Review,* 11, no. 2 (Summer 1987), pp. 127–46.

4. David Lavender, *The First in the Wilderness,* (Garden City, N.Y.: Doubleday, 1964), p. 262.

5. *Ibid.* p. 262.

6. Quoted in Joseph M. Pitulla, *American Environmental History: The Exploitation and Conservation of Natural Resources* (San Francisco: Boyd and Fraser, 1977), p. 220.

7. "Efficiency/Equity/Esthetics," pp. 129–33.

8. Quoted in Samuel P. Hays, *Conservation and the Gospel of Efficiency: The Progressive Conservation Movement, 1890–1920* (Cambridge, Mass: Harvard University Press, 1959), p. 42.

9. For a wonderful picture of the workings of Forest Service management at the local level in Montana in its beginning, 1905–15, see the novel *Dancing at the Rascal Fair* by Ivan Doig (New York: Atheneum, 1987).

10. Marston Bates, *The Forest and the Sea* (New York: Vintage Books, 1960), p. 247.

11. Barry Commoner, *The Closing Circle: Man, Nature, and Technology* (New York: Knopf, 1971), pp. 294–95.

12. "National Policy for the Environment: Politics and the Concept of Stewardship," in *Congress and the Environment,* ed. Richard A. Cooley and Geoffrey Wandesforde-Smith (Seattle: University of Washington Press, 1970), p. 208.

13. Bill McKibbin, *The End of Nature* (New York: Random House, 1989), p. 58.

14. Senator Albert Gore, Jr., in his recent book *Earth in the Balance: Ecology and the Human Spirit* (New York: Houghton Mifflin, 1992) lays out a plan to save the earth. But one reviewer upon studying the plan was overwhelmed. His reaction: it will never happen.

15. Vernon W. Ruttan, *Sustainable Growth in Agricultural Production: Poetry, Policy, and Science,* Department of Agricultural and Applied Economics, University of Minnesota, Staff Paper P91-47, November 1991.

Chapter 15

1. Adam Smith, *An Inquiry into the Nature and Causes of the Wealth of Nations,* ed. Edwin Cannan (New York: Modern Library edition by Random House, 1937), p. 651.

2. For a fuller account of this effort refer to chapter 6 of this volume and to Murray R. Benedict, *Farm Policies of the United States, 1790–1950* (New York: Twentieth Century Fund, 1953), chap. 10.

3. As will be recalled from chapter 7, the original AAA was declared unconstitutional by the Supreme Court in 1936, but new and modified versions of the AAA were substituted for the original act in 1937 and 1938.

4. Benedict, *Farm Policies of the United States,* chap. 12.

5. This struggle is told in chapter 7 of this volume and told also by Willard W. Cochrane and Mary E. Ryan in *American Farm Policy, 1948–1973* (Minneapolis: University of Minnesota Press, 1976), chaps. 2 and 3.

6. This action and development of the Federal Land Bank system are discussed in chapter 6 and in Benedict, *Farm Policies of the United States,* chaps. 8 and 12.

7. Robert L. Tontz, "Foreign Agricultural Trade Policy of the United States, 1776–1976," United States Department of Agriculture, Economic Research Service, ERS-662, Washington, D.C., January 10, 1977, pp. 7–9.

8. U.S. Department of Agriculture, Economics, Statistics, and Cooperatives Service, "An Analysis of American Agricultural Movement Proposal," *Issue Briefing Paper,* March 3, 1978, pp. 3 and 4.

Chapter 16

1. By capital deepening we mean that the amount of capital employed in producing a given amount of product has increased.

2. This section is based on the ideas and writings of John M. Brewster. The most complete treatment of American beliefs and values by John Brewster in one place is to be found in the essay "The Cultural Crisis of Our Times," from the volume *A Philosopher among Economists* (Philadelphia: J. T. Murphy, 1970).

3. The source of most of the numbers and estimates in this section is *Annual Energy Review, 1990,* U.S. Department of Energy, Energy Information Administration, Washington, D.C., May 1991.

4. For a discussion of the reasons for this planning approach on the part of governments, as well as a discussion of the concept of national development planning, see Willard W. Cochrane, *Agricultural Development Planning: Economic Concepts, Administrative Procedures, and Political Process* (New York: Praeger, 1974), chap. 3.

Chapter 17

1. The Economic Research Service has recently revised its historical productivity index—changing to an entirely new index called the Tornquist Productivity Index. We did not employ the Tornquist series in table 17.4 for three reasons: (1) the revised Tornquist series goes back only to 1948; (2) at the time this book was being revised the ERS was having problems with the Tornquist Index for the decade of the 1950s; and (3) most important, although there are year-to-year discrepancies between the old series presented in table 17.4 and the new Tornquist Index series, the basic trends since 1948 in both series are similar. And the purpose of the productivity index series in table 17.4 is to show trends over the long period 1870–1990, which the new Tornquist series could not do.

2. The discussion in this section is based upon the work of Yujiro Hayami and Vernon W. Ruttan to be found in *Agricultural Development: An International Perspective* (Baltimore: Johns Hopkins Press, 1971), chap. 6.

Chapter 18

1. It could be argued that it has crossed three. The third, the rejection of a plantation agriculture based upon black slavery, as a result of the Union victory in the Civil War, will not be discussed in this volume because the implications of that watershed crossing reached far beyond agriculture and because the crossing did not alter the basic extensive development of American agriculture in the nineteenth century. It represented a watershed in the total social development of the nation, but not in an economic developmental sense.

2. For a good brief discussion of these policies with maps see Ross M. Robertson, *History of the American Economy,* 2nd ed. (New York: Harcourt, Brace, and World, 1964), pp. 90–94.

3. This information regarding different yield rates by size of farm was provided to the author by Lloyd Teigen in a personal letter.

4. Reported in *Ag Week*, Monday, February 3, 1992, p. 36.

5. U.S. Department of Agriculture, *Yearbook of the United States Department of Agriculture, 1910*, p. 9.

6. For a discussion of this process see the section entitled "The Engine: Farm Technological Advance" in chapter 10 of this book.

Chapter 19

1. We define demand in the usual manner. By demand we have in mind the amount of product that buyers in the market stand ready to purchase at varying prices. This concept can be, and often is, expressed as a functional relation between price and quantity or geometrically as a curve.

2. See G. E. Brandow, *Interrelations among Demands for Farm Products and Implications for Control of Market Supply*, Agricultural Experiment Station, Bulletin No. 680, Pennsylvania State University, 1961; and P. S. George and G. A. King, *Consumer Demand for Food Commodities in the United States with Projections for 1980*, Giannini Foundation Monograph 26, University of California, Berkeley, March 1971.

3. The price elasticity of the export demand for American farm products continues to be a much debated subject. Some analysts believe this elasticity is much higher than is implied in the above paragraph. But the author shares the view of Dr. Abner Womack, codirector of the Food and Agricultural Policy Institute (FAPRI) when he writes that our trial-and-error process with national and international models consistently leads us in the "direction of inelastic export demand for major U.S. commodities." The use of relatively high elasticities of export demand causes their models to "spin out of control."

4. For a review of these cost concepts in the traditional theory of the firm see any standard economics textbook.

5. We use the term *size* here rather than the conventional theoretical term *scale* because the term *scale* implies a strict proportional increase in all inputs, and farms typically do not grow along a true scale line; as they grow in size they are likely to follow an expansion path that involves the use of more capital than labor.

6. Since the fixed costs of the firm are not shown on this chart, one cannot say whether profits are increased or losses are reduced.

7. For the reader interested in a more theoretical underpinning of asset fixity in farming, two references could be helpful. Oliver E. Williamson in his volume *The Economic Institutions of Capitalism* (New York: Free Press, 1985), chap. 2, has an insightful discussion of the role of asset specificity on asset fixity. And Glenn L. Johnson's discussion of agricultural factor markets in the volume *The Overproduction Trap in U.S. Agriculture* (Baltimore, Md.: Johns Hopkins University Press, 1972), chap. 2, could prove useful.

8. For the farmer who purchased his land at a low price in an earlier period, this devaluation process is only a bookkeeping operation; but for the farmer who purchased his land at a recent high price, the deflation process is real indeed.

9. For a more detailed discussion of this possible course of events, see Frederick J. Nelson and Willard W. Cochrane, "Economic Consequences of Federal Farm Commodity Programs, 1953–72," *Agricultural Economics Research*, 28 (April 1976), pp. 52–64.

10. Mordecai Ezekiel first developed the cobweb idea in the article "The Cobweb Theorem," *Quarterly Journal of Economics*, February 1938, pp. 255–80. The idea was further developed by Willard W. Cochrane in *Farm Prices: Myth and Realty* (Minneapolis: University of Minnesota Press, 1958), chap. 4

Chapter 20

1. The government makes a loan to a participating farmer on the commodity produced by him at the guaranteed price support level. If the price of the commodity in the market falls to or below the loan rate, the farmer can, if he wishes, turn the commodity over to the government and keep the monies obtained by the loan. If the price of the commodity in the market rises above the loan rate, the farmer can sell his commodity, pay off the loan, and pocket the difference.

2. On the condition that the mandatory control provision was approved in referendum by two-thirds of the producers of that commodity.

3. The market clears when the amount demanded is equal to the amount supplied at the equilibrium price — at price P_M in the free market situation in chart A of figure 20.1 and at price P_S with government intervention.

4. The costs of all these programs to the government can be reviewed in detail in Willard W. Cochrane and Mary E. Ryan, *American Farm Policy, 1948–1973* (Minneapolis: University of Minnesota Press, 1976), chap. 8.

5. These purchase operations typically occur only at or near the level of price support; hence the demand curve D_2D_2 in figure 20.1, chart A, is drawn to extend over a limited range of prices.

6. The most famous of those studies was *Report from the United States Department of Agriculture and a Statement from Land Grant Colleges, IRM-1, Advisory Committee on Farm Price and Income Projections, 1960–65, under Conditions Approximating Free Production and Marketing of Agricultural Commodities,* S. Doc. 77, 86th Congress, 2nd Sess., January 20, 1960. For a full list of such studies, see Cochrane and Ryan, *American Farm Policy,* chap. 9, n. 1.

7. *Reforming Farm Policy: Toward a National Agenda* (Ames: Iowa State Press, 1992), chap. 6.

8. This theory was first expounded by the author in his volume *Farm Prices: Myth and Reality* (Minneapolis: University of Minnesota Press, 1958), chap. 5.

9. The price solution presented in chart B of figure 19.3 illustrates the maximum price decline possible in response to the industry-wide adoption of the new and improved technology. For this solution to occur there must be an entry of new firms into the commodity enterprise to sustain the increase in marketable supplies, where the supplies offered on the market by each adopting firm decline along the marginal cost curve, MC_2, as the price declines from P_1 to P_2. A more probable solution would involve a final price at some level between P_1 and P_2, where (1) each adopting firm offers more on the market following the adoption of the new and improved technology than it did before, (2) the entry of new firms augments marketable supplies, and (3) the cost structure of firms rises somewhat as a result of increased prices of scarce inputs.

10. The available evidence suggests that the long-run planning curve is flat over an extended range, as is suggested in chart A of figure 19.5. See *Public Policy and the Changing Structure of American Agriculture,* U.S. Congress, Congressional Budget Office, August 1978, pp. 29–34; and Bruce F. Hall and E. Phillip LeVeen, "Farm Size and Economic Efficiency: The California Case," *American Journal of Agricultural Economics,* 60 (November 1978), pp. 589–600.

11. Professor Philip M. Raup has also used the term *cannibalism* to describe the situation in American farming in which the strong consume the weak. He argues that farm expansion buyers have been the dominant force in the recent upsurge of land values; his evidence suggests that farm expansion buyers accounted for 63 percent of all land purchases for the year ending March 1977. Professor Raup thus concludes that the current threat to smaller

family-type farms does not come from outside investors; the threat is from large neighboring farmers in the same community. See "Some Questions of Value and Scale in American Agriculture," *American Journal of Agricultural Economics*, 60, no. 2 (May 1978), p. 307.

12. The case history of one of these aggressive, innovative farmers, Mr. Pat Benedict, as he expanded the size of his farm operation by gobbling up the productive assets of his less able neighbors, is well told in "The New American Farmer," *Time, the Weekly Newsmagazine*, 112 (November 6, 1978), pp. 92–102.

Chapter 21

1. For a treasure of economic information on this and earlier periods see Cheryl D. Johnson, *A Historical Look at Farm Income*, U.S. Department of Agriculture, Economic Research Service, Statistical Bulletin No. 807, May 1990.

2. Kenneth E. Boulding, *Economic Analysis*, rev. ed. (New York: Harper & Brothers, 1948), p. 511.

3. Joseph A. Schumpeter, *The Theory of Economic Development*, (Cambridge, Mass.: Harvard University Press, 1936).

4. To raise the long-run level of world grain prices would involve the insuperable task of raising the price of grain to every producer around the world. This would induce an increase in production and world supply, and further increase the costs to the governmental agency so engaged. To move in this policy direction would drive the United States back again to a system of production controls and market isolation.

Chapter 22

1. This had to be the approach to national economic development taken by the early classical economists: Adam Smith in his *The Wealth of Nations* (particularly books III and IV) and Thomas R. Malthus in his *Principles of Political Economy* (particularly book II). It was the exclusive approach of Karl Marx. Historical description and knowledge of social and economic evolution, or process, play important roles in the theorizing of many modern economists concerned with economic development: Joseph Schumpeter (see particularly his *Capitalism, Socialism and Democracy*, 3rd ed. [New York: Harper and Row, 1950]); W. W. Rostow (see particularly his *The Stages of Economic Growth: A Non-Communist Manifesto* [London: Cambridge University Press, 1961]); W. Arthur Lewis (see his *The Theory of Economic Growth* [London: George Allen & Unwin, 1955]); Gunnar Myrdal (see particularly his *Asian Drama: An Inquiry into the Poverty of Nations*, 3 vols. [New York: Pantheon, Random House, 1968]); P. N. Rosenstein-Rodan (see "Problems of Industrialization of Eastern and Southeastern Europe," *The Economic Journal*, 53 (June-September 1943), pp. 202–11; Vernon W. Ruttan (see his book with Yujiro Hayami, *Agricultural Development: An International Perspective* [Baltimore: Johns Hopkins Press, 1971]). The historical underpinning of theories of economic development is well documented in the volume by Benjamin Higgins entitled *Economic Development: Problems, Principles, and Policies*, rev. ed. (New York: Norton, 1968), pts. 2, 3, and 4.

2. This is what happened in the study of the American farm economy from 1932 to 1953 under the assumption of free market conditions, by Daryll E. Ray and Earl O. Heady, *Simulated Effects of Alternative Policy and Economic Environments on U.S. Agriculture*, Center for Agricultural and Rural Development, Report 46T, Iowa State University, Ames, Iowa, March 1974; and in the study of the American farm economy from 1953 to 1972 by Frederick J. Nelson, "An Economic Analysis of the Impact of Past Farm Programs on Livestock

and Crop Prices, Production and Resource Adjustments" (Ph.D. diss., University of Minnesota, 1975).

3. This method was employed in this volume. The conceptual model formulated and presented in part IV was constructed from literally hundreds of historical studies, parts and pieces of which were reported in parts II and III.

4. A recent and important source of this evidence is Donella H. Meadows, Dennis L. Meadows, and Jørgen Randens, *Beyond the Limits: Confronting Global Collapse, Envisioning a Sustainable Future* (Post Mills, Vt.: Chelsea Green Publishing, 1992).

Index

Index

Compiled by Robert J. Grogan

Page references to figures and tables are shown in boldface.

Willard W. Cochrane graduated in 1937 from the University of California at Berkeley with a major in agricultural economics. He received a master of science degree in agricultural economics from Montana State College in 1938. He was a Littauer Fellow at Harvard University in 1941–42 and received from that institution a master's degree in public administration in 1942 and a Ph.D. degree in economics in 1945. He was employed as an agricultural economist in the U.S. Department of Agriculture in 1939–41 and 1943–47. He worked as an economist for the Food and Agricultural Organization of the UN in 1947–48 and was a member of the UN Mission to Thailand (then Siam) in 1948.

Cochrane was appointed associate professor of economics and agricultural economics at Pennsylvania State University in 1948 and was promoted to professor in 1949. He was appointed professor of agricultural economics at the University of Minnesota in 1951 and has been associated with that university in various capacities to the present time except while away on leave.

He was chairman of the Governor's Study Commission of Agriculture for Minnesota in 1957–58 and visiting professor at the University of Chicago in 1958–59. In 1960 he served as agricultural adviser to Senator Kennedy in the presidential campaign and was appointed director of agricultural economics in the U.S. Department of Agriculture in 1961 — a position he held through 1964. He was appointed dean of the Office of International Programs at the University of Minnesota in 1965 and served in that capacity through 1970. During the period 1965–70 he traveled widely in the less-developed world on university business and as a consultant for the Ford Foundation.

Professor Cochrane was elected vice-president of the American Farm Economic Association in 1954–55, president in 1959–60, and a Fellow in 1965.

He has written numerous articles and bulletins. In addition, he is the coauthor of four books: *Economics of American Agriculture* (3rd ed., 1974); *Economics of Consumption* (1956); *American Farm Policy, 1948–1973* (1976); and *Reforming Farm Policy: Toward a National Agenda* (1992); and author of four books: *Farm Prices — Myth and Reality* (1958); *The City Man's Guide to the Farm Problem* (1965); *The World Food Problem: A Guardedly Optimistic View* (1969); and *Agricultural Development Planning: Economic Concepts, Administrative Procedures and Political Process* (1974).